THE QUEEN

THE QUEEN

A Revealing Look at the Private Life of Elizabeth II

Douglas Keay

St. Martin's Press
New York

Library of Congress Cataloging-in-Publication Data

Keay, Douglas.
    The Queen : a revealing look at the private life of Elizabeth II /
Douglas Keay.
       p.   cm.
    ISBN 0-312-07776-9
    1. Elizabeth II, Queen of Great Britain, 1926– . 2. Great
Britain—Kings and rulers—Biography. I. Title.
DA590.K36   1992
941.085′092—dc20
    [B]   92-4035
                                                                    CIP

First published in Great Britain as *Elizabeth II: Portrait of a Monarch* by Random Century Ltd.

First U.S. Edition: July 1992
10 9 8 7 6 5 4 3 2 1

Contents

For Marianne

Acknowledgements

In his study in Buckingham Palace, the Duke of Edinburgh was explaining why he didn't think I, or anyone else for that matter, would
ever be granted an interview by the Queen. 'It's partly a matter for
her own decision,' he said, 'but I think it's also that the sovereign is in
a much more difficult situation than some others because of the problem
of misunderstandings or opinions which . . .' He paused, sensing perhaps
that he was on tricky ground as he was being interviewed himself. As
usual, he wanted to help – if he could. 'So much of it is involved in a
sense with . . . I don't know what you would call it . . . official attitudes.'
He smiled, before summing up what were almost certainly the Queen's
views as well as his own. 'I think probably the risks would be greater
than the benefits,' he concluded.[1]

In fact, since that particular interview, in 1981, the Queen has granted
two interviews of a kind for what one of her aides might deem 'the public
prints' – or, in this case, the public media. Godfrey Talbot, the doyen of
court correspondents, was fortunate enough to be in a position to introduce the Queen reminiscing on BBC radio about the Victory Night
celebrations after the Second World War when she and Princess Margaret went out into The Mall in front of Buckingham Palace and mingled
with the cheering crowds. Peter O'Sullevan, the horse racing commentator, made a film about the breeding of thoroughbreds in which the
Queen, an acknowledged expert, gave her views. However, in both cases
she was talking to people she knew and the conversations were not
allowed to stray or expand into forbidden fields.

Nelson Mandela, commenting in a letter on an authorized biography

vii

of himself, *Higher Than Hope*, which came out before he was released from prison, noted: 'Writing a biography without access to the subject of study can be a very difficult matter . . .'[2]

One of the many obstacles confronting anyone wishing to write authoritatively about the Queen is that the lady herself happens to believe, fairly strongly, that biographies should not be written until after the person's lifetime. So this book is not a biography, or at least certainly not an official one. It is not even authorized, in so far as it did not have to be vetted by Buckingham Palace before publication – although, in the interests of accuracy, parts of the manuscript were read by senior Members of the Queen's Household. The Queen herself was aware of the project almost from the outset, and discussions took place among her advisers early on as to the amount of access I should be granted. Fortunately, this turned out to be more than I had hoped for – although, as for anyone with responsible curiosity who wishes to write about royalty, it was never to be enough.

Unlike Mr Mandela's biographer, I did get to see the Queen, and to talk to her – albeit at media receptions – but nothing that passed between us could be said remotely to constitute an interview. It was always understood beforehand that any conversations, which were necessarily short, light and cheerful but nonetheless revealing to an author trying to piece together a mosaic, were to remain strictly off the record.

Sir Harold Nicolson, who wrote the official biography of King George V, the grandfather of Elizabeth II, was told that he would be expected to 'omit things and incidents which were discreditable to the royal family'. Fortunately, I was not expected to labour under any such restriction, and no one ever said – least of all any member of the royal family – that he or she would be happier if I steered clear of certain areas.

Above all, I must record my gratitude for the generous help I have received from those people who have been very close to the life and work of the Queen over a period of many years, and who have given unstintingly of their time and listened patiently to my endless string of questions. I am gratified that a good number of them have felt able to speak freely and, in some cases, for the first time, about aspects of the Queen's life which up until now have been hidden from general view. Invariably, they have done so out of a sense of loyalty and admiration for the Queen, plus a desire to help paint a picture that is not merely 'chocolate-box-pretty'. Critics of the Queen herself have been hard to find, although a minority – including one or two well-known politicians – have expressed displeasure at the behaviour of certain younger members of the royal family during the recent past. A few criticize the monarchy as an archaic institution and would like to see it replaced within the first quarter of the twenty-first century by a presidency. However, this group is definitely in a minority, not only among those I talked to but, polls show, in the country as a whole. For the foreseeable future the monarchy in Britain seems safe, although it may have to change quite a bit if it is to survive another fifty years into the next century. But people have been saying that sort of thing for the *past* fifty years.

This book is based largely on interviews. A few of these, notably those with members of the royal family themselves, took place over a period of years. The majority were given within the eighteen months to two years before this book went to print. In practically every case I have used a tape recorder. However, this has not meant that all the interviews were 'on the record'. Some of the most valuable sources have requested no acknowledgement of any sort. Others have asked that certain parts of what they have told me should be 'non-attributable'. It is not the best arrangement, but it has sometimes proved to be the only way of gaining access to information and opinion that might otherwise remain totally private.

'I think interviews and the extent to which members of the family expose themselves to the media,' Prince Philip once told me, 'is a matter for their own judgement, and trial and error.'[3]

When it comes to those actually in the employ of the Queen, the judgement about when to say something and when to say nothing is even harder to make. Those present Members of the Queen's Household – her extremely loyal courtiers – who did agree to see me did so on the strict understanding that they would not be named. As one of them put it, in words that might almost do justice to a *Yes, Minister* script: 'I think anybody who is by virtue of office admitted to a greal deal of intimacy with somebody else, wants to go on being able to do their job without prejudicing it, by not appearing as the source of a whole lot of information which the principal figure might prefer not to have made public.' ... Quite.

Notwithstanding such understandable reservations, present and former Members of the Queen's Household have put themselves out to a considerable extent to give me a great deal of help and I wish, above all, to acknowledge my debt to them and express my gratitude. I wish especially to thank the Rt Hon. Sir William Heseltine, GCB, GCVO, AC, QSO, until August 1990 the Principal Private Secretary to the Queen, and Mr Robin Janvrin, LVO, the Queen's Press Secretary, who was promoted in July 1990 to the post of Assistant Private Secretary. I also wish to acknowledge my debt to certain other Members of the Households, and to the ladies of Buckingham Palace Press Office.

Seventeen years ago in *Majesty* (surely one of the most enjoyable and informative books ever written about the monarchy), the author Robert

Lacey wrote: 'For many good reasons – and a few bad – great secrecy surrounds the Queen.'[4] Nothing, or at least very little, has changed in that respect since Lacey published his book. Despite the ever increasing exposure to television and the inspired guesswork of some other parts of the media, an air of mystery still hangs about the monarchy, if not the sovereign herself, like the aroma of some powerful medieval perfume.

Prince Philip insists that any mystique remaining is created from outside the Palace, not from within. His explanation for its continuance is typically to the point. 'There is a sort of inevitability about it if there's only one of you and lots of everybody else,' he once said. 'You're bound to be different, and looked at differently.'[5]

One of my aims in writing this book has been to attempt to lift a few veils and to let in a little more light on to a subject that has universal and continual fascination. Another aim, perhaps more important, is to draw the reader's notice to the service that a remarkable woman who appears unremarkable, has given to her country, her family, and to the Commonwealth over a period of forty years.

So my thanks to all of the following, and also to those who wished not to be named here, but who helped me in so many ways, not least by entrusting me with their confidence. I am glad that others, who have been equally helpful in drawing together the different strands, have allowed me to express my gratitude in a small way by recording their names here:

Mr Ronald Allison, CVO; Mr Charles Anson, LVO; Dr W.E.K. Anderson, B.Litt., D.Litt., FRSE; Her Grace the Duchess of Beaufort; the late Mr Richard Cawston, CVO; Lt.-Col. the Lord Charteris of Amisfield, PC, GCB, GCVO, OBE; Mr Alan Hamilton; Lord Home of The Hirsel, KT; The Rt Hon. R.S.G. Hattersley, MP; Sir William Heseltine, GCB, GCVO, AC, QSO; Mr Robin Janvrin, LVO; the Rt Revd Michael Mann, KCVO; Sir Oliver Millar, GCVO, FBA, FSA; the Rt Hon. J. Enoch Powell, MBE; Sir Shridath Ramphal, OE, OM, GCMG, QC; Commander Bryan Rayner; Mr Christopher J.E. Trevor-Roberts, LVO; the Rt Hon. the Viscount Whitelaw, KT, CH, MC, DL; the Rt Revd Robin Woods, KCMG, KCVO.

I am in deep debt to Their Royal Highnesses the Duke of Edinburgh and the Prince of Wales whom I have been privileged to interview on a number of occasions in the past and whose words, as they are sometimes painfully aware, live on for ever.

I should also like to express my thanks to Mr Oliver Everett, LVO, the Librarian and Assistant Keeper of the Royal Archives at Windsor Castle, and to Lady de Bellaigue. I am grateful for the gracious permission of Her Majesty the Queen to use material from the Royal Archives. My thanks, too, to the ever-helpful staff of the London Library.

ACKNOWLEDGEMENTS

Finally, I should like to thank Simon Master of Random Century for having the faith to commission when so many other, hopefully different, books are being written about members of the royal family; Hilary Arnold, editorial director of Century, and Sophie Figgis and Mary Remnant, my indefatiguable and helpful editors; Carole Blake, my equally indefatiguable agent; and most of all my patient wife, Marianne, whom I can now take on the holiday that I promised her two years ago.

Prologue

Anyone who has ever seen a British postage stamp has a fair idea of what Queen Elizabeth II looks like, albeit when she was a few years younger than she is now. Similarly anyone in the remotest corners of the Commonwealth who has ever tuned in to one of Her Majesty's Christmas Day broadcasts knows what she sounds like – or at least what she sounds like when she is reading from a prepared text. But only a minute proportion of those millions of people spread around the world who have seen and heard her have very much idea of what kind of woman she is. 'Are you going to deal at all with her grumpiness?' enquired a certain duchess. 'It would make it a more interesting read if you did.' Is the Queen grumpy? 'She can be', replied the duchess, with a knowing look. Others closer to the sovereign than Her Grace said that Her Majesty was of an unusually equable nature, though one of her cautious courtiers saw no reason not to add, 'The Queen can get very sharp at times, yes. She's only human after all.'

Four years after she came to the throne, 34 per cent of those questioned in a poll believed that the Queen was someone specially chosen by God; by 1964 the figure had only dropped to 30 per cent.[1] Even today traces of medieval mysticism remain. Reporters covering a 'walkabout' by the Princess of Wales in a provincial town grow bored with hearing the same response from those who have shaken Diana's hand. Invariably, the lucky few nurse the hand that held the hand while exclaiming excitedly: 'I won't wash it for a week!' Perhaps it is just as well that the Queen rarely, if ever, shakes hands unless she is meant to, and even then usually does so with her gloves on.

In a number of ways, Elizabeth II is an enigma. Throughout an un-completed reign lasting some forty years, she has managed to remain aloof yet not remote. While her eldest son openly creates controversy over architecture or the environment – 'throwing a pebble into a pond and seeing how far the ripples spread out' is what he calls it – the Queen's personal opinions on broad issues are very rarely publicly ex-pressed. The Princess of Wales may be photographed hurling about in a dodgem car with a dare-devil Prince William at the wheel, but the Queen takes care that there are no pictures taken of her off duty, except possibly when she is on a horse – and even then she grows furious if her privacy is encroached upon. Presumably, she has at some point built sandcastles with her grandchildren, but if so the family snapshots remain under lock and key as far as the outside world is concerned.

At the same time we already own to a pot-pourri of minutiae about this self-contained lady, gathered up from here and there. We know, for instance, that she gets her milk delivered daily to Buckingham Palace in monogrammed bottles from a farm near Windsor; that her corgis obey her, even if they pay little attention to anyone else; that she feels the cold but not the heat; that, after forty years, she is still not completely used to people staring at her, and 'always gets butterflies in the stomach' before performing the State Opening of Parliament; that, much to the fury of animal-rights protesters, she wears fur coats and stoles, and, to the des-pair of pony-club instructors, does not wear a protective helmet when out riding; that she has been to see television's most popular soap opera, *Coronation Street*, for herself; that she has come to terms with advancing age – 'I look so old,' she commented when seeing her face on the new, smaller, five-pound note, 'but then, I suppose I am'. We know that she actually owns the royal box in the Albert Hall; that she prefers not to wear artificial flowers for decoration, and that she is not partial to beards – when one of her closest advisers began cultivating one at Balmoral during the holiday season, the Queen merely remarked, 'I suppose it's all right for up here,' and by the next morning it was 'orff'.

The Queen cannot be sued in court, nor can she give evidence - because it is *her* court. She does not need to own a passport, pass a driv-ing test, nor have licences for her numerous dogs. In Lancashire she is the Duke of Lancaster, because Queen Victoria thought it proper for the holder of the title to be called a man. In the Isle of Man she should be toasted 'The Queen, Lord of Man'.

Despite a sometimes glum expression (a hangover from the Hanovar-ian dynasty), the Queen has a wry sense of humour which can catch out those not accustomed to meeting it or its owner – as when she enquired of a weekend visitor to Windsor Castle: 'You found us all right?' Or, when emerging from a shop in Sandringham village, and being told by a perfect stranger that she resembled the Queen of England: 'How very re-assuring'.[2]

When you first meet the Queen you are immediately aware of the loveliness of her blue eyes, and of her flawless complexion. Next you may be surprised by her height. Somehow, like Margaret Thatcher, she always appears to be the smallest person in the room. She is, in fact, five feet four inches, which is still some five inches taller than her great-great-grandmother, Queen Victoria. In that initial nervy conversation, the Queen has a knack of making you feel that you have been on friendly, if not exactly close, terms for several years, and at the same time shows that you have not been, by being curious to know something about you.

'What do you do?' she asked of a scientist at an investiture.

'I kill mosquitoes.'

'Good' seemed exactly the right response.[3]

On the first occasion that the present author had the honour of being presented to the Queen, as a journalist covering the state visit to Sri Lanka in 1981, he tactlessly touched on the subject of immigration and mentioned the name of Mr Enoch Powell, a controversial figure in politics because of his well-known views on immigration. Without saying a word or betraying any expression, the Queen slowly swivelled round to talk to someone else in the group, before returning face to face once more a few moments later. 'I gather that they had snow at Balmoral yesterday, which is very early,' she said.

Earl Mountbatten of Burma, who always tended to wave the flag for the Mountbattens more vigorously than for the Windsors, once described the Queen as being 'extremely sound – not brilliant – and that comes from her mother'.[4]

The Duchess of Beaufort, at whose home, Badminton, the Queen has been a frequent visitor through the years, particularly during the lifetime of the 10th Duke, believes that the Queen has become above all 'a very wise person'.

One of the Queen's former advisers said: 'She is not an intellectual and would not pretend to be, thank God. But she has a lot of common sense. She may not immediately appreciate the subtleties of a complicated paper when it is presented to her, but she will spot the weaknesses in the argument, and the typing errors, quicker than most.'

Several years ago, a commentator wrote that the Queen was an ordinary woman in an extraordinary position. A nicely turned description it may be, but it is doubtful whether it was ever true in any sense. The Queen may at times look like a housewife, or, particularly as she gets older, a *hausfrau*. When she is bundled up in some tweed winter coat and wearing a felt hat, she could possibly be mistaken for a million other well-to-do grannies out window shopping in one of Britain's more prosperous high streets. But the concept is wide of the true mark.

Horace Smith, in his memoirs, *A Horseman Through Six Reigns*, wrote that Princess Elizabeth, whom he taught to ride, once told him that if she had not been born who she was she would have liked to have been a lady living in the country with lots of horses and dogs. In which case, instead of window shopping, it is more likely that she would have bowled in to the local high street in a Range Rover, parked on double yellow lines, popped in to the bank, and got out of town and back to peace and calm as soon as possible. In the afternoon, duty might require her to present prizes at the Women's Institute, and weekends would be taken up with a house full of guests and required worship at the parish church on Sunday morning.

In some respects the Queen has realized her childhood ambition to be a country lady. For something like three months and several weekends each year she resides either at Windsor Castle or in one or other of her two very large privately owned homes, Sandringham and Balmoral, with lots of horses and dogs to give her exercise and pleasure. However, that is where the parallel with any other prosperous landowner ends. For even when she is technically on holiday, the red dispatch boxes keep on arriving from London with official papers to read and inwardly digest. Among the weekend guests there are often important foreign guests whom, the Foreign Office might suggest, it would be diplomatic to entertain. At least once a year, in the summer, the Prime Minister travels to Balmoral to spend a bracing weekend in the bosom of the royal family. The Queen is a seriously religious person, so she would wish to worship in church every Sunday, but it must make some difference that she is Supreme Governor of the Church of England. As sovereign, the whole of Britain's Armed Forces owe allegiance first to her, not to the government of the day. All laws are carried out in the name of the sovereign. ('The Queen only signs Acts of Parliament', a tall equerry gently advised a small boy seeking an autograph outside St Paul's Cathedral at the time of the Queen's Silver Jubilee.)[5] But if she did not accept her ministers' advice and act upon it, it would be necessary for all of them to resign. A general election would follow and the people themselves would then decide who should have power – Crown or Parliament.

Sir Antony Jay in the 1969 television documentary film, *Royal Family*, made the point that 'the strength of the monarchy does not lie in the power that it has, but in the power that it denies to others.' The Prince of Wales some time later told the present author that he 'did not think people realize just how much influence the monarch does and can have. And its influence is very often more effective than direct power.'[6]

None of this, of course, necessarily accounts for the popularity or otherwise of the sovereign. Basically, most people either agree with the view that 'the use of the Queen, in a dignified capacity, is incalculable' (Walter Bagehot, 1867), or that the royal family in general are 'expensive lunatics that are kept in motors and stables by an industrious nation's toil' (Vera Brittain, social reformer, mother of Shirley Williams, 1913).[7] Even approaching the end of the twentieth century, both these views are current, although polls show that the first is still held by the great majority of people, even if to a lesser extent than it was.

Critics point to the fact that the Queen is said to be the wealthiest woman in the world, with a private fortune estimated to be almost £8 billion, yet she pays not a penny in income tax. Some people say that money – too much of it – will be the downfall of Britain's monarchy. Champions of the royal family, on the other hand, and of the Queen in particular, point to the millions accruing each year to the national exchequer from foreign tourists whose first stop in England is almost invariably Buckingham Palace.

The Queen never takes a holiday abroad, and very rarely makes a private visit to friends or acquaintances living outside her own shores. On the other hand, she has travelled more miles and seen more different places in the world than any other monarch before her. With her husband beside her, she has made over 120 state visits, and has reciprocated by entertaining the kings, sultans, and presidents of about an equivalent number of nations, ranging from Emperor Hirohito of Japan to President Vigdis Finnogadottir of Iceland. At the time of writing, she has still to take up President Gorbachev's invitation to visit Russia, thus being the first British monarch to step on to the soil of the country whose rulers murdered her great uncle and the whole of his young family in the revolution of 1917. Despite the sad associations for her, it is said that the Queen is looking forward to the visit enormously.

While politicians continue to argue about the merits and demerits of 1992 and the full union of the European Community, in public at least the Queen holds silent on the subject. Not so surprisingly, the question of national sovereignty, once so assiduously defended by Prime Minister Margaret Thatcher, is something else on which Elizabeth II has personal views but, once again, her counsel is for private ears only.

As the monarch who came to the throne in time to preside over the demise of the British Empire, Elizabeth II holds a touching affection for, and belief in, that loose connection of independent states spread around the world and somewhat grandly termed the Commonwealth. She would probably agree, even so, with her former Foreign Secretary, the good and urbane Lord Carrington, that 'many people find the present concept of Commonwealth an irritant'.[8] It does not bother her particularly that she is acknowledged as Head of the Commonwealth but is not sovereign of those Commonwealth countries which are republics. Far more important to her is the feeling of family which the Commonwealth engenders – family meaning honest rows as well as friendships – and also the sense of lasting loyalty which spreads over from one generation to the next. The Queen was thrilled when Pakistan rejoined the Commonwealth in October 1989 after an absence of twelve years. Were a new and totally non-apartheid South Africa to apply for membership renewal (the republic left the Commonwealth in 1961), she would doubtless be overjoyed.

Both the Queen and the Duke of Edinburgh have always insisted on leading their own family life as they see fit, with due regard being given to the future role of their eldest son, but without undue attention being given to current fads and fashions. They abhor intrusion into private lives, their own or anyone else's, and have crossed swords with the media on a number of occasions. They have become experts at preserving their distance while appearing to be more accessible.

Above all, the Queen has kept a level head throughout forty years of social and political upheaval, both national and international. She has known great secrets and known how to keep them. She has been attracted to one person more than to another and that person, world statesman, politician or courtier, has never been aware of being held in different esteem from another. She has warned and advised but seldom interfered, and has never been the cause of a constitutional crisis. If sometimes she has appeared to be unmoved, it is because she believes a monarch must show impassiveness and solemnity, for that is part of being regal. Loyalty and service have always been her lodestars, and a sense of the ridiculous the chaser away of pomposity. Over the years, she has probably amassed more inside knowledge of world events than any of her Prime Ministers (after all, she was there before they arrived and is still there after they have gone) and is constantly alert to the latest developments. Experience and the nature of her character mean that she is not inclined to rush at fences – she leaves that sort of thing to her husband. The great thing about the Queen, according to members of her staff is that in essence she doesn't change very much, although over the years the longer serving of them have sensed that she has become a little less stiff in her approach to people, and a little more confident of her own position.

The same calm good sense and forgiveness of *most* transgressions applies generally. Within her own family, she has experienced more heartache than many of her subjects have had to bear, and at the same time has been placed in the position of having to decide whether to put a sovereign's duty before a woman's natural inclination. She has known the pain of seeing her young sister give up the man she loved, marry another, and become divorced; and witnessed her only daughter's marriage fail. She has had a son who has risked his life in war, and another who has been falsely rumoured to be a homosexual. Two daughters-in-law have given her anxiety and annoyance as well as pride, and, so far, six grandchildren have rewarded her with simple unalloyed escape from the treadmill of her work. Throughout the whole of her life she has been blessed with the presence of a mother who brought sunlight into any room she entered, and unswervingly supported by a sometimes crotchety husband whom she is still in love with after forty-four years of marriage. Above all, she has watched her eldest son grow in and out of phases and mature into a good and likely future king, with an almost fierce sense of independence. Whether or not she should forsake the solemn oath that she took at her coronation and step down from her throne in order that he might inherit before he is old, is the one unresolved question that may concern her subjects more than it does the Queen herself. For both the Queen and the Prince of Wales, the question may not even require consideration. The monarch is monarch until death intercedes.

Of all her predecessors the Queen most admires her grandfather, King George V, and before him her great-great-grandmother, Queen Victoria, who reigned for nearly sixty-four years.

When he was receiving instruction in constitutional history at Cambridge in 1894 – that is, before he came to the throne – King George V wrote in his careful hand in a notebook still preserved at Windsor:

> Though it would be possible to construct a system of political machinery in which there was no monarchy, yet in a State where a monarchy of the English type already exists, it is still a great political force and offers a splendid career to an able monarch; he is independent of parties and therefore impartial; his position ensures that his advice would be received with respect; and he is the only statesman in the country whose political experience is continuous.[9]

King George V's official biographer, Sir Harold Nicolson, wrote of his subject: 'His faith in the principle of monarchy was simple, devout even; but selfless. All that he aspired to do was to serve that principle with rectitude; to represent all that was most straightforward in the national character; to give the world an example of personal probity; to advise, to encourage and to warn.'

Those words might equally have been written of Elizabeth II, for they equally apply, but, as she becomes older, the questions that her younger subjects may wish to ask in the later 1990s are these: does Britain still have need of a monarchy at a time when the country is being drawn further and further into a community of European nations? If it does, should it not be in some way modernized to bring it more into line with the twenty-first century? And following the celebration of forty years of the reign of Queen Elizabeth II, in February 1992, should not serious consideration at least be given to the idea of abdication in favour of the Prince of Wales? Or should we forget all such notions, in favour of a monarch who has already served so well and so long?

THE QUEEN

I

Accession

 ❧

In Government House, Nairobi, on 13 October 1951, the Governor of Kenya, His Excellency Maj.-Gen. Sir Philip Mitchell, summoned his secretary from the outer office and dictated a letter under the heading 'Secret and Personal'. The letter was addressed to Sir Thomas Lloyd at the Colonial Office in London.

> My dear Lloyd,
> Thankyou very much for your letter of the 9th October, personal and secret, about the possibility of a visit by Princess Elizabeth and the Duke of Edinburgh to the Colony *en route* to Australia and New Zealand in February next. This is *very* good news.
> After the strenuous tour in Canada and all the heavy duties that will fall especially on the Princess after her return and the even more strenuous time ahead in Australia and New Zealand, the object of the exercise will, I assume, be that they should have as complete a rest as possible.[1]

Sir Philip was correct in his assumption, but naive in thinking that any part of a royal tour could ever be really restful. Nor could he, or Sir Thomas, have had any perception of the tragic drama that lay ahead. In a later letter, the Governor of Kenya confessed to 'knowing little or nothing of court procedure', and the lists of programme suggestions he bombarded at Buckingham Palace during the following weeks practically ensured that the royal couple would have very little chance of relaxing totally on their own.

Princess Elizabeth at twenty-five years of age, and her husband just five years older, were quite young enough to withstand the rigours of a journey into the African bush, but, when Sir Philip wrote his letter, they were already less than halfway through a thirty-five day journey across North America, covering nearly 10,000 miles in Canada alone. The press had not got a whisper of the planned trip to Africa, and then on to Ceylon, Australia, and New Zealand by the steamship *Gothic*. The Princess and the Duke were themselves as yet very hazy about the details. They were much more concerned about the health of the Princess's father, King George VI, in whose place they had undertaken the tour of Canada and America on the advice of the King's doctors.

In the autumn of 1951, Britain was still suffering from austerity measures as a result of the war, although the giant Festival of Britain on London's South Bank was, according to Herbert Morrison, 'the people giving themselves a pat on the back'. In October, Winston Churchill was returned to power as Prime Minister at the age of seventy-seven. From the White House, after entertaining Princess Elizabeth and her husband, President Truman was prompted to write to King George VI, 'We've just had a visit from a lovely young lady and her personable husband. They went to the hearts of all the citizens of the United States...As one father to another we can be very proud of our daughters. You have the better of me — because you have two!'[2]

The letter must have cheered the King, coming as it did not long after he had undergone an operation for the removal of a lung. Although he was never told that he had cancer, perhaps he guessed. When he was asked, he put his illness down to 'the incessant worries and crises through which we have to live'.[3]

Because of a high risk of thrombosis in the days following the operation, the King's daughter and son-in-law had postponed their trip to Canada and America. When they finally flew off on 7 October 1951 (the journey of 3,400 miles to Montreal took sixteen and a quarter hours in those days), a sealed packet containing accession documents was placed in the locked case containing other official papers.

During the six weeks that the Princess and her husband were out of the country, the King's health showed a remarkable improvement. On 14 November he was able to put in an appearance at his grandson's third birthday party. A photograph of Prince Charles sitting on a sofa with the King, the only memory Charles retains of his grandfather, has stood ever since on the Queen's desk in her sitting-room at Buckingham Palace.

After their return home, to show his appreciation of his daughter and son-in-law's successful tour, the King made both of them Privy Counsellors. And the country expressed its thanks for the King's recovery with a special day of National Thanksgiving on Sunday, 2 December.

While all this was happening, preparations were going ahead for the visit to Kenya, with letters and telegrams buzzing backwards and forwards between Government House, Nairobi, and Buckingham Palace. Sir Philip Mitchell wrote in October:

Assuming Their Royal Highnesses arrive in Nairobi about noon and that their visit is to be classified as private, my wife and I would meet them at the airport with the Mayor and Mayoress, the GOC and AOC and their wives. It might be desirable to put in the Chief Justice and possibly the Chief Secretary and the Administrator, but we can decide that later.

Come to Government House for lunch, and rest in the afternoon. The only engagement I suggest would be an informal visit to the Princess Elizabeth hospital, which is five minutes drive from Government House. By informal I mean a visit of which the hospital would have been warned, but there would be no notice to the press and therefore no crowd, and the Princess would be expected to do no more than just walk around.

After that no engagements except dinner at Government House, the nature of which depends entirely on the Princess's wishes. Could be a full dress party with about fifty people, or a dinner jacket party of any dimensions they like. It could indeed be nobody at all, except of course ourselves, or if they preferred it, they could dine in their own quarters.[4]

So much for an informal, complete rest – on the very day that the Princess and the Duke were due to arrive from London after a flight lasting some eighteen hours.

Any royal tour involves hundreds of people, reams of paperwork and protocol, and not a few mini-crises along the way. It is so now. It was so then.

The visit to Kenya was planned to last just six days, from 1 to 7 February. The high spot was to be a visit to the hunting lodge on the banks of the Sagana river, a car ride from Nairobi, which the people of Kenya had presented to the Princess and Prince Philip as a wedding gift in 1947, but which the couple so far had not had a chance of seeing.

The Governor did not think that a handing over ceremony was necessary – 'but it might be a good thing, if HRH would agree, that I, the Speaker, and the principle members of the Legislature concerned, together with the architect and the people who built the Lodge were waiting at the Lodge.' Sir Philip said that if this were approved he 'should like a newsreel man to be there'.[5]

The Princess would then open the Lodge and walk in – 'and I suggest

3

that without further ado the party disappears. If, however, the Princess would like them to have a glass of sherry, that, of course, can be laid on.'[6]

Sir Philip was a military man who had spent a large part of his life in Africa, hunting game and generally running things, so having the heir to the throne come to visit him in his colony was something rather major that needed planning down to the last detail. It also required a good deal of confirming with the Colonial Office and the Princess's staff back in London on matters of protocol, if the whole operation were to go off without a hitch.

Among the flurry of letters and cablegrams that flew between Government House, Nairobi, and London were urgent requests for information about such things as the crests or monogram that should be embroidered on the bed linen at the Lodge. Then there was the matter of the writing paper on the desk. Could the Colonial Office possibly obtain a specimen monogram and coronet, wrote Sir Philip on 30 October, that would go in the centre of each page and on the flap of the envelope? And what colour should the notepaper be?

The reply from the Colonial Office, dated 12 November, enclosed samples of what was required. There should be 'two sizes of notepaper, four different sizes of envelopes, and one postcard'.[7] Their Royal Highnesses' badge and letter heading should as usual be in green, and the quantity required was four dozen of every kind. *And,* Buckingham Palace had requested, would Sir Philip please send a separate bill for all this as it would be paid for by the Crown Agents for the Colonies.

Next, there was the question of the flagpole in front of Government House: 'I am having the flagstaff erected in front of the staff which flies my flag to fly HRH's flag. Could you please get it sent to me in advance by BOAC' [the forerunner of British Airways].

The question of the car that would carry Princess Elizabeth and the Duke of Edinburgh also occupied a good deal of attention: 'I have been making enquiries both locally and in the United Kingdom for a more suitable car for Their Royal Highnesses than those we have in our present fleet. The chances of obtaining a tourer or one with a cabriolet body are fairly remote in the time at our disposal, so it looks as if TRH will have to use the Rolls and one of the new Humber limousines.'[8]

In the end an order was placed with Rootes, the English manufacturers of the Austin range, for a Humber Laundolette. The chairman himself promised to have it shipped out to Mombasa by mid-January, with all the royal fittings, such as flagstaff and crests, already attached.

None of these important details needed to concern Princess Elizabeth directly, of course, but, as with any royal tour right up to the present day, they ensured the smoothness and efficiency which never fails to impress.

Nearer home, the well-honed preparations were under way for the royal family's traditional Christmas and New Year gathering at the King's private, and favourite, home at Sandringham in Norfolk. George VI had celebrated his fifty-sixth birthday quietly at Buckingham Palace on 14 December and travelled down to the country a week later. He was experiencing some difficulty in speaking for any length of time because the doctors' examinations of his chest and throat had left him hoarse. The one benefit of this was that he had been allowed to record his Christmas Day message for radio in stages, a task that always made him extremely nervous, instead of broadcasting it live. And so, like millions of his subjects, he would be able to sink back in his chair after the festive lunch with all his family around him, and switch on the wireless . . .

On the world front, the dawn of the new year, 1952, brought a warning from Mr Winston Churchill to Egypt that no amount of terrorism would drive Britain out of the Suez Canal Zone. Churchill himself was on his way by sea to the United States for consultations with President Truman.

The *Daily Mail*, 'For King and Commonwealth', price three half-pence, on Tuesday, 1 January 1952, reported that the two doctors who had operated on the King had been made Commanders of the Victorian Order, and on another page the newspaper speculated whether 1952 might be leap-to-fame year for three unknown and aspiring young actresses – Audrey Hepburn, Susan Stephen, and Joan Collins. The last, according to the *Daily Mail*, 'radiates a quality of which not even the British film's best friend would boast . . . sex.'

Centre stage in Britain, however, during the first twelve days of January 1952 was the drama of a sea captain, Henrik Carlsen, who had stayed with his doomed ship, the *Flying Enterprise*, as it lay battered by heavy seas on Cornish rocks. He eventually dived into the rough seas and was rescued, just before his ship finally slid beneath the waves.

Princess Elizabeth and the Duke of Edinburgh were due to leave London for Africa on 31 January. As a treat, King George VI decided to take the whole family on an outing to the theatre on the night before the young couple set out on their journey, partly to celebrate his own remarkable recovery – his doctors had expressed themselves well satisfied after a thorough examination only two days earlier – but mainly as an expression of *bon voyage* to his daughter and son-in-law. He had chosen Rodgers and Hammerstein's *South Pacific*, a particular favourite with them all, which was playing to packed houses at London's Drury Lane Theatre.

The evening was a huge success. The following morning, before she set out for the airport, Princess Elizabeth wrote to her grandmother (Queen Mary, the widow of King George V) thanking her for a present of three fans, and telling her how much everyone had enjoyed the evening at the theatre, and how everyone had been so touched by the reception given to her father.

The letter finished with a note about the weather – it seemed to be all right for flying, and so the Princess hoped all would go well – and a promise to write again when there was a chance.[9] Written in a rounded, open hand, it is quite probably the last letter Queen Elizabeth II wrote to a member of her family prior to her father's death, and almost certainly the last written from England as Princess Elizabeth.

King George, Queen Elizabeth, Princess Margaret, the Duke of Gloucester, and Lord and Lady Mountbatten were all there at London Airport on a bitterly cold January morning to see Princess Elizabeth and the Duke of Edinburgh set off on their tour, which was scheduled to last five months. So, too, were 3,000 other spectators – a measure of the King and Queen's popularity more than anything else.

The next morning, when these and millions of other well-wishers scanned their newspapers over breakfast, they were shocked by pictures of the King, as he waved goodbye to his daughter, his thin hair blown into a peak by the icy wind. He looked so drawn and haggard that, as people were to recall later, really for the first time, there was a general awful feeling that their King might not have very long to live.

The flight to Nairobi in a piston-engined Argonaut aircraft took over sixteen hours, with a stopover in Libya for refuelling and change of crew. The Princess and the Duke whiled away some of the time going over once again the programme for their first day in Kenya which they already knew almost off by heart.

Item one of their notes read: 'Everyone says Africans never demonstrate their feelings by cheering. Silence therefore does *not* indicate indifference.' (If it was true at that time, then Nelson Mandela's supporters proved it was not the case in 1989.)

Item four informed the Princess that the small black boy who was to present her with a bouquet on arrival at the maternity hospital was born on the same day as Prince Charles, and the boy's mother was presently in the hospital and about to have another baby. This is the sort of inside information and detailed briefing that is invaluable to visiting VIPs, royalty included.

However it was Item eight that probably gave the Princess the most pleasure. It informed her that a telephone call had been booked to Buckingham Palace at 4pm. She would be able to talk to her two children Charles and Anne (although she couldn't expect to get much sense out of her daughter because she was only eighteen months old) and find out the latest news about her father, who had returned to Sandringham for some end-of-season coot and hare shooting.

After the phone call, the royal couple would be requested to step out through the French windows for Item nine on the agenda: a garden party for some 2,500 guests. . . . Almost as if he could hear the stifled groans, the author of the notes had thought to add: 'Although the party goes on till about 6pm it will be pleasantly warm throughout.'[10]

In all of this His Excellency the Governor of Kenya and his wife, Sir Philip and Lady Mitchell, played their dutiful part. Indeed Sir Philip could be said to have excelled himself in preparing the details. He had happily offered, and had had accepted, the loan of his personal fishing tackle for use by the Princess and the Duke. Through the good offices of a Mr C.N.L. Fernandes, he had laid on four good ponies for Their Royal Highnesses to ride, even establishing beforehand that Princess Elizabeth would wish to sit astride in preference to side-saddle – 'if she would prefer to sit side-saddle would you inform me fairly soon so that a horse may be trained for the purpose'. He had retained a small Hungarian string orchestra for the dinner party on the first night at Government House – 'refugee, displaced persons, very deserving, excellent musicians and rather a sad lot', he informed General Sir Frederick Browning, Comptroller of Princess Elizabeth's Household.[11]

If Sir Philip had committed any *faux pas* – and no one would seriously accuse him of doing so – it had been when, almost at the last moment, he wrote in longhand enquiring whether both Sir Philip's brother and nephew might be allowed to be added to the list of guests at the dinner party on the evening of 2 February. 'Please have no hesitation in saying No without embarrassing Their Royal Highnesses by asking them. If you think it should be No, I suggest the signal might simply be 2 February Yes or 2 February No, as the case may be.'[12]

Unfortunately for Sir Philip's relatives, within a day, a reply cable arrived from General Browning in London with the cryptic message: 2 February No. Charteris[*] will explain. Browning'.[13]

Sir Philip Mitchell's most historic suggestion, had he but known it at the time, was his proposal early on in the planning of the visit to Kenya that the Princess and the Duke might like to spend a night at a hotel called Treetops, the unlikely location of which was the branches of a giant fig tree overlooking a pond and salt lick. The hotel, which was little more than a rest-house, was only about ten miles from the Lodge where the royal couple would be staying after leaving Government House. It would provide a wonderful opportunity, especially after dark, of seeing several species of wild animal close-to.

---

* Lt.-Col. the Hon. Martin Charteris, Assistant Private Secretary to Princess Elizabeth, who became the Queen's Principal Private Secretary until his retirement in 1977. Today he is Lord Charteris of Amisfield, and up until mid 1990 was Provost of Eton College.

'Even I, after the life that I have led among all the wild animals in Africa, get a thrill from Treetops,' Sir Philip informed his superiors in London, 'and I am sure that Her Royal Highness would enjoy it enormously. It really is something not to be missed. Full moon is the best night, or perhaps a day or so before.'[14] It was decided to take up Sir Philip's suggestion and make a visit to Treetops a part of the programme.

The plan as finally worked out was that Princess Elizabeth and Prince Philip should spend their first two days in and around Nairobi, fulfilling engagements and visiting the game reserve of the Nairobi National Park. The next morning they would set out on the ninety miles dusty drive to the Lodge on the Sagana river for four days of complete rest before flying to Mombasa to join the liner *Gothic* and the main part of their tour. Using the Lodge as a base, they would go to Treetops and spend one night there, the night of 5/6 February.

When the time came, all went smoothly and according to plan. The hospital was visited, the dinner at Government House was taken, and Princess Elizabeth spent the morning of 5 February watching her husband play polo before having lunch. Everyone then got into their cars and together they arrived at the forest path approaching Treetops shortly before 3pm. They were greeted by the alarming din of trumpeting elephants that sounded as if they were only a few yards away.

Accompanying the Princess and the Duke were Lady Pamela Mountbatten, the Princess's lady-in-waiting, Commander Mike Parker, the Duke's equerry and Private Secretary, and Mr Windley, the Provincial Governor.

Unsure of what danger they might be facing, the party began their cautious advance along the 600-yard-long path that led to Treetops. Meanwhile, in the best tradition of Hollywood movies of the time, Colonel Jim Corbett, a big game hunter, watched their progress from the observation platform of the hotel.

To his considerable consternation, he reported later, he had counted over forty elephants unexpectedly massed in the glade below him just minutes before the Princess and her party were due to arrive. Among them were three jealous bulls who were screaming with rage and getting dangerously close to the path the visitors were on. Apparently, there was very little the Colonel could do about it, apart from raising a white pillow case on the hotel flagpole as a warning signal. This he did.

After some hurried consultation, Prince Philip gave the order to the royal party to 'go ahead'. There was some fifty yards of open ground in front of them, with the narrow forest path to the rear. By now they had come so far it would be just as dangerous to turn back as to go on. On some of the trees there were rope-ladders to scramble up. There were three guns in the party, including Prince Philip's.

It was decided to split the group up. Lady Pamela Mountbatten and Mike Parker would bravely wait behind for a few minutes, each standing beside an escape ladder, while the others advanced silently towards the rough wooden steps that would take them up into the thirty-foot-high tree cradling their sanctuary.

In what can only have been a minute or two, but must have seemed much longer, the ordeal was safely over. As the Princess clambered on to the platform, her face beaming, an extremely relieved Jim Corbett and the owner of the hotel, Mr Eric Sherbrooke Walker, hastened forward to greet Her Royal Highness and the Duke and offer congratulations on a fair display of courage. (The others in the party were no cowards either.)

According to those there at the time, Princess Elizabeth showed absolutely no sign of fear. She seemed thrilled by the adventure and was chiefly interested in hurrying to get pictures of the elephants before they moved away. She spent the next hour sitting on the balcony directing her small cine-camera at the scene below. And when teatime came she asked that she might have hers where she was.

The whole party went on watching the animals long into the night.The air was warm, the feeling magical. Now and then Princess Elizabeth spoke of her father, and how much he would have enjoyed doing what she was doing. She recalled the day, just four days ago, when he had come to see her off at the airport, even though it was freezing cold – 'He's like that, never thinks of himself'. She told her friends that she felt his health might be improving. She surmised that he might have turned the corner when recently he raised a walking stick to his shoulder, saying: 'I believe I could shoot now!'[15]

Although Colonel Corbett was to record that 'the young Princess who spoke of her father that night with such affection and pride never had the least suspicion that she would not see him again',[16] it seems likely that Princess Elizabeth was more aware than she admitted about the state of George VI's health. It is likely that she had been prepared for the shock of bad news for several months now.

It was somewhere around 2am when the Princess and the Duke finally retired to their sparsely furnished room at the back of Treetops, pleasantly exhausted.

Kenya time is three hours ahead of British time, so by now King George had already gone to his own bed in Sandringham. A valet took the King a cup of hot chocolate at about 10.30 pm and it is believed that he read for an hour and a half until midnight, when a watchman noticed him fastening the latch of his bedroom window.

Then the King turned out the light and drifted into a sleep from which he never woke. The valet entered the room early on the morning of

Wednesday, 6 February 1952, and found his master at perfect peace.

Although the exact moment of George VI's death could never be established precisely, it seems likely that the Crown of Britain passed from father to daughter while both were sleeping 4,000 miles apart from one another, and that a young mother of twenty-five became sovereign over nearly 650 million people congregated in twelve countries and many colonies around the world while perched in a wild fig tree in Kenya. A tree called *mgumu**.

News of her father's death did not reach Princess Elizabeth until several hours after the event. She woke before dawn, after less than three hours sleep, and was soon out on the balcony again, filming and photographing rhinoceroses and water-buck in the clearing below.

When the time finally came to drag herself away and return to the Lodge, she told her hosts that she had enjoyed 'my most thrilling experience yet'. Eric Sherbrooke Walker responded, 'Ma'am, if you have the same courage in facing whatever the future sends you as you have in facing an elephant at eight paces, we are going to be very fortunate.'[17] It was the kind of compliment which always makes Prince Philip laugh, and his wife give a little smile. Both are slightly embarrassed by compliments.

The rest of that morning was spent fishing, with Sir Philip Mitchell's borrowed tackle, and after lunch, quietly pleased that she had caught more fish than her husband, Princess Elizabeth went to lie down for a while.

Because the Lodge had only four bedrooms, only the lady-in-waiting, the Princess's dresser, and Prince Philip's Private Secretary and valet were in constant attendance. (Inspector Clarke, the security officer, found himself sleeping in a tent.)

The Comptroller, General 'Boy' Browning, (husband of the novelist Daphne du Maurier), was on board the *Gothic*, tied up in Mombasa harbour, double-checking preparations for departure. Sir Philip Mitchell and his staff were already entrained for Mombasa, expecting to wish the Princess and the Duke *bon voyage* the following afternoon. Lt.-Col. Martin Charteris, the Princess's Assistant Private Secretary, was driving from the Lodge to the Outspan Hotel across the valley for a bite of lunch before going up to Treetops himself – a chance he had been told he shouldn't miss.

---

* Thirty-one years later, in 1983, when Elizabeth II and Prince Philip returned for the first time to the historic site, their disappointment was visible. The original Treetops hotel had been burned down by the rebellious Mau Mau, and replaced by a much larger hotel on the opposite side of the pond. Prince Philip's reaction was: 'They've cut down the trees!' An almost disbelieving Elizabeth II asked: 'Is this where we came before?'[18] They were not exactly the dramatic quotes the attendant press had been hoping for.

When the phone call came it was a reporter from the *East African Standard* who took the message – the press party covering the royal tour were staying at the Outspan. A colleague intercepted Martin Charteris as he was about to leave for Treetops, and hurriedly brought him to the phone booth. Almost forty years later he has a clear picture of the correspondent, his hands shaking as he fumbled with a cigarette packet. The reporter simply said: 'The King is dead'.

The news came as a profound shock, especially to those who did not know the full extent of the King's illness, but it was not totally unexpected. What Members of Her Majesty's Household found somewhat baffling was the fact that the new Queen had not been the first to be informed of the King's death. The reporter had received the news through a Reuter agency message from his office in Nairobi. In Government House, it later transpired, cipher telegrams from London had been piling up, but with the Governor and most of his staff on the train and heading for the coast, there was practically no one left who knew what to do about them.

Colonel Charteris's first action was to contact Prince Philip's Private Secretary with the news, as yet not officially confirmed. Before going to the Prince, Lt.-Cdr Michael Parker turned on the radio, but all he got was solemn music – an indication in itself.[*]

By this time several reporters at the Outspan Hotel had been rung up by their offices in London and Nairobi and there was no longer any need for official confirmation. Martin Charteris held a press conference at which he spoke of 'the lady we must now call Queen'.

Commander Parker went round to the lawn at the side of the Lodge and managed to attract Prince Philip's attention through the wide window without his wife seeing him. A few moments earlier she had spoken to two of her servants who were sitting on a doorstep cleaning shoes. She had thought, if there were to be time the next morning before they set off for Mombasa, she and the Duke might go for a ride. Would the servants please arrange for the horses to be ready?

Prince Philip came out on to the lawn and Commander Parker broke the news of the King's death to him. He 'looked as if the whole world had dropped on him. I never felt so sorry for anyone in all my life,' the Commander said later.[19] In the beat of a heart the course of the Duke of Edinburgh's life, as well as that of his wife, had changed for ever. He was

---

[*] The BBC Home Service, the highly respected 'voice of the nation' at that time, was unsure of how to announce the King's death, even after consulting a file marked 'Demise of Crown'. The Overseas Service was less hesitant. Listeners in Indonesia were the first to hear the news of the King's death. On the way to Buckingham Palace, Godfrey Talbot, the BBC's court correspondent, dropped off at Jermyn Street to purchase a black tie and a new bowler hat.

not yet thirty-one. But, as it has been ever since, he was aware that his first duty was to the Queen. He went inside the Lodge and gently informed his wife of her father's death.

Like most of those in the royal party, Lady Pamela Mountbatten, the Queen's lady-in-waiting who is also her cousin,* realized that she could not find the right words to express her true feelings. 'I suppose one's only reaction was that it was her father who was dead – it didn't sink in that it was the King.'[20]

In those first hours of sovereignty, 'the lady we must now call Queen' made a deep impression on all those around her, by her extraordinary composure and thought for others. She said that she was sorry that returning to England meant upsetting everybody's plans.

Lord Charteris remembers 'with diamond clarity' the moment he first saw his new sovereign. After giving the press conference, he had driven straight from the Outspan Hotel to the Sagana Lodge. 'I walked into the sitting-room. At the far corner, sitting at a writing table, was the Queen. Prince Philip was sitting on the sofa, with *The Times* held up like a barrier in front of his face. I bowed, and said, "I'm so sorry, ma'am." The Queen smiled and said, "I think we'd better get this telegram off." Immediately, it was down to business. She was absolutely somebody who had accepted her destiny without question.'[21]

Apologies to those awaiting her arrival in Ceylon, Australia and New Zealand were drafted. How would Her Majesty wish to be known, Colonel Charteris asked. It was not a formality that she would use her own name. After all, George VI's first name was Albert, and King Edward VIII's was David within the family. But the Queen replied without hesitation: 'I'm Elizabeth. I'll be Elizabeth.'[22]

Like many another equally well-ordered family, when a crisis suddenly hits Britain's royal family, those surrounding and servicing it – most of them military or naval trained at some stage in their careers – move swiftly and, usually, efficiently. Within an hour of learning of George VI's death, his successor was packed and ready to leave for the long journey home.

Not, however, before the proper courtesies had been observed.

Those who had looked after the Queen and Prince Philip in the game reserves and at Treetops were presented with the customary tokens of appreciation, ranging from much treasured signed photographs to cufflinks and ashtrays. And the Queen and Prince Philip made a special point of thanking the African servants they had known for only a few hours but who had shown particular devotion.

Afterwards, one of these Africans, Hussein bin Abdulah, wrote down

* In 1960 Lady Pamela married David Hicks, a highly successful interior designer.

his own personal report of the day's events. The touching account is still carefully preserved in the Royal Archives at Windsor.

'After two minutes Inspector James Cosma came to us, Hussein, Waithaka, and Juma, and said "Perhaps the Princess and the Duke will go to Nairobi". Waithaka asked why. He answered and said: "Our King, His Majesty King George, is dead. Be ready. I hope we shall go back to Nairobi today."

'Hussein took to his heels to where Martin was and found him packing up. Hussein told Martin, "Pack up all the luggage. Sad news has just come. The King is dead." Martin sighed and asked "Where?" "In England," said Hussein.'

The almost biblical account ends: 'We who are her servants and who were with her in her lodge in Sagana pray for Their Royal Highnesses, that they may live long in safety.'[23]

The logistics of transporting Elizabeth II back to London as quickly as possible presented a formidable challenge. The nearest airport was at Nanyuki, ten miles distant and lying directly on the equator, but it was little more than an airstrip and quite incapable of accommodating a large aircraft.

By sheer good fortune the Argonaut which had flown the royal party out to Kenya was at Mombasa, having returned to England to pick up a second group of Household staff and officials who were now on board the *Gothic*. Also on board the ship, hanging in one of the tall upright steel trunks inscribed HRH The Princess Elizabeth, was a set of mourning clothes – a precaution taken on all royal tours.

The Queen left the Lodge at 5pm and, all along the red-dust road to Nanyuki, groups of Africans offered their silent sympathy.

At the airport the few newspaper cameramen who had managed to get there in time were asked not to take pictures – partly because the Queen was still wearing a flowered summer frock with white hat and gloves – and respectfully they rested their cameras on their arms, the lenses dipped to the ground. (It is extremely unlikely that such a request would be made, or agreed to, today.)

From Nanyuki a piston-engined Dakota, the faithful workhorse of all small airlines after the war, flew the Queen the 500 miles to Entebbe. Out of the small windows she could look down on orange patches of bush fires gleaming here and there, and above the horizon a sky brilliant with stars. Very little was said, except that at one point the Queen beckoned Martin Charteris to come and sit beside her. 'Now tell me, what's going to happen when we get home?' she asked.

An hour or so into the flight the pilot received a radio message from London which was passed to the Queen. 'The Cabinet in all things awaits Your Majesty's command', signed Winston Churchill.[24]

Soon after the Dakota touched down at Entebbe a violent thunderstorm swept the area, delaying the Argonaut's departure for London by three hours and leaving the Queen no alternative but to wait in the small airport building and make conversation with the Governor of Uganda and his wife who, because of a family bereavement of their own, were in deep mourning.

Finally, shortly before midnight, the Argonaut *Atlanta* climbed into the sky and the Queen and Prince Philip retired to their sleeping berths at the rear of the aircraft at the start of the 4,127-mile-long flight home. But when the plane landed at El Adem, in Libya for refuelling, both the Queen and the Prince got out to stretch their legs and spent several minutes talking to RAF ground crew. When the flight path arrived over the Alps, the Queen went forward to the cockpit and sat in the second pilot's seat for twenty minutes taking cine pictures. 'We chatted for quite a while about the wonderful view,' said Captain R.C. Parker. 'The Queen spoke softly, but clearly.' Others were also to remark on the Queen's composure.

London on the following afternoon was in its full February melancholic state. A pall of grey cloud kept the cold in.

As the Argonaut circled to land (only ten minutes late despite the hold-up at Entebbe), the Queen finally changed out of her bright summer dress into black. Lady Pamela Mountbatten thought she understood why her cousin had been so reluctant to do so until the last possible moment. 'The sort of feeling, "If I put my black on now, that's admitting he's dead." '[25]

Down on the ground, taxi-ing towards the receiving party, the Queen noticed the black limousines drawn up in perfect line. 'Oh, they've sent those hearses,' she remarked.[26] It was the description the Queen and Princess Margaret gave at the time to all the stately black cars used by royalty. But perhaps the comment gave a glimpse of what was passing through the young Queen's mind: a realization that the whole of the rest of her life was destined to be boxed up in stately motor cars and receiving lines. She had enjoyed little personal freedom in the twenty-five years of her life. Now she would be given the chance of even less.

'Shall I go down alone?' she asked her uncle, the Duke of Gloucester, who had come aboard the aircraft to greet her and was likely to know more about these matters. Yes, he thought she should. Prince Philip waited inside in the shadow as his wife slowly descended the fifteen steps of the gangway, holding on to the handrail.

Waiting in a line at the foot of the stairway were four men more than twice the Queen's age who had come to pay homage: Lord Woolton, her burly Leader of the House of Lords; Harry Crookshank, Leader of the

House of Commons; the tall and handsome Anthony Eden, Foreign Secretary; the shorter, bald-headed Clement Attlee, Leader of Her Majesty's Opposition; and, on the left of the group, his walking-stick held at an angle like a sword in its scabbard, the squat, reassuring figure of her Prime Minister, Winston Churchill. In his turn, Churchill bowed to his Queen and took her outstretched hand, the fifth sovereign that it had been his honour and privilege to serve in a long life.

Shortly after the Queen arrived back at her home, Clarence House, at about 5pm, Queen Mary came to call. The mother of the dead King had made the short journey from Marlborough House next door because, she said, 'her old grannie and subject must be the first to kiss her hand'.[27]

The following morning, Elizabeth II held her first privy council at St James's Palace, walking across the courtyard from Clarence House in a light flurry of snowflakes. Lord Woolton thought she was 'very serious, but completely composed', while Harold Macmillan, one of her future Prime Ministers, remembered thinking that some of the Privy Counsellors gathered to do obeisance looked 'scruffy' in their wartime ration-book suits.[28]

The youthful Queen crossed to the oak table and picking up the copy of her declaration, 'in a clear and controlled voice' spoke to her subjects: 'Your Royal Highnesses, My Lords, Ladies and Gentlemen. On the sudden death of my dear father I am called to fulfil the duties and responsibilities of sovereignty . . .'

The long road and reign had begun.

Eleven days later, another young woman, newly married and in the early stages of reading for the Bar, was invited to contribute to a popular newspaper series about the new role of women in public life: 'If, as many earnestly pray,' she wrote, 'the accession of Elizabeth II can help to remove the last shreds of prejudice against women aspiring to the highest places, then a new era for women will indeed be at hand.'[29] The author of the article was an ambitious young politician by the name of Margaret Thatcher.

2

Preparation

❦

O ne of the more intriguing aspects of the Queen's life is that, up until almost the time she reached the age of eleven, it was never intended, and hardly dreamed of, that she would one day become Queen Elizabeth II. (Queen Elizabeth I of Scotland.) It was always assumed that her uncle David, the Prince of Wales, would marry and have children – certainly more than one – to ensure the succession. However, as the whole world now knows, fate intervened. In 1935, the Duke of Windsor, as he will for ever be known, was in love with a twice-divorced American, Mrs Wallis Simpson and, after a period of several months and much arguing with his ministers, he eventually took the crucial decision to abdicate his throne as King Edward VIII after a reign lasting only 326 days, the second shortest in English history. This in order that he might go and marry the woman whose slave he had seemingly become.

In the precise moment that a clerk rose to his feet in the House of Commons to read aloud the royal assent to the Instrument of Abdication – 1.52 pm on 10 December 1936 – Princess Elizabeth passed from being a Princess of the royal blood to being also heir presumptive to the throne of the United Kingdom of Great Britain and Northern Ireland and of Britain's possessions beyond the seas.

'Who is she?' the ten-year-old Princess Elizabeth asked her governess in the spring of 1936.[1] Her uncle David – the name by which the family knew King Edward VIII – had unexpectedly turned up one afternoon at Royal Lodge, her parents' home outside London in Windsor Great Park, driving a new-fangled American station wagon. At his side was a thin, spikily glamorous woman who spoke with an American accent.

Lilibet, the name which Princess Elizabeth gave herself as a child, was too young to be fully aware of the ramifications of her uncle's involvement with Mrs Wallis Simpson, or even the distraught look on his face which the governess, Marion Crawford, noticed – the King 'made plans with the children and then forgot them'.

By the end of the year, despite the efforts of the Duke and Duchess of York to protect Princess Elizabeth and her young sister, Princess Margaret Rose, from the drama that was unfolding almost by the hour, the two girls had managed to winkle out of various people what was going on. On the day that the King finally made his irrevocable decision, Princess Elizabeth, writing up her notes on her latest swimming lesson, put at the top of the piece of paper: 'Abdication Day'. And spotting a letter on the hall table at 145 Piccadilly, the Yorks' London address, addressed to HM The Queen, she remarked to a visitor, Lady Cynthia Asquith, 'That's Mummy now, isn't it?' Princess Margaret Rose, who was at the stage of practising how to sign her name, complained: 'I had only just learned how to spell York, and now I am not to use it any more.'[2] (At least she was soon able to dispense also with the suffix 'Rose'.)

Picking out these two anecdotes may make it seem as if Princess Elizabeth was at the best unconcerned, at the worst plain smug about her new situation. Neither is at all likely to have been the case. Even as a child, Elizabeth II rarely showed her innermost emotions but took a calm, balanced view of most events – even of an abdication which, historians agree, threatened to bring down the monarchy itself. When she heard crowds cheering in the street outside her house, Elizabeth dashed downstairs from the nursery to find out from a footman what was going on. Told that assent had just been given to the Act of Abdication, she tore back upstairs to the nursery to give her little sister the news.

'Does that mean that you will have to be the next Queen?' asked Margaret.

'Yes, some day,' her sister replied.

'Poor you,' said Margaret.[3]

The Princesses' mother, the Duchess of York, who had suffered months of strain and despair over the thought of what would happen if her brother-in-law did abdicate – her dislike of Mrs Simpson amounted to loathing – also remained remarkably calm when news of the King's final decision was brought to her. She was lying in bed, doing her typical level best to get over a bout of influenza, when the messenger called at 145 Piccadilly in the form of the dowager Queen Mary. The mother of four royal princes and one princess, and the widow of King George V, this redoubtable old lady, as ramrod straight as one of her furled umbrellas, was incapable of believing that any of her children could put love of any woman before duty to the Crown and their inheritance. Yet, somehow, despite all her own efforts to 'talk sense' into Edward, her worst fears had come to pass and the wife of her second son was now to be Queen. Even at her lowest, as the Duchess was now, Queen Mary recognized that this young woman was to be the saviour of her second son. He was weak. She was strong.

After her visitor had left, the Queen – as almost everyone now assumed the Duchess of York to be – called in the Princesses' governess. 'I am afraid there are going to be great changes in our lives, Crawfie,' she said. 'We must take what is coming to us, and make the best of it.'[4]

This much repeated remark, with more than a touch of Mrs Miniver about it, was recorded by Marion Crawford some time later for her book, *The Little Princesses*, and has always been taken to mean that Queen Elizabeth, as we shall call her, was referring to her new life at Buckingham Palace as the Queen to King George VI.

Yet, according to the records so far available, there is a suggestion at least that it was not absolutely certain at this stage that George V's second son Albert, who took the name of George, would in fact be crowned king. Or that, in consequence, Princess Elizabeth could correctly be titled heir presumptive.

The mystery lies in the application of the Act of Settlement, which governs the succession of the Crown, and also in the belief held by some influential people at the time that the Duke of York was both an unwilling and an unsuitable person to become monarch.

What is certainly true is that the Duke of York had a dread of succeeding to the throne that went in tandem with an almost crucifying sense of duty to his country. 'Dickie, this is absolutely terrible,' he cried despairingly to his cousin Lord Louis Mountbatten on the eve of Edward VIII's departure. 'I'm quite unprepared for it . . . I've never even seen a State paper.' King George VI's official biographer, Sir John Wheeler-Bennett, speaks of him being 'emotionally disturbed' at the thought of having to face his new responsibilities. Shock was followed by 'merciful numbness'.

Throughout the latter part of 1936, both country and Parliament had been split over what should be done about Mrs Simpson's love affair with the King. In the House of Commons, during the abdication debate, the Independent Labour Party MP, James Maxton, had warned: 'We are doing a wrong and foolish thing if, as a House, we do not seize the opportunity with which circumstances have presented us of establishing in our land a competely democratic form of government which does away with old monarchial institutions and the hereditary principle.' When he moved an amendment to the Abdication Bill, calling for 'a more stable and dignified form of government of a republican kind, in close contact with, and more responsive to, the will of the mass of the people,' he was defeated by 403 votes to five.[5] However, that may have had something to do with Party pressure. A Conservative MP, Sir Arnold Wilson, thought that in a free vote as many as one hundred might have been in favour of a republic. If so, the new King did indeed face problems.

There were other tell-tale signs of uncertainty about the succession. When the as yet uncrowned king left London with his family for the Christmas holiday at Sandringham in 1936, a reporter from the *New York Herald Tribune* was on hand at the railway station. 'King George VI, and his family walked bowing across the platform. Perhaps half the men in the little throng raised their hats. There was a subdued murmur which might have been a suppressed cheer – or might not. . . . In short, on his first public appearance after his succession to his brother, King George VI was given an extremely cold shoulder.'[6]

As the world was to discover, King George turned out to be the ideal monarch to succeed the King whom most people were eventually to look back on as the weakling Duke of Windsor. But at the moment of accession, the Duke of York, it was feared by many in high places, was even weaker in characer and resolution than his elder brother, and without any of the ex-King's redeeming personal charisma.

The new King always looked nervous. He seemed unduly strained. He had such an appalling stutter that it was doubtful whether he would ever be able to speak in public. 'He would be a recluse or, at best, a "rubber stamp",' said his biographer, reporting current fears. About the best that could be said about this slightly-built, unfortunate man, then aged forty-one, was that he had had the sense to marry the beautiful and vivacious Lady Elizabeth Bowes-Lyon, (although, rumour had it, this canny daughter of a Scottish earl had turned him down twice before finally accepting his proposal), and their two daughters, the Princesses Elizabeth and Margaret, were a delight. When they were still tiny tots, photographs of the two girls, their hair curled in the bubble style of Shirley Temple, the child actress who was all the rage at the time, had been carefully scissored out of magazines and pinned up in the bedrooms of thousands of small children, in the same way that today's youngsters put up posters of pop stars.

As George V's first grandchild with the status of Royal Highness, Princess Elizabeth had been a focus of press interest ever since her birth a fortnight after Easter 1926 at her maternal grandparents' London house in Bruton Street. When, four years later, the Duchess of York gave birth to another girl and the two sisters began being seen together in public, the nation took to them in much the same fashion as they did to Prince

William and Prince Harry two generations later. And in their case the parents responded to the extent of inviting the press inside their private home at 145 Piccadilly, and allowing a tour of the children's nurseries, showing them their menagerie of pets which was said to include several corgis, Shetland collies, and fifteen budgerigars.

Considerations of security apart, is it likely that that sort of public relations exercise could happen today? Interestingly, the answer is Yes. In the summer of 1990 the present Duke and Duchess of York invited the Spanish-owned magazine *Hello* into their home to take some exclusive and intimate pictures of their two young daughters which had the Queen gasping. But we shall come to that episode later. The reason facility was offered in the early part of the 1930s was almost certainly due to the shaky state of the monarchy in Britain at the time, and the need to bolster the image of happy royal family life. The Princesses had instant appeal. Even so, nobody seriously thought of little Princess Elizabeth in terms of being a future monarch.

However, as the abdication of King Edward appeared more and more likely to happen, the children themselves gradually became part of the problem of accepting the Duke of York as possibly the new king. The trouble was, they were both *girls*. The rules of succession to the British throne insist that the departed sovereign is succeeded by his sons in descending order of age. Only if there are no sons to inherit does the eldest daughter get a chance. In 1936, when the Duke of York was forty-one and his wife the same age as the century (which, even when she reached ninety, made her sound much older than she appeared), it was not thought likely that they would have any more children. At the same time, the Duke was extremely distressed at the prospect of his beloved Lilibet one day having to take up the burden of sovereignty. If there were any way to escape that route without failing in his duty to his country, which he put above all else, he was likely to accept it.

There is, in fact, evidence to suggest that discussions did take place in December 1936 to consider whether the Duke of York might not step aside in favour of one of his younger brothers. In both Palace and government circles there was serious anxiety both about the Duke's ability to undertake the arduous duties of a monarch, and the age of the child who would inherit from him should tragedy again strike the royal family within the space of a few years.

Next in line to the throne after the Duke of York was his younger brother, the Duke of Gloucester, but generally he was not thought likely to be a suitable or willing person to take up the burden. He, too, did not possess the strongest constitution. However, this still left the youngest surviving son of King George V and Queen Mary,* the young Duke of Kent, who in many eyes and in many ways was thought to be the ideal candidate. In addition to having the outward-going personality of his eldest brother, David, he already enjoyed the bonus of a male heir to succeed him.

The Duke of Kent's marriage to Princess Marina of Greece in November 1934 – 'she has not a cent to her name,' King George V cheerfully told his Prime Minister[7] – had met with great public approval. Princess Marina was not only beautiful to look at, she also possessed an elegance and intelligence that made men her adoring slaves. (Her daughter, Princess Alexandra, has much the same effect on both men and women today.) Their son Edward was just one year old. Would this not be the perfect young family to start off a bright new reign?

Although the public were unaware of it at the time, there was just one serious defect in the idyllic picture. In his youth the Duke of Kent had been inveigled into taking drugs, and prior to his marriage had been prone to periods of deep depression. But, the Prime Minister of the day, Stanley Baldwin, was assured that the young man had won his fight against these twin afflictions – interestingly enough, largely through the help of his eldest brother, and was said now to be completely recovered. Reformed in his behaviour, and with a son already there to succeed him, perhaps the order of succession should be altered to bypass the Duke of York and, thereby, the Yorks' daughter Elizabeth, also?

We shall not know for sure how serious this proposition was, or how far it was taken, until the time comes for the official life of Elizabeth II to be written down with all the private papers made available. But as long ago as 1947, strong evidence was published to support the allegation, and today it is hard not to speculate on what the outcome might have been if the suggestion had been implemented.

Among other things, it would have meant that the present Duke of Kent would now be King – either Edward IX or, more likely, George VII – and his very attractive wife, the former Katharine Worsley, would be the Queen. Their only son, the present Earl of St Andrews, would have become heir apparent, with the inherited title of Prince of Wales. And 'that little local difficulty', Marina Ogilvy, who caused her parents, Princess Alexandra and the Hon. Sir Angus Ogilvy, such anguish during 1989 when she left home to have a baby out of wedlock, (eventually she and the father decided to marry some months before the birth) would be a niece of the King and thus closer in line of succession to the throne.

As for the Queen and Prince Philip, if what was discussed at the

---

* Prince John, the youngest son of King George V and Queen Mary, was subject to epileptic seizures and died in 1919 at the age of fourteen.

highest levels over half a century ago had been put into operation, then they might indeed be living today the private life of country landowners that they both enjoy so much, seldom seen outside of State occasions and hardly known by the world at large.

In 1947, Dermot Morrah, late Fellow of All Souls College, Oxford, published a celebration of the first twenty-one years of Princess Elizabeth's life. When the account reached the period of the abdication crisis, Mr Morrah stated:

> It was certainly seriously considered at this time whether, by agreement among the royal family, the crown might not be settled on the Duke of Kent, the only one of the abdicating King's brothers who at that time had a son to become Prince of Wales, and so avoid laying so heavy a future burden upon the shoulders of any woman. The possibility of such a course was debated by some men of authority in the State who believed that it would accord with the wishes of the royal persons concerned.[8]

What is particularly significant about this account is that Mr Morrah's book was written 'by gracious permission of His Majesty the King'.

However, Mr Morrah went on to point out that 'whether it was ever seriously considered in the royal household itself is of course a matter of which nothing is ever likely to be publicly known.'

Some eleven years later, in another book which also spelled out his royal credentials and access to Members of the Queen's Household, Morrah saw fit to return to the subject:

> Since Parliament must be asked to alter the laws of succession so as to transfer the Crown from the heir designated by the Act of Settlement to some other person, it was not a legal necessity that the person selected should be the next in hereditary order; and there are veteran officers of the Household who remember how much persuasion had to be brought to bear upon the Duke of York in order to persuade him that he was the man that the nation and Empire overwhelmingly desired to see as their head. ... At that time the only prince near to the line of succession who had a son was the Duke of Kent, and the draftsmen preparing the Abdication Bill at least tentatively considered what to do if his two elder brothers asked to stand aside in his favour.[9]

All these years later, it is worth reflecting on the fact that if the then Duke of Kent had been made king in his brother's place, his reign would have lasted less than seven years. For, tragically, he was killed at the age of forty in a Second World War crash while serving with the RAF. If he had been king at the time, his death would have led to his eldest son Edward, today the Duke of Kent, ascending the throne at the age of seven, and quite possibly his uncle, the Duke of York, would have been made Regent.

It would be an exaggeration to say that the life of Princess Elizabeth changed completely after her parents became the King and Queen. But, not surprisingly, the accession meant some major alterations to a lifestyle she had become accustomed to, even at the age of eleven. For a start, the whole family had to up sticks and move house.

King George VI and Queen Elizabeth moved into Buckingham Palace on 15 February 1937, and Princess Elizabeth and her little sister two days later. Princess Elizabeth had lived there before, as a six-month-old baby, while her parents were sent on a six-month tour of the Empire. The Duchess of York, as she was then, had been so upset at having to leave her baby behind that she had had to ask the driver taking her to Victoria Station for the departure to drive twice round Grosvenor Gardens so that she could compose herself – a reason perhaps why, some forty-six years later, as Queen Elizabeth the Queen Mother, she was in favour of the Prince and Princess of Wales taking their six-month-old son, Prince William, on their tour of Australia and New Zealand.

Apart from the all-too-brief years of young married life that she spent in Clarence House and on the island of Malta as the wife of a naval officer husband, Buckingham Palace has been the main residence of Elizabeth II ever since she reached the age of eleven – in other words for over half a century.

At first she did not much like the place. It was too big, too grand, and too reminiscent of her awesome grandmother, Queen Mary, to whom the little princesses had to curtsy whenever they were received into her presence. The awesome granny – who, in fact, was less formidable and more at ease with her grandchildren than she had been with her own children – had moved down the road to Marlborough House after the death of her husband, and the new King and Queen made it a rule from the outset that their children should not have to curtsy to them.

Up until the time she moved into Buckingham Palace with her parents and young sister, Princess Elizabeth had spent seven cheerful years at 145 Piccadilly, four doors along from Hyde Park Corner in an area that at that time was still comprised essentially of exclusive private houses with hardly any hotels or offices in sight.*

* Number 145 was destroyed by bombs in the Second World War and the site was subsequently used to build the London Intercontinental Hotel and the Inn on the Park.

The Princesses' nursery was on the top floor of the house, with large windows overlooking the plane trees of Hyde Park. The night nursery had no plumbing, just a ewer and basin for washing hands. There was a circular landing, with a huge glass dome above, and through the gaps in the bannisters the children could peep down on the comings and goings of important visitors three floors below.

Lilibet kept a collection of toy horses on iron wheels which had regular feeding times and which she 'stabled' at night in neat rows on the landing outside her bedroom. At the age of three she was given her first real pony and could soon ride well, to the pleasure of her grandfather George V who had told his own eldest son as a child: 'If you can't ride, you know, I am afraid people will call you a duffer.'[10] The six-year-old Princess was sitting up in bed riding an imaginary horse when the governess, Marion Crawford, was first introduced to her.

'Do you usually drive in bed?'

'I mostly go once or twice round the park before I go to sleep, you know,' the Princess solemnly explained.[11]

As small children, Margaret was regarded by parents and servants alike as mischievous, even wilful, while her elder sister was much more 'ordered' within herself. Neatness was everything, and nothing was wasted. Lilibet folded up wrapping paper, kept a box for discarded ribbon and, until she was teased out of it by her young sister, would get out of bed more than once before going to sleep, to make doubly sure that her shoes were meticulously placed together and her clothes properly arranged over a chair – something, curiously enough, which Lady Diana Spencer was also credited with doing, when hurriedly prepared biographies came to be written about her.

Up until the arrival on the scene of Miss Marion Crawford, Princess Elizabeth was looked after, as far as the nurseries were concerned, by four women. The first was the nanny, Mrs Knight – known to everyone as Allah* – who had been nanny to Princess Elizabeth's mother, and who, in the manner of nannies of the day, held the title of Mrs but had never been married. Nobody could remember ever seeing her out of uniform and it was rumoured, incorrectly, that she never took a holiday. She was always calm, always deliberate, and always to be obeyed – instantly. She was also greatly loved, except by Miss Crawford when she arrived. The two women had different ideas about upbringing. It was said that rumours about Little Princess Margaret being deaf and dumb were caused because Allah refused to let her out of her pram when they were out walking in Hyde Park.

---

* The name has been variously spelt 'Alah', 'Allah' and 'Ala'. The Queen's personal preference is not known.

However, Dermot Morrah, the favoured royal chronicler, was never in any doubt about Mrs Knight's value:

It is the peculiar good fortune of the English that there is always an abundance of men and women of simple and upright character who can undertake in obscurity the tasks of which the consequences will become of world-wide significance, though their contribution will be forgotten; and among these Miss [*sic*] Knight is entitled to an honourable place, as the first of a succession of tried and trusted friends who have helped their future sovereign on her way.

The second person to have a deep influence on the young Princess was Margaret MacDonald, the under-nurse, whose mother came from the Sutherland fishing village of Durness and whose father was a gardener and coachman at Cromarty in 1904, when his eldest daughter was born.

After the birth of a little sister to Princess Elizabeth, Mrs Knight needed to concentrate on the new arrival, and so 'Bobo' MacDonald, as she came to be known, looked after Elizabeth. In time, Bobo knew most of the Princess's secrets and learned to judge what and whom she liked and did not like. Nurse and charge occupied the same bedroom right up until the Princess was eleven years old. Sixty years later, Miss Mac-Donald was still living in the same house as the Princess who was now the Queen. In her later years Bobo held a unique position in Bucking-ham Palace, having her own suite, no duties, and enjoying a closer personal friendship with the Queen than practically anyone else, in-cluding some of the Queen's closest relatives. After a lifetime of service as personal dresser to Elizabeth II, she is held in awe by even the most senior other Members of the Queen's Household.

'Do you know what she said to me the other day?' the Queen exclaimed to one of them, before proceeding to tell the person a quite astonishing tale. 'Of course, she has every right to say that,' said Eliza-beth II. 'She has been with me such a long time.'

Bobo's sister, Ruby, joined the nursery staff at 145 Piccadilly, and the fourth person to surround the future Queen at this early stage of her life was somebody known in the annals as simply 'Smith the nursery-maid'.

This muster of the nursery staff takes no account, however, of Marion Crawford who in any case, as governess, would place herself in a slightly different category from the others. Miss Crawford was in charge of the education of both Princesses.

'Crawfie', as she soon became known (for some reason the aristocracy have a greater than normal propensity for abbreviating the names of their staff and their animals) is one of those somewhat sad figures to be found wandering around the footnotes of almost any family history.

Immensely fond of her charges, and by all accounts excellent at her job, she made the elementary mistake of believing that, because her employers were friendly, she was their friend. Royalty has few close friends, and fewest among its staff. It has loyalty, but that is not the same. And it expects loyalty to be returned. Crawfie, in the end, had no loyalty – or very little, it would seem – and that is what finally finished her off in the eyes of most, if not all, members of the royal family who knew her. Even before her death, mentioning the name of the Queen's governess in certain company brought forth a stony silence.

Among those grateful to her memory, however, are a succession of authors. Without Crawfie's illuminating account, *The Little Princesses*, published by Cassell in 1950, it is doubtful whether royal biographers would know half of what they do know about the early years of Elizabeth II and the events leading up to her enthronement. Long before it became a requirement for anyone employed in royal service to sign an undertaking under the Official Secrets Act, Crawfie walked out through the gates of Buckingham Palace one day, spilled the beans – or some of them – and, sweet and harmless though they were, paid the price for doing so.*

Crawfie was born in the Scottish town of Kilmarnock and trained as a teacher, though she envisaged a career in child psychology. A chance invitation to tutor Lord Bruce, the seven-year-old son of the Earl and Countess of Elgin, led to a recommendation to the Leveson-Gowers and their daughter Mary, the young niece of the then Duchess of York. For many weeks the tall, sparely-built Miss Crawford found herself striding the three miles from her home to the Elgins, three miles further on to the Leveson-Gowers, and three miles home for tea.

When he came to hear about it, no doubt through his wife or one of his huntin'-shootin'-and-fishing friends, the energetic youthfulness of Miss Crawford appealed to the Duke of York, who, in his own upbringing, had suffered agonies under crusty old tutors who could barely conceal their impatience at his acute stutter.

With the approval of his wife, the Duke engaged the twenty-two-year old progressive nursery teacher and brought her to London as governess to his then six-year-old elder daughter. 'Why have you got no hair?' Princess Elizabeth enquired on first seeing Miss Crawford's mannish hairstyle.[12]

After a successful month's trial, the Scot was given full responsibility for the child's education. 'For goodness sake, teach Margaret and Lilibet to write a decent hand, that's all I ask you,' growled the princesses'

---

* She married Major George Buthlay and retired to Aberdeen where, a widow, she died in 1987. None of the royal family attended the funeral or sent a wreath.

grandfather King George V, 'I like a hand with some character in it.'[13]

Princess Elizabeth's parents were not so demanding. Their governess was surprised to find what a free rein she was given. 'No one ever had employers who interfered so little. I had often the feeling that the Duke and Duchess, most happy in their own married life, were not over concerned with the higher education of their daughters. They wanted most for them a really happy childhood, with lots of pleasant memories stored up against the days that might come and, later, happy marriages.'

A room on the floor below the nursery, next to the Duchess of York's drawing-room, was set out as a schoolroom. There was a blackboard, maps on the wall, and a small desk with a hardbacked chair for the one pupil in the class – a second desk would be placed alongside the other in a few years time when Princess Margaret joined her sister for lessons.

A strict routine was followed each day, without the slightest complaint, it seems, from the young Princess. At 7.30am she got up, dressed, and had breakfast in the nursery. At 9am she went downstairs to visit her parents. At 9.15am lessons began, with half an hour's religious instruction every Monday morning. At 11am there was a half-hour break for a glass of orangeade and a biscuit before lessons resumed. At 1.15pm the Princess joined her parents for luncheon – provided they were not out attending to some duty or other – and in those early days of the Princesses' education the afternoons were always spent out of doors, if weather permitted. If it did not, then there were drawing or music lessons. Tea was at 4.45pm in the schoolroom, and between 5.30pm and 6.30pm the Duchess of York insisted that both Mrs Knight and Crawfie should allow her to enjoy the company of her children as she wished. After supper, at 7.15pm on the dot, Princess Elizabeth went to bed, having claimed the elder sister's privilege of staying up almost an hour longer than Princess Margaret.

In the days long before television governed young people's lives and wearied parents acquiesced, it was a routine followed in millions of other homes up and down the land, where a mug of Ovaltine and a rubber hotwater bottle carried up to bed warmly put the day away.

On Friday afternoons the family climbed into the box-shaped Daimler and drove down to Royal Lodge in the grounds of Windsor Castle. Apart from a Saturday morning of revising and a Sunday morning at church, the weekends were spent riding, playing, or helping Papa to build bonfires from the acres of wild rhododendron and scrub that he thoroughly enjoyed hacking away at in order to make a new garden. 'I am only a very ordinary person when people let me be one,' the Duke of York once said. Certainly, especially before the abdication crisis, he and his wife tried hard to bring up their children to be as much like any other children of the same class as possible.

Of course, there were differences, and not only the most obvious ones. Just now and then a chink of light reveals that the children were not expected to move away entirely from the traditional behaviour of their charmed circle. For instance, although fox hunting has never been part of Elizabeth II's life, as a child she did ride with the Beaufort, and when she was only five her father asked that she should be 'blooded' with the Pytchley. She was probably very relieved that on the day it was supposed to happen the fox got clean away.

To prepare her for a future public life, Princess Elizabeth was occasionally treated to outings into 'the real world'. She pestered her governess into taking her to Tottenham Court Road for a two-stop ride on the Underground followed by tea at the YWCA. On another occasion, she rode on the top deck of an omnibus. She was frequently taken for walks in Hyde Park by either her nanny or Miss Crawford, running the gauntlet of the press photographer (usually only one in those days and not a pack), who was soon seen off like some unwelcome cur. 'I'm sure he thinks that Crawfie bites!' declared a delighted Princess following one of these skirmishes.

As any child would, Princess Elizabeth was beginning to realize that she and her young sister attracted considerable attention from total strangers whenever they stepped outside their front door. An incognito ride on the Underground was exciting for its rarity alone, but a public appearance causing crowds to gather could very easily turn a young girl's head. No one was more aware of this danger than the children's paternal grandmother, Queen Mary. As has been said already, she had never been able to form a close relationship with her own children, particularly when they were small, so perhaps she tried to make up for the deficiency when grandchildren arrived. In any event, she by no means ignored them, although she could be strangely shy in their presence.

If anything, King George V was the more favoured grandparent. Like Queen Mary, he had been awkward with his own children – 'I'm a bad hand at saying what I feel,' he admitted. But he was devoted to his grandchildren. For a long time a favourite story was that they called him 'Grandpa England' – a cuddly sort of title – but Princess Margaret has knocked that one of the head. 'We were much too frightened of him to call him anything but Grandpapa,'[14] she has said. She has also spoken of any summons from Queen Mary bringing on a 'hollow, empty feeling in the pit of the stomach'.[15]

But as with many grandparents of the time, brought up on a diet of Victorian discipline, their intimidating manner often only covered over kind intentions. Queen Mary saw it as her duty to give an early grounding in the arts to her granddaughters and would lead them on long exhausting tours of portrait galleries and museums. It was on one of these outings, to an afternoon recital at the Queen's Hall, that the Queen first had evidence that her eldest granddaughter might be reacting the wrong way to the fact that she had been born famous. Queen Mary had suggested that, as Lilibet was wriggling so much instead of sitting still like a good girl should, it might be prudent if they just slipped quietly out of their seats and left before the recital ended. 'Oh no, Granny,' was the response, 'we can't leave before the end. Think of all the people who'll be waiting to see us outside.' Queen Mary's very straight back must have stiffened to rigidity. A whispered instruction to her lady-in-waiting, and the offending child was promptly led out by a back door and taken home by taxi. A taxi! Queen Mary cannot have meant to give her granddaughter this unexpected treat.

Another story of about this same period – the mid-1930s – tells of how the Lord Chamberlain, coming across the King's granddaughter in a corridor of Buckingham Palace, greeted her pleasantly with 'Good morning, little lady', only to be corrected with 'I'm not a little lady, I'm Princess Elizabeth'. Later that same day the Chamberlain received a visit from Queen Mary accompanied by a small child held firmly by the hand. 'This is Princess Elizabeth, who hopes one day to be a lady,' said the Queen.[16]

Viewed from the standpoint of current royal thinking, it may seem extraordinary that Princess Elizabeth and Princess Margaret were not sent away to school for at least part of their education. At least they would have made more friends that way, and any chance of big-headedness would have been knocked out of them at a very early stage. As it was, apart from sometimes inviting their cousins, George and Gerald Lascelles, to Buckingham Palace to play, or occasionally going out themselves to the homes of neighbouring aristocrats for tea, the two girls spent most of their time in the company of adults.

'Other children,' recalled Crawfie, 'always had an enormous fascination, like mystics from a distant world, and the little girls used to smile shyly at those they liked the look of. They would so have loved to speak to them and make friends, but this was never encouraged. I have often thought it a pity. The Dutch and Belgian royal children walked about the street in their countries as a matter of course.'[17]

The idea of their children attending school was an improbable notion to the Duke and Duchess of York, and practically inconceivable to King George and Queen Mary. Even twenty years later, in 1951, Princess Elizabeth's father was to chuckle at the very idea of his going into hospital to have a serious operation. 'I've never heard of a king going to a hospital before,' he protested.[18]

The objection to his children going to school was partly to do with the fact that they were girls. Daughters of the upper classes very often had to rely on governesses, which at least had the benefit of giving them individual tuition. But the main objection in the case of Princess Elizabeth, and to a lesser extent with Princess Margaret, was that school would mean mixing with other children whose parents the royal family might not even know!

An attempt was made to alleviate the situation through the formation of the 1st Buckingham Palace Company of Girl Guides, to which two Brownies were attached so that Princess Margaret could join in with her sister. However, the idea was not an immediate success. A contemporary recalls how doors were flung open to the troop by scarlet-coated footmen and 'nannies treated the whole affair as they would a dancing class, bringing their charges in party frocks with white gloves.'

The children, all carefully vetted and from families well known to the Princesses' parents, naturally showed their very best behaviour once inside the Palace. '*They* won't be able to roll about and get dirty,' said Princess Elizabeth scornfully on first meeting them. There was one game in which the children had to pile their shoes up in a heap and then sort them out. The Princess stood amazed when it came to the end. Quite a few of her fellow Guides could not even identify their own footwear!

To her grown-up observers, Princess Elizabeth very often seemed old for her age and self-possessed. Compared with her little sister, who was a chatterbox and into everything, Lilibet was always more restrained. It was partly to do with the problem facing all first-born, that of setting an example to those who follow. But the sisters were, and have remained, strikingly different in personality. A typically 'Crawfie' illustration is provided by the governess: 'The two little girls had their own way of dealing with their barley sugar. Margaret kept the whole lot in her small, hot hand and pushed it into her mouth. Lilibet, however, carefully sorted hers out on the table, large and small pieces together, and then ate them very daintily and methodically.'

Despite, or possibly because of their differences, an immensely strong bond of mutual love and dependence developed between the sisters from very early on. Each could see in the other, even as small children, facets of character they admired and wished they had themselves. Princess Margaret has always admired her sister's sang-froid and, according to a friend, 'the Queen sometimes wishes she was a little better at "unbending"'. As children, like the best of friends at that age, they sometimes had fierce squabbles. Margaret only had to twang the elastic of Lilibet's hat, or provoke her in some other way, and tempers flared. At such times, according to Princess Margaret, the elder sister would pinch and the younger would retaliate with a sharp kick to the shin. But 'I never won,' Princess Margaret remembers.[19]

It came as a considerable shock to both children when the death of King George V, followed a year later by the abdication of King Edward

VIII, resulted in their being uprooted from their home in Piccadilly and plonked down, as it must have seemed to them, among the overstuffed impedimenta of Buckingham Palace. Informed that this was to be her new home, the seven-year-old Princess Margaret was incredulous. 'What! Do you mean for ever?' Her sister was just as unexcited by the prospect. She seriously wondered if a tunnel could not be burrowed between the Palace and 145 Piccadilly, which was less than a mile away.

The change of address brought with it other, more far-reaching changes. Up until this point the sisters, despite the four-year age gap, had been brought up almost as twins. Their mother dressed them in practically identical outfits – short fitted coats over jumpers and pleated skirts. The public had grown used to seeing the two girls in tandem, either in photographs or out walking with their governess, and the Duke and Duchess of York had encouraged this togetherness as part of their desire that, in the words of King George VI's official biographer, 'Princess Elizabeth and Princess Margaret should look back upon their early years as a golden age'.[20]

The pity was that the golden age couldn't have lasted just a little longer.

From the moment King George VI returned home from his Accession Council in December 1936 to be greeted by his two daughters sinking to the floor in a deep curtsey (meticulously rehearsed by Miss Crawford), the relationship was bound to change. There was very little likelihood that the new Queen would have any more children. Apart from any consideration of age, she was faced with the exhausting task of supporting a husband who, despite a remarkable improvement to his stutter, was nonetheless terrified of failing at his job. With no prospect of a Prince, Princess Elizabeth at almost eleven years of age was expected to succeed to the throne.

Princess Margaret has always maintained that her sister's new situation did not affect their close relationship. It simply meant that Lilibet now had *official* seniority and would increasingly be privy to State matters. Where it could have caused serious problems, as we shall see, was when the elder sister, as Queen, had to make agonizing decisions about Princess Margaret's future happiness. For the time being, the sisters carried on very much as before, although interest outside the Palace increasingly focused on Princess Elizabeth.

While the King still had much to contend with – 'there's a lot of prejudice against him,' said Prime Minister Stanley Baldwin – his eldest daughter made a favourable impression from almost the outset. In the opinion of the *Daily Mail*, 'This little lady has in her the qualities of greatness'. *The Times* went further: 'Her self-possessed yet perfectly unspoilt and childish deportment when she appears with her mother in public shows that the training of this little girl is proceeding on the right lines for the happiness of the country over which she may one day have to rule.'

The first big test was King George VI's coronation. In her usual way, Lilibet took utmost care in preparing. Her governess planned a pre-coronation course of reading that included Queen Victoria's youthful journal and H. E. Marshall's history, *Our Island Story*. Along The Mall from Marlborough House, where she had taken up residence after King George V's death, came Queen Mary in her huge old-fashioned Daimler car, bearing a prized item from her hoard of antiques. It was a panorama of King George IV's coronation which, when unfolded concertina-fashion, revealed a procession thirty feet long of all the leading luminaries taking part in the ceremony. Lilibet was delighted by it. She was even more excited by 'a very, very special book' which was a surprise gift from her papa. Bound in beige linen, with the title 'Her Royal Highness The Princess Elizabeth' embossed in gold, it was her own private copy of the illustrated 'Order of the Service of the Coronation'.

On the great day itself – 12 May 1937 – practically everyone in Buckingham Palace was woken at 3am by the din of loudspeakers being tested on the route from the Palace to Westminster Abbey. At 5am, Princess Elizabeth was woken again, this time 'by the band of the Royal Marines striking up just outside my window'. She could hardly sleep for excitement anyway. Preserved in the Royal Library at Windsor is an exercise book tied in pink ribbon in which Princess Elizabeth wrote down in red pencil her memories of Coronation Day 'To Mummy and Papa,' it reads, 'In Memory of Their Coronation, from Lilibet By Herself.'

> I leapt out of bed and so did Bobo. We put on dressing-gowns and shoes and Bobo made me put on an eiderdown as it was so cold and we crouched in the window looking on to a cold, misty morning. There were already some people in the stands and all the time people were coming to them in a stream. . . . Every now and then we were hopping in and out of bed looking at the bands and the soldiers. At six o'clock Bobo got up and instead of getting up at my usual time I jumped out of bed at half past seven. When I was going to the bathroom I passed the lift as usual, and who should walk out but Miss Daly! [her swimming instructor]. I was very pleased to see her. When I dressed I went into the nursery.[21]

Both princesses wore specially designed lace gowns with purple cloaks edged with ermine. But when Lilibet lifted her skirt to show off her silver slippers it was noticeable that she was still wearing her schoolgirl white ankle socks. What worried her almost more than anything was the thought that Margaret might fidget or do something silly like laugh during the long service, which evidently their father had done at King Edward VII's coronation. However, Princess Margaret's behaviour turned out to be nearly impeccable. 'I only had to nudge her once or twice, when she played with her prayer books too loudly,' said Princess Elizabeth afterwards[22] – which makes it sound as if she were a real bossy-boots at this early stage in her life.

Queen Mary was gratified by both granddaughters' behaviour. 'They looked so sweet, expecially when they put on their coronets.'[23] The elderly Queen – she was never to take the title of Queen Mother as her widowed daughter-in-law was to do one day – had broken with tradition by attending the coronation of her son. Hitherto, a queen-dowager had stayed away from a successor's crowning, but Queen Mary had rightly judged that a display of family solidarity would not come amiss after her eldest son's shameful behaviour. The Duke of Windsor wisely remained in France, where he had gone into exile.

'Grannie looked too beautiful in a gold dress patterned with golden flowers,' wrote Lilibet. She thought the act of coronation 'very, very wonderful, and I expect the Abbey did too. . . . The arches and beams at the top were covered with a sort of haze of wonder as Papa was crowned, at least I thought so. . . . What struck me as being rather odd was that Grannie did not remember much of her own coronation. I should have thought that it would have stayed in her mind for ever.'

The young Princess's only criticism was that the service went on too long and got rather boring because, towards the end, there were rather a lot of prayers. There was also 'the most awful draught coming from somewhere'.

'Grannie and I were looking to see how many more pages to the end, and we turned one more and then I pointed to the word at the bottom of the page and it said "Finis". We both smiled at each other and turned back to the service. . . . When we got back to our dressing room we had some sandwiches, stuffed rolls, orangeade and lemonade.'[24]

More than anything, the coronation put the tottering monarchy safely back on to its pedestal. As always, the public lapped up the pomp and ceremony and were inspired by the history and tradition. But King George VI personally came out of it very well too. Just as his father had been moved by the size and affection of the crowds who had come out to greet him and Queen Mary on the celebration of their Silver Jubilee – 'I'd no idea they felt like that about me. I am beginning to think they must really like me for myself'[25] – so King George VI too was touched by the warm reception of his people. With his quite amazing wife, Queen Elizabeth, at his side, encouraging, correcting, supporting, above all showing love, he gradually emerged, sooner than anyone had expected, from his prison of uncertainty to give the nation the kind of unassuming integrity it needed. Like his father, he was to be loved for possessing 'the majesty of the ordinary man', to quote author Robert Lacey.

George VI's children were devoted to him and, for his own part, the King found exceptional enjoyment in watching them grow up. He had had a fairly miserable childhood himself and his daughters' genuine affection warmed him greatly. According to Sir John Wheeler-Bennett, the King saw in his elder daughter certain traits of his own character: 'His own combination of humour and dignity, his common sense and eagle eye for detail'. And in Princess Margaret, 'the same quick mind and with it a vivacious charm, a sparkling sense of wit, an appreciation of the ludicrous.'[26] She it was who could always make her father laugh, even when he was angry with her. The King had a temper quick to rise and just as quick to ebb. Among the family the outbursts were known as 'gnashes'. His eldest grandson has inherited the trait. But when Sir John Wheeler-Bennett talks of Princess Margaret's appreciation of the ludicrous he should really have included her sister. Elizabeth II's sense of the ridiculous is equally pronounced, although in the company of pompous mayors or craven officials it may have to be curbed and is normally only apparent to those in her household who have learned how to recognize the Queen's coded messages.

The coronation of George VI was to be the last embroidered piece of pageantry that Britain was to see for a long time to come. Just two and a half years later the glowering threat of Nazi Germany became a hideous reality with the outbreak of the Second World War on 3 September 1939.

At the time the Princesses were on holiday at Birkhall, on the Balmoral estate. The King and Queen had already broken off their holiday to return to London. Lilibet and Margaret, it was decided, would be safer for the time being remaining in Scotland. Miss Crawford was left with instructions to 'stick to the usual programme as far as you can'. That just left the King with the problem of what to do with his mother, by now seventy-two.

At first, Queen Mary was adamant that she should remain in London to face anything that was coming, but she was persuaded to evacuate to the depths of the country, along with all the city children.

The Duke and Duchess of Beaufort graciously, and perhaps a trifle rashly, offered Queen Mary the use of their home 'for the duration of the war'. The Duchess was a niece of the dowager Queen – her father was the German Prince Teck – and Badminton had been the Beaufort family's stately mansion in Gloucestershire since the seventeenth century. The Duke and Duchess were very fond of Queen Mary, but in offering her their home it is perhaps not too unkind to suggest that they may have reckoned that the presence of royalty would circumvent any suggestion that the house be commandeered by the Army. However, they may not have known quite what they were letting themselves in for.

Near pandemonium broke out shortly after the dowager Queen's arrival. She had journeyed from London with no fewer than seventy-one pieces of personal luggage and fifty-three servants. Though it was said that only ten of them looked after the Queen, fifteen looked after the ten, and the rest looked after the fifteen, they all had to be found somewhere to sleep and the locals revolted at being kicked out of their rooms. The Duchess of Beaufort reported to her husband's cousin, Osbert Sitwell, the author and poet: 'They refused to use the excellent rooms assigned to them. Fearful rows and battles royal were fought over my body – but I won in the end and reduced them to tears and to pulp ... I can laugh now, but I have never been so angry! ... The Queen, quite unconscious of the stir, has settled in well, and is busy cutting down trees and tearing down ivy. Tremendous activity.'[27]

Queen Mary had a phobia about climbing ivy. Wherever she saw it, she ripped it down, or had someone do it for her. 'Lovely morning,' she wrote in her diary on 26 September, 'which we spent clearing ivy off trees. We watched a whole wall of ivy of fifty years standing at the back of Mary B's bedroom being removed – most of it came down like a blanket.' No one dared to object. In fact, everyone – lady-in-waiting, private secretary, equerry – was roped in to help. They became known as Queen Mary's 'Ivy Squad' and when their mission was not within walking distance they would commandeer a farm cart in which were placed two wickerwork chairs. 'Aunt May,' called out her niece one day, 'you look as if you were in a tumbril!' 'Well, it may come to that yet, one never knows,' the Queen responded, giving a little royal wave as the cart jolted off.[28]

Another of Queen Mary's phobias was waste of any kind. Whenever she saw farm equipment lying in a corner of a field she would track down the owner and demand that the old iron be sent for scrap to help the war effort. Just because the ploughs were rusty she assumed that they were no longer used. She really had no idea about country life. On watching long grass being mowed in May she is said to have remarked: 'So, *that's* what hay looks like.'[29]

Her host and hostess, who were slightly eccentric themselves, were very fond of the Queen, even though for something like five years, perforce, they had to be content with being more or less guests in their own house. Until she settled in properly, which meant taking over entirely, Queen Mary was at a loss herself. 'I long to be at Home,' she wrote to Lady Bertha Hawkins. 'I feel rather useless here but I can visit Evacuees & Work depots, they seem to like to see one which is a mercy!'[30]

On dry days she always managed to get out into the open air. On very wet days she sat in the Music Room and sorted through Beaufort family papers, putting the more interesting items in separate envelopes and signing the outside Mary R., followed by the date. Many years later, when the Severn Bridge was being built across the Bristol Channel, someone in the Beaufort family remembered that John of Gaunt had originally granted their ancestors rights to the river Severn bed. Prove it, said the authorities. A frantic search, and three weeks later the Duchess came across a faded envelope signed Mary R., 1940, and titled 'Papers of Interest'. Inside was the agreement, signed in his own hand by John of Gaunt in 1360. As a result of the find the Beauforts were able to arrive at good terms with the bridge contractors, so Queen Mary need not have felt at all useless.

With Queen Mary settled in, King George VI and Queen Elizabeth now had to decide what to do about their daughters. The 'phoney' first few months of the war, when mass bombing raids had been expected but didn't happen, were over. But there still remained a very real threat of a German invasion. Raids by enemy parachutists with specific targets was another possibility. The little Princesses were obviously at great risk. The first move was to get them to Windsor Castle where, in theory at least, the massive walls and deep cellars would give them protection. Gun emplacements circled the castle and specially briefed troops were never more than a few yards away. That, at least, was the assurance given to the King and Queen. Alternatively, as Princess Margaret was to recall many years later, 'they dug trenches and put up some rather feeble barbed wire, and the feeble barbed wire of course wouldn't have kept anybody out but it kept us in.'[31]

Prime Minister Winston Churchill, newly appointed and at this stage not particularly favoured by the King, had a plan to spirit the Princesses away to a 'safe-house' in Worcestershire if Hitler invaded. But the King was not in favour. Neither did he like the idea, mooted by the Dutch Queen Wilhelmina, herself a recent evacuee from Holland, that the children should be sent as far away as Canada where they would be completely out of harm's way. Quite apart from the almost insufferable separation, he felt that he could not have his children spend the war safely out of the country while millions of other children were staying put. If there were to be a successful invasion, the King wished personally to lead an armed resistance movement and have his family close at hand. Any sneaking feeling among the public that there might be one law for the rich, (several of whom had, in fact, sent their children abroad with government approval), and one law for the rest, was finally dispelled by the Queen in an official statement: 'The children won't leave without me; I won't leave without the King; and the King will never leave.'[32] One could almost hear the silent cheers.

The two sisters settled down quickly in the castle that was to become Elizabeth II's favourite home. (Balmoral Castle runs a close second.) In some ways it was an odd choice as a refuge. Within striking distance of London, it was almost on the Germans' direct flight path to the important ports of Bristol and Plymouth. By the end of the war 300 high-explosive bombs and innumerable incendiaries would have fallen within a three-mile radius of the castle. Hygiene and good manners were not among the casualties, however. Princess Margaret remembers dropping a ginger biscuit the first time a bomb exploded close by, and not being allowed to eat it after picking it up off the floor.

The King and Queen, at Buckingham Palace, were soon also in the thick of it. 'We were both upstairs,' the King wrote in his diary on 13 September 1940, 'talking in my little room overlooking the quadrangle. All of a sudden we heard an aircraft making a zooming noise above us, saw two bombs falling past the opposite side of the Palace, and then heard two resounding crashes as the bombs fell in the quadrangle about thirty yards away.'[33]

Altogether six bombs had been dropped by an aircraft diving below the clouds and flying down The Mall. 'It was a ghastly experience and I don't want it to be repeated,' wrote the King. 'It certainly teaches one to "take cover" on all future occasions, but one must be careful not to become "dugout-minded".'[34] The Queen thought that a direct hit meant that at least they could look London's bomb-battered East End in the face. When the King and Queen visited the area, clambering over the rubble in their smart clothes, there was a noticeable feeling of camaraderie and defiance to Hitler between King and countryman. Winston Churchill wrote to his sovereign: 'This war has drawn the Throne and the people more closely together than was ever before recorded, and Your Majesties are more beloved by all classes and conditions than any of the princes of the past.'

This sense of service and common cause was infectious. Princess Elizabeth, like a great many other children at the time, was furious that she was not yet old enough to join one of the armed forces, and she cast around for some other contribution to make. There is some debate as to whether it was completely her own idea, or whether Derek McCulloch, 'Uncle Mac' of children's radio made the suggestion. Whichever, Lilibet gained her father's approval to make a broadcast – something which the King himself was always terrified of doing. With Margaret sitting at her side the future sovereign gave her very first address to the nation and the Empire on 13 October 1940. Reading her words today, over half a century later, the cadences of Christmas messages to come are clearly apparent.

'I can truthfully say to you all,' she informed her audience in places as far apart as Canada and Australia, 'that we children at home are full of cheerfulness and courage. We are trying to do all we can to help our gallant sailors, soldiers, and airmen, and we are trying, too, to bear our own share of the danger and sadness of war. We know, every one of us, that in the end all will be well.' When she had finished, the Princess invited her ten-year-old sister – listeners had had no idea that she was also there – to add a word. 'Come on, Margaret.' There was a slight pause before a tiny voice piped up, 'Good night, and good luck to you all'.[35]

There could hardly have been a dry eye in the country, certainly not at Badminton where even Queen Mary's stern composure was threatened. 'Excellent . . . so natural and unaffected,' she wrote. Five thousand miles away, the South African novelist, Sarah Gertrude Millin, thought the broadcast was perfectly done. 'If there are still queens in the world a generation hence, this child will be a good queen,' she forecast.

In the meantime, the heir presumptive, now fourteen years old and cautious of compliments, was not being allowed to neglect her studies. A year or two earlier it had been felt by her parents, her mother especially, that the Princess would benefit from the kind of specialized tuition that Miss Crawford was not really qualified to give. On the recommendation of a Member of Queen Mary's Household, Sir Henry Marten had been engaged to instruct Princess Elizabeth in constitutional history. The Vice-Provost of Eton, a gentle scholar, with attractive eccentricity – he used to chew the corners of his handkerchief and crunch sugar lumps while contemplating – Sir Henry received his very special pupil in his study at Eton College where the books were piled up in columns like so many leaning towers of Pisa. Later, at the start of the war, when the Princess was first at Birkhall and then at Sandringham before coming to Windsor, he posted his lectures to her. And finally, twice a week, he would toil up to the castle to imbue the future Queen with a grounding in the role of monarchy. Princess Elizabeth became very fond of the old man – his death in 1948 was compared to the fall of an old tree. During the war, knowing of his sweet tooth, Sir Henry's star pupil used to make sure he regularly received a pot of heather honey from Scotland.

Princess Elizabeth's other tutor was Mme. de Bellaigue, who had been recommended by Sir Alexander Hardinge, Private Secretary to the King and to King Edward VIII before him. She was known for her exceptional merits as a French conversationalist. She was to remain with the royal family for six years, improving both Princesses' French and exciting their interest in that nation's literature and art. In later life Princess Margaret was to acknowledge the debt that she owed Mme. de Bellaigue – one of the most powerful cultural influences she had ever come across, she said.

'In our general conversations I endeavoured to give the Princesses an awareness of other countries, their way of thought and their customs – sometimes a source of amusement,' Mme. de Bellaigue told the royal biographer Lady Elizabeth Longford. 'Queen Elizabeth II has always had from the beginning a positive good judgement. She had an instinct for the right thing. She was her simple self, *tres naturelle*. And there was always a strong sense of duty mixed with *joie de vivre* in the pattern of her character.'[36]

This opinion complements that of the Princess's dance teacher, Miss Betty Vacani, who thought Princess Margaret a lively pupil but her elder sister a better dancer because she concentrated so hard until she got the steps absolutely right. By the time she was fifteen, her piano teacher, Miss Lander, predictably nicknamed 'Goosey Lander', reported that the Princess could play Beethoven sonatas 'with real musical feeling'.

But as the war progressed and both Princesses advanced through teenage years, there was not a great deal other than schoolwork to keep them amused or stimulated. One could take only so much of Beethoven or Bagehot, the nineteenth-century writer of *The English Constitution* which formed a large part of Princess Elizabeth's history diet – and has, incidentally, formed an indispensable fund of quotation for students of monarchy ever since.

In company with millions of other children the sisters had already gone through almost five years of wartime food rationing, where butter for a week amounted to what most people would nowadays spread on three slices of bread. They knew all about blacked-out windows – at the start of the war all the bulbs in Windsor Castle were replaced with ones of lower wattage to save on fuel. And as with everyone else, new clothes were a luxury governed by rationed clothing coupons – some of Princess Elizabeth's own clothes were handed down in the family to such needy children as her cousin Princess Alexandra.

Even so, it almost goes without saying that in some respects the Princesses were much better off than most children in Britain at that time. For one thing, their father had not been sent away from home for months on end, or made a prisoner of war, or killed in action. Princess Elizabeth especially, being just that much older than her sister, was conscious of all of this. The death of her uncle Georgie, the Duke of Kent, killed when his plane crashed into a Scottish hillside, had brought the war that much closer to her. She prayed for her widowed aunt and the seven-week-old Prince Michael of Kent who would be brought up without a father. And at the same time she felt that she was not doing enough herself to give service to her country.

With the end of the war hopefully just in sight, King George VI finally surrendered to Princess Elizabeth's persistent requests and gave permission to his daughter to join one of the services.

In March 1945 she became 'No 230873, Second Subaltern Elizabeth Windsor of the Auxiliary Territorial Service' and put on the khaki uniform. Admittedly, although it was not her wish, she was not treated quite as other recruits. For instance, she did not have to share sleeping quarters or sleep in a camp-bed. Instead she returned to Windsor Castle each evening. But she did learn how to work on, in, and under cars and heavy vehicles. She got her hands dirty, and for an all too short time she mixed on equal terms, or almost equal terms, with other eighteen-year-old women not all of whom were from her own kind of background. Her commandant wrote in her report: 'Her Royal Highness is a very good and extremely considerate driver.' It happened to be true, and is still so today, according to members of her family. Even so, one wonders if the senior officer would have dared to write anything else.

On 8 May 1945, the country celebrated the unconditional surrender of Germany, and on the same spring evening the King led his family out on to the balcony of Buckingham Palace time after time, in order to acknowledge the cheers of the crowds numbering several thousands who were pressing up to the Palace railings below. They had come, almost by instinct, to join with the King and Queen and their two children in saying, 'Thank God it's all over'. The mood was so electrifying that, even if he had wished, the King could not refuse his daughters' request to go outside and join in the fun.

Fifty years later, in a radio broadcast, Queen Elizabeth II was to recall those wonderful moments: 'I remember the thrill and relief after the previous day's waiting for the Prime Minister's announcement of the end of the war in Europe. My parents went out on the balcony nearly every hour, six times, and then when the excitement of the floodlights being switched on got through to us, my sister and I realized we couldn't see what the crowds were enjoying . . . so we asked my parents if we could go out and see for ourselves.

'I remember we were terrified of being recognized, so I pulled my uniform cap well down over my eyes. A Grenadier officer amongst our party of about sixteen people said he refused to be seen in the company of another officer improperly dressed, so I had to put my cap on normally. We cheered the King and Queen on the balcony and then walked miles through the streets. I remember lines of unknown people linking arms and walking down Whitehall, all of us just swept along on a tide of happiness and relief. I remember the amazement of my cousin, just back from four and a half years in a prisoner-of-war camp, walking freely with his family in the friendly throng.

'After crossing Green Park we stood outside and shouted 'We want the King', and we were successful in seeing my parents on the balcony, having cheated slightly because we sent a message into the house to say we were waiting outside. I think it was one of the most memorable nights of my life.'[37]

King George's final entry in his diary for 8 May 1940 speaks of his daughters: 'Poor darlings, they have never had any fun yet.'[38]

Their night out apart, they probably would not have entirely agreed with their papa. After all, although they had had no chance to experience a normal peacetime childhood, there had been excitement as well as deprivation in a wartime upbringing. Furthermore, apparently the King had not spotted the look that had recently appeared in Lilibet's eyes – the look that Crawfie had been quick to catch. Or if he had noticed, he had tried to ignore the implication. Like many fathers, he did not consider that at eighteen his daughter was old enough to contemplate the thought of marriage, or even to have a serious boyfriend. Like many fathers, he was certainly not ready to give her up to another man.

3

Philip

◦⫶∾◦

Mabell, Countess of Airlie, whose husband, the 11th Earl, died leading a cavalry charge against the Boers, had been a close friend of Queen Mary since childhood and her lady-in-waiting and confidante for over forty years. So when the two women were discussing the future of Princess Elizabeth, then just nineteen, it seemed appropriate for Lady Airlie to mention that Queen Mary herself had fallen in love at the same age and that her devotion had lasted for ever. Queen Mary nodded. 'Elizabeth seems to me that kind of girl,' she agreed. 'She would always know her own mind. There is something very steadfast and determined in her.'[1]

Lilibet's parents would not have quarrelled with that assessment, but her father was not sure that young Prince Philip was the right man for their elder daughter. Not at this stage anyway. She needed to meet more men before making up her mind about whom she wished to marry. That was why he had arranged for a succession of suitable sprigs of the aristocracy to be invited to private dances at Buckingham Palace and weekends at Balmoral or Sandringham. These young men – mostly Guards officers and the like – were quickly dubbed Princess Elizabeth's 'Body Guard'. She was charming to all of them, but singled out none. In that quiet, patient way that has never deserted her, she was waiting for the return from the wars of that Viking figure – as Miss Crawford described Prince Philip on first meeting – who had made her heart flutter when she was an impressionable thirteen-year-old.

There are various versions of precisely when the first meeting took place. Philip was a guest at the wedding of his cousin Princess Marina to the Duke of Kent in 1934, and was present at the coronation of his second cousin, George VI, in 1937. So he was almost bound to have seen his third cousins, Elizabeth and Margaret, on both of these occasions, although whether he talked very much to small children at that stage seems unlikely. He was not quite sixteen himself at the time of the coronation.

The moment of first meeting favoured by most royal chroniclers occurred in 1939, just before the war, when King George VI took his family down to Dartmouth Royal Naval College in Devon, where he had been a cadet himself before the First World War. He wanted to show his wife and daughters some of his old haunts. Unfortunately, on this occasion he was prevented from doing so because the college had been hit by a combined outbreak of mumps and chicken-pox among the trainee officers.

As a result, the young ladies found themselves confined to the commanding officer's house – where Miss Crawford did her best to keep them amused – until in breezed 'a fair-haired boy, rather like a Viking, with a sharp face and piercing blue eyes'.[2] He knew his manners, but he soon got bored with kneeling on the floor playing with clockwork trains (the Princesses are unlikely to have been madly excited either), and suggested going to the tennis courts and having 'some real fun jumping the nets'.

'She never took her eyes off him the whole time,' was how Crawfie described the interaction between Elizabeth and Philip. 'I thought he showed off a good deal, but the little girls were much impressed. Lilibet said, "How good he is, Crawfie! How high he can jump!" He was quite polite to her, but did not pay her any special attention. He spent a lot of time teasing plump little Margaret.'[3]

When the moment came for the visitors to say their farewells and to sail away in the royal yacht *Victoria and Albert*, Prince Philip was among those cadets who furiously rowed after the ship in dinghies and skiffs. As, one by one, the others finally fell away exhausted, he kept going for another half-mile. Princess Elizabeth 'watched him fondly through an enormous pair of binoculars'.

'The young fool,' exclaimed the King, looking back from the bridge; all this according to the ubiquitous Miss Crawford. Characteristically, Prince Philip's own memory of that day is more prosaic. 'As far as I was concerned it was a very amusing experience, going on board the yacht and meeting them, and that sort of thing, and that was that.'[4]

No one has been closer to Elizabeth II or more supportive of her for over forty years than Prince Philip: in public, always a step behind his sovereign; in private, sometimes a step ahead – his boundless vigour and curiosity usually takes him there. As a husband, the Queen would point to no serious fault. As a father, he has set sights for his children to aim at and has then become reconciled to the fact that they sometimes chose to aim at different targets. He is a man much kindlier than his public persona sometimes suggests. His abrasive, almost aggressive opening gambits, seemingly calculated at times to bludgeon strangers or even those people he knows well, are suspiciously like those of a man who is superior or, alternatively, instinctively feels that he is not. Extremely knowledgeable over a wide range of subjects, he nonetheless protests that he does not know the answer to many of today's universal problems. 'You tell me!' is frequently his response to questions. The older he gets, the less certain he is about most things – although he's still adamant about a few, such as the threat to the world posed by uncontrolled population growth. Renowned for his outspokenness, especially during the 1960s, he has rather taken a back seat as his eldest son has taken over, in this role at least. Unlike Prince Charles, who tends to see the best in people until proved wrong, Prince Philip often appears suspicious of other people's motives. Invite him to make comment, or pay tribute to Elizabeth II, and he bridles. 'I don't think it would be either reasonable or proper to make any comment,' he said in an interview with the author in April 1986.

'Not in any sense?'

'Well, it's bound to be misunderstood or whatever,' he replied. 'After all, we've been living as husband and wife very happily for I don't know how many years it is, and that's enough. That's comment itself.'

One day a student of the human psyche might be tempted to write a thesis on Prince Philip and his position as subject and husband of Elizabeth II. If the research began with his childhood, it would not be a waste of time.

Although he is generally credited with being Greek before he became British, Prince Philip's line of ancestry is more complicated than that. Just how complicated it is may be judged by the number of birthday reminders sprinkled through his diary – some 150 a year to relatives spread around the world. In his study at Windsor Castle he keeps a family tree, executed in concentric circles rather than with names hanging from the branches of an oak. Although he would think it not a terribly important distinction, the ancestry shows visitors that the Queen's husband has more blue blood running through his veins than Elizabeth II herself. He has ancestors who were kings, queens, emperors of practically any European country one cares to mention, dating back to Charlemagne himself. Yet, when it came to it, Prince Philip had the most awful job becoming a naturalized British subject.

He was born on 10 June 1921 in an imposing if somewhat neglected villa called 'Mon Repos' on the island of Corfu. Because the only doctor on the island thought his highly nervous patient would stand a better chance on a hard surface than in a bed, Prince Philip was brought into the world with his mother lying on a dining-room table. Princess Alice, who was thirty-six at the time, already had four daughters who were to give her a total of twenty grandchildren. The eldest of her daughters was sixteen and the youngest seven when their only brother was born. Their father, Prince Andrew of Greece, had sailed to war in the battleship *Lemnos* only the previous day, with his brother King Constantine.

For many years the Greeks had fought hard to retain their independence after centuries of Turkish domination. To help restore stability they had invited several members of the Danish Royal Family to occupy the throne, with a succession of unfortunate consequences.

The first to accept, in 1863, was the eighteen-year-old Prince William of Denmark – Prince Philip's grandfather – who took the title of King George I. He was assassinated in 1913. Prince Philip's uncle, Constantine I, was deposed in 1917; his cousin, Alexander I, died of blood poisoning in 1920; and King Constantine, having returned to the throne, abdicated in 1922. This was when Prince Philip also left Greece.

Being barely one year old at the time, Philip was quite unaware of dynastic upheavals going on around him, but in a dramatic operation, orchestrated by King George V in England, the Royal Navy cruiser *Calypso* was sent secret orders to rescue Prince Andrew and his family from Greece. In the best Hollywood style, the navy arrived only just in time. Lt.-Gen. Prince Andrew was in an Athens prison under threat of execution, blamed along with others for a massive military defeat by the Turkish revolutionary leader, Mustapha Kemal Atatürk. However, gunboat diplomacy was enough, in those days, to secure release, and Prince Andrew was able to rush his family aboard the cruiser. The baby Philip made his escape to Sicily in an orange box for a cot.

His childhood thereafter was almost as topsy-turvy, although he himself has said that he doesn't 'think it necessarily was particularly unhappy'.[5] At least one of his sisters, Princess Sophie, might not agree. She once acknowledged to a friend that her little brother had had 'a very rough and tumble upbringing'.

In a profile of the Prince, published to mark his engagement to Princess Elizabeth in July 1947, *The Times* pronounced that 'Mr Mountbatten left Greece in early childhood and since then has known no home but England'. The title of 'Mr' may have been technically correct but the rest was not.

Apart from being shifted around for long holidays with various relatives in Europe, Philip spent most of his first eight years in Paris. His parents, their characters very different, grew further and further apart from one another following their banishment from Greece. Princess Alice was to return there later, and refused to leave throughout the Second World War. But Prince Andrew, his spirited energy slowly souring into cynicism, became a well-known figure among Monte Carlo's debonair set – even though he could hardly afford the champagne that he liked to have to hand. Prince Philip was greatly attached to both his parents, his father in particular, but following the German occupation of France in 1940 he was never to see him again. Prince Andrew died in 1944, a year before the war ended.

Prince Philip has inherited something of his father's love of clubland company, and humour of the rollicking kind – it has passed down the line once more to another Andrew, his son. From his mother comes the caring side that some people say they have difficulty in seeing. It is often suggested that Prince Philip cares more for causes than for individuals. There is no doubt that he has never suffered fools gladly – including himself when he believes he has been a complete ass over something through not doing his homework. He has certainly never been the utter tyrant, even when younger, that some people privately imagine him to be. 'He is self-contained to a fault – it makes people think he's colder than he is,' decided the late Basil Boothroyd who wrote what he called an 'informal' biography of Prince Philip. One of the Prince's equerries once volunteered this: 'What people don't realize is that he's immensely kind. No one has a bigger heart, or takes greater pains to conceal it.'[6] A small example of this: when Prince Philip heard that his mother was ill in Munich, he flew from Aberdeen (he was staying at Balmoral), saw to it that her stretcher was loaded gently on to the aircraft, and stayed by her side giving encouragement throughout most of the bumpy return flight to England. The whole operation took sixteen and a half hours.

Princess Alice was born at Windsor sixteen years before her great-grandmother Queen Victoria died. Her father was Prince Louis of Battenberg, and one of her three brothers became Earl Mountbatten of Burma but, although she lived to the age of eighty-four and died in Buckingham Palace, the British public hardly knew she existed. This was partly at her own request. 'My mother's life is her own business,' Prince Philip once told off a reporter. She had had a hard life and towards its end became practically a recluse, a mysterious lady in the grey habit of the Mary and Martha order of nuns which she had founded. Servants newly employed at Buckingham Palace found it difficult to believe at times that this quiet lady silently walking the corridors was the mother of the less than quiet Duke of Edinburgh. Since childhood she had been hard of hearing and in later life became profoundly deaf, but she had learned to lip read in four languages – English, Greek, French and German – and despite her apparent frailty there were few important decisions regarding Prince Philip and his new family that did not require her tacit agreement. It is from his mother rather than from his father that Philip inherited his strong resolve.*

Apart from his mother, the chief Battenberg influence in Prince Philip's youth was his uncle George, 2nd Marquess of Milford Haven, elder brother of the more extrovert Louis Mountbatten. Uncle George had retired from the Royal Navy when Philip was nine, and had taken a house on the river Thames near Maidenhead. This was to be the young boy's main base when he was at Cheam preparatory school and until he was well into his stride at Gordonstoun, the spartan school in the Highlands of Scotland where Prince Philip was later to send his own sons.

Uncle George died in 1938, when he was only forty-eight, and after that Philip was drawn increasingly into the orbit and ambitions of his other uncle, the dashing, brilliant, scheming, autocratic and highly placed Lord Louis. On leaves from Dartmouth Naval College and later from the wartime Navy, he would doss down on a camp-bed in the drawing-room of the Mountbattens' London home at 16 Chester Street.

Prince Philip is a naval man through and through (despite the fact that his aim as a young man was to join the RAF), and he is more at home in the wardroom of a frigate than in the ballroom of a palace, although now that the Navy has decreed that its women can go to sea, his eye can be caught by a pretty woman in either place. Fellow officers – technically, the Duke of Edinburgh has never retired from the senior service – grow nervous at his coming aboard. He wants to be into everything. Some years ago, the rear-admiral, or captain, of the royal yacht *Britannia*, grew sufficiently impatient with the Queen's husband that he found the courage to more or less order him from the bridge by pointing out that in this case he was in charge. 'Fortunately he went quietly and without any fuss. Otherwise things might have been a trifle awkward.'

As a young man just out of Gordonstoun, the Navy offered the clean challenge that Prince Philip has savoured throughout his life. His headmaster in an early report had pointed out that 'Prince Philip's leadership qualities are most noticeable, though marred at times by impatience and intolerance.' In his final report, before the school's head boy left for Dartmouth, he warned future instructors: 'Prince Philip is a born leader, but will need the exacting demands of a great service to do justice to himself. His best is outstanding – his second best is not good enough.'[7]

Fifty years later, a close friend of the Duke's was to make this assessment: 'His true brilliance is that in spite of having to take second place he has carved out for himself a niche which doesn't in any way interfere

---

* Princess Alice was buried in Jerusalem at her own request, a reinterment that took eight years of patient and secret negotiation to achieve.

with the Queen's position, but enables him to excel in whatever it is he is doing.'

When the thirteen-year-old Princess Elizabeth met the eighteen-year-old naval cadet at Dartmouth Royal Naval College, the outbreak of the Second World War was only two months away. Their meetings during the war were fleeting and taken aboard, as far as Philip was concerned, more or less as welcome breaks from a somewhat more demanding life. He would spend the occasional weekend at Windsor – on one occasion sitting in the front row with the King and Queen for a Christmas panto-mime in which Elizabeth and Margaret were the stars. He would drop in to see his grandmother, the widow of the first Lord Louis Mountbatten, at Kensington Palace. And now and then his little green sports car could be seen parked in the forecourt of Buckingham Palace.

Like any young naval officer he took his pleasures where and when he could, in between long periods at sea and the occasional chance to see some real action. (Prince Philip earned a Mention in Dispatches for his part in the Battle of Matapan in March 1941.) If he gave much thought to Princess Elizabeth at all, it was probably as a second cousin who had grown up a little more each time he saw her. At this stage in their re-lationship his ambitions were no higher than that.

Princess Elizabeth's emotions were quite different. When the dashing young naval lieutenant came to watch her playing the part of Prince Charming in *Aladdin* – 'weather-beaten and strained', according to Crawfie; 'rolling in the aisles at the appalling jokes', according to biog-rapher Basil Boothroyd – Miss Crawford thought she had 'never seen Lilibet more animated. There was a sparkle about her none of us had ever seen before.' Sir John Wheeler-Bennett, King George VI's official biog-rapher, was quite adamant that 'this was the man with whom Princess Elizabeth had been in love from their first meeting'.[8] And as Queen Eli-zabeth II, as far as we know, made no amendment to his draft manu-script when it was presented to her, we may take it to be true. In other words, the Queen fell in love with her future husband when she was a girl of no more than thirteen – official.

Her father was bound to hear of it eventually. As many a parent would, he imagined the affection to be infatuation and put it all down to puppy love. As with some fathers also, there was probably an element of jealousy lurking in there somewhere. Although he occasionally found his daughters 'strange and odd', he was devoted to both of them, particu-larly to Lilibet because he recognized some of his own strengths, and faults, in her. But as to love and marriage, he thought that there was plenty of time for all that sort of thing when Lilibet was older. Although he never specified, as far as we know, he was probably thinking of her early twenties as a ripe time to marry.

However, over the years there has been a suggestion, with some evidence to support it, that Elizabeth II's marriage to Prince Philip of Greece was arranged long before the moment of actually popping the question. Or, if it was not arranged in the way that royal marriages used to be organized to suit political alliances between nations, then at least it became the subject of some judicious matchmaking behind the scenes.

As early as January 1941, Henry Channon (later to become Sir Henry Channon) returned from a cocktail party at which Prince Philip was present and noted in his diary: 'He is extraordinarily handsome ... He is to be our Prince Consort, and that is why he is serving in our Royal Navy.'[9]

The almost dilettante style of the bold entry suggests that the author rather enjoyed making outrageous statements that might or might not be true. On the face of it, it seems extremely doubtful if anything about a marriage between the future Queen of England and a somewhat impoverished Greek princeling had been seriously discussed, although the topic might have been thrown into the still pond of an unusually dull cocktail party – by Channon himself perhaps – just to see what happened.

Channon was a 'character'. Even his nickname 'Chips', by which he was universally known, had a nice cavalier ring to it. It is said that he acquired the sobriquet simply because a good friend of his had the name of 'Fish'. In fact Henry Channon was born in Chicago, the grandson of a Somerset man who had emigrated and made himself a fortune in shipping. 'Chips' settled in England at the end of the First World War and, after coming down from Christ Church, Oxford, shared a house in London with Prince Paul of Yugoslavia and Lord Gage, who became a lord-in-waiting to King George V. He went on to marry Lady Honor Guinness, second daughter of the 2nd Earl of Iveagh, and practically inherited the safe Conservative parliamentary seat of Southend-on-Sea which had been held by both his father-in-law and his mother-in-law before him.

By the time he was forty he had all the credentials to glide effortlessly around the highest reaches of society. His talents were social rather than political. He had two impressive houses. The one in London's exclusive Belgrave Square had a dining-room of blue and silver copied from the Amalienberg, near Munich. The other mansion, Kelvedon Hall in Essex, is where his son Paul and his wife now live. Paul was also to become Member of Parliament for Southend-on-Sea, and did rather better than his father in politics by serving as a Minister in the governments of both Edward Heath and Margaret Thatcher. Tragically the Channons' daughter, Olivia, died in 1986, following a party at Oxford where drugs were circulating among fellow students.

The 'Chips' diaries, excerpts from which were published in 1967, are peppered with anecdotes about parties. He was a friend of kings and a confidant of prime ministers' cronies, and he revelled in his popularity. 'We were invited to eleven dinner parties tonight. The Iveaghs, while amused by our royal activities, are nevertheless impressed. Their gangster son-in-law from Chicago has put their daughter into the most exclusive set in Europe.'

Today, some of Chips Channon's summations have a curious ring to them – he described Field Marshal Goering on first meeting as 'disarming' – but his early tip-off about a marriage between a very senior member of the House of Windsor and a fairly low-ranking scion of the Greek royal family apparently came from Philip's aunt, Princess Nicholas. She had the closest links with the British royal family through her daughter Marina's marriage to the Duke of Kent.

Unfortunately, things become a trifle complicated when attempts are made to untangle the skein of relationships spread across the face of Europe by the plethora of Queen Victoria's descendants, coupled with the ambitions of the various royal houses. But it does appear, at least as far as the Greeks were concerned, that Philip's marriage to Elizabeth was a sensible liaison. Indeed, when King George II of Greece (once more in exile), met King George VI at the wedding of King Peter of Yugoslavia (also in exile) in London in 1944, he evidently thought it worthwhile to have a quiet word in the English king's ear, and was most surprised when King George VI displayed precious little enthusiasm at the suggestion of a marriage between the two royal houses.

It was not that King George and Queen Elizabeth had anything against Prince Philip. On the contrary, both of them had taken to him from the outset. 'I like Philip,' wrote the King. 'He is intelligent, has a good sense of humour and thinks about things the right way.'[10] Queen Mary added her invaluable blessing: 'A nice little boy with very blue eyes,' she recalled.[11]

It was just that there was no need to hurry. And, also, there was no particular reason (was there?) why Elizabeth should marry someone of royal blood like herself? Or a foreigner? The days when the royal houses of Europe inter-married as a matter of policy were over. For one thing, there were few royal houses left, and most of them were in exile and impoverished. The King himself, as Duke of York, had married a commoner and his marriage had proved uncommonly successful. He could see – mostly because he was told – that Lilibet was in love. She kept a photograph of Philip on her bedroom mantelpiece, and when Crawfie had pointed out that this was perhaps a little indiscreet, she had replaced it with one of him beaming out from behind a beard. Her parents weren't fooled. Nor were they unaware that Lord Louis Mountbatten, who was particularly popular with some leading politicians, Churchill included, had been promoting the marriage of his nephew Philip to Elizabeth for quite some time. There is evidence for this, among other places, in the diary of Prince Philip's first commanding officer at sea.

Captain Baillie-Grohman had recruited the bright cadet as a midshipman after he left Dartmouth, at the request of Lord Mountbatten. So there was a special interest in the young man's progress. In the course of a conversation about his career prospects, Prince Philip volunteered that 'my uncle Dickie has ideas for me; he thinks I could marry Princess Elizabeth'. Astonished by this admission, the captain gently enquired whether the midshipman was fond of the Princess. 'Oh yes, very,' came the breezy reply. 'I write to her every week.'[12]

Prince Philip himself either has a hazy memory of the precise order of events, or was not aware of what others were planning, or simply does not wish to tell. His response to Basil Boothroyd, when the author raised the subject of Chips Channon's prophesy, went like this: 'It had been mentioned, presumably, that "he is eligible, he's the sort of person she might marry". I mean, after all, if you spend ten minutes thinking about it – and a lot of these people spent a great deal more time thinking about it – how many obviously eligible young men, other than people living in this country, were available? Inevitably I must have been on the list, so to speak. But people only had to say that, for somebody like Chips Channon to go one step further and say it's already decided, you see what I mean?'[13]

Apart from the King who, by law, had to give permission for his daughter to marry, (and all he genuinely wanted was her happiness), there was another obstacle facing Prince Philip's promoters. This concerned nationality. In his own self-interest, Philip wanted to become a naturalized British subject because that was the only way he could gain promotion in the Royal Navy. As a foreigner he could go no further than the rank of acting sub-lieutenant. But in addition, Britain had become his home since he was eight or nine years of age and this was where he wanted to stay. Dammit, he could have said, and almost certainly did, he had fought for his adopted country for six whole years! Why couldn't he be British?

No reason at all, except that there were a few snags. At the conclusion of the war against Germany, British troops became involved in a Greek civil war, so there was potential embarrassment lying ahead if a Greek Prince became engaged to the heir to the British throne. Furthermore, as the public gradually became aware of a budding romance between *their* Princess Elizabeth and a blond Greek prince, press enquiries revealed that all four of Philip's sisters had married Germans. One of them, Cecilie, had been tragically killed with her family in an air crash before the war. But the husbands of the others had presumably served under Hitler. What's more, genealogists could point to the fact that Prince Philip's family name was Schleswig-Holstein-Sonderburg-Glucksburg. At the start of 1946, with a name like that, and with the effects of a long war still fresh in people's memories, it was not the most propitious moment to announce a royal engagement, or at least not this one. Not yet. The King consulted his Home Secretary about naturalization papers for Prince Philip, and was advised to await the outcome of a plebiscite of the Greek people as to whether or not they wished to restore their monarchy. In March 1946 the Greeks decided they did want a king, but even though Prince Philip was a long way down in the line of succession, the British government still thought it might be undiplomatic for him to renounce his Greek nationality so close to the royalist restoration. Interestingly, Philip's mother, Princess Alice, had once proudly harboured a hope that her son might one day become King of Greece. Waiting for her fifth child to be born, she wrote to her brother Dickie in 1921: 'If the child will be a boy, he will be sixth in succession to the Greek throne. As things are today, with Alex dead, Tino threatened by Venizelos, and George and Andrew unacceptable, my son if God wills could become one day the king, if monarchy prevails.'[14]

It was all highly hypothetical, of course. And the hypothetical is a minefield Princess Alice's son has always steered away from. Just short of sixty-five years after his birth, when asked if his marriage had in any way impeded success in a career – the questioner had a Royal Navy career in mind – the Duke of Edinburgh replied that did not think so. 'Whatever position you're in, there are advantages and disadvantages and one balances out the other. I'm delighted to be where I am for a great many reasons, and I regret it for a great many other reasons.' Could he enumerate those reasons? 'No, because it's all hypothetical. I'm here now. There's no point in worrying about what might have been.'[15]

According to her friends, this is exactly how the Queen thinks, too. At least Prince Philip was born with many paths ahead of him. Elizabeth II has never had any choice about her position in life, except through renouncing her inheritance. The most important choice she has had to make in sixty-five years is deciding whom she wished to marry.

By the summer of 1946 Princess Elizabeth had grown impatient with all the 'this and that' reasons why she and Philip should postpone their engagement. When they went to Balmoral for the traditional royal family summer holiday it was clear to everyone that they were very much in love.

There have been many guesses as to who actually popped the question, and where, but the only reliable account yet available comes from Prince Philip himself, couched in his own very British, very understated way.

'I suppose one thing led to another. I suppose I began to think about it seriously, oh, let me think now, when I got back in '46 and went to Balmoral. It was probably then that we, that it became, you know, that we began to think seriously, and even talk about it.'[16] When one day they come to make the feature film, you can be sure that is not the way they will tell it.

The King and Queen *still* thought that their daughter was too young to marry. She was twenty and a half. Since the age of sixteen she had been quietly growing into maturity and showing at every stage a gravity alternating with sunshine bursts of infectious humour that in later life were to be even more pronounced.

Shortly before her fifteenth birthday the Princess was confirmed into the Church of England by the Archbishop of Canterbury, Dr Cosmo Lang, who when Elizabeth was a little younger had insisted, to her great but self-controlled annoyance, on patting her head, and also Princess Margaret's and saying, 'Bless you my child' every time he saw her. As he prepared the heiress presumptive for her initiation into the Church he found that 'she showed real intelligence and understanding', although by nature she was 'not very communicative'. Perhaps it is not hard to understand why.

Lady Airlie, Queen Mary's friend, coming up from the country specially for the confirmation service, was impressed by the transformation from small girl to shapely adolescent in the space of just three years. 'I saw a grave little face under a small white net veil, and a slender figure in a plain white woollen frock. The carriage of her head was unequalled, and there was about her that indescribable something which Queen Victoria had.'[17]

During the five years following the confirmation, the preparation for a future role had advanced step by careful step. In the week following her eighteenth birthday, Princess Elizabeth attended her first official banquet for the Prime Ministers of the Dominions. She was seated between Prime Ministers General Smuts of South Africa, and Mr Mackenzie King of Canada who thought she was 'not in the least shy and looked very pretty and very happy and graceful'.

In the same month she was given her own lady-in-waiting and accepted an invitation to become President of the National Society for the Prevention of Cruelty to Children. At her installation she made the first of a thousand speeches carrying the same familiar ring: 'I would like you to know that the all-important work which the Society has done and is doing for the children of this country lies very near my heart . . . I trust that in the days to come we may hope that every child's life may be a free and happy one.'

All of this work, which she enjoyed more than she would have done if it had been simply a duty, was carried out with grace and some solemnity. At the same time, concealed behind the sweet young face there was an excited young woman who couldn't wait for the next letter from Philip, or, better still, a chance of seeing him again. Their engagement, however, which was still quite unofficial and known only to close family, was to be put to a further test before the public was allowed to share the secret – at this point the Buckingham Palace press office was poker-facedly denying any serious romance.

On 1 February 1947, King George VI, Queen Elizabeth and their two daughters sailed from Portsmouth aboard HMS *Vanguard*, the newest and most powerful capital ship in the Royal Navy which Princess Elizabeth had commissioned just a few months earlier. They were bound for South Africa on a tour that was scheduled to last three months. There was no question of Prince Philip accompanying them, although curiously enough someone who was aboard was Group Captain Peter Townsend, the man Princess Margaret was later to fall in love with. He was there as the King's equerry.

Six days after *Vanguard* sailed, Prince Philip's naturalization papers came through, at last. The final obstacle to be overcome had been one of name. What should he call himself in his new life? The College of Heralds had suggested the ancestral name of Oldenburg might be anglicized to 'Oldcastle', but that didn't sound quite right – even if one didn't know that its owner was one day to become consort to the sovereign.

The Home Secretary at the time, Mr Chuter Ede (strongly prompted by Lord Mountbatten, it has to be said), came up with the answer. Why not choose the surname from the mother's side of the family? After all, Princess Andrew of Greece was born Princess Alice of Battenberg. Her father, Prince Louis of Battenberg, had come to England at the age of fourteen, joined the Navy and risen to the high post of First Sea Lord as a British subject. All of which, in a roundabout way, made sense of Prince Philip of Greece becoming Lieutenant Philip Mountbatten, a naturalized British subject.*

Princess Elizabeth received news of Philip's citizenship by ship's radio. Naturally she was delighted. It seemed that the final barrier to her becoming married had been removed. However, there were still weeks and weeks of arduous travel and public engagements around South Africa, and then the long sea journey home, before she could see her fiancé again. Typically, she just tried to put all thought of him to the back of her mind while she got on with the tour.

There were consolations, the climate being one. While South Africa

* The style and title of a Prince of the United Kingdom was not formally accorded until 1957 when Queen Elizabeth II bestowed it on her husband in recognition of his work.

basked in sunshine, Britain was having its coldest winter for sixty-six years. Coal – the main form of heating – was in short supply. Food was still rationed to little above subsistence level. Elizabeth and her sister meanwhile were being pressed by their hosts to gorge on huge meals: 'We feel (I say we, but I really mean I) guilty to be away from it all.'

The King felt so badly about leaving the people who had gone through the war with him that he suggested to Prime Minister Attlee that he should abandon the tour and return home. He wrote to his mother: 'I am very worried over the extra privations which all of you at home are having to put up with in that ghastly cold weather with no light or fuel.'

Clement Attlee thought a hurried return would only serve to underline the impression of a crisis. Besides, the King needed the warm sun to build him up. The war years had worn him out, and there were already signs of the circulation problems in his legs which were soon to lead to serious illness and eventually to his premature death.

As the two princesses walked dutifully in the path of their parents at seemingly endless parades and presentations – 'Princess Elizabeth looked a little stolid, her little sister more animated' – it was perhaps just as well that the elder daughter had no inkling that in less than five years' time she would be monarch of all her father's dominions.

On the evening of her twenty-first birthday, as was thought fitting, Princess Elizabeth made a memorable broadcast on the wireless to five million of the King's subjects across the world. Speaking from Government House, Cape Town, in a thin, high-pitched voice, she proclaimed an act of solemn dedication, to devote a lifetime of service to each of her future subjects.

'I declare before you all that my whole life, whether it be long or short, shall be devoted to your service and the service of our great Imperial Commonwealth to which we all belong. But I shall not have the strength to carry out this resolution unless you join in it with me, as I now invite you to do; I know that your support will be unfailingly given. God bless all of you who are willing to share it.'[18]

Today it seems ironic that such a noble pledge should have been given in South Africa of all places. Strangely, its tone and message, in the latter part at least, has echoes in some of the speeches made by Nelson Mandela after his release from prison over fifty years later, in particular the line 'I shall not have the strength to carry out this resolution unless you join in it with me'.

When the royal party arrived back in London in May 1947, Princess Elizabeth could have expected that her father would give immediate permission for a public announcement of her engagement. Instead, he somehow managed to hold out for yet another two months. His biographer tried to find excuses for King George VI: 'He had always liked Prince

Philip and had grown to esteem him highly, but he still found it difficult to believe that his elder daughter had really fallen in love with the first young man she had ever met, and perhaps he also dreaded losing her from that compact and happy family circle which had been his delight and solace since his early married days in Royal Lodge.'[19]

He could not hold out for ever, especially not in the face of such patent love. Apart from any other consideration, there was also the gentle pressure from both his wife and mother. *They* wanted the marriage to go ahead. And so 'there could no longer be any question as to the wishes and affections of both parties, and their pertinacity and patience were rewarded.'

On 10 July 1947, the customary framed notice was wired on to the railings of Buckingham Palace:

> It is with the greatest pleasure that The King and Queen announce the betrothal of their dearly beloved daughter, The Princess Elizabeth to Lieutenant Philip Mountbatten, R.N., son of the late Prince Andrew of Greece and Princess Andrew (Princess Alice of Battenberg), to which union The King has gladly given his consent.

There could be no going back now.

4

The Carefree Years

⟪⟫

There is a common fascination about other people's marriages, particularly if one or both of the partners is famous. Where the Queen is concerned, most people, if they were being completely honest, would own up to slightly more than an idle curiosity. They feel that her marriage must be different and yet in some ways very similar to that of millions of her subjects. They are aware, many of them, that Elizabeth II and Prince Philip have occupied separate bedrooms – with an interconnecting door – since the start of their marriage. Yet they have a sense that it is an impertinent invasion of privacy to know this, since they are talking about the Queen. (The same is not so likely to apply to younger and more junior members of the royal family.) They are intrigued to know whether there is any truth in the rumours, persistent over the years, that Prince Philip has had a string of mistresses. And they wonder whether at home it is the husband or the wife who wears the trousers. In other words they are nosy.

The reality is that the condition of the sovereign's marriage is a heavily protected area and, unless ructions inside it in some way threaten state security or the stability of the monarchy itself, family and close friends properly insist that it remain that way. Apart from Prince Philip's judgement that 'we've been living as husband and wife very happily for I don't know how many years',[1] about the only other oblique insight into the marriage came when he was asked whether he agreed with the fairly general view that he might be a male chauvinist. He laughed (fortunately for the interviewer), before replying, 'I'd find it a bit difficult in my position, wouldn't I?'[2]

No one ever knows the whole truth about anyone's marriage, including their own, and sometimes they have less difficulty understanding other people's. In its proper time, history will dissect the marriage of Queen Elizabeth II as it has done with each of her predecessors. In the meanwhile, from their own personal observation through the years, most people would hazard a guess that the relationship between Elizabeth II and the Duke of Edinburgh is like a calm sea covering a few rocks. Someone who has known the Queen since the days when they were both Brownies and Girl Guides together in the Buckingham Palace pack gave this assessment: 'The Queen was very much in love with Philip when she married him. Then there was a slight disillusionment and a bit of compromising on both sides. But since then, and for many years now, it has been a very steady relationship. They can spend hours happily talking to one another, and in how many marriages can you say that happens?'

By nature the Queen is inclined to be a one-man woman, and in any case her position rules out any serious contemplation of divorce.

As for Prince Philip, he bows to no one in his forthright admiration of and devotion towards the woman he married. She likes to rely on him, and he enjoys being protective. In that sense it is an old-fashioned marriage. As to love, as with many other men, including his eldest son, he might find this more difficult to define in words. But countless examples of his attentiveness to his wife, observed by courtiers and non-courtiers alike, give witness to a genuine bond. After forty-four years, their marriage is not one that has hollowed out into dusty dereliction or become boring. They laugh together, which is not a bad sign. And, if the truth be told, both partners are too busy in their separate and combined ways to give the state of their union a great deal of thought. They certainly do not agonize over it. It is the condition of other people's marriages, within their own family, that over the years has given them the most cause for concern.

In 1947, Winston Churchill, in typically fine flow, had dubbed the engagement of the future Queen as 'a flash of colour on the hard road we have to travel'.[3] Thrown out of power by the very people he had led to victory in the war, he was in sombre mood and convinced that Britain was heading for economic crisis.

When the forthcoming marriage was announced, the country as a whole welcomed it. People were ready for a bit of love and laughter after years of deprivation. They approved when the House of Commons voted £50,000 for Clarence House to be refurbished for the young couple, even though thousands of ex-servicemen were homeless and Buckingham Palace had something like 400 spare rooms going begging. They queued up in the winter cold outside St James's Palace for a chance to gasp over the plethora of expensive wedding presents: a full-length mink coat from Canada, a filly from the Aga Khan, a golden coffee service from the Emir of Transjordan, a loin cloth from Mr Gandhi and, oh yes, a pair of nylon stockings (catalogued no. 351) from a Mrs David Mudd.

Of course, not everyone was jubilant about the wedding. Among the dissenting voices was that of the Camden Town First Branch of the Amalgamated Society of Woodworkers. Their branch secretary wrote direct to the King that 'any banqueting and display of wealth at your daughter's wedding will be an insult to the British people at the present time, and we consider that you would be well advised to order a very quiet wedding in keeping with the times. ... May we also remind you that should you declare the wedding day a public holiday you will have a word beforehand with the London Master Builders' Association to ensure we are paid for it.'[4]

There is no available record of whether they were paid. Everyone was too caught up with the unaccustomed celebration to bother about such important trifles. 'A week of gaiety such as the court has not seen for years' preceded the wedding day. No fewer than five kings, six queens, and many more princes, princesses, counts and countesses, attended a magnificent evening party at Buckingham Palace. King Michael of Romania was there, and his government back home took advantage of his absence to declare their country a republic.[*]

At the same party, according to Sir John Colville, Princess Elizabeth's Private Secretary at the time, 'an Indian Rajah became uncontrollably drunk and assaulted the Duke of Devonshire (who was sober), but otherwise there were no untoward events. However, Queen Mary, scintillating as ever in a huge display of jewellery, without giving the least impression of vulgarity or ostentation, was somewhat taken aback when Field Marshal Smuts (South Africa's leader) said to her, "You are the big potato; the other Queens are small potatoes".'[5]

Such indiscretions were easily forgiven. Everyone was enjoying themselves too much at endless cocktail parties to harbour grudges. Two nights before the wedding, Queen Mary wrote in her diary: 'Saw many old friends. I stood from 9.30 till 12.15. Not bad for eighty.'[6]

The wedding itself, on 20 November 1947, went off *almost* without a hitch. Two hours before the bride was due to leave for Westminster Abbey, the frame of the diamond tiara she planned to wear snapped as she was putting it on. It was rushed away for repair and returned just in

---

[*] Following the execution of Romanian President Ceauçescu in 1989, the exiled King made an, at first, unsuccessful attempt to visit his country after an absence of fifty-three years.

time. Then it was discovered that the two pearl necklaces, the wedding gift of her parents, had been placed on display at St James's Palace. Sir John Colville was dispatched to recover them off the stand. Finally, there was a minor panic when the bride's bouquet went missing. It had been put away in a cool cupboard.

Fortunately for everyone, an early ban on filming the wedding was lifted. King George VI had decreed, on a notepad in pencil, 'Photography and broadcast commentary, yes. No Filming or Television. G.R.' Presumably he was still trying to protect his beloved daughter. However, he relented.

The King also announced, on the morning of the wedding day itself, that he had created the bridgegroom Baron Greenwich, Earl of Merioneth and Duke of Edinburgh. It was too late for anything to be done about the printing on the order of ceremony, so, according to the programme, Princess Elizabeth married her Lieutenant Philip Mountbatten of the Royal Navy and saw, courtesy of the government this time, his income instantly jump from around £11 a week as a naval officer to £10,000 as her husband.

The Archbishop of Canterbury, Dr Geoffrey Fisher, intoned in his address that in essence the marriage ceremony of Philip and Elizabeth was 'exactly the same as it would be for any cottager who might be married this afternoon in some small country church in a remote village in the dales'.[7] Any other fine considerations apart, this was not quite so. As the Archbishop had previously pointed out to the King in a letter, it appeared that while regarding himself as an Anglican, Prince Philip had in fact been baptized into the Greek Orthodox Church. While there was no problem about this – 'we are always ready to minister to members of the Orthodox Church and to admit to the Sacrament,' said the Archbishop – there would, of course, be certain advantages if he were to be officially received into the Church of England.[8]

Interestingly, a similar question mark arose when Sir Angus Ogilvy and Princess Alexandra, Queen Elizabeth II's cousin, were married in November 1962. The Hon. Angus Ogilvy, as he was then, although a devout believer in Christian principles, has never felt the need to become a member of any Church. Perhaps not so surprisingly, the Archbishop wished to remedy this situation also, as he saw it, before the wedding took place. But Mr Ogilvy declined and, certainly up until recently, when they are together in church and his wife takes communion, Sir Angus undemonstrably does not do so, preferring either to stay away altogether or to remain quietly aside. He is possibly unique in being the only member of the royal family who is not a member of Queen Elizabeth II's Established Church.

King George VI was clearly moved and saddened by his daughter's wedding. He wrote to her: 'I was so proud of you and thrilled at having you so close to me on our long walk in Westminster Abbey, but when I handed your hand to the Archbishop I felt I had lost something very precious.'[9]

Princess Elizabeth was probably too excited and too nervous to think about it at the time, but later she too was to reflect on the separation from a father whom she loved very deeply.

The reception took place at Buckingham Palace. Beside each placing there was a little bunch of white heather, specially picked and sent down from Balmoral the previous day. The honeymoon was to begin at Broad-lands, the Mountbatten's Hampshire home, and then continue at Birkhall, the house on the Balmoral estate that was to become the home of Queen Elizabeth the Queen Mother. In the cold November air, as the newlyweds' open carriage passed along the cheering crowds on London's streets, few were aware that a thoughtful servant had placed hot water-bottles at the feet of bride and bridegroom, and Princess Elizabeth's favourite corgi, Susan, was concealed beneath the travelling rugs.

The next four years were to be the most carefree, relaxed and, at the same time, in some ways the most anxious years, that Elizabeth II has ever known.

Less than a year after her wedding, Princess Elizabeth, as of course she still was, gave birth to her first child, a son whom she and her husband had decided long before should be named Charles Mountbatten. (If it had turned out that the baby was a girl, she was to be known as Lady Anne Mountbatten.) Just in time, King George VI made sure the baby would qualify for the title of prince or princess.*

The birth took place, with the aid of anaesthetic, in the Buhl Room in Buckingham Palace. The date was 14 November 1948. There was never any suggestion but that the mother should feed the baby herself.

The child's grandparents were naturally over the moon to have news of their first grandchild. King George VI, always a stickler for detail, was perhaps less interested in the fact that the infant weighed in at seven pounds six ounces than that he was the first royal child to be born at Buckingham Palace for sixty-two years (the last being the daughter of Arthur, Duke of Connaught).

Prince Philip had grown impatient with waiting for the baby to arrive and had to be brought off the Palace squash court where he had been

---

* Less than a week before the birth, on 9 November 1948, George VI issued letters patent under the Great Seal conferring on all children born to the Duke and Duchess of Edinburgh the style and title of Prince or Princess. Up until then, according to the edict issued by George V in 1917, only the children of a sovereign and his *sons* could hold these titles.

thrashing a ball with his friend and Private Secretary, Lt.-Cdr Michael Parker. When he reached the Buhl Room, taking the stairs three steps at a time, he found his wife still sleeping off the effects of the anaesthetic. So he went to the nursery to admire his baby son. Within minutes he was back again with his wife – Prince Philip has never been one to coo over babies – this time bearing a huge bunch of red roses and carnations.

No one would have imagined that Queen Mary could be left out of the celebration. Shortly before 11pm (Prince Charles was born by Caesarean section at 9.14pm precisely), the crowd of well-wishers outside the Palace railings spotted the old lady's limousine progressing down The Mall from Marlborough House. 'I am delighted at being a great-grand-mother!' she wrote in her diary.

A day or two after she had first inspected the baby (she stayed until after midnight, even though she was recovering from influenza), Queen Mary and her friend Lady Airlie spent a whole afternoon going through old photo albums to see whether Charles took after Queen Victoria or Prince Albert – Queen Mary favoured Prince Albert. And she took special pleasure in hunting out and making her first present to the new baby a silver gilt cup and cover which King George III had given to a godson in 1780 – 'so that I gave a present from my great-grandfather to my great-grandson 168 years later'.[10]

Princess Elizabeth was as proud as any other mother of her baby. 'Don't you think he's quite adorable?' she wrote to a friend. 'I still can't believe he's really mine, but perhaps that happens to new parents.' She was particularly intrigued by Charles's tiny hands. They were 'fine with long fingers,' she told her old music teacher. 'Quite unlike mine and certainly unlike his father's. It will be interesting to see what they become.'[11] They were to become rather thick and stubby actually, but even so the hands of a gifted painter and a sensitive man.

Anyone who enquired of the child's father what the baby looked like was told by Prince Philip that he resembled nothing so much as a plum pudding.

The Edinburghs had been due to move out of Buckingham Palace and into Clarence House after Charles was born, but the royal residence was not yet ready. In the meantime they had rented a house at Windlesham, near Windsor, after the house that they were supposed to have moved into at Sunningdale mysteriously burned down. (Some forty years later, Queen Elizabeth II was to lease the same land to her son and daughter-in-law, the Duke and Duchess of York, and pay for the house that they built there.)

Clarence House was in a real mess. It had been left derelict since the first Duke of Connaught retired to Bagshot, not far from Aldershot – an area of heath and sandy earth in Surrey where the Army practised firing.

That had been soon after the First World War. King George VI had lent the house to the British Red Cross for the duration of the Second World War, but they cannot have found it comfortable. Unbelievably, there were no real bathrooms and no electricity. It is no wonder that it took over a year to renovate.

However, when Princess Elizabeth and the Duke of Edinburgh finally moved in, in July 1949, they were as delighted as any young couple with a baby to have a home of their own. Prince Philip worked for some time just down the road at the Admiralty, 'shuffling ships around' was how he termed it. Princess Elizabeth had the old perambulator that her own mother had used brought down from Windsor – Prince Charles can still remember being encased within its high walls – and the same hairbrush and silver rattle that belonged to the baby Princess Elizabeth were put back on the nursery dressing-table.

Occasionally, one or other of the two nannies would take Charles over to neighbouring Marlborough House to visit the Prince's great-grandmother – he called her 'gan-gan'. He was enthralled, he remembers, by the sight of the dignified old lady sitting bolt upright in her chair, with her feet resting on an embroidered footstool. When he was old enough to walk, Queen Mary permitted her great-grandson to unlock, very carefully, the glass door of one of the display cabinets in which she kept her priceless collection of *objets d'art*. He was, furthermore, allowed the enormous privilege of taking out, very carefully, whichever glistening item engaged his curiosity. It was something neither his mother nor his aunt Margaret had ever been allowed to do when they were children, but then Charles was someone very special. The old Queen, now approaching her eighty-fourth year, had endured the death of her husband, of two of her sons, and the exile of a third son. Now it was plain to her that another son, the King, was a very sick man. Charles was special because he represented the future and the continuation of the monarchy which she had fought so hard to sustain all through her married life.

The news had been kept from Princess Elizabeth during the last weeks of her pregnancy, but tests showed that George VI was suffering from early arteriosclerosis and there was a danger that his right leg might have to be amputated. It had been found neccessary to postpone a royal tour of Australia and New Zealand, and every effort was being made to persuade the King to rest as much as possible.

In the following spring, a right lumbar sympathectomy operation was performed, in the same room, transformed into an operating theatre, where Prince Charles had been born. The results were encouraging. In a matter of weeks the King had recovered sufficiently to lead a fairly normal life, even to the extent of giving a magnificent Waterloo Day ball at Windsor Castle. He insisted that nothing should stand in the way of his

son-in-law furthering his naval career by taking up a posting as first lieutenant of HMS *Chequers*, command ship of the first Mediterranean destroyer flotilla. He even suggested that his wife should join him on station
in Malta. Perhaps King George already knew that this was likely to be
the young couples' last chance of experiencing the kind of freedom
denied to those in his own position.

In fact, provided her father's recovery continued and he returned to
full health, there seemed to be no reason why Elizabeth and Philip could
not look forward to several years of near-perfect existence. He could
pursue his career while she, quite happily, would play the part of the
naval officer's wife, and bring up the children. (Princess Anne was born
just under two years after Charles, on 15 August 1950). There would be
some royal duties to attend to, but nothing like the number that the King
and Queen had on their plate. Inheriting the throne and all its burdens
was something hopefully in the far distant future, say in the 1970s or
even the 1980s.

When Princess Elizabeth flew out to Malta to join her husband for
Christmas 1949, it was a happy coincidence that Lord Mountbatten was a
Flag Officer commanding the First Cruiser Squadron in the Mediterranean. He invited the young couple to stay at his house, the Villa Guar-
damangia, overlooking the harbour. Inevitably, despite their wishes,
Lieutenant Mountbatten and his wife were treated differently from other
junior officers and their wives. People bowed or curtsied to the King's
daughter, and the Duke of Edinburgh's captain addressed him as 'sir'
until, that is, his first lieutenant pointed out that on board ship the captain was the only officer entitled to be addressed as sir.

Prince Philip found it difficult to adjust to his new position as the husband of the heir to the throne. When he discovered that a 'failed' mark in
an exam might be 'reconsidered', he smelled favouritism. 'If they try to
fix it,' he told his equerry, 'I quit the Navy for good.'[12]

Gradually, protocol relaxed and at least the royal couple were spared
the daily round of civic receptions, presentations and provincial tours –
although the Princess was conscience-pricked into visiting a local hospital and a school. Young habits die hard.

It was on Malta that Prince Philip learned polo from his uncle Dickie
Mountbatten, who had a passion for the game. Princess Elizabeth, who
has never shown more than the spectator's required enthusiasm, learned
how to hang around the polo field and gossip with the other wives and
girlfriends, and be on hand to present prizes, of course. At least she liked
the horses and could tolerate the players, a virtue which her eldest
daughter-in-law has somehow not always managed to share.

There were parties, picnics, shops to wander in and out of, carrying
her cane basket over her arm. In her Jacqmar headscarf, dirndl skirt and

sunglasses it was easy for others not to recognize the future Queen, and just as easy for the future Queen to feel completely relaxed. It is probably the only time that she went to a hairdressing salon and sat alongside other women under the driers: 'It was the natural thing to do.'

By May 1950, Princess Elizabeth was pregnant once more. She returned to London where her husband joined her a month before the birth of their second child. Princess Anne was born by happy chance on the same day as her father was made-up to Lieutenant Commander and given command of his first ship, the frigate HMS *Magpie*, a worthy though small part of the Mediterranean Fleet.

Basil Boothroyd, in his 'informal biography' of Prince Philip, quotes the Prince's cousin, Princess Alexandra of Yugoslavia, remembering an officer who was 'glowing with warm enthusiasm as he told me how popular Philip was with his crew'. One of them said: 'He worked us like hell, but treated us like gentlemen.' Boothroyd himself mentions one of these gentlemen as claiming that he would rather die than serve on *Magpie* again. Another that Prince Philip 'stamped about like a —ing tiger.' 'Still, they privately called him "Dukey", and that sort of tiger doesn't usually attract the inoffensive nickname,' Boothroyd concluded.

The Foreign Office, always willing to work the royals hard in the interests of commerce and improved international relations, got together with the Admiralty and worked out a way in which the Duke could command his ship and show off the heir to the throne to advantage. Provoking a little envy among the other naval wives of Malta, Princess Elizabeth was given the use of the Commander-in-Chief's supply vessel, HMS *Surprise*. With Prince Philip's frigate as escort, the two ships paid courtesy calls at a number of Mediterranean ports, notably Athens, which did much to improve Graeco-Anglo relations. They stayed with Philip's cousins, King Paul and Queen Frederica, who had the Parthenon specially floodlit for their guests. In private moments, Prince Philip took his wife to see points of (his) family interest. They went swimming from deserted coves, and once arranged with the wife of the British Ambassador to have a small midnight barbecue at her beach house. Unfortunately, the good lady forgot to mention the matter to her husband and as a result the pots-and-pans-carrying 'raiding party' struggling up the cliff from the shore was greeted by Sir Clifford Norton, KCMG, CVO, bellowing out of a bedroom window 'Who's there?' Later, still wearing his pyjamas, he happily left his warm bed to join the party, equipped with his own knife and fork.

When they were at sea, each in their separate ships, the Prince and Princess communicated by radio message. The Prince was naturally anxious to learn how his wife was faring. (Elizabeth II, in fact, has always had fairly good sea legs.) The resultant dialogue was reminiscent of a Tony Hancock script:

> *Surprise* to *Magpie*: 'Princess full of beans.'
> *Magpie* to *Surprise*: 'Is that the best you can give her for breakfast?'[13]

Probably these idyllic days could not have lasted very much longer. The likelihood is that Prince Philip, ambitious in his career, would have had to serve prolonged periods at sea and his wife would not have been able to accompany him – in the same way that the present Duchess of York has had to put up with long separations from her naval officer husband.

Princess Elizabeth, in any case, would have wanted to spend more time with her two children at home. But it is interesting to note that there was no public outcry when she left them in the company of their grandparents over Christmas and New Year 1950/1 in order to be with her husband in Malta – the kind of criticism which neither the Princess of Wales nor the Duchess of York have managed to escape in their time.

Princess Elizabeth telephoned New Year greetings from *Magpie* to her son at Sandringham after receiving a letter from her father telling her: 'Charles is too sweet, stumping around the room. We shall love having him at Sandringham. He is the fifth generation to live there, and I hope he will get to like the place.'[14]

Tragically, grandfather and grandson were to be together for little more than another twelve months. The fun was to end abruptly, too, for Princess Elizabeth and her husband. In July 1951, the Duke of Edinburgh left the Navy on indefinite leave. Through no fault of his own, his command of a ship had lasted less than a year and the only sign of *Magpie* today is the model of the ship encased in glass in Prince Philip's study aboard the royal yacht *Britannia*.

When the King's illness forced his elder daughter and her husband to return home and take up other duties, firstly their tour of Canada and the United States, and then their planned mammoth trip to Australia and New Zealand, it must have seemed just possible to Philip and Elizabeth – he hardly thirty and she only twenty-five – that one day they might be allowed to return to living the way they had, before the King's illness, even if it were only for a few more years. They had enjoyed such carefree times and they had so many plans for the future. Sadly, it was not to be. The news that reached them in Kenya put an end to all their dreaming.

5

Moving Back

⤷∾⥥⤶

'ow we've got to live behind railings,' said the Queen[1] dejectedly when she moved back into Buckingham Palace with her husband and two children early in 1952, following the funeral of George VI. She had been happy living at Clarence House and now there was to be yet another turn around.

Prince Philip could not see why they could not continue to stay where they were, using the Palace as an administration headquarters and for official State functions, but Prime Minister Winston Churchill would not hear of it. Buckingham Palace was not only the place where the sovereign worked, it was where she and her family lived. It was the focal point for the nation and a great attraction for tourists.

So the Queen moved back into the building that she knew so well, and a few weeks later Queen Elizabeth the Queen Mother and Princess Margaret moved out and down the road to Clarence House. Queen Mary remained where she was, at Marlborough House.

All three residences are within five minutes walk of one another, which, as far as Queen Mary was concerned, was just as well because, while the rest of her family spent a good deal of time chatting away to one another on the telephone, Queen Mary never did. She steadfastly refused ever to use the instrument, insisting on either face to face conversation or a short note, hand delivered. She was perfectly happy living in the past. It suited her. To Queen Mary there was nothing particularly strange about coming down to dinner each evening wearing a tiara.

Elizabeth II is something of a traditionalist herself (although she stops short of headgear at meals) but, when she entered her old home once more, this time as monarch, she could see that some changes needed to be made. Although the words don't quite ring true – the Queen is not a natural coiner of phrases – she is supposed to have said that she wanted to be rid of all those 'greybeards in satin breeches'.

Prince Philip is usually given the credit for most of the innovations that were introduced into Buckingham Palace over the next few years, but this is not entirely fair. The Queen had a hand in many of the ideas, curbing some of her husband's wilder plans as well as suggesting improvements to others. 'Nothing', says Sir Oliver Millar, Surveyor of the Queen's Pictures for many years, 'is altered – even the position of a picture – without the Queen knowing about it and approving.'[2]

During the first months of the Queen's reign, her husband found it extremely difficult to adjust to his new life. He felt himself to be trapped, almost, in a sticky web of outdated protocol and sterile thinking. Immediately after King George VI's funeral, his depression was so deep that his elder sister, Margarita, was worried that he spent so many hours shut away in his room. 'You can imagine what's going to happen now,' he told her.[3] He feared that the dramatic change of circumstance would bring about his own almost total eclipse as an individual.

Speaking of his relationship with the Queen up until that time, he told his biographer Basil Boothroyd: 'Within the house, and whatever we did, it was together. I suppose I naturally filled the principal position. People used to come to me and ask me what to do. In 1952 the whole thing changed, very, very considerably.'[4]

A courtier present at the time said, 'The truth is, the King's death was good for Elizabeth, bad for Philip. She was almost instinctively ready, he was not.'

In a different way, Queen Elizabeth the Queen Mother's life was also drastically altered by the death of George VI. She was still a comparatively young woman – only fifty-two – but the grief of losing her husband went so deep that her strong inclination was to withdraw from public life altogether and spend the rest of her days in a derelict castle that she was having renovated on a windy cape in the far north-west of Scotland.

When he came to hear about it, Winston Churchill was so horrified at the idea of this self-imposed exile that he hurried to speak with his friend before it was too late. It is said that the Prime Minister's timely eloquence played a major part in the Queen Mother changing her mind.

Another contributing factor may have been a literary anthology which the poet Dame Edith Sitwell sent to the Queen Mother. On 15 September 1952, in thanking her friend for the book, Queen Elizabeth wrote:

I started to read it, sitting by the river, and it was a day when one felt engulfed by great black clouds of unhappiness and misery, and I found a sort of peace stealing round my heart as I read such lovely poems and heavenly words.

I found a hope in George Herbert's poem, 'Who could have thought my shrivel'd heart, could have recovered such greenness. It was gone quite underground' and I thought how small and selfish is sorrow. But it bangs one about until one is senseless. . . . I found so much beauty and hope, quite suddenly one day by the river.[5]

Forty years on, it seems almost inconceivable to imagine the royal family without the fortifying presence of Queen Elizabeth the Queen Mother. As Edith Sitwell wrote to Cecil Beaton after a lunch he gave for the Queen Mother in November 1962, 'She has a kind of genius for making everyone feel particularly happy.'*

Everyone in the family was affected by the King's death in different ways. Princess Margaret, whose youthful effervescence had so rejuvenated the King, was devastated. Her religious faith gave her some solace. She attended post-confirmation classes at St Paul's Vicarage in Knightsbridge and had long talks with an old friend, Simon Phipps, at that time a curate and latterly Bishop of Lincoln. She drew comfort also from the companionship of another friend, Group Captain Peter Townsend. The two of them were thrown together by the Queen Mother's decision to promote the equerry to the office of Comptroller to her Household. Clarence House was to become not only the Princess's home but also the Group Captain's base. 'I wonder what will happen to her,' Chips Channon had mused on meeting the Princess, aged eighteen. 'There is already a Marie Antoinette aroma about her.'[6]

Queen Mary, the fourth member of the family most affected by the King's death, who had endured more than the average amount of personal tragedy in her long life, was aware that she did not have a great deal of time left, but she was not prepared just to lie back and wait. The day after George VI's death she told her lifelong friend, Lady Shaftesbury, 'One must force oneself to go on until the end.'[7] However, three months later, on her eighty-eighth birthday, the indomitable old lady was writing to Osbert Sitwell in a quite different vein. 'I am beginning to lose my memory, but I mean to get it *back*.'[8]

Elizabeth II out of all the family appears to have borne the death of George VI with the most equanimity. It was not that she felt his loss any less deeply than the others, but rather that the self-discipline which had been a hall mark of her character since childhood came to the fore, as it

---

* Within Palace circles the Queen Mother is invariably called 'Queen Elizabeth', while her elder daughter is always simply 'The Queen'.

was to do again and again in the future. She was sensitive to Philip's situation, and let him know how much she still relied on him. She realized that Margaret, however much she might wish to deny it, also found her position subtly changed. From being one of two daughters of the King she was now the unmarried sister of a monarch with two children. Elizabeth had *official* seniority, with all that that entailed. The Queen Mother and Queen Mary also had to move back a row, or along the pew at least.

At the same time, Queen Mary, Queen Elizabeth and Princess Margaret were like pillars of strength to a young and nervous woman embarking on what amounted to a new career – a career in which she had been catapulted straight into the top job. To help her meet the unique challenge, the four women – three Queens and a Princess – quickly formed themselves into a solid square from which even Prince Philip was sometimes excluded. They were one separate family. Elizabeth and Philip and their small children were another. As titular head of both families now, as well as being Head of State and Commonwealth, Elizabeth II moved into what must be one of the loneliest jobs there is. She was governed, then as now, above all by a sense of duty to others and a genuine humility which strangers least expect in one so exalted.

The first duty to perform was the sacred act of coronation.

The date finally set for the grand occasion was 2 June 1953. Prime Minister Winston Churchill was so pessimistic about Britain's current economic climate that he had wanted the date put back. 'We can't have a coronation with the bailiffs in the house.' But he relented and was soon being whirled along in the nation's torrent of celebration with everyone else.

As always with the Queen, before anything happened, the detail had to be got right and as far as possible nothing should be left to chance. Chief among her guides and mentors (there were several) was her Earl Marshal, the portly Duke of Norfolk, who had to decide on such things as whether rabbit-trimmed robes would do instead of ermine – yes, all right – and whether the Prime Minister should be allowed to ride in an open coach – no, it must be enclosed; but, all right, as he insisted, it could be fitted up with interior lights so that he could be seen.*

The Queen had lights placed in her golden coach (but then she was the real star) and brackets to help to support the heavy orb and sceptre that she would be required to cradle in her arms on the way back from Westminster Abbey.

---

* A number of the superfluous fleet of horse-drawn carriages from the Royal Mews had been sold to Sir Alexander Korda for use in costume films and had to be hurriedly retrieved and repainted in the royal colours.

White sheets were brought to the ivory and gold ballroom of Buckingham Palace and, pinned together, gave the Queen and her attendants an idea of the length, but not the weight, of the sixty-foot coronation train. Posts and tapes on the carpet marked out the route the Queen would take in the Abbey. Two small silver stars were attached to the front of the crown so that the Archbishop of Canterbury would not place it on his sovereign's head back to front. Like a rehearsal for a village pageant, the whole rigmarole of rehearsal might have easily descended into hilarious farce, but the Queen would never allow that to happen. She took it all very seriously and was snappy to anyone tempted to introduce a note of levity. 'Don't be silly,' she said to her husband at one point. 'Come back here and do it again properly.'[9] At Westminster Abbey, where several rehearsals took place in great secrecy, with the Duchess of Norfolk standing in for the Queen, the Duke of Norfolk barked at a procession of clergy: 'If the bishops don't learn to walk in step we'll be here all night!'

Norman Hartnell submitted, in all, nine proposals for the Queen's coronation gown, which she wanted to be of similar design to her white wedding dress, but with embroidered floral emblems depicting the four parts of her United Kingdom, and the national flowers of her Commonwealth countries worked around the hem. As Robert Lacey, author of *Majesty*, wrote in 1977: 'She did not find it demeaning to be a doll dressed for her subjects' pleasure. She saw it as the essence of her job. The holy puppet clothed in magic robes for the people's comfort went back to the very roots of primeval monarchy.'[10]

In 1953 the total population of Britain and the Commonwealth numbered almost 650 million. A good proportion of these millions, black and white, became increasingly excited at the idea of a woman, barely twenty-six years of age, being raised above all others and crowned with due ceremony in the church where her forebears had been crowned for centuries past. Americans especially were intrigued by this phoenixlike manifestation of their wartime ally rising above its post-war austerity. *Time* magazine put Elizabeth II on its cover and wrote about 'the aspirations of the collective subconscious' – something which, like monarchs of old, she was recapturing on an international scale, according to America's biggest-selling news magazine.

In Britain, newspapers promoted the idea of a 'New Elizabethan Age'. Some deep-searching reporter even came up with the 'fact' that Elizabeth I became Queen while sitting under a tree a Hatfield House, the home of William Cecil, Elizabeth I's Lord High Treasurer. Linking this with the fact that Elizabeth II had acceded to the throne while perched in a fig tree he arrived at a neat conclusion: considering the glory that had been England's in the sixteenth century, was not this an omen for Britain in the second half of the twentieth century? 'The Signs Are Bright for a Great Revival' ran one newspaper headline.

In private, the Queen pooh-poohed all this nonsense. She was even embarrassed, and perhaps a little unnerved, by the comparison with her ancient forebear. Quite apart from the fact that she, Elizabeth II, was a constitutional monarch with little or none of the power enjoyed by Elizabeth I, she did not see herself as a 'gleaming champion' (the words later used by Winston Churchill to describe his sovereign) but rather as a servant and, if insisted upon, a symbol. It was all to the good of tourism and the Exchequer for the crowds to pour into London, and mugs, plates, teacloths, and balloons – all bearing the Queen and Prince Philips's impression – to be sold in their hundreds of thousands. She welcomed these demonstrations of the popularity of monarchy, and she was glad that people were organizing street parties up and down the length and breadth of the country, and that flags and banners covered practically every building. But for her personally, if she were to be asked, the coronation held a much deeper significance within the pageantry and popularity surrounding it. It was to be a solemn religious act of dedication and commitment. She had shown her feelings, and her anxieties, very clearly in her first Christmas broadcast to the nation in December 1952, as she looked towards her coronation in June. 'Pray for me on that day. Pray that God may give me wisdom and strength to carry out the solemn promises I shall be making.'

Forty years on, the vows Elizabeth II made at her coronation still held their brightness and seemingly put any thought of abdication out of court.

The Rt Revd Michael Mann, Dean of Windsor and domestic chaplain to the Queen for thirteen years until 1988, has often spoken to his sovereign about that period in her life. In his words, 'The Queen looks upon her coronation in much the same way as I would look upon my in-ordination as a priest, or my consecration as a bishop. It is something that is indelible, that is hers, and she feels that she was called to it by God. To give it up would be an abdication of her responsibilities.'[11]

The morning of 2 June 1953 opened up with one of Britain's thin summer drizzles, which did nothing whatsoever to dampen the spirits of the 30,000 subjects of the sovereign who had spent the night camped out on the pavements around Buckingham Palace and along the route to Westminster Abbey. During the next few hours, hundreds of thousands more were to join them.

Some people stayed at home to watch the ceremony on television – although nothing like as many as would today, for the simple reason that most people did not have television. Those who did possess a black and white set with a nine-inch screen invited friends and neighbours in and discovered, perhaps too late for some of them, that the coronation coverage went on, live and non-stop, for seven and a half hours.

Those whose most recent indelible memory of a major televised royal event is 'when Charles and Di got married' may be surprised to learn that the coronation was a far, far bigger affair than that. The London Metropolitan Police estimated the crowds at over one million. Tented camps were erected in the royal parks to accommodate the 60,000 troops brought in to line the route, and also the special contingents from every section of the Commonwealth forces. More than a hundred foreign radio commentators came to London to report in forty-two different languages. The Post Office installed an extra 3,280 telephone circuits 'for use by the biggest international assembly of commentators ever gathered for a single event'. And 60,000 feet of film, rushed by specially chartered aircraft to countries around the world, ensured that by the end of the day an estimated audience of 300 million people had witnessed the coronation of Elizabeth II.

Although the Queen wanted everything to be done according to what had gone before ('Did my father do it? Then I will too' was a frequent comment during the coronation preparations), she made one major and historic departure from precedent. She allowed live television into the Abbey for the first time so that as many people as possible could be witness to what went on. Her decision caused a furore.

George VI had forbidden television cameras recording his daughter's wedding some six years previously, and it was assumed by Churchill and his cabinet that his daughter would follow her father's example in this as in most things. Among the older politicians and some of the more fuddy-duddy advisers surrounding the Queen at the time, there was deep antipathy towards television. It was thought to be rather vulgar. It was an upstart that would worm its way into everything if not curbed. Besides, 'I don't see why the BBC should have a better view of my monarch being crowned than me,' grumbled Churchill.[12]

Sir Norman Brook, the Secretary of the Cabinet and a wily old bird, prepared a paper, setting out the dilemma facing the government. 'What arguments will remain for refusing T.V. facilities of e.g. royal funerals or weddings, religious services, or even proceedings in the House of Commons?' he asked. On the other hand, he conceded, 'Television has come to stay and unless it is fully used on an occasion like this it will be said that we are not moving with the times.'

A rumour had gone around early on in the planning stages that it was the Queen's expressed desire that live television should *not* be allowed at her coronation and, to be fair to him, this was partly why Churchill urged the Cabinet to inform the Queen that they were strongly against her being televised. With all the lights and other paraphernalia, it would place too great an additional burden on her young shoulders, they warned. Much better that it should be filmed, and the film vetted by the Archbishop of Canterbury before being viewed by the general populace. Live transmission 'would mean that any mistakes, unintentional incidents or undignified behaviour by the spectators would be seen by millions of people without any possibility of cutting or censorship.'

But the Queen *did* want her subjects to have the chance of seeing her being crowned, and was prepared to take the risk that something might go wrong. Only the most sacred moments, such as the communion, were to be for herself alone. A second meeting of the Cabinet reversed its earlier decision. 'Thus it was,' wrote Sir John Colville, Churchill's Private Secretary, 'that the new twenty-six-year-old sovereign personally routed the Earl Marshal, the Archbishop of Canterbury, Sir Winston Churchill and the Cabinet, all of whom submitted to her decision with astonishment, but with good grace.'[13] Churchill came round to Colville's view that 'it was the Queen who was to be crowned and not the Cabinet. She alone must decide.'

In its way, it was an important victory for Elizabeth II. Along with Prince Philip, she had been quicker than most to appreciate the value of television, not only to show monarchy at work but also to protect its future by letting in a little light on its mystery. Ever since the coronation the royal family has made use of television in preference to any other branch of the media to show off its wares. And television, in turn, by making absolutely sure that it never blots its copybook, has found entertaining programmes for, mostly, afternoon viewers, and a ready market overseas for its exclusive material.

The BBC television commentator for the coronation was the legendary Richard Dimbleby whose style was unique. Today's more sophisticated viewers might find it cloying, but in 1953 it struck exactly the right note. Hushed, almost reverential, rising and falling like the music of a church organist waiting for the bride to progress down the aisle, Dimbleby's commentary missed no detail and was meticulously prepared. 'Over the years,' writes the biographer John Pearson, 'he [Dimbleby] had become a convinced evangelist for the British monarchy, believing in his earthly sovereign rather as Billy Graham does in his heavenly one.'[14] Malcolm Muggeridge, a fellow journalist and broadcaster, dubbed him 'Gold Microphone in Waiting'. But Dimbleby's younger son, Jonathan, who along with his brother David was to follow in his father's footsteps and become a successful television interviewer himself, has said of Richard Dimbleby, 'His belief in the monarchy was not dispassionate; it was to partake in an emotional experience in which his whole being was involved.'[15]

Dimbleby was a superb professional who could make the dullest picture sing with his words, and translate grandiose pageantry into a simple stirring language that rarely failed to move. He was the best public relations officer the monarchy ever had. Why then was he not honoured with the knighthood his friends expected? In 1946 he received the OBE, and in 1959 he was made a CBE, but the Queen never bestowed on him any grade of the Royal Victorian Order for personal services, which is entirely in her gift. All that happened was that, in 1965, when he lay in hospital dying of cancer, a Buckingham Palace footman was dispatched to his bedside with half a dozen bottles of champagne.

All these years later, someone who was close to the Queen at the time of the coronation offered this explanation when asked about Dimbleby's missing knighthood: 'He got the CVO didn't he? I think that was probably considered quite enough for a reporter in those days. I think that would have been the Queen's attitude. She made old Perkins, her police officer, a KCVO – and that was unheard of – but that was twenty years later.*

One of the best examples of Dimbleby's eye for detail was contained in an article he wrote for a Sunday paper the weekend following the coronation service. Although he must have been exhausted by his marathon commentary and smothered by colleagues' compliments, he had time to observe that

one little thing slightly marred the glorious memories ... the melancholy sight of the litter left by the peers.

It seemed to me amazing that even on this occasion we could not break ourselves of one of our worst national habits. Tiers and tiers of stalls on which the peers had been sitting were covered with sandwich wrappings, sandwiches, morning newspapers, sweets and even a few empty miniature bottles.

Let us be fair however, and remember that the peers, many of them elderly men, had sat in their places, some of them seeing very little of the ceremony, for seven hours.[16]

When Elizabeth II arrived at Buckingham Palace and posed for the photographer Cecil Beaton in her purple robes and crown, she admitted, 'Yes, the crown does get a little heavy'.

She had worn the solid gold St Edward's crown, made in 1661 for Charles II, for the actual crowning ceremony, but during the coronation procession had chosen instead the Imperial Crown of State. This was the

* In November 1990, twenty-five years after his death, Richard Dimbleby became the first broadcaster to be honoured with a memorial plaque in Westminster Abbey.

crown that she wore when she stepped out on to the balcony of Buckingham Palace to receive the roar of approval of thousands of her subjects
who pressed towards the railings, and who simply refused to go home.
Altogether, the Queen and the Duke of Edinburgh made six appearances, the last at midnight. Behind and above them, in their respective
nurseries, Charles and Anne – their parents hoped – slept peacefully at
the end of an exhausting day. Princess Anne had been considered too
young to go to the Abbey, but Prince Charles, who was four, had been
slipped in by a back door and allowed to stand between the Queen
Mother and Princess Margaret. Not surprisingly, he seemed to be fairly
bemused by the whole business of coronation and was more interested in
exploring the contents of his granny's handbag, where he knew he would
find an Imperial peppermint.

The Queen Mother had followed the precedent set by Queen Mary
some seventeen years earlier by being present at the coronation of the
new sovereign, but Queen Mary herself was absent, having made her excuses some time earlier. Soon after her grand-daughter's accession she
had let it be known at Buckingham Palace that in the event of her untimely death there should be no question of the coronation being postponed. 'I feel weary and unwell,' she wrote to a friend on 18 March
1953.[17] On the morning of 24 March she slipped into a coma. At 11pm
Winston Churchill rose in the House of Commons and, moving the
adjournment of the House, announced the death of Queen Mary half an
hour previously.

In its way, the end of Queen Mary's long life – she was eighty-five
when she died – and the coronation of her granddaughter less than three
months later clearly defined the change from the old to the new. Queen
Mary and the lifestyle she followed belonged to the Victorian age. Elizabeth II was opening up a reign that encompassed the jet engine, mass
television, and upheavals both social and political across the world that
would seem, to some people, to make the monarchy increasingly irrelevant, not to say obsolete.

For one of the bishops attendant on the Queen at her coronation, the
most moving moment came when the Sovereign offered her great Sword
of State upon the High Altar: 'She never thought of the crowds of
people. She was completely taken up in her Act of Dedication. The most
wonderful thing I ever saw in my life was the moment when she lifted
the sword and laid it on the altar – she was putting her whole heart and
soul to the service of her people.'

Those who are closest to Elizabeth II today say her feelings have not
changed one jot from then, even if the world has.

Within weeks of the coronation and all its national acclamations of
Vivat! Vivat!, the young Queen was to learn what it was to be *for* the

people yet not *of* the people, to be *for* the family yet above it. She was to be plunged into political and personal upheaval.

On 24 June her seventy-nine year old Prime Minister, Winston Churchill, suffered a severe stroke which partially paralysed his left side and affected his speech. Two days later, his heir apparent, Anthony Eden, had a bile duct operation in the Lahey Clinic in Boston that would require several months of convalescence. And on the day of the coronation itself, as the VIPs were lining up to leave Westminster Abbey at the end of the ceremony, one or two reporters were quick to spot and interpret the moment when Princess Margaret, laughing and playful, picked a speck of dust off the breast jacket pocket of one Group Captain Peter Townsend, DSO, DFC.

6

The First Crisis

୧∾୨

Winston Churchill was Elizabeth II's first Prime Minister and her father's close wartime friend. The two men lunched together at Buckingham Palace every Tuesday, serving themselves from a side table so that they could discuss the progress of hostilities without footmen overhearing. When King George VI died, his first minister was so distraught, tears running down his cheeks, that he could not bring himself to write the speech that he knew he had to make.

However, the notion of serving a sovereign young enough to be his granddaughter filled him with apprehension. 'I don't know her,' he confided to his Private Secretary, Sir John Colville. 'I knew the King so well.'

Churchill was almost certainly the greatest all-round Englishman of his century: statesman, politician, writer, painter. He had led his country to victory in a war that it had been near to losing. In 1953, he was venerated almost as a god. Yet, like many very old men, he was nervous and ill at ease at the prospect of being in the company of a pretty young woman who might make him feel slightly antediluvian.

The Queen was just as nervous. On the grand old man's first visit to Balmoral, everyone under thirty was petrified by the thought of what to say without sounding stupid.

No one need have worried. In common with not a few of those at her court, Churchill immediately fell under the spell of the modest, unassuming and charming young person who was his monarch. 'What a very attractive and intelligent young woman,' he informed friends. On

Tuesdays, before he set out for his regular weekly audience at Buckingham Palace, he would take great care in putting on his frock coat and brushing the cigar ash from his lapels. When he returned and his secretary tried to get a hint of what had been discussed, Churchill would merely mumble, 'Racing mostly'.

Churchill, the romantic whose youth, he declaimed, 'was passed in the august, unchallenged and tranquil glare of the Victorian era' admitted to a thrill 'in invoking once again the prayer and anthem, "God Save the Queen!".' The accession 'aroused in him every instinct of chivalry,' said his daughter Mary Soames,[1] but Sir John Colville detected something else as well. 'Churchill,' he wrote, 'was an old man whose passions were spent, but there is no doubt that at a respectful distance he fell in love with the Queen.'

Some time before the premierships of James Callaghan and Margaret Thatcher, the Queen was asked: 'Which of your Prime Ministers, ma'am, did you enjoy your audiences with most?'

'Winston, of course, because it was always such fun.'[2]

Asked a similar question at a different time by another court confidante, the Queen said she found Churchill 'rather obstinate'.[3] The contrast in views is probably accounted for by the change in Churchill himself. At the time of the Queen's accession he was still fairly active and bushy-tailed but, following his stroke, his health if not his spirit went steadily downhill.

Lord Whitelaw, who was a sprig of an MP at the time but who, as Home Secretary, Deputy Prime Minister and Leader of the House of Lords, was later to come to know the Queen well, imagines that there was a grandfatherly relationship between Churchill and the Queen.

Some politicians and historians surmise that it was similar to that which existed between Queen Victoria and her Prime Minister Lord Melbourne, although towards the end of his second term of office Churchill's conversations tended increasingly to be monologues – from him.

At the outset of their relationship, Elizabeth II and Winston Churchill were confronted with a problem that neither of them envisaged developing into the crisis that it did. For the Queen it was the worst kind of problem – the kind that, unfortunately, she has had to deal with on more than one occasion in her reign – where her personal feelings and her position as a constitutional monarch cut across one another. She must take advice from her Ministers, and at the same time listen to the teachings of her heart and of her Christian faith.

The story of the ill-fated love affair between Princess Margaret and an RAF officer, Group Captain Peter Townsend, has been told many times, and each time a new facet has been added to the multifaceted mosaic. The complete story, if such a thing is possible where two people's love is concerned, will not be told until after the lifetime of the Queen and of Princess Margaret, if then. A contributing factor undoubtedly will be the diaries assiduously penned by Sir Alan Lascelles, the Queen's Private Secretary at the time – who became the sworn enemy of Princess Margaret – and which have never been published. The purpose here is to examine what occurred, to reflect on the impact it had on the royal family, the Queen in particular, and to ask what would happen if a similar situation were to arise either today or in the foreseeable future. Would the country split into two camps as it did in the 1950s?

For Princess Margaret, the attraction began when she was a mere girl of sixteen. But then again, the attraction was there for practically every woman of whatever age. Peter Townsend was the kind of man women fell for. He was good-looking in a fragile, underfed-looking kind of way. He was a wartime hero, a fighter pilot, winner of the DSO, DFC and Bar, whose nerve had been shattered by his bravery in overcoming fear. He was a talker, mostly about himself in a tormented self-deprecating way which appealed to some women but not to most men. Prince Philip, for one, was not particularly drawn to his sort. He was a mixture of Trevor Howard in *Brief Encounter* and Leslie Howard in *Gone With the Wind*, which meant, with women at least, that he could hardly go wrong *.

King George VI liked him. He is supposed to have said that Peter was the kind of son he would have liked to have had. He took him on as an equerry in March 1944 on a three-month secondment from the RAF, extended the period indefinitely and even stood as godfather to his second son. This was the nub of the matter, of course, the fly in the fragrant ointment. Group Captain Townsend was already married when he took up his appointment and first met Princess Margaret.

He made steady progress at the Palace. Like a good courtier he was always at hand but never acted out of place. In 1947, following the royal family's tour of South Africa, the King made his favourite equerry a Commander of the Royal Victorian Order for personal services to the sovereign. Other Heads of State quickly followed suit. The King of Denmark made him a Knight of Dannebrog. President Auriol of France sent him, by post, the insignia of an Officer of the Legion of Honour. At the express wishes of King George and Queen Elizabeth, Townsend and his family moved into Adelaide Cottage, once the tea house of Queen Adelaide, in Windsor Park. In 1950, the Group Captain was promoted to the post of Deputy Master of the Household.

---

* A superior officer once described Townsend's shyness as 'a reluctance to attempt anything which might make him noticeable'.[4]

It seemed as though nothing could dim his dazzling career, but life at court for outsiders (and Townsend was still an outsider, desite the affection royalty showed to him) almost invariably restricts itself to the person employed, and rarely includes that person's spouse. Long hours and lengthy travel for Peter meant that his wife saw less and less of him. Eight years after taking up the job that was going to be the making of them both, she un-made her marriage. On 20 December 1952, ten months after King George's death, Townsend was granted a divorce on the grounds of misconduct by his wife with an export merchant. They married two months later. In those days, a clear distinction was made at court between those 'innocent' and those 'guilty' in a divorce case. Townsend was adjudged innocent and thus was not required to resign. In fact, following the King's death, Queen Elizabeth the Queen Mother promoted him to the office of Comptroller to her Household, and he moved into Clarence House to be near his new mistress, and to Princess Margaret who also lived there.

Viewed from a distance of some forty years, it may seem odd that the romance between the Queen's sister and one of her mother's staff was not spotted sooner and, in view of the inherent consequences, discouraged. But this would be to fail to take proper account of the personalities of the three main royal participants involved in the drama – Princess Margaret, the Queen Mother and the Queen herself – and, also, of the way these things tend to be handled by Elizabeth II, equally today as then.

The Queen is a great one for taking the long-term view. She is also, perhaps above all, a pragmatist. And she wants people, especially those nearest and dearest to her, to be happy. In other words, she is like a great many other sound and sensible people.

The Court – two words which like the Establishment are extremely difficult to define – comprises a number of Households. There are Members of the Queen's Household, the Prince of Wales's Household, the Queen Mother's Household, and so on. Each Household operates largely in isolation and, occasionally, in serious jealousy of one another. Each is like a small business company, or Civil Service department, with clearly defined levels of authority. The main difference in the case of royal Households, of course, is that the boards of directors hold their jobs for life, and pass them on to their children. Another difference is that senior members of staff often live in houses belonging to their employers, are sometimes related to their employers and, much more than in other companies, tend to be wrapped up in the lives of their employers. Life at court tends to be not only exclusive but introvert as well. In this small self-contained society attachments are not unknown and are sometimes even a necessary part of staving off isolation and loneliness.

Older members of the royal family have always known this. That is why they have not just turned a blind eye but have more often approved of younger members of the family forming friendships outside their normal circle, though still inside the castle walls, so to speak. Before he married, Prince Charles associated with a number of women, not all of them aristocrats, whom his parents never really expected to see him marry. Prince Andrew had a well-publicized affair with the actress and photographer Koo Stark, who came from outside the castle walls, but there is no evidence that the Queen strongly disapproved. Though Miss Stark did not come into this category, friendships with married women – for instance, Prince Charles and Lady Tryon - were considered almost fail safe, and especially useful to someone as shy as Prince Charles was then.

When signs of affection between Princess Margaret and Peter Townsend were first spotted – credited to Continental journalists covering the Princess's visit to Amsterdam in 1948 – there was no reaction in Britain, either in the press or within the royal family. Margaret already had a host of admirers of her vivacity and beauty. Townsend was just one more, although, in his case, Princess Margaret seemed at first to be the one who was making the moves. But the Group Captain was a man of honour and he was already married. So that was all right. It was only after he ceased to be married and signs of mutual affection grew stronger, that the matter began to assume a different complexion.

In his memoirs, *Time and Chance*, Townsend gives a description of the woman he fell in love with that is both complimentary and at the same time probably the most accurate picture there has been of this much troubled lady.

He wrote of the Queen's sister at that time:

She was a girl of unusual, intense beauty, confined as it was in her short, slender figure and centred about large purple-blue eyes, generous, sensitive lips and a complexion as smooth as a peach. She was capable, in her face and in her whole being, of an astonishing power of expression. It could change in an instant from saintly, almost melancholic, composure to hilarious, uncontrollable joy. She was, by nature, generous, volatile. She was a *comedienne* at heart, playing the piano with ease and verve, singing in her rich, supple voice the latest hits, imitating the famous stars. She was coquettish, sophisticated. But what ultimately made Princess Margaret so attractive and lovable was that behind the dazzling façade, the apparent self-assurance, you could find, if you looked for it, a rare softness and sincerity.

It was hard for anyone not to like Princess Margaret, in spite of her sudden switches of mood and occasional shafts of haughtiness. Both the Queen and the Queen Mother held a special affection for her. 'She is so outrageously amusing that one can't help encouraging her,' Mabell, Countess of Airlie wrote. She had been the apple of her father's eye, but her elder sister had never shown any signs of jealousy. Now that she was happily married with two lovely children, Elizabeth II just wished for her little sister to find happiness too.

Shortly after the coronation, Princess Margaret chose the moment during a weekend at Windsor to tell the Queen of her deep love for Peter Townsend, and of their desire for her permission to marry. Although Margaret was twenty-three years of age, she still needed her sister's consent, for under the Royal Marriages Act of 1772 members of the royal family in line of succession to the throne had to secure the sovereign's authority if they wished to marry before the age of twenty-five.

As far as the laws affecting royalty, and the moral outlook of the nation were concerned, the possibility of a marriage between the Queen's sister and a divorced commoner was to be the first real test of the new reign. Privately, the Queen was delighted for her sister. Peter Townsend was popular with the whole family, with the possible exception of Prince Philip who could see difficulties ahead. The government and the country as a whole was still to be drawn into the affair.

In 1953, a person who had been divorced, whether or not he or she was the guilty party, was held in some way to be tainted when it came to holding a position in public life. And, although there was no direct parallel, memories of the furore caused by Edward VIII's passion for the twice-divorced Wallis Simpson still haunted the corridors of Windsor.

After careful reflection following her meeting with Princess Margaret, the Queen called both the Group Captain and the Princess together for a further talk, when she informed them that she could give no personal directive either way with regard to marriage. They would have to resolve the matter for themselves, but must realize that they would almost certainly run into strong opposition from some quarters. Pragmatic as ever, she suggested that 'under the circumstances, it isn't unreasonable for me to ask you to wait a year'.

Queen Elizabeth the Queen Mother joined the Queen in trying to find the best solution for all. 'If disconcerted, as they had every reason to be,' Townsend recalled, 'they did not flinch, but faced it with perfect calm and, it must be said, considerable charity.'

However, where Sir Alan Lascelles, the Queen's Private Secretary, was concerned 'charity' was not a word Princess Margaret was likely to rush to. Were it not for a respect for the dead, contempt might be her favoured choice of word, even to this day.

Perhaps unfairly, perhaps not, Sir Alan, who was always known as

'Tommy' and who in old age grew a beard and looked rather jolly, has been cast as the 'baddie' in what, predictably, the newspapers called 'the great royal romance'. It may have been that he was simply carrying out his duty to his sovereign as he, and the law, saw it, but his actions, and certainly his attitude, may have also owed a smidgen to that more incurable of British afflictions: class distinction.

Lascelles, who died in 1981 at the age of ninety-four, was a grandson of the 4th Earl of Harewood and cousin of the 6th Earl who married King George VI's sister, Princess Mary. In 1920, he married Joan Thesiger, eldest daughter of the 1st Viscount Chelmsford, Viceroy of India. He had been Assistant Private Secretary to George V and Edward VIII, and Private Secretary to George VI. Now he was Private Secretary to Elizabeth II. He was very much of the old school. Peter Townsend, son of an Indian Army officer serving in the Burmese administration, educated at Haileybury (Alma Mater of Clement Attlee, the former socialist Prime Minister), pilot in the RAF and a divorcee, was of the new.

The two men did not dislike one another, as far as one can gather, but Sir Alan Lascelles was far more concerned with the Queen's interests than he was with Princess Margaret's affairs, romantic or otherwise. As the Queen's principal adviser, his chief concern was always that his sovereign should not be put in a position that would in any way be detrimental to the throne.

When Townsend sought Lascelles's informal advice about marriage, as a Member of one Household to a Member of another, he was sent away with his ears stinging. 'You must be either mad or bad,' stormed the Queen's Private Secretary. 'Though not entitled, perhaps, to any sympathy from him, it would all the same have helped,' Townsend wrote later. 'He was a friend and I was asking for his help.'

The most infuriating part, as far as Princess Margaret was concerned, was that while Lascelles was clearly not in favour of such a union, he did not actually say she could not marry Townsend, for constitutional or any other reasons. In fact, he did not say anything to her at all, and for the rest of his life Princess Margaret refused to exchange a single word with him, so disgusted was she with his behaviour. 'Had he said we *couldn't* get married, we wouldn't have thought any more about it. But nobody bothered to explain anything to us.'[5]

At the time, both the Princess and Peter Townsend believed that there was at least a chance of their getting married with the Queen's approval, even though they might have to wait a year. What, apparently, they never bargained for was the hornet's nest that their romance stirred up in the world outside the Palace.

At first the British press behaved precisely as it did when the love affair between the Prince of Wales and Mrs Wallis Simpson was first rumoured. In other words it gossiped in bars and maintained a discreet silence elsewhere. It placed nothing in print. American and Continental newspapers and magazines, however, suffered from no such inhibitions. They took hold of every rumour and wrung it out like a dishcloth. However, once all the patriotic fervour of the coronation was out of the way, and royal stories were beginning to get thin on the ground, one newspaper, the Sunday *People*, decided to act. In the classic style of the 1950s, the paper went for a denial, rather like a footballer deliberately looking for a foul in the penalty area: 'It is high time for the British public to be made aware of the fact that newspapers in Europe and America are openly asserting that the Princess [Margaret] is in love with a divorced man and that she wishes to marry him. The story is of course utterly untrue. It is quite unthinkable that a royal princess, third in succession to the throne, should even contemplate marriage with a man who has been through the divorce courts.'[6]

This time it was Buckingham Palace that kept a discreet silence, but behind the walls the wheels were whirring. Sir Alan Lascelles's advice to the Queen was that Townsend should 'move on' – as most equerries normally do, anyway – to another posting. He suggested that Townsend might be found an appointment abroad, how far abroad he did not specify. The Queen, typically, preferred the middle way. She agreed that Group Captain Townsend should be moved from Queen Elizabeth's Household, and thereby from Clarence House, but he should not be sent abroad. Instead, she would appoint him to her own personal staff as equerry.

Presumably disappointed by this suggestion, Lascelles went away to talk with John Colville who for a time had been Private Secretary to Princess Elizabeth and had now returned to Winston Churchill's side as his Private Secretary. The Prime Minister would need to be put in the picture, Lascelles advised Colville. It was a skilful move, taking the matter out of the Queen's hands. However, the ploy almost backfired, for instead of shaking his head, Churchill greeted the news of a possible engagement with exuberance. 'What a delightful match. A lovely young royal lady married to a gallant young airman, safe from the perils and horrors of war!'[7] Churchill was on the verge of being carried away by his own romanticism, until Colville pointed out that this was not at all the message that he had meant to convey. Lascelles had spoken of the Royal Marriages Act, and of the impossibility of Princess Margaret marrying anyone before the age of twenty-five without the permission of the sovereign. The Cabinet would need to discuss the matter and express a firm point of view. Churchill looked suitably crestfallen. His wife, Clementine, overhearing the conversation, looked towards the two men and added her own storm-cloud warning: 'Winston, if you are going to begin the Abdication all over again, I'm going to leave! I shall take a flat and go and live in Brighton.'*8

The Cabinet duly met the next morning and unanimously decided to advise against any such royal marriage. Churchill put their feelings to the Queen at his audience the following day.

Coming less than a fortnight after her coronation, this was likely to have been a hard blow for Elizabeth II to take, not in respect of herself, but on behalf of her sister. All her sympathy would have been for Margaret and for the man with whom she was so obviously in love. Both people were very dear to her. If her father had been alive, he would almost certainly have taken steps to end the affair. But, for once, possibly the first time, the Queen appeared not to wish to ask herself: What would the King have done? The clear thinking and innate wisdom that were to be so apparent in the future were already making an appearance. The Queen Mother also desperately wanted her younger daughter to be happy, although some thought she strangely distanced herself from taking decisions or offering clear advice. Perhaps it was all too painful, or perhaps she did not want to interfere with what she knew must be finally the Queen's decision. Or perhaps it was simply that, with her facility to look on the bright side, she thought that, given time, the clouds would somehow miraculously float away.

Time was the card that the Queen played. The Princess and Peter Townsend had already reached the conclusion that a temporary separation was probably unavoidable. Even before the coronation, Townsend had offered to take up a new posting, but now it was inevitable that he went. Churchill and the Cabinet insisted on it, Lascelles strongly urged it, and the Queen could not easily or safely ignore the advice of her Ministers. In any case, she was all for giving matters a breathing space and thus hopefully avoiding any crisis.

It so happened that in the summer of 1953 there were Foreign Office vacancies for air attachés in Johannesburg, Singapore and Brussels. Not very surprisingly, Townsend chose Brussels, by far the nearest of the three to London. On the morning of 30 June 1953, he and Princess Margaret said their goodbyes. The Princess was due to leave Heathrow Airport with the Queen Mother in two hours' time, bound for Salisbury, Rhodesia. As Townsend recalled, 'the Princess was very calm for we felt certain of each other and, though it was hard to part, we were reassured by the promise, emanating from I know not where, but official, that my departure would be held over until her return on 17 July.'

In fact, while the Princess was still in Africa, struck down by an attack of 'Bulawayo flu', Townsend was ordered to have his bags packed and be

---

* Winston Churchill had supported Edward VIII in the Abdication Crisis of 1936.

in Brussels by 15 July, two days before Princess Margaret was due back in London. Nobody, it seemed, was taking any chances.

By now, through press reports, the British public was *au fait* with the situation and was beginning to take sides. This as much as anything disturbed the Queen and her advisers. The last thing anybody wanted so early on in the reign was a return to the divisions caused by Edward VIII's love affair with a divorced woman.

'*Tribune* believes that Princess Margaret should be allowed to make up her own mind about whom she wants to marry,' wrote the magazine's editor, Michael Foot, the MP and future leader of the Labour Party. 'Most people, we imagine, would agree with that simple proposition. But the British Cabinet does not agree.' The objection was based on the fact that Townsend had been involved in a divorce case, Foot continued, even though he was the innocent party in the action. 'This intolerable piece of interference with a girl's private life is all part of the absurd myth about the royal family which has been so sedulously built up by interested parties in recent years. . . . The laws of England say that a man, whether he has divorced his wife or been divorced himself, is fully entitled to marry again. . . . If those laws are good they are good enough for the royal family.'[9]

More and more people outside of the main body of the Church of England were coming round to this point of view. The pictures of a tragic-looking young Princess Margaret, deliberately picked out by some newspapers, served to reinforce sympathy, but by now the powder had been removed from the explosive situation. Townsend was to all intents and purposes exiled – although the Queen had agreed that the couple should stay in contact by telephone and letter – and it was now just a question of waiting until Princess Margaret reached the age of twenty-five, or so most people thought, when she would be able to marry whomsoever she chose, unhindered by the archaic Royal Marriages Act of 1772.

During the two-year separation, quite a sizeable proportion of the public apparently were of the opinion that the exotic butterfly Margaret – a sort of Vivien Leigh character in the mould of Scarlet O'Hara – would soon alight somewhere else, and that the affair with Peter Townsend was largely a press invention anyway. But it wasn't, and the Princess did not look to anyone else. On 21 August 1955, when she reached her twenty-fifth birthday, she still wished to marry Peter Townsend.

However, if she had hoped for a rapid recall of her loved one, and a joyful acceptance of their plans, she was in for a cruel disappointment. After two years, nothing had changed in any direction. The objectors still objected. If anything, their opposition to a wedding was even more deeply entrenched. The Queen Mother was perhaps the only one to have modified her views, but not in the way her younger daughter would have wished. She had had time to ponder on the implications of the proposed marriage, and she had also listened to the advice of her friend the Marquess of Salisbury, a grandson of Queen Victoria's last Prime Minister, and a descendant of Elizabeth I's Lord High Treasurer. 'Bobbety' Salisbury, a High Anglican who pronounced 'r' as 'w' so that Harold Macmillan became 'Hawold', was Lord President of the Council and leader of the House of Lords. Under the premiership of Sir Anthony Eden, who had taken over from a physically exhausted Churchill, Salisbury threatened to resign from the government if wedding plans were approved. His influence, and that of the Archbishop of Canterbury, Dr Geoffrey Fisher, bore down heavily and could not be shaken off. However much affection the Queen and the Queen Mother might have for both Princess Margaret and Peter Townsend, and however much they wished to see them happy together, they could not ignore the twin influences of Church and Cabinet. Public clamour was being whipped up, too. 'Come on Margaret!' headlined the *Daily Mirror*, 'Please Make Up Your Mind!'

In the late summer, as over 250,000 visitors to the Royal Academy Exhibition in London queued up to see Pietro Annigoni's romantic portrait of the Queen ('I don't think I really look like that'), Anthony Eden and his wife were invited to Balmoral for the Prime Minister's traditional annual Scottish visit. The Queen still hoped a way could be found to allow her sister's marriage to go ahead without impairing the standing of the monarchy. The irony of receiving a Prime Minister who himself had divorced and then happily remarried was not lost on her. Nor was the fact that two other members of the Cabinet in opposition to the marriage – Thorneycroft and Monckton – were also divorcees. At the same time, she realized that these private arrangements had no real relevance where her sister was concerned. There, she still counted on time solving the problem. She told the Prime Minister of her sister's desire for Parliament to give consent to her marriage, and of her own wish that the couple should be given six months of normal life together before finally making up their minds. Anthony Eden listened but said very little and, when he set off back to London on the Monday morning, he cannot have left much optimism behind.

However, on 12 October a surprisingly cheerful Princess Margaret travelled from Balmoral to London by train. On the same day, as she already was aware, Peter Townsend was flying in from Brussels. The Princess went straight to Clarence House. Townsend drove from Lydd airport in Kent to 19 Lowndes Square in Knightsbridge, where a close friend of the royal family, the Marquess of Abergavenny, had placed his apartment at Townsend's disposal.

The following day, one of Princess Margaret's cousins lunched with him at the flat, and afterwards the two of them went on a shopping expedition, pursued by a gaggle of press men and women. Shorly after 6pm, the Group Captain drove himself to Clarence House for his first open meeting with Princess Margaret in two years (there was a strong suspicion that there had been one or two clandestine meetings during that time). The press checked their watches when Townsend went in, and again when he finally emerged. He had been with Princess Margaret for one hour and forty minutes it was reported the next morning.

The more popular papers could not get enough of the story and neither could most of their readers. A survey carried out by one newspaper in October 1955 showed that 59 per cent of its readers actively approved of a marriage taking place, while only 17 per cent were against the idea.

During the next two and a half weeks every visit by Townsend to Clarence House (five in all), was scrupulously logged by reporters; every dinner party (four) was doorstepped. The couple 'strolled gaily through the wooded parkland of the Wills's lovely country estate'; 'Princess Margaret left for church in a Rolls Royce at 10.35'. It was reported that the Wills's butler had been offered £1,000 to tell of what he saw, but sternly declined.[10] *Paris Match* even published a picture of a small cairn, supposedly on a hill above Balmoral, where over the years Margaret and Townsend were said to have placed a stone each time they passed. The story was pure fiction.

Not for the first or last time Buckingham Palace had underestimated public interest in a royal romance. Any thought of a six-month period of 'normal' life was beyond wishful thinking.

Commander Richard Colville, the Queen's tight-lipped Press Secretary (about whom, more later) issued a statement:

The Press Secretary to the Queen is authorized to say that no announcement concerning Princess Margaret's personal future is at present contemplated. The Princess has asked the Press Secretary to express the hope that the press and public will extend to Her Royal Highness their customary courtesy and co-operation in respecting her privacy.[11]

Clearly, the statement had been read and approved by the Queen before being issued, but once again it was simply a method of playing for time, and the inclusion of the words 'at present' only served to fuel the speculation. Did it mean that eventually Margaret would marry Townsend? The phrase could equally mean that a decision had already been made, but that the public would have to wait a little longer for an announcement. The whole matter was still a confused mess.

On the evening of 18 October, following a Cabinet meeting that morning, Anthony Eden went to Buckingham Palace with some firm and painful advice for the sovereign. If Princess Margaret insisted on marrying Peter Townsend she would voluntarily have to renounce her rights to the succession – she was at that time third in line to the throne – and waive all claims to her official income. This stood to be more than doubled, to £15,000 per annum, once she married.

A Bill would be introduced into Parliament to bring all this into effect, and would undoubtedly be passed. The Prime Minister felt bound to tell the Queen that in his opinion, if Princess Margaret did not make the right decision – that is, give up all thought of marriage to Townsend – the whole issue would irreparably damage the standing of the Crown.

The Queen listened to her First Minister, and at that point almost certainly must have known that the marriage was doomed not to take place. It was now up to Margaret, after the situation had been explained to her, to make the final decision. But surely, remembering the Duke of Windsor, she would not make the same mistake of putting love before duty? Surely she would make the sacrifice and, if hesitant, would be persuaded to do so by her sister, her mother, and her brother-in-law?

Lord Charteris, who was an Assistant Private Secretary to Elizabeth II at the time, believes that in today's climate there would have been no problem about a marriage going ahead. 'The Queen was very fond of Peter herself, and I suspect she was pretty sorry for her sister. But you've got to remember that it all happened almost forty years ago, and people were pretty strait-laced. No government would have supported the marriage.'[12]

On 24 October *The Times* weighed in with an editorial which, considering the influence that it has always had, probably helped to make up a few minds.

After stating that in the twentieth century the monarchy had come to be the symbol of every side of British life, with the Queen 'its universal representative in whom her people see their better selves ideally reflected,' the paper pointed out that the Queen's family 'has its own part in the reflection'.

> If the marriage which is now being discussed comes to pass, it is inevitable that this reflection becomes distorted. The Princess will be entering into a union which vast numbers of her sister's people, all sincerely anxious for her lifelong happiness, cannot in conscience regard as a marriage. This opinion would be held whether the Church of England were established or not, and extends to great bodies of Christians outside it.

There would be profound sympathy with the Queen, said *The Times*, 'who would be left still more lonely in her arduous life of public service', but 'if the Princess finally decided, with all the anxious deliberation that clearly she has given to her problem, that she is unable to make the sacrifice involved . . . then she has a right to lay down a burden that is too heavy for her.'

The peoples of the Commonwealth, whose governments had taken a keen interest in all that was going on in London, 'would see her step down from her high place with the deepest regret. [But] these things said, the matter is, in the last resort, one to be determined solely by Princess Margaret's conscience.' Her fellow subjects would want to wish her every happiness, but 'not forgetting that happiness in the full sense is a spiritual state and that its most precious element may be the sense of duty done'.[13]

By now the Princess and Peter Townsend were reeling under the onslaught of public debate about their private relationship. They might have felt inclined to agree with the *Daily Mirror* that *The Times* spoke 'for a dusty world and a forgotten age. . . . Would *The Times* have preferred this vivacious young woman to marry one of the witless wonders with whom she has been hobnobbing these past few years? Or to live her life in devoted spinsterhood?

It was becoming altogether too much. 'We were both exhausted, mentally, emotionally, physically,' Townsend wrote later. 'We felt mute and numbed at the centre of this maelstrom.'

Princess Margaret spent 23 October at Windsor Castle, mainly in contemplation and in consultation with the Queen and Prince Philip. Late in the day she telephoned Townsend 'in great distress'. She did not say what had passed between herself and her sister and her brother-in-law, but doubtless the stern truth was dawning on her.

The following evening Townsend and Margaret came together alone in the drawing-room of Clarence House and openly faced up to the situation as it was. They talked about it, and around about it, and could find no way out of it. In Townsend's words, they had arrived at a 'no deal situation'.

'For a few moments we looked at each other; there was a wonderful tenderness in her eyes which reflected, I suppose, the look in mine. We had reached the end of the road.'

The Queen took the news with the equanimity of a fair judge, though in this trial she had never been a judge, nor a prosecutor or defender, but simply a devoted sister who must pay heed to the man in the Anthony Eden hat who came to call.

The first person outside the immediate family to be told of the decision was the Archbishop of Canterbury. Princess Margaret went alone to Lambeth Palace, almost directly opposite the Houses of Parliament, on the opposite side of the Thames.

Over the years there have been at least two versions of the actual words used on that occasion. Princess Margaret's own account, as told to the biographer Lady Elizabeth Longford, must hold favour.

'After she and Dr Fisher had exchanged greetings, he put on his spectacles, went over to the bookcase and began to haul out a large reference book. "Put it back," said Princess Margaret. "I have come to give you information, not to ask for it." So he sat down again and she told him she had decided not to marry Peter Townsend. The Archbishop's comment was made with a beaming smile: "What a wonderful person the Holy Spirit is!"'[14] Dr Fisher was to inform the author James Pope-Hennessy some two years later that Princess Margaret 'is a thoroughly good churchwoman who really understands doctrine'[15] and perhaps not enough attention has been paid in the intervening years to the influence her very deep religious faith may have had on her decision not to marry Peter Townsend.

Certainly, in her statement of renunciation on 31 October 1955, Princess Margaret conceded that 'it might have been possible for me to contract a civil marriage. But, mindful of the Church's teaching that Christian marriage is indissoluble, and conscious of my duty to the Commonwealth, I have resolved to put these considerations before any others.'

At the time there were some people, cynics no doubt, who said that Margaret loved being a princess too much, and that once she realized that she would have to give up her royal status and her income in order to marry, Townsend's chances were reduced to dust under the foot. That seems too harsh a judgement, and takes no account of her loyalty. 'She minds about people, and is a better friend than the Queen is in that way,' according to someone who knows both of them well.

Princess Margaret herself believes that the whole question of whether or not she and Peter Townsend could marry, and under what circumstances, should have been spelled out to her much earlier. Peter Townsend also thinks he might have been warned sooner of the deep waters he was getting into. It was not good enough for Sir Alan Lascelles simply to damn the young equerry as 'either mad or bad'. 'I was describing to him a state of affairs,' wrote Townsend, 'which, if thoroughly undesirable, reprehensible even, in his eyes (and, eventually, in a good many others'), was, equally, impossible to ignore.'

Within the royal family the epithet most frequently applied to Princess Margaret is 'poor'. 'Poor old Margaret,' said one courtier who has

known the Princess since she was a young girl, 'has simply got a very difficult destiny. Everything goes wrong for her. Her father died just at the
wrong moment for her, when she was coquette of the walk. Suddenly,
instead of being, as it were, the only operating child of the sovereign, she
becomes the sister of the Queen. And then she wasn't allowed to marry
Peter – whether or not it would have been a good thing if she had is
another matter; I simply don't know. And then she married Tony [Arm-
strong-Jones, now Lord Snowdon] and that looked all right, but it
wasn't . . .' And another view from close-in: 'She was a very sexy girl,
although she drank too much and smoked too much. I'm very fond of
her. She can be terrible really, a bit imperious, but she sometimes surprises you by being much better than she appears. I was going to say
she's profoundly superficial, but she's really rather a good friend. But I
don't terribly want to spend a lot of time with her. Why? Well, she's
quite boring really. She's not scintillating at all.'

Princess Margaret once described to a friend how she had spent one of
her birthdays at Balmoral in the late 1970s. She said that the Queen and
she had spent the day making bonfires. The Queen had succeeded in getting her bonfire to light straight away and it blazed for hours, whereas
Princess Margaret's bonfire had refused to light properly and kept fiz-
zling out. 'Story of my life,' the Princess commented.

When this anecdote was related to Lord Charteris, he said he thought
it showed great perspicacity on the part of the Princess, and told a great
deal about her. 'The person who supports the Queen and is more loyal
than anyone I know is Princess Margaret,' he said. 'Which is rather remarkable because you would think she must be jealous of her sister
psychologically. I have never heard her say anything but that she loves
the Queen, trusts her, and thinks she has got marvellous judgement.'[16]

The two sisters have remained extremely close over a span of sixty
years, with few serious disagreements. Time has changed them both, but
not very much. Family loyalties still come first, linked to the duty
attached to their destiny.

As for Peter Townsend, as he says in his memoirs, he outflew the
storm. Four years after he said goodbye to Princess Margaret he married
an attractive Belgian heiress named Marie-Luce Jamagne and they had
three children. He is still occasionally in communication with Buckingham Palace, but for those old enough to recall the heady romantic days
of the Margaret-Townsend affair it may come as a slight shock to realize
that in 1990 Peter Townsend arrived at his seventy-sixth birthday.

The 1991 edition of *Whitaker's Almanack* still lists among the extra
equerries to Her Majesty the Queen the name of one Group Captain
Peter Townsend, CVO, DSO, DFC.

7

Inside the Palace

⁓⁕⁓

The Queen's car sweeps in through the gate at the right of Buckingham Palace, within inches of the knot of tourists standing on the pavement, and disappears through an archway at the side of the building. This leads to the Garden Entrance, the Queen's private front door.

The bevelled glass inner door is held open by a footman dressed in a blue battledress tunic with red facings. The Queen's Page stands just inside the door.

A covey of corgis* bound out of the car and into the dark interior of the Palace almost before the Queen has had time to make sure that she has left nothing behind.

She crosses the deep red carpet to the small lift, capable of carrying four people at a squeeze, that will take her up to the royal apartments on the first floor. In passing, she may notice that the small pile of towels on a shelf near the lift has been replenished. These are for wiping the corgis' paws after they have been out in the garden to spend a penny. In really wet weather, sharp-eyed visitors are sometimes mystified too by the sight of grubby dogs' towels drying out on a radiator.

Stepping out of the lift, the Queen turns left and goes into her private sitting-room which also acts as her office. What happens after that depends on the nature of the Queen's diary, entries in which are made at least six months in advance, for home engagements, and up to two years

---

* At the time of writing, the Queen has seven corgis: Spark, Fable, Diamond, Kelpie, Myth, Phoenix and Pharos.

in advance of overseas tours. When she is working in London, Elizabeth II frequently may have to make three changes of clothes in a day, make visits to three entirely different types of environment – say, a hospital, a factory and a university – and receive in audience senior diplomats from three different countries.

Nowadays Elizabeth II tends to keep evening engagements to a minimum – the occasional charity premiere perhaps – whereas her husband's workload entails attending several official dinners each month. Elizabeth II spends more evenings alone in her Palace, with a TV supper and her dogs, than most people might imagine. There is no 'popping-in' of relatives or friends. Even her children, who are out on official engagements themselves most evenings, ring up first before dropping in on Mummy.

The pattern of the Queen's working week at the Palace has hardly changed in forty years. Provided one or other has no appointments outside London, requiring an early start or an overnight stay, the Queen and Prince Philip take breakfast together before going their separate ways. Prince Philip's office, although 1950s in interior design, is up to the minute in gadgets and computer software. He revealed to a trio of young reporters in an interview for a children's newspaper in March 1990 that he particularly enjoys a magnetic pattern game. The Queen's private sitting-room is much more homely and at the same time elegant. Visitors often comment on the sweet smell that fills the room, coming from the vases of fresh flowers and the bowls of pot-pourri standing on the various pieces of priceless and at the same time well-worn furniture.

The antique desk at which the Queen sits – on a Chippendale elbow chair with a tapestry seat – is festooned with photographs in silver frames. Some are of her children and grandchildren, but there are also one or two of horses and dogs, including one of her favourite corgi, Susan, who died in 1957, aged ten. The Queen always has a vase of flowers on her desk, often pink carnations of a special kind grown in one of the glasshouses at Sandringham, or, in their season, lily of the valley.

The walls, as one might expect, are hung with fine paintings, including a charming little picture by the seventeenth-century Flemish artist Teniers, some nice horse pictures by Hondecoeter and – a special favourite of the Queen – a tranquil scene of a Normandy beach with fishermen and children, by Bonington, that was given to her by the Plunkett family after the tragically early death in 1975 at the age of fifty-one of Lord Patrick Plunkett, Deputy Master of the Household, who was a close personal friend of the Queen.*

---

* The Queen personally picked out the ground for a memorial to Lord Plunkett in the Valley Gardens of Windsor Great Park. It takes the form of a small wooden temple where a person can sit and look out over Virginia Water.

After she has glanced – and sighed – at the pile of official papers waiting in their special red box to be studied and/or signed, or passed on to a
Private Secretary for reply, she may turn more eagerly to the large pile of
letters that have arrived with the morning post. These can number up to
some two hundred each day.

Once the whole post has passed through the screening process that
detects any possible explosive device, the Queen's Page sorts through the
letters and packages addressed to the Queen personally and puts aside
junk mail and circulars, and what is suspected to be 'mad mail'. Over the
years the Palace has developed a sixth sense about letters from crackpots,
although the clue of green ink is not infallible because Chiefs of Staff also
use green ink. The Page then divides what is left into two piles, those
letters that bear the tell-tail initials of the sender in the bottom left-hand
corner of the envelope, and the others. Those with the initials are from
personal friends of the Queen and are almost invariably recognized by the
Page, but the others – the great majority – might be from anyone from
anywhere in the world. Every communication addressed to HM The
Queen, with the exception of the aforementioned, lands up on her desk.

Like most people, she begins by reading the letters from personal
friends. Then she moves on to the larger pile, and by a process of reading
the post marks and the style of handwriting on the envelopes she has
learned over the years how to pick out a fair sample of her mail. Depending on the time available, she might read up to twenty or thirty letters
from total strangers each morning. She is quite proud of boasting that
because of this practice she reckons she knows more about what ordinary people in the street are thinking than does any member of her family.
She is quite likely to flourish a letter from one of her subjects as her
Private Secretary enters the room: 'Do you know about this?' If he
doesn't, he soon will. She is also very good at remembering events and
when they happened. If neither she nor her Private Secretary can recall a
date precisely, she will reach for a drawer in her desk and extract her
private diary in which, it is said, she records not only what happened but
also what she thought of what happened.

When she is ready, the Queen flicks a small lever or key, one of a number in a row, on a somewhat antiquated intercom system standing to the
side of her desk. This puts her in touch with one or other Member of her
Household, each of whom has a similar box of tricks on his desk. In their
offices, on the ground floor directly below the royal apartments, a bulb
lights up above a tiny ivory plaque that reads simply 'The Queen'. Sitting
alongside the intercom, and looking somewhat incongruous on the large,
highly polished antique leather-topped desks of the Private Secretaries
and other senior Members of the Queen's Household, are the plastic
boxes and staring green faces of the computer system which was installed

in Buckingham Palace in the early 1980s and is constantly being updated. Elizabeth II, while not averse to modernization, is happy to go on using her old and well-tried system. So, too, are her courtiers, even though there has been some jealousy in the past about who has a 'master' system and who a 'slave'. The difference between the systems is complicated to the outsider, but apparently the advantage of the 'master' system is that it tells you who is calling, and so you don't need to answer if you don't want to. Naturally, the Queen has a 'master' system.

'Can you come up for a moment please, Robert?' All Members of the Queen's Household are addressed by their first name from the first day of their appointment. In the case of Sir Robert Fellowes, Principal Private Secretary to Elizabeth II since July 1990, it would be rather surprising if she didn't. He is married to the elder sister of the Princess of Wales.

A slim, studious-looking man of fifty who wears horn-rimmed spectacles, he was with a London City firm of discount brokers and bankers, Allen Harvey and Ross, before going to the Palace. Before that he held a short commission with the Scots Guards. He was appointed an Assistant Private Secretary to the Queen in 1977, and nine years later was promoted to the post of Deputy. A naturally reticent person, with a gentle but ready smile, he likes to relax by watching or playing cricket and golf. Friends say he is not at all a bad shot. His clubs are Whites, Pratt's, and the MCC.

The Queen has always liked to have about her men who are the quintessence of loyalty, who are non-obsequious, intelligent, efficient and, preferably, have a sense of humour. When she was younger she liked them to be tall and slim, but nowadays the character counts for much more than the looks. She used to recruit, or often inherit, her staff mostly from among the ranks of officers and aristocrats – very often they came recommended by a relative or friend. Then she began bringing into her service people whose talents she had spotted and made a mental note of on an overseas tour, or who were from one of the Commonwealth countries, Australia and Canada in particular. More recently, she has tended to recruit men with a Foreign Office or even a City background. But sometimes she is quite relaxed about appointments, simply saying to her senior advisers: 'I leave you to choose'.

Unlike the Prince of Wales, who never seems to keep his Private Secretary for more than two or three years at a time, Elizabeth II is most loathe to see anyone leave her service – former Private Secretaries are hard put to think of a single example of dismissal – and usually her senior advisers remain with her for at least twenty years.

Her Principal Private Secretary before Sir Robert Fellowes was Sir William Heseltine who first came to her notice when he was seconded for a year from the Department of the Australian Prime Minister in Canberra to be an Assistant Information Officer at Buckingham Palace in 1960. He returned to London in 1965 and became one of the Queen's most popular and successful Press Secretaries before moving up to become Assistant Private Secretary and then Principal Private Secretary to the Queen from 1986 to 1990. He was sixty when he retired from the post and moved back to Australia after serving the Queen for a total of twenty-seven years.

The longest serving of all the Queen's men when he retired in 1977 was Lord Charteris of Amisfield, who in turn was Assistant and then Principal Private Secretary to the Queen. He remains one of the sovereign's Permanent Lords-in-Waiting, and in his capacity as Provost of Eton he welcomed Elizabeth II to the College's 500th anniversary celebrations in May 1990.

Forty-one years earlier, in November 1949, Major Martin Charteris, as he was then, was second-in-command of an army training battalion in the cathedral city of Winchester, in Hampshire.

Unlike many of the Queen's Household at that time, he had no family history of royal service – although he will admit that he did have one or two family advantages. One of his grandfathers was the 11th Earl of Wemyss, the other being the 8th Duke of Rutland. In 1944 he married the Hon. Mary Gay Hobart Margesson, whose father was the 1st Viscount Margesson. It is said, mostly by Charteris himself, that Montague Corry, Disraeli's Private Secretary, was caught up by his coat tails somewhere in the Charteris family tree.

The young Charteris – he was thirty-six when he received the royal invitation – was also a friend of 'Tommy' Lascelles, King George VI's Private Secretary, and both Charteris and his wife were friends of 'Jock' Colville, who had been seconded from Winston Churchill's staff to be Princess Elizabeth's Private Secretary.

A letter from Colville asking, 'out of the blue', whether he would accept the post of Private Secretary to Princess Elizabeth, if asked, should not perhaps have surprised him too much, although it did. Today he admits with a characteristic chuckle, 'It was pure old boy net'.

Charteris went along to Clarence House for an interview, 'in a nice suit and a hard collar', he remembers. The appointment was for 11.30am but, like a good soldier, he turned up a quarter of an hour early. 'Boy' Browning, the Princess's Comptroller, himself an Army general with a distinguished war record, chatted with Charteris until 11.25am, when he rang through to Princess Elizabeth on the intercom.

'Yes, Boy?'

'For the first time in my life I heard the voice of the future Queen,' Charteris recalls with almost the same excitement in his voice that he confesses to feeling all those years ago.

'Boy speaking. Good morning, ma'am. I have Martin Charteris here.

Shall I bring him along?'

'Yes. At 11.30.' The line went dead.

Lord Charteris's bushy eyebrows shoot up, and his jaw drops. He barks out a laugh, and takes a pinch of snuff. 'She can be like that,' he says.

The interview lasted three-quarters of an hour and went well. The Princess talked to the Major about his war service with the King's Royal Rifle Corps, and his short time in Whitehall after the war – 'I knew something about that, not very much about anything else. But I knew quite a lot of people that she knew; in a sense I was in the same walk of life.'[*]

However, Charteris heard nothing back from Clarence House for four weeks, even though, it later transpired, he was the only one interviewed for the position. Eventually he decided to ring his friend Tommy Lascelles.

'Oh God, hasn't anybody let you know?' It appeared that he had got the job.

'The only question that it never occurred to me to ask was what was I going to be paid. One didn't ask in those days. I assumed I'd be getting what I got in the Army, which is what happened. £1,200 a year and promotion to Lieutenant-Colonel.'

In talking at great length with present and former Members of the Queen's Household, it is easy to reach the conclusion that everyone who works for Elizabeth II, if not actually besotted by her, is certainly brimming over with admiration for their sovereign lady. And, equally, it is soon apparent that the feelings expressed owe everything to honesty and little or nothing to sycophancy. Indeed the comments can be measured for honesty against what some people say privately about working for one or two other members of the royal family. No royal boss, with the possible exceptions of Queen Elizabeth the Queen Mother and Princess Alexandra is as popular.

Words like inspiring, fascinating, and hard work – as well as privileged – are the ones most often employed to describe what it is like being in the Queen's senior employ. Although it may not always be apparent from their greyly solemn expressions on public or State occasions, most of those working close to the Queen find it can be a lot of fun. There is a sense of good fellowship which emanates from the top, but which also owes something to long service, comradeship under fire ('the Queen can be quite niffy at times, if things go slightly wrong'), and, it has to be said, the soft living. The pay may not be very good – most of the Queen's staff could earn very much more outside the Palace, as one or two from time to time have discovered – and wives of men working for the Queen see

---

[*] One of the many stories related about the delightful and invariably courteous Martin Charteris tells of how, in the Second World War, after being torpedoed in the mid-Atlantic and cast adrift on a raft, he apologized to his fellow castaways for being seasick.

less of their husbands than they would if they were in most other jobs. But there are compensations. For these invariably suave men, there are opportunities to travel abroad, first class, with 'The Queen's Household' printed on one's baggage tag, and a small royal coat of arms pinned to one's lapel, ensuring – although this, of course, is not the purpose – that head waiters look twice, and policemen – which *is* part of the purpose – wave one through. As one well-satisfied courtier said, 'The feeling of being on the other side of the railings is still quite pleasant even after a number of years. I don't think one ever becomes totally blasé about it.'

Up until a few years ago, the working day began with a free breakfast at Buckingham Palace for Members of the Household. The practice was thought to make for rather a congenial start to the morning, with a chance to catch up on overnight political or other news events, and perhaps the opportunity for a quick informal word with a Private Secretary before he disappeared into a meeting. When, on 1 January 1982, on grounds of economy, a stop was put to the free devilled kidneys on silver salvers, it was thought by some to be a particularly rotten way to start the new year.

Had it not been for the spirited last-ditch stand taken by a lady Member of the Household, Members might also have been forced to sacrifice their traditional afternoon tea-break, or, more precisely, the cakes and cucumber sandwiches that went with it. This pleasant little interlude in the long working day takes place in the Equerries' Room around about 4pm.

Lunch is served in another room, some way distant, where the only place unofficially reserved is for the Master of the Household. He has a small silver bell at his setting. The menu is written in French if the court is in residence, and not at all when the court is out of London. The charge for the meal is minimal, and beer is free, although you pay for spirits.*

There is another lunch room, known as the canteen, for those working for the Queen who do not qualify as Members of the Household. They are known as 'Officials' and include those holding such positions as Clerks and Office managers.

A third group, by far the largest, comprises the Palace Staff, which includes footmen, cleaners and gardeners. Up until not long ago the staff called everyone who was not staff 'sir' or 'madam'. Officials addressed staff as Mr, Miss, or Mrs and Household referred to officials by their surnames, with no prefix. These rules are no longer rigid, but Members of Household continue to be on first-name terms with one another,

---

* This has quite recently been changed. To avoid confusion, or possible embarrassment, everything is now free.

irrespective of seniority. Until they reached the age of eighteen, on the express instruction of their mother, the sovereign's own children were also always addressed by everyone within the Palace walls by their first names.

To the outsider looking in, the ground-floor offices of the Private Secretaries and other Heads of Department at the Palace have the atmosphere of a well-ordered club that is extremely difficult to get into. There is no noise, and anyone encountered in the corridor looks as if he (there are very few women) is either on the way to the Library to return a valuable tome, or to one of the lavatories which have mahogany seats, hairbrushes, and a stack of white linen hand-towels. In either case, the demeanour is preoccupied and the gait unhurried. Courtesy and good manners count for everything.

The late Basil Boothroyd told how, when he was writing his biography of Prince Philip, he ran into Sir Michael Adeane, the Queen's Principal Private Secretary at the time, as they were both about to leave the Palace. Boothroyd thought he would take the opportunity to tackle Adeane about a minor problem that was worrying him. Adeane listened sympathetically for a good two minutes before showing signs of wanting to move on. 'I do hope you'll forgive me,' he said, 'but I've just heard that my house is on fire. I wouldn't mind, but as it's a part of St James's Palace . . .'[1]

Old-world charm may not be *quite* so apparent as it was twenty years ago. As in the City, new blood moves faster than it once did, and there is a greater tendency than there was, perhaps, to take a glance over one's shoulder from time to time. Despite efforts towards greater camaraderie, rivalries do develop between the Queen's aspiring courtiers, and jealousies are sometimes evident where Members of, say, the Queen's Household and that of the Prince of Wales are concerned. Usually the petty fracas are over communication, or what may appear to be a deliberate lack of it.

A former Member of the Queen's Household recalls being offered this piece of advice – wise but difficult to follow – by Lord Charteris: 'Never let anyone come between yourself and direct access to the monarch. Never believe that the Queen has said anything unless you've actually heard her say it yourself. Thirdly, keep your counsel.'

Among the great majority of the 250 people employed at Buckingham Palace, most of whom may not set eyes on the Queen from one six months to the next, a somewhat different relationship necessarily applies. As one of the scores of electricians working in and around the Palace observed: 'There's nothing blue blood about a bit of wiring when it's down a hole in an awkward place.' Many of those employed in servicing Buckingham Palace and its chief occupants look upon their jobs as no different from other people's, although most would probably admit to getting some sort of kick out of working for the Queen, even if it only amounts to putting down as place of work: Buckingham Palace.

Those higher up in the pecking order count themselves much luckier than that.

Sir Oliver Millar, who succeeded the traitor Anthony Blunt as Surveyor of the Queen's Pictures in 1972, is one of those who has always found the Queen an inspiration to work for. 'When one talked to her about any one of a variety of things, one was always sharply impressed by an astonishing mixture of common sense, and an extreme niceness in dealing with one. No time was wasted, but everything was friendly and unpretentious. I always went away wishing I could see her more often.'²

Bishop Michael Mann, who was the Queen's Domestic Chaplain for many years, believes his service with the 1st King's Dragoon Guards helped to develop a very close relationship with both the Queen and Prince Philip. 'It is very much the sort of relationship one has with one's colonel, in the sense that when you're on parade it's one sort of relationship. And when you're in the mess it's a completely different kind of relationship.'³

Others speak of the Queen's strong dislike of any form of snobbery, and of her finely tuned ability to show no favouritism to one member of her court above another. An Australian on secondment to the Palace is unlikely to forget the day that he was invited to have lunch with the Queen à deux in her private apartments. The hour or so passed very pleasantly. The Queen wanted to know all about his family back home, and sympathized with him for having a bad cold. However, the next morning, when the two happened to pass one another in a corridor, the Australian's smile was met with a stony stare and not the smallest flicker of recognition.

Another servant speaks of the Queen's innate sense of dignity. On a State visit to Iceland in June 1990 – the first ever by a British monarch – she was enveloped in a cloud of steam from a bore-hole when the wind unexpectedly changed direction. Some of her entourage made an undignified run for it and were soaked. The Queen, unlike Canute, waited for the wind to change direction once more – and for someone to come to the rescue with umbrellas and plastic macs – before calmly walking back across duckboards to the road. She had found it all rather fun, she told her hostess. What caused mild irritation, however, was the small ripple of applause that greeted her emergence from the steam. The Queen glowered, as if to make plain that there was no need for such a demonstration. She had done nothing remarkable.

'I've known the Queen for forty years now,' says Lord Charteris, 'and I've never seen her lose her dignity, ever. Whether she's coming into the house wet and covered with mud from deerstalking, or coming down the steps of the aircraft in her dressing-gown to give me a message on our way back from Kenya after the accession, she's always *the* Queen.'

His Lordship is equally admiring of the Queen's business sense – 'she'd have made a very good businesswoman'.

An important part of the job of the sovereign's Private Secretaries is to open the large red, green, black , or blue leather-covered dispatch boxes that arrive at the Palace at all times of day and night and with overpowering frequency from Number 10 Downing Street, the Cabinet Office in Whitehall and all the other various government ministries and departments. The boxes contain multifarious official papers, all for the Queen's personal attention. They may range from Bills of Parliament requiring the Royal Assent to memos from the Prime Minister about the advisability or otherwise of a forthcoming foreign visit; requests to visit this factory, open that hospital; and, just very occasionally, a recommendation from the Home Office for a Royal Pardon. Quite a few of the telegrams from British embassies around the world tell the Queen the secret background story to the news that she, and we, may have seen reported on television the night before.

All the papers are carefully read and sorted through by the Private Secretaries. Those of special or necessary interest to the Queen are placed altogether in one red box and taken up to her. The Queen holds one key to this box, her Principal Private Secretary the other. On the table at the side of her desk there may be at least three other boxes containing papers from the Master of the Household or the Keeper of the Privy Purse, and a third box in which she keeps her own personal papers. Although she is painstakingly diligent in 'doing the boxes', as she calls it, the amount of paperwork to be got through means that the Queen's desk, and sometimes the floor around it, is practically 'bricked up with boxes'. And, like her corgis, the boxes follow the Queen everywhere, be it to Windsor, Balmoral or Sandringham. When she is out of the country, those requiring urgent attention are flown out in sealed diplomatic bags. The boxes take no account of holidays.*

The Queen rarely shows impatience at this workload. As with most things, she just gets on with it. More than that: after forty years she appears to have lost none of her enthusiasm for knowing what is going on, very often in her name, in her realm and throughout the Commonwealth.

'In thirty-seven years of doing business with her,' says Lord Charteris,

---

* The Prince of Wales also has his 'boxes'. Some years ago, when the author interviewed him in his 'office' on board the royal train – somewhere between Preston and Blackpool – he was invited to 'squeeze in between the boxes, if you can find room'.

'I can think of no occasion when I haven't actually felt better for it. She stiffens the back. She wastes no time. She's a very quick reader, and very quick to spot possible mistakes in planning.'

Another former Private Secretary bears this out. 'A box of work sent up in the evening is invariably read, signed where necessary, and back waiting on one's desk with comments first thing the next morning.'

'Her transparent honesty is so encouraging,' says Lord Charteris. 'You need never have any hesitation about telling the Queen about anything. Never need to wrap anything up, whether it be about her children's behaviour or whatever. All you say is, "Ma'am, this is what people are saying". And she listens carefully, and is glad to be informed. Usually.'

Lord Charteris is known to be one of the most ardent admirers of Elizabeth II. His eyes positively sparkle when he talks about his former employer. But he is not totally uncritical. An amateur sculptor of no mean distinction, he is perhaps more aware than some others that no one's character is as smooth as a pearl. 'One must say what is wrong with people as well as what's right. Otherwise there are no shadows.'

It is the opinion of this grand old man that 'the Queen is courageous, honest, humble, truthful, but mean. She is not a good giver, and she doesn't particularly like saying thank you. Her mother is cornucopia. The Queen, no. I don't know why. It may be shyness, but she doesn't get any pleasure out of saying thank you. I remember she said "thank you very much" after I'd conducted her round the Outer Hebrides. But she never said thank you after we came back from long foreign tours. And yet I know she valued me. When I retired from her service she said, "Thank you for a lifetime".' Martin Charteris smiles contentedly. 'That was enough for me. But I'm telling you this because the Queen, like everyone, has faults. She has fewer than most people, in my estimation, but that is one of them.'

When he retired, the Queen gave her faithful servant a magnificent silver salver and two signed silver-framed photographs. In 1978, he was created The Lord Charteris of Amisfield, taking the title from the house in the Scottish Lowlands that had once belonged to an ancestor. He was given the honour of the Grand Cross of the Victorian Order, which is in the Queen's personal gift, and he particularly treasures a silver snuff-box, with the Queen's name inscribed inside, which Princess Elizabeth gave him in 1951. Lord Charteris has no complaints whatsoever.

Another loyal servant also admits, although reluctantly, that Elizabeth II is not without faults as an employer. Apparently, she is mean with her praise and unaware of how often people might respond better if they were given a pat on the head now and then. She is not always forgiving either. Newcomers to her service who have transgressed in some small way are advised to 'bounce upstairs straightaway and apologize' before they can be accused of neglecting to carry out a duty.

As we shall hear later, Elizabeth II is capable of forming deep prejudices against individuals or groups of people, and once formed they are practically impossible to dislodge. By nature a compassionate woman, she may forgive but seemingly she never forgets. As evidence of this, there is a certain elderly duke living in the shires whom the Queen will have no dealings with. 'I think he may have gone a little too far when courting the Queen as a young girl,' explains one of the duke's relatives delicately. 'Whatever, over forty-five years later, she will still have nothing to do with him.'

Sir John Colville, the Queen's first Private Secretary, found his young mistress had what he termed 'superb negative judgement'. As she has grown older others have confirmed this assessment. 'The Queen is not good on taking imaginative initiatives,' said one of her advisers. 'She's frightened of her own emotions, I think.'

In all or any of these assessments the role and influence of Prince Philip should never be overlooked. No one has been closer to the Queen for almost half a century than the person, now in his seventy-first year who has always held first place in her heart. 'I dread to think what would happen if anything were to shorten his natural life,' observed someone close to them both. 'The Queen would be absolutely shattered. I am not sure, even with all her inner strength, that she would be able to recover.'

Over the years much has been spoken and written about the support given by Prince Philip to his wife, especially during the early part of the Queen's reign. Much less has been said about the support she has given him. Or, more accurately, tried to give her husband.

Adore him as she undoubtedly does, Elizabeth II, no less than others, can find Prince Philip at times argumentative to the point of exasperation. 'Have you noticed how many of his sentences begin with "No"? Even if he agrees with you, he first has to challenge you.'

The Queen has been heard to admit that 'sometimes he riles me'. On occasion she has resigned herself to one of his more ambitious plans, practically all of which call for an extra burst of mental or physical energy, with the words 'Oh, let him get on with it'. Husband and wife are rarely if ever seen to squabble in public, though there was one famous occasion in the 1980s in Stockton-on-Tees when it appeared to bemused well-wishers lining the royal route that their sovereign and her better half were having a spirited battle behind the bullet-proof glass of their limousine. In the corridors of Buckingham Palace, footmen and other members of staff are accomplished at fading into the walls at the approach of the Queen and the Duke of Edinburgh wearing what they call 'the acid drop look'.

According to some of those who have worked for, or alongside, the Duke of Edinburgh in his work for various charities, he has mellowed considerably over the past five years - this despite the nagging pain he gets from arthritis, especially in his hands. He is slightly less likely to erupt than he was, although, as one veteran committee man put it: 'You should always approach a volcano with care, even if it seems extinct, which this one isn't.' Others, including the author, who has been privileged to interview Prince Philip on a number of occasions over the years, believe that you should do your best to stand up to him when he tries to put you down, which he does.

'He's very easy to talk to, and very provocative,' according to Lord Whitelaw who, when Home Secretary, had the awesome task of providing security for the royal family. 'I've heard him say, "Can't move for police surrounding us". And on another occasion complain that "there doesn't seem to be any security round this place at all, Home Secretary". Poor old Home Secretary, can't please either way. But I greatly admire Prince Philip for what he has achieved in what must have been a very difficult position for him, especially at first.'[4]

Even his detractors admire Prince Philip's fight for many causes, and have done so increasingly as the years have passed. He is no longer thought of simply as the royal who told industrialists, in 1961, that it was 'about time we pulled our fingers out' – although that first example of robustness set the pattern for the future. To his eternal credit he managed to carve out a niche for himself in a royal enclosure where no one was alive who could remember exactly how it had worked with Queen Victoria and Prince Albert.

If he found difficulty in adjusting to being the husband of a Princess, he experienced even greater problems in adapting to being consort to the sovereign, in all but name, after they moved into Buckingham Palace. Perhaps if Elizabeth II had elevated Philip to Prince Consort early on, the road might have been easier for him as far as his dealings with court officials were concerned. But she did not, and it is said that in any case he never wished to be Consort with a capital 'C', believing it might only be a handicap to his personal initiatives and independence. All he really wanted was to be allowed to take some share in the too-heavy load, as he saw it, that had been suddenly placed on his young wife's shoulders.

In the early days, some of those surrounding the Queen were suspicious of Prince Philip's motives. Courtiers who had been used to serving a monarch who was male soon discovered that they experienced little or no difficulty in serving one who was female, especially one who was like her father in so many ways and who took up the reins of her destiny with shyness but also with inbred assuredness. She was, after all, the sovereign, and sex did not come into it. Her husband, on the other hand,

The first portrait of the future Queen Elizabeth II—the baby
Princess in 1926 in the arms of her mother, the then Duchess of
York, with the Duke of York, who was to become King George VI.
The Queen's mother reached her 91st birthday in August
1991.   *(I.L.N./Camera Press)*

Ten-year-old Princess Elizabeth in the garden of her home at 145 Piccadilly, London, with the first of a long line of Corgis. In 1992 she owned seven. *(Hulton-Deutsch Collection)*

Princess Elizabeth and Prince Philip, still a lieutenant in the Royal
Navy, were married in Westminster Abbey in November 1947. The
Princess fell in love with the Prince when she was thirteen. By all
accounts their marriage has been a success, despite marked
differences in character.   *(Camera Press)*

One of the earliest pictures of Squadron Leader Peter Townsend, standing behind Princess Margaret (with cigarette holder) and Princess Elizabeth. After the Queen's coronation the relationship between Princess Margaret and Peter Townsend caused a constitutional crisis.
(Hulton-Deutsch Collection)

Buckingham Palace—Trooping the Color Ceremony in June 1991.
(Photographers International)

Christmas Day 1991—the Queen and Princess Diana after attending family morning service at Sandringham, the Queen's country home.

(Photographers International)

A family portrait to mark the 40th birthday of Prince Charles in 1988. Rumours of problems within the marriage continued to threaten the stability of the monarchy into the 1990s.

(Photographers International)

Three generations of royals: the Queen, Princess Diana, the Queen Mother, and Princess Margaret outside Clarence House, the Queen Mother's London home, on the occasion of her 90th birthday party in August 1990.
(Photographers International)

The Queen and Prince Philip are at their happiest in the country and with horses. Prince Philip was a proficient polo player until arthritis forced him to give it up.

(Photographers International)

Elizabeth II's reign has so far lasted through eight U.S. presidencies. She visited the West Coast of America in March 1983 and was the guest of President Reagan as Head of State.

(Photographers International)

President Bush welcomed Queen Elizabeth to the United States in April 1991.

(Photographers International)

As she enters the fourth decade of her reign, Elizabeth II has indicated that she will never abdicate. If she lives to be 90, which her mother has, Prince Charles will be 68 before he becomes King, and Princess Diana will be 55. *(Photographers International)*

whom one or two of the courtiers had never exactly taken to – 'a German princeling, *not* whom she should have married', it was whispered – was an outsider with ambitions no one had yet been quite able to define.

Prince Philip was excluded from certain important planning meetings, and generally given a cool shoulder. Relations grew so bad that he was heard once to complain angrily, 'I'm just an amoeba, here to procreate members of the royal family'.[5] For a time he was not even allowed a throne beside the Queen when she ceremonially opened Parliament and had to stand to one side of her.

The cockiness of the young man, his bounding energy, and his seem-ing desire to shake out Palace procedures like a fusty blanket irritated some of the older courtiers such as Sir Tommy Lascelles, and even gave some concern to the Prince's mother-in-law who also wished things to continue very much as they had done in George VI's day.

Not long after her accession but before she moved into Buckingham Palace from Clarence House, the Queen was heard to remark, '*That's what's stopping it all*', as she watched Queen Elizabeth the Queen Mother's car draw up outside. The comment was taken to mean that the Queen Mother was the force behind the attempts to block the reforms that both Prince Philip and the Queen desired to happen.

Forty years on we are in a better position to understand the problems raised when a wife gains promotion over her husband, because increas-ingly it is known to happen. In the 1950s it was an extremely rare occur-rence and, for someone like Prince Philip - even though it was not quite the same kind of promotion – especially difficult to adapt to.

What Prince Philip, a practical man, found so absurd was that the Palace hierarchy seemed incapable of adjusting to the ramifications of having a monarch who was a woman. 'If you have a king and a queen,' he would argue, 'there are certain things people automatically go to the queen about. But if the queen is also the *Queen*, they go to her about everything. The fact that they report to the Queen is important to them, and it's frightfully difficult to persuade them not to go to the Queen, but to come to me.'[6]

The point Prince Philip missed, or perhaps he did not really, was that the wife of King George VI had been crowned Queen in her own right, and was treated accordingly. Prince Albert had been officially pro-claimed Consort (although not until seventeen years after his marriage to Queen Victoria), and Prince Philip had not. He held no keys, had no access to 'the boxes' and, although King George VI had appointed him to the Privy Council, he did not attend its meetings because they were purely formal and allowed for no discussion.

Whether or not the young Queen Elizabeth would have wished to proclaim officially her husband to be Prince Consort, or whether she took the advice of those who did not, we shall have to wait to see. At a calculated guess, based largely on what we have learned about her since then, she might have perceived the dangers of sharing matters of State secrecy with someone as argumentative and forthright as her husband and, for this reason alone, might have wished to remain alone to work things out for herself. Perhaps, from a constitutional standpoint, she saw no reason for there being anyone on near-equal terms with the monarch. Perhaps, simply, she saw that her destiny had made her the sovereign, and that was that. As an individual, the Queen is a very humble person, but as a monarch she has always been extremely conscious of the majesty of her position. Philip might rule the roost at home – a role, incidentally, he was to find increasingly difficult to maintain as the years went by – but she, as Elizabeth II, would reign over the United Kingdom. This was not to say she did not think that her husband had an important role to play. In 1957, making clear to everybody where her affection and admiration lay, she formally made her husband a Prince of the United Kingdom for his services to the Commonwealth and herself.

Among the courtiers, Lord Charteris was one of a comparatively small number who had sympathy for Prince Philip, although, with hindsight, he thinks the Queen's husband might have tried a little harder to accommodate the views of Household Members. 'Because of the way he was treated, especially before his marriage, he had a certain amount of prejudice against the old order. He thought it was stuffy and needed shaking up, in which I think he was right. He came to being the consort of the sovereign as opposed to the husband of a princess with a certain amount of antipathy and impatience. He sulked quite a bit.'[7]

Sulkiness, however, is not something we associate with the Duke of Edinburgh. More in character, within a comparatively short time after he moved inside Buckingham Palace he was launching out in several directions, somehow without upsetting the old order too much. The Queen was there to give him support and suggest more subtlety at times, and he was at his wife and sovereign's side, or three paces behind when protocol proscribed, to make the quip that made her smile, and shout at bureaucrats who made her life any more arduous than it needed to be. The couple made – make – a good combination, both in and out of public view, and of all Prince Philip's many achievements some believe that his greatest was eventually succeeding in adapting to being husband of the monarch.

The Duke of Edinburgh Award Scheme for young people was one of Prince Philip's first and most enduring successes, but it nearly failed to get off the ground. Prince Philip had what he has described as 'rather a difficult interview' with a Minister of Education at the time. The Ministry was highly suspicious. 'As with all our organizations,' he said in

November 1970, 'it worked on the "not invented here' syndrome. Anything you haven't thought of yourself is bound to be wrong. Everybody does this: I do it myself. But gradually, as they came to realize what the scheme was about, and that it wasn't a new Hitler youth movement, people began to realize that there was some merit in it.'[8]

Since its formation in 1956, over two million young people in Britain have won Duke of Edinburgh awards. Though he refuses to count the formation of the scheme as a personal achievement – 'they decided to call it after me, but that's about the extent of it'[9] – Prince Philip confesses it is the single venture that has developed beyond anything he expected. Typically, when asked whether he would wish to be remembered for the scheme above all of his other achievements, he replied: 'I shall be dead and gone when that is necessary, and so it doesn't interest me very much.'[10]

Usually Prince Philip finds it almost impossible not to give an opinion when asked for one, and sometimes when not. During his ten years as President of the Automobile Association, he deluged its offices with his thoughts on everything from motorway landscaping to better lighting on lorries. He argued for vertical exhaust pipes to reduce ground-level pollution. 'How do we know it won't work? Opinion was divided about the shape of the world until it was proved to be round.' Anything which doesn't make sense to him, he queries. Officials who prevaricate are speared by a look. A smile and a chuckle are often only the reassuring preface to a shuddering comment. But, most of the time, he means well. He is one of those rare men blessed with an excess of energy, combined with high principles, a good brain, and a deep concern for those issues which should, but don't always, concern the rest of us. 'Pious resolutions,' he is fond of saying, 'are not enough.' He told the committee of the National Playing Fields Association at his first meeting as President: 'Gentlemen, I want to assure you that I have no intention of being a sitting tenant in this post.'[11]

It was the message that the old guard at Buckingham Palace also received and eventually understood. In the first few years of the Queen's reign, Prince Philip managed gradually to introduce new ideas. Communication was speeded up by the use of dictaphones, tape recorders, and a peculiar electric filing system which revolved like a chicken on a spit. Administration was pushed out beyond the quill-pen frontier – 'It's more difficult to get Prince Charles's cot from Windsor to Buckingham Palace than to move an army across the Rhine!' General 'Boy' Browning complained.[12] Prince Philip gave his wife an electric kettle so that she would be spared the long wait for tea (tepid), to arrive from the kitchens in the basement which has a mile of circular passageway known as the M1. (Even today there is a notice in the service lift saying it must not be used between certain times, when staff are trying to get food piping hot up to the Private Apartments.)

On the wider front, and in keeping with a joint desire of both herself and the Prince to modernize the monarchy in a strictly limited sense, the Queen decided to abolish the traditional presentation parties for debutantes. No longer would young society 'gels' queue up in a long line to be formally presented to their sovereign, thus assuming a pseudo-superiority that was supposed to launch them out into the world in search of suitable husbands.

Before the war there had been strict rules about who could and who could not be presented at court. But after the war, when things were slightly lax, aspiring mothers only had to pay hard-up ladies who had already been presented to sponsor their precious daughters and lead them to their all-important first curtsy before the Queen. A season of 'coming-out' is still favoured to this day by some doting mothers and wealthy fathers, frantic for their daughters to meet the *right* man. But the Queen no longer plays any part in this antiquated marriage market.[*]

Even before the presentation parties were abandoned, the Queen and Prince Philip hit on another idea to make the monarchy seem somehow more democratic.

Unlike her husband, the Queen has never relished lengthy dinner parties with strangers – 'too tiring, too late' – although duty has decreed that she be the honoured guest at many. But she does enjoy meeting people from different walks of life, and so the idea of holding luncheon parties at Buckingham Palace for a dozen or so guests from a wide cross-section appealed greatly.

The first informal lunch took place in 1956. They are still taking place today, and the mixture of guests is much as it was thirty-five years ago. The main difference is that, while at that time the hostess was much younger than most of those she had invited, today the opposite is the case.

The lunches began at 1pm, and ended shortly after 2pm at the appearance of the Queen's handbag from under the table, where it apparently hung on a hook. At first the guests tended to be leading industrialists, senior churchmen and, say, the Editor of *The Times*, with perhaps someone from the racing world added for the Queen's personal interest. But gradually the net widened until today the fortunate dozen is likely to include a television personality, a bestselling author, and an Olympic athlete.

---

[*] It took three years to implement the change – an illustration of the resistance of 'the old school'. One courtier warned that doing away with the presentation parties would mean that the royal family would be stranded between the meritocracy and factory workers.

As they step back into everyday reality, chirpy and cheered by their brief brush with royalty – and unlikely to do very much else but talk about it for the rest of the day – the guests might spare a thought for their host and hostess. Before they have arrived back at their offices, or even the nearest Underground station, the Queen is quite likely to have changed clothes, made a phone call (to discover how one of her horses did in the 3.10 at Goodwood), and be on her way to visit a hospital in north London where a plaque is waiting to be unveiled, or to a violin recital where eager young children who have been practising for weeks are waiting to perform. The Duke of Edinburgh, meanwhile, is just as likely to be piloting a helicopter of the Queen's Flight to carry out a couple of engagements in the Midlands before returning to London to host a reception at the Palace, then change into white tie and tails and go on to a banquet given by a City Guild.

Perhaps the Queen's engagement book is kept not quite as full today as it was in the early years of her reign. But then again, there are now plenty of younger members of the family to help share the load. And over 400 official engagements during 1990, not counting overseas tours, is still not bad going for a woman four years past the official retirement age for other women.

Today the Queen rarely agrees to arriving at any engagement before 10am, just as she preferred, as a young mother, to be back at Buckingham Palace in time for the children's bath and bedtime story. And, of course, whenever possible she likes to be home in time for the ritual of the dogs' supper in her sitting-room. At 5pm, a footman carries in a tray of bowls containing the individual diets of her seven corgis. (The numbers go up or down depending on a variety of circumstances, such as mating.) The bowls are placed on a plastic sheet and, with silver fork and knife, the Queen sets about mixing the various portions.

For a woman in her middle sixties, Elizabeth II leads an extremely busy and varied life, always at a measured pace. But it is not very surprising that her day-to-day schedule in the 1990s, and that of the Duke of Edinburgh, is not quite as hectic as it was when they were both in their middle thirties and when both the monarchy and the Commonwealth needed constant attention, and their children were nowhere near old enough to take up their share of the burden. Each in their individual way worked hard at what they saw as their bidden duty to Britain and the Commonwealth. However, it seemed that they could not please everyone, although the majority remained loyal. The outbursts of a vociferous few, taken up and boosted by a media always on the look-out for controversy, caused an uproar in the mid-1950s that led to some radical rethinking about how the monarchy should operate. By 1957, the honeymoon period of Queen Elizabeth II's reign was over.

111

8

Troubled Times

❧

In the spring of 1956 Britain was in a funny sort of state. Eleven years after the end of the Second World War a generation not old enough to have fought in that war was beginning to make its influence felt. The term 'teenager' suddenly started appearing everywhere and a whole new commercial market opened up to cater for its needs, causing fall-out in a good many homes. Humbert Humbert's *Lolita* suggested that even a nice girl did not need to wait for the man to make the first move, and a new play called *Look Back in Anger* by a hitherto unknown writer, John Osborne, tore apart conventions that had lasted well enough since Victorian times. Its hero, Jimmy Porter, was a ranting young misfit, but the theatre critic Kenneth Tynan thought he represented post-war youth 'as it really is'.

On the political scene, the Chancellor of the Exchequer, Harold Macmillan, had issued a warning in February 1956 that holds a familiar ring for Britons living in the 1990s: 'The nation must pause in its pursuit of a higher living standard. Inflation is obstinate and serious.' The previous autumn the first commercial television channel had opened up, exhorting viewers to buy household goods and Murray Mints, 'the too good to hurry mints'. Jingles were the latest novelty. Clement Attlee, who as Labour Prime Minister immediately after the war had presided over sweeping social reform, was created an earl by the Queen. A Prince – Rainier of Monaco – married a film star – Grace Kelly of Hollywood; and Nikita Khruschev, the roly-poly partner of the Bulganin-Khruschev joint Soviet leadership, proclaimed that if he were British he would vote Tory – this after a lengthy and apparently argumentative dinner party with George Brown, Labour's Shadow Foreign Secretary.

While some of this was going on, 'wildly excited crowds running alongside the royal motorcade raised billowing clouds of red dust when the Queen and the Duke of Edinburgh made the thirteen-mile drive from the airport into Lagos at the start of their visit to Nigeria yesterday.' The dateline on the news report was 29 January 1956.

In the winter following her coronation the Queen and Prince Philip had undertaken a massive world tour that acted as a natural follow-up to the crowning itself. Millions had seen their sovereign on television. Now they had a chance of seeing her live. She visited Bermuda, Jamaica, Fiji and Tonga, where Queen Salote greeted the Queen and the Duke riding in a London taxi that she had purchased during her visit to London for the coronation. The tour continued to Australia and New Zealand and, at each stage, Elizabeth II emphasized that she was arriving in each of her dominions not as *the* Queen but as *their* Queen. On the way home, the royal couple visited the Cocos-Keeling Islands, Ceylon and Aden; and flew to Uganda before joining the newly completed royal yacht *Britannia* and being reunited off the North African coast with their children, Charles and Anne, who had been staying with the Mountbattens in Malta.

Even though, quite happily and properly, Prince Philip found himself always three paces behind his wife on these journeys, and thus it could be said playing second fiddle, he so enjoyed being away from the fustiness of court life and courtiers that the overseas tours quite made up for it. He was fascinated by seeing new places and talking with national leaders about challenging problems. His mind was put to work, which is what he likes, and he was spending a lot of time in the open air, which is also his preference.

After they returned from Nigeria in January 1956, the Queen and Prince Philip put their heads together and jointly worked on a plan for a solo tour by Prince Philip which would take him to some of the more outlying parts of the Commonwealth.

Initially, he would fly to Melbourne in October to open the 1956 Olympic Games, and from there he would board *Britannia* to sail to New Zealand, Malaya and the Gambia, as well as venturing to Antartica, the Galapagos Islands, and the Falklands. Altogether he would travel some 39,000 miles and be away from home for four months.

At the time of his departure on this massive trip, in October 1956, the royal couple were coming up to their ninth wedding anniversary. Prince Philip was thirty-five years old and had arrived at that stage in married life when many husbands (and wives) would give almost anything to *get away* for a while.

The Queen couldn't get away, but perhaps she thought that it would be better all round if her husband did. It might help to cure the frustration and impatience he apparently still felt deep down at being forced to abandon his naval career. Although she could not possibly be held to blame in any way, it is even conceivable that she felt a hidden sense of guilt about some of the effects her father's untimely death had caused. Perhaps there *was* a strain in their marriage. Or perhaps the Queen, being wise beyond her years (she was thirty at the time), foresaw a serious breakdown in relations with her husband, and thereby with those in daily contact with them both, if she did not agree to, encourage even, the idea of a long trip abroad. Or yet again, perhaps there was not even a smidgen of truth in the rumours of a rift in the royal marriage that were widely circulated during the four months that Prince Philip was out of the country.

Considering his good looks, which if anything improved between the ages of thirty and thirty-five, and his win-over charm where almost any lady was concerned, it is not so surprising that there was gossip about Prince Philip's alleged affairs. He was supposed to have acquired a flat in South Kensington to which he slipped away for romantic assignations. He was supposed to have one girlfriend who was a well-known musical comedy actress. He had another who was French and might possibly be the mother of an illegitimate child. These falsehoods popped up like bread from a toaster to enliven breakfast-time banter. One creative woman journalist writing from as far away as Baltimore, from whence hailed the Duchess of Windsor, reported 'whispers that the Duke of Edinburgh had more than a passing interest in an unnamed woman and was meeting her regularly in the apartment of the royal photographer'.[1] This was taken to be Baron Nahum, who did take pictures of the royal family and who, with Prince Philip, attended meetings of something called the Thursday Club. But these jolly little outings happened before the Duke of Edinburgh's marriage and, in any case, according to a Member of the Queen's Household who was once invited to join in as a guest, 'it was all boyish stuff really. They used to drink and eat too much and tell one another dirty stories. Personally, I found it all rather boring.'

However, the newspapers were not prepared to let go. Towards the end of Prince Philip's four-month-long ramble round the world, word leaked out that his companion and Private Secretary, the Australian Michael Parker, was being sued by Mrs Parker for divorce on the grounds of her husband's adultery. For some reason a few foreign newspapers took this as clear indication that both Michael Parker and his boss had been up to some fair high jinks and that the royal marriage was also in danger of falling apart as a result.

Although it would have been much wiser in the circumstances to preserve its more customary silence, Buckingham Palace, or rather, the

Queen through the words of her Private Secretary, Sir Michael Adeane, decided to counter the rumours with a denial.

'It is quite untrue that there is any rift between the Queen and the Duke of Edinburgh,' it was stated. Instead of issuing a denial, which only fuelled the rumours, it would perhaps have been more sensible for the Palace to let the press into a few other secrets. For instance, the fact that Prince Philip had arranged for a huge bunch of white roses to be delivered to his wife on the morning of their ninth wedding anniversary; that he had spoken to her and their children many times by radio telephone from various locations around the world; and that he had specially sent his wife a photograph that he had taken of two iguanas with their arms round each other. These did not sound like the actions of a man who had lost his love for his wife.

As for those of a more cynical disposition who might wish to quote a line from the song that goes, 'You know what sailors are', someone who has been close to the Queen's husband for over forty years gave this as his opinion: 'I don't think that Prince Philip was ever unfaithful. It is just not his line.'

In a Mansion House speech on 26 February 1957, marking his return from his 40,000-mile tour, Prince Philip told his audience of dignitaries:

> It would be quite easy to claim that this journey was all part of a deep-laid scheme, but I am afraid it all came about because I was asked to start off the Olympic Games in Melbourne. In fact, it would have been much simpler to have flown out and flown back, but if I had done that I could not have visited several remote communities who are loyal members of the Commonwealth, and I could not have inspected some of our bases in the Antarctic.
>
> I might have got home for Christmas, but I could not have entertained nearly 1,400 people in the Queen's yacht from Australia, New Zealand and those remote communities at twenty-six lunches, dinners and receptions, and thereby strengthened I hope the close links which exist between the Crown and the people of the Commonwealth.

So there.

In the ensuing year life returned to its calm, controlled course, as it tends to where the Queen is concerned. There were State visits to Portugal in February, to France in April, and to Denmark in May. Then, in August, while the Queen was taking her summer break in Balmoral, prior to setting off with Prince Philip on a tour of Canada and the United States in October, controversy once more disturbed the complacent scene. This time it did not emanate from a popular tabloid – although the papers were quick to pick it up – but from an obscure little magazine called the *National & English Review* which devoted the whole of its August issue to an examination of 'The Monarchy Today'.

The author of the article, who was also the owner of the magazine, was a young Lord Altrincham, the son of a former Governor of Kenya and government minister who, as James Grigg, had been given his peerage by a grateful Churchill in 1945.

Altrincham was no critic of the Queen herself, but of those surrounding her, and of the system which kept the whole monarchial institution tottering along on its high heels of privilege. He did not mince his words. He wrote of his sovereign: 'Like her mother she appears to be unable to string even a few sentences together without a written text.'* In her speeches, 'the personality conveyed by the utterances which are put into her mouth is that of a priggish schoolgirl, captain of the hockey team, a prefect and a recent candidate for confirmation.'[2]

The manner in which the court was presently run bode ill for the future, Altrincham warned. 'When she has lost the bloom of youth, the Queen's reputation will depend, far more than it does now, upon her personality. It will not then be enough for her to go through the motions: she will have to say things which people can remember and do things on her own initiative which will make people sit up and take notice.'

'The Queen's entourage,' wrote Altrincham, 'are almost without exception the "tweedy" sort. . . . [The Buckingham Palace hierarchy] has lamentably failed to live with the times. . . . [The court remained] a tight little enclave of English ladies and gentlemen'.[3] Dear oh dear. It was enough to put a fella shooting grouse at Balmoral quite off his aim.

Of course, there was more than a grain of truth in what Lord Altrincham said, and one or two of the Queen's younger courtiers at the time silently thanked him for saying it.† But, predictably, there were those who did not agree. 'I would like to see the man hanged, drawn and quartered,' boomed the Duke of Argyll.[4] 'Young Altrincham is a bounder,' declared the Earl of Strathmore. Fifty-five per cent of the *Daily Mail*'s stoutly pro-royal readers felt that the magic circle surrounding the Queen should be widened to include people from various walks of life.[5]

---

* The left-wing MP Tony Benn, who like Altrincham also renounced his peerage, made a similar comment in a volume of his memoirs, published in the autumn of 1990. Describing a presentation to the Queen marking her Silver Jubilee in 1977, he wrote of her response: 'The Queen, who can't say good morning without a script, referred to a bit of paper and said, "Prime Minister, thank you very much indeed".'

† Many years later, introducing Altrincham at a debate at Eton College, Lord Charteris acknowledged: 'You did a great service to the monarchy, and I'm glad to say so publicly.'

And the *Daily Mirror*, echoing a worry of many about the considerable disquiet that Altrincham's article had caused, posed the stark question in a front-page headline: 'Is the New Elizabethan Age going to be a Flop?'

Reflecting on his words a long time afterwards, John Grigg, as he had now become,* blamed the 1957 controversy on the 'Shintoistic atmosphere of the post coronation period. . . . There was a tendency – quite alien to our national tradition – to regard as high treason any criticism of the monarch however loyal and constructive its intent.'[6]

It was this same pious attitude to the whole tabernacle of monarchy that landed the much-loved pundit and former editor of *Punch* magazine, Malcolm Muggeridge, in such deep trouble. For his comments, Altrincham had his face slapped on television by a representative of the League of Empire Loyalists, and was verbally mauled by many other people. But Muggeridge had a lucrative contract with the BBC terminated and was made *persona non grata* by many of those who had hitherto been his admirers. And all for an article which, if read, was not critical of the Queen herself, or even the monarchy, but did point out that in an increasingly materialistic society the royal family, and the Queen as its head, was in danger of replacing Christianity as the nation's recognized religion.

Originally, the article had been written in 1956 for the radical thinking *New Statesman* and entitled 'The Royal Soap Opera' – arguably the first time the appellation was used. But, to coincide with the visit of the Queen and Prince Philip to the United States in October 1957, the American *Saturday Evening Post* bought the article and reprinted it under the title 'Does England Really Need A Queen?'

With that interpretation of what Muggeridge had been trying to point out, the British papers back home saw scope for further controversy. 'Out of context' was a foul one or two of them did not recognize. In bold headlines, Muggeridge was accused of calling his monarch, 'Dowdy, frumpish and banal', when he had actually written that 'it is duchesses, not shop assistants, who find the Queen dowdy, frumpish and banal'.

Compared with the cost of nuclear submarines or guided missiles, the monarchy could not be considered expensive, 'though,' wrote Muggeridge, 'there are those who find the ostentation of life at Windsor and Buckingham Palace little to their taste'. This, according to the *Sunday Express*, meant that Mr Muggeridge said that the Queen 'leads an ostentatious and tasteless life at Buckingham Palace and Windsor Castle'.[7]

In another part of the article Mr Muggeridge had said that Elizabeth II, with her 'charming personality', played a necessary role. 'The British

---

* Lord Altrincham became John Grigg in 1963, when a law was passed allowing peers to renounce their titles.

monarchy does fulfil a purpose. It provides a symbolic head of state transcending the politicians who go in and out of office.'

So why was Muggeridge pilloried for expressing an honest opinion, which many people would have shared, and making a few satirical comments of the kind which today pass unnoticed on television and hardly less so in newspapers?

When he complained to the Press Council about the damage the misrepresentations had done him professionally, he was told: 'The Council believes the impression of the article (in the *Saturday Evening Post*) conveyed by the *Sunday Express* and the *People* was honestly held and those papers had a right to put their case that the article contained a number of unfair, untimely and wounding disparagements of the royal family.'[8]

And what about the reaction inside Buckingham Palace? Looking back, a former Cabinet minister recalls, 'I don't think anyone was exactly quaking in their shoes, although they took some of it quite seriously.' The Queen's reaction to Altrincham's outburst is supposed to have been, 'Has he gone mad?' But then, as we shall see later, that is an exclamation the Queen is wont to use on exasperating occasions.

Certainly, there was truth in Lord Altrincham's allegations that Elizabeth II was confined within an enclave of English ladies and gentlemen. And why not, she would be likely to argue. The Queen much prefers to have about her those who largely share her interests and to a certain extent her background. And as long as they can do their job, what's wrong with that? Even today, some thirty-five years after Altrincham's criticisms, a fair proportion of the Queen's Household could be said to be what Altrincham termed 'tweedy'.

'It is England's homogeneity and class insularity which makes it seem small,' wrote William Manchester in his account of Winston Churchill's life between 1932 and 1940. 'In the public school network, referrals by mutual friends to mutual friends may lead anywhere, even to the sovereign.'[9]

Even in the so-called more egalitarian 1990s, this is something that it is hard to refute. As has been previously mentioned, Elizabeth II's Private Secretary, educated at Eton, is married to the future Queen's sister. Her Lord Chamberlain, the Earl of Airlie, is the eldest son of the 12th Earl who himself was Lord Chamberlain to Queen Elizabeth for almost thirty years, and grandson of Mabell Countess of Airlie, Queen Mary's confidante for more than fifty years. The Earl of Airlie's younger brother is the Hon. Sir Angus Ogilvy, the husband of Princess Alexandra, a cousin of the Queen.

The Mistress of the Robes to Elizabeth II is the Duchess of Grafton, and an Extra Lady of the Bedchamber is the Marchioness of Abergavenny. The Queen's Master of the Horse is the Earl of Westmoreland,

and the Keeper of the Privy Purse and Treasurer to the Queen delights in the splendid name, for that particular post, of Major Sir Shane Blewitt, KCVO.

However, despite the presence of these worthy aristocrats, there are not as many 'tweedy' persons at the court of Queen Elizabeth II today as there were in the 1950s and 1960s. There are fewer majors and colonels, and a few fewer Honourables. This is largely because many of those who served the Queen in the early part of her reign had been 'passed down', so to speak, from her father. These men and women have now retired or died in old age, and there is less inclination than there was for sons and grandsons to follow their parents into royal service. Recruitment nowadays comes more from other areas and is sometimes treated as a very useful stepping-stone to another quite different career. However, word-of-mouth recommendation from someone already working for the Queen can still be of help, and the one question that is always asked about an aspiring candidate for royal service is, 'Is he [or she] *sound*?' It is a description tweedy people can interpret instinctively.

The person within the Palace who tended to sympathize with a great deal of what Altrincham and Muggeridge were saying was, of course, Prince Philip. Had he not himself been struggling to blow some fresh air through the wide corridors?

To a certain extent he did this through making the sort of speeches that someone in the position of sovereign could not make. Altogether, between February 1956 and December 1959, Prince Philip accepted no fewer than 242 speaking engagements.

'Some people speak because they want to, and others speak because they have to,' he wrote. 'Some people speak because they have a special knowledge of a particular subject; others are expected to have something suitable to say on any occasion. I belong to the latter group in both instances.'[10]

He preferred writing out his speeches beforehand, rather than rely on scribbled notes, 'because then I feel I can develop any particular point with a greater economy of words and without fear of repetition.' He rehearsed delivery on a bulky Grundig tape recorder in his study, but did not memorize the words because he had seen too many instances of speakers doing this, forgetting their lines, and becoming totally stuck.

'Some people have what I can only describe as a positive genius for saying absolutely nothing in the most charming language. Neither my English nor my imagination are good enough for that, so I try to say something which I hope might be interesting or at least constructive.'[11]

In the 1950s and 1960s, Prince Philip enjoyed the kind of reputation that Prince Charles was to forge for himself in the 1980s and early 1990s. He, too, spoke out on matters of public concern although, whereas

Charles often reflected what many of the public were already thinking (about most modern architecture, for instance), his father's speeches tended more to prod people into reflecting anew about forgotten intentions. Where Charles liked to believe he was casting a pebble into a pond and seeing how far the ripples spread, some of Prince Philip's speeches (the 'pull your finger out' message to industrialists being the most famous), hit the ear with the force of a schoolmaster's cuff. He encouraged youth and deplored apathy. 'If anyone tells you that there isn't a better way of doing something, he is either a supernatural being or a supernatural clot.' He promoted science and technology, and began his warnings about wildlife extinction. He encouraged young artists, with whom he got on well. They had no 'fundungus', the Duke's term for meaningless trappings.

Perhaps Prince Philip's most inspired idea, in concert with Lord Patrick Plunkett, was to suggest the creation of a public art gallery, the Queen's Gallery, on the site of the Buckingham Palace private chapel which was bombed to destruction during the Second World War. Sir Oliver Millar, formerly chief adviser to the Queen on pictures, recalls being led through the ruins by an enthusiastic Prince Philip who pointed out how, in his mind's eye, the gallery might be constructed and what it would look like. 'As it turned out, the building proved a little too small, but we were provided with a great challenge in setting out a new exhibition each year.'[12]

At the very outset the Queen made plain to Sir Oliver that 'it is only going to work if you can have anything you like for the exhibition'. This would entail a constant change-around of pictures and works of art throughout the royal palaces, which Sir Oliver and others did not think the Queen would appreciate. But, on the contrary, she did not mind at all. Although by nature she is uncomfortable with change, she enjoyed seeing pictures in unfamiliar settings. It gave her something different to look at.

9

Likes and Dislikes

❧

onsidering the armies of tourists who climb the hill to her castle each day (a total of some 800,000 in 1990), it seems strange that Elizabeth II should think of Windsor as the place she 'can escape to'. But once she has driven inside the castle's massive walls she is totally cut off from the 'tourist section', and when she has a foreign Head of State to stay she can always stop public access to the State Apartments. Windsor is her home. Buckingham Palace is much more her office. The castle is where she spent her formative years as a child during the war. It is where she first got to know her husband when he had leave from the Navy ('I once or twice spent Christmas at Windsor, because I'd nowhere particular to go').[1] It is where her father is buried. When she stands at a window of her drawing-room, which has the most beautiful Gainsborough in the Royal Collection (an oval portrait of the Duke and Duchess of Cumberland walking in a glade), she can look out and down on wide acres of parkland and oak trees, some of which were there when Henry VIII hunted wild boar in the Great Park. She can also hear the incessant drone of jumbo jets going in and out of Heathrow, less than five miles away.*

The court moves to Windsor for the whole of April and half of May. June centres around Ascot Week, and up until the builders arrived in August 1988 to undertake huge renovations costing £20 million – which included

---

* There is a very old joke about an American tourist who said what a pity it was that Windsor Castle had been built so close to a very busy airport. The origins of the castle go back over 900 years.

121

a complete rewiring and major work to the Round Tower – there was room for all the family to come for Christmas. But more than that, the Queen spends approximately thirty-five weekends a year at Windsor. If it were not in an entirely different league, the castle could be said to be her weekend cottage.

The routine varies, but usually she arrives from London some time between three and four on a Friday afternoon, driving up a part of the three-mile-long avenue of the Long Walk and through the arch of St. George's Gate to the Sovereign's Entrance. Sometimes she is at the wheel of her own car, but always well protected by her policemen. (When she is at Windsor for any length of time the Queen likes to have her own policemen, the ones she knows by sight, transferred from Buckingham Palace.) She has tea, brewing it herself from Earl Grey leaves, *never* tea-bags, then puts on her headscarf and takes the dogs for a walk.

Coming out on to the wide terrace from the Lancaster Tower in the Private Apartments, she descends the two short flights of wooden steps to her own private garden.

Actually, it is not a garden in the sense that most people know a garden. It has only one wall – the castle rampart wall – and beyond that it is open to the wide acres of the Home Park, with only a narrow road running parallel to the wall some fifty yards in.

Turn left, and a twenty-minute stroll takes you to the Queen Mother's home, Royal Lodge.

In the Queen's garden itself there are several small trees dotted about the grass, which is deliberately not a manicured lawn. There is a wide, well-stocked herbaceous border and, near the steps, the same aviary that she and Princess Margaret knew as children. In fact, this is where they were photographed during the war, doing their school lessons sitting at a table, with a youthful Queen Elizabeth watching their progress.

What both the Queen and Prince Philip like most about Windsor Castle is the amount of privacy that they can enjoy there. Unlike the garden at Buckingham Palace, which is overlooked by tower blocks of hotels and offices, the Queen's garden at Windsor, despite being unfenced, is completely private. Parts of it cannot even be seen from the Private Apartments, which themselves, on the south side at least, are never visible to the general public.

Even on the north side, which faces into a grassed courtyard and can be seen by tourists using the souvenir shop in Engine Court, the windows are at such an angle to inlookers that they appear opaque. The only way that the Queen can be overlooked is from the air, and care is taken that the jumbo jets lumbering in and out of Heathrow stay well above or to the sides of the castle - although nothing much can be done apparently about their infernal whine.

Prince Philip frequently 'choppers in' to Windsor Castle from an engagement, parking his helicopter beside the nine-hole golf course that Prince Andrew has begun using for practising his swing.

On Friday evening, husband and wife will usually have a quiet supper on their own, and perhaps watch television for an hour or so, though this can be less relaxing than it is meant to be if Prince Philip jumps up from his chair shouting, 'What a load of rubbish' at the screen.

On Saturday morning the Queen goes riding, sometimes before breakfast, in what is known as 'Home Park Private'. She may be out all morning, returning for lunch, or to change clothes before going to visit one of her tenants on the estate perhaps. She takes a keen personal interest in all that is happening, to the extent of wanting to know if a stable boy's wife has had her baby yet, or whether one of her footmen is still having an affair. When the wife of a junior member of her staff began drinking heavily and eventually slashed her wrists in despair and nearly died, the Queen went to great lengths to help, listening, sympathizing and eventually convincing the lady to seek the help of Alcoholics Anonymous. The woman, who recovered and later became the president of a local branch of Alcoholics Anonymous, still speaks of her gratitude to the Queen personally.

At least part of the Queen's afternoon and evening is taken up with 'the boxes', and walking the dogs. On a pleasant summer's afternoon she and the Duke may have the 'loungers' put out on the South Terrace, so that they can lay back and browse through the newspapers. The Queen brings out her spectacles. The Duke has worn contact lenses for many years now, but may put on dark glasses against the sun.

The garden beyond the East Terrace was always uncharacteristically messy, until Prince Philip took a hand at redesigning it in a kind of cartwheel system with a fountain at the hub. He did not much care for the original fountain – 'a sort of huge black figure of a man strangling a snake'[2] – and spent several hours working out the most attractive lotus-leaf design familiar to visitors today. He can look out at his handiwork from his study, which overlooks the garden.

Around about teatime, members of the family start arriving. Prince Charles, before he broke his arm so badly in the summer of 1990, might have dropped in prior to going on to the polo practice ground. The Duke of York, if he had managed to get weekend leave from the Navy, might tear himself away from his brand new house, Sunninghill Park, just a mile or two away, and bring Sarah and the children over to see granny and grandpapa. Or, alternatively, the Queen, as interested as most mothers to see what a daughter-in-law has got up to in the way of interior design, might go over to see them – 'though the Queen would never visit anyone, even a close relative, without telephoning first,' said a friend.

On Sunday morning, without fail, everyone goes to church.

When she was married to Lord Snowdon, Princess Margaret would tease her husband that the reason he sometimes liked arriving at the castle just in time for lunch was because in that way he could avoid 'church parade'.

When staying with her sister or her mother at Royal Lodge, Princess Margaret, being theatrically and musically inclined, prefers worshipping in St George's Chapel, within the castle walls, where she can be assured of a highly polished professional choir. The Queen, on the other hand, although she would never *not* go to a particular church because of the type of service followed, prefers a Low Church service, the kind she might expect to find in a thousand village churches throughout her realm. On Sundays at Windsor, she worships in the chapel of the Great Park, where the choir is comprised largely of estate workers and the congregation is a mixture of courtiers, clerks, and farmers and their families.

Bishop Michael Mann, who was Dean of Windsor and domestic chaplain for thirteen years, will tell you that the Queen has a very deep and sincere faith that never questions. 'If anyone were to ask me what were the particular attributes that I associated with the Queen I would say: common sense, compassion and generosity, self-discipline, complete integrity, an enormous sense of duty, and a deep, deep but very simple faith. Her faith is the whole basis of her existence, and under strain it is that on which she depends.'[3]

Of all those who served Elizabeth II over a considerable number of years and came to know her and the Duke of Edinburgh well, the Right Reverend Michael Mann is one of the most interesting, and the most perspicacious.

In the spring of 1976, Michael Mann, a former officer with the King's Dragoon Guards, was leading a busy life as Bishop Suffragan of Dudley, in the diocese of Worcester, when he was astonished to receive a letter from the Chaplain of the Great Park at Windsor inviting him and his wife to spend a weekend at Windsor Castle. The invitation came on behalf of the Queen, and gave the Manns a choice of three dates.

'I knew that the Dean of Windsor, Launcelot Fleming,* was about to retire, so it was quite obvious *why* one had been invited, but it still came as a complete surprise,' he recalls.

The Bishop and his wife Jill were told that they would be expected to

---

* The Rt Revd William Launcelot Scott Fleming, KCVO, died on 30 July 1990, aged eighty-three.

arrive on Saturday at about teatime. That same evening the Queen gave a small dinner party for her guests, who were under no illusion that they were being scrutinized.

The following morning Bishop Mann celebrated communion in the chapel in the Great Park, and preached at Matins. He and his wife were then invited back to Royal Lodge, the Queen Mother's home close to the castle, for drinks and a chance for the principal members of the royal family (apart from Prince Philip, who was out of the country) to make their acquaintance.

'After about half an hour of convivial talk, Jill and I were extracted by the Queen and Princess Margaret and driven at break-neck speed down the Long Walk to the castle where just the four of us sat down to lunch.'

During lunch, Bishop Mann found himself engaged in a fairly fierce argument with Princess Margaret. He cannot recall what it was over – 'probably High and Low Church services' – which led Mrs Mann to predict to her husband on the way home that he had almost certainly 'blown his chances' of ever becoming Dean of Windsor.

After lunch, Michael Mann found himself led off into one room by the Queen, while Princess Margaret took Mrs Mann into another room. From 2.15 until 3pm, when they were dismissed kindly but firmly, the Manns found themselves being grilled. What were their hobbies? What were their views on various controversial Church matters, such as the new Church of England prayer book? (Prince Charles was known to be against it.)

'It was a discreet but an extremely professional sounding out,' Bishop Mann recalls. 'And then, about six weeks later, when I had more or less forgotten all about it, I answered the phone one morning when I was feeling particularly bad-tempered, and heard the voice at the other end say: 'This is the Queen. Will you come and be my Dean?' I'm afraid I replied, "I must have twenty-four hours to discuss it with my wife, ma'am."'

There were two other candidates for the appointment, interviewed on consecutive weekends. Bishop Mann does not know why he was chosen over the others, although he suspects it might have had something to do with the fact that he had had another career before entering the Church.

With hindsight I realize that it is important that anyone who goes to Windsor isn't one-track minded, because Windsor Castle is like a little medieval village. Within those stone walls you can become very isolated and very parochial.

The Queen is a very discreet but direct person. She does not beat about the bush. In my interview she was wanting to know my views on things such as family matters, marriage and divorce, pastoral care, but also did I keep any link with my background? I think she was determined to have someone as her Dean who had outside interests, and wouldn't be too narrow.

The position of Dean of Windsor at 'The Queen's Free Chapel of St George within Her Castle of Windsor' is, as the title says, 'A Royal Peculiar'. A Papal Bull of 1384 frees the Dean from all allegiance to either of the two Archbishops in England, Canterbury and York, as part of the checks-and-balances mechanism operating between sovereign and Church. The monarch's domestic chaplain and confidant must avoid being placed in a position where his arm might be twisted by his ecclesiastical superiors. On the whole, there is generally a friendly relationship between a Dean of Windsor and an Archbishop of Canterbury. The Archbishop gives his views to the monarch officially, but at the same time he may have a sneaking suspicion that the monarch has sought the views of her domestic chaplain beforehand. And this exchange, of course, is confidential.

During his thirteen years at Windsor, Bishop Mann calculates that he had between 750 and 800 transactions of one sort or another each year, by letter, telephone call or personal meeting, with the Queen and members of her family, 'so one did get to know them fairly well'.[*] He likened the job to that of a parish priest or local vicar, to whom people could come with their problems.

In addition to members of the royal family, the Dean of Windsor cares for the spiritual needs of some 300 employed in the castle and mews, and another 200 living in the Home Park. During his period of office, Bishop Mann part-officiated at the funerals of George Duke of Cambridge and of the Duchess of Cambridge; of Princess Alice of Athlone; and of the Duchess of Windsor. He played his part at the weddings of Prince Charles and Princess Anne, and was presently at hand at the time of Princess Margaret's divorce from the Earl of Snowdon, and the estrangement of the Princess Royal from Captain Mark Phillips. Since his retirement in 1989, his close association with the Queen and certain members of her family has continued. More than one of the Queen's children has sought out the advice of Michael Mann, travelling down to see him in his cottage in a remote West Country hamlet.

Bishop Mann finds Elizabeth II a person who in many ways has a simple, straightforward character, but in other ways an extremely complex one. Her faith is simple and bedrock, but as a woman she sometimes has to conceal her true feelings because of who she is. 'With you or I, if

---

[*] All his correspondence with the royal family has subsequently been sealed in boxes and placed in the Royal Library with a fifty-year embargo on inspection.

there's someone we don't like, we can avoid them. The Queen can't. She's got to live with people that she doesn't like and not show that she doesn't like them. That's a complexity.'

In some ways Prince Philip is exactly the opposite. He tends to say what he thinks and make plain to people his opinion of them. Interestingly, however, right up until a few years ago, after he had reached his sixties, he wrestled with deep doubts about his Christian faith.

In December 1983, a pile of papers appeared on Bishop Mann's desk, along with a note in the Duke of Edinburgh's handwriting: 'I think you'd better publish these.' The papers turned out to be letters that Prince Philip and the Bishop had exchanged over a period of months on the vexed subject of certain Christian beliefs.

Michael Mann wrote back to the Duke saying he did not think the letters should be published, and when Prince Philip asked why not, he was told: '(a) because your language is unpublishable, and (b), these letters are domestic chaplaincy business and should not be made open to the public.'

Prince Philip responded, 'Nonsense! You can edit them.' He thought that they should be published 'so that people can see that we do think about these things.'

The outcome was a slim, paperback of seventy-nine pages, called *A Windsor Correspondence*, price £2.50. Although it had a fairly modest sale, considering whose name was on the cover, it can still be obtained, amongst other places, in the souvenir shop at St George's Chapel, Windsor.

The interchange of letters, which ranged over aspects of Darwin's theory of evolution to science and religious conservatism, had been sparked off by Sir Fred Hoyle's Omni Lecture in January 1982. The letters, according to the book's publishers, demonstrated 'Prince Philip's familiar capacity to stimulate', and what Bishop Launcelot Fleming, who provided the introduction, called 'the able and undogmatic response of a Christian apologist'.

Picked out almost at random, some of Prince Philip's thoughts and expressions make particularly interesting reading at a time when a new, evangelistic Archbishop of Canterbury, the Most Revd George Carey,*

* George Carey, the son of a hospital porter in the East End of London, was enthroned the 103rd Archbishop and Primate of All England in April 1991, having previously been the Bishop of Bath and Wells.
In the week of his enthronement, one of the Queen's bishops told the author that he thought that the Queen – possibly urged on by Prince Philip – would welcome an Archbishop of Canterbury who wished to move the Church of England forward. But another cleric was of the opinion that while the Queen was likely to decide whether or not she liked George Carey personally after she had got to know him, she would certainly not change her views on the way she personally preferred to worship. 'I don't think you will find the Queen dancing in the aisles,' he remarked.

has taken up his appointment and is expected to spearhead a moral
crusade among the young and the doubting.

'It seems to me,' wrote the Duke of Edinburgh, 'that the argument between Darwin and creation has taken place because churchmen have felt that while God, according to Genesis, invented
creation – and therefore they had to defend it - Darwin somehow
"invented" evolution.

In fact all Darwin did was to show that God had invented the
process of evolution which achieved the same result but over a
longer period of time. . . .

Whether "God became man in Jesus Christ" is a philosophical
question; what is a matter of fact is that Jesus tried to show us how
to live so that the world would become a better place. . . .

I would prefer to follow his teaching because I am convinced that
it is right, than simply as a means of getting a better deal in
Heaven. . . .

To me, at any rate, the concept of instant creation is not tenable,
for a number of practical reasons, and also because it is too sim-
plistic.'

From the outset Prince Philip was aware that there were certain forms
of institutional worship that, being married to the Queen, he would be
required to observe. And also he started out on his quest for a complete
faith already believing in the basic ethical principles that govern religion.
It was the things like the resurrection and the carrying out of miracles
that really troubled him. He is inclined not to accept anything without
tearing it to bits first, like a terrier. However, he may eventually have resolved most if not all of his doubts. Bishop Mann especially treasures the
Queen's message to him shortly before his retirement: 'If I have nothing
else for which to thank you,' she said, 'it is for bringing Philip to a
Christian faith.'

Windsor Castle is an overwhelming but at the same time a magnificent
place for parties and weekends that are out of town, but not too far out
of town. Its silicate and crystalline stone washes clean as new with every
shower of rain, so that floodlit, with the royal standard languidly furling
out from its staff atop the Round Tower, the castle has the appearance of
every child's dream of a toy fort. In the year following the Restoration of
the Monarchy in 1660, Samuel Pepys recorded his impression of a visit to
Windsor thus: 'It is the most romantique castle that is in the world.'

Those who can remember parties at the castle in King George VI's
time, not long after the Second World War, say that there was more

formality and, in some ways, more fun then. The fun, it's no surprise to learn, largely emanated from the presence of Queen Elizabeth the Queen Mother. 'She has a genius for making everyone feel particularly happy,' Dame Edith Sitwell told Cecil Beaton.[4]

The Duchess of Beaufort, daughter of the Marquis of Bath, recalls arriving as a young woman at the castle at about 5pm, being shown to a very grand room, and being made to feel very uncomfortable by her own shyness.

> But then, as others began to arrive, one met friends and there was corridor talk before one went downstairs for drinks before dinner.
>
> Changing clothes was the most difficult part. You had your cocktails and then the Queen would say, 'See you in a quarter of an hour'. Well, the Queen Mother has always been a quick changer, but our rooms were a long way away and I can remember Lady Willoughby and I picking up our skirts and simply flying down the corridor in order to change and be back in time for dinner, before the King and Queen returned.
>
> It is different now, but in those days you dressed in one thing for breakfast, changed into another for Ascot, changed again when you came back for tea, and then changed again for dinner. I remember it was the time of the New Look, so my nanny worked overtime adding pieces to the afternoon dress to make it long enough for fashion.[5]

Rules have relaxed, and an invitation from the Queen to spend a few days, or even an evening, at Windsor no longer holds any horrors but remains an honour. A former Labour Cabinet minister found the evenings when the Queen gives musical soirées more enjoyable than those which end up with guests playing a form of charades – 'nice music and nicer people on the whole'. But an opposite number on the Tory benches thought that 'all that miming-games stuff after dinner is awfully good for the digestion, and tremendous fun'. One thing everyone agrees about is that however relaxed Elizabeth II may be, her guests must always take care to mind their Ps and Qs. 'Anyone who thinks they are getting on famously with her,' commented one courtier, 'and is tempted to become more pally is very likely to find a frozen face. While the Queen may occasionally throw her great caution to the winds, the next time one meets her she may not, and you will find yourself back at square one.'

Everyone has sympathy for the Queen. Normally, a hostess receives her guests as they arrive at a party, but, when Her Majesty entertains, the guests are generally already standing around nervously when she enters the room. Even on the least formal occasions no one is completely at ease, each person silently wondering when and how often one should address the sovereign as 'Ma'am'.

The Duchess of Beaufort used to have fun settling on who was 'an oily' and who was a show-off at Windsor parties. She found anyone, high or low, in the presence of royalty was invariably one or the other. She put herself down as a show-off. 'Nobody's natural with royalty – except perhaps when they're with the Queen Mother. She talks to you as if saying, "Come on now, tell me all". But then she's a commoner. She knows how we all are.'[6]

Others have found that even the Queen Mother can be reticent. As the biographer Elizabeth Longford once cleverly pointed out: 'In every royal person there is a private person trying to keep in.'[7]

In the company of her family or those others she has known for a very long time, the Queen can be witty and unrestrained – although she will always use five words when others may use ten and has a habit of ending in mid-sentence. She is a very pithy person. A true story is told of how, driving home from a picnic in the grounds of Balmoral Castle, with a young Prince Charles in the back seat, she spotted in her rear-view mirror a window being lowered and something being thrown out. The Queen eased the Range Rover to a halt, and looking straight ahead simply enquired: 'Do you think you can find it?'

On the whole, relations between the Queen and Queen Elizabeth have always been good. The Queen adores her mother, though just now and again a grit of irritation enters into the relationship. 'The Queen has never been prepared to play-act,' said a courtier, 'although, as a matter of fact, she's a very good play-actor and a frightfully good mimic. But she'll never play to the crowd, partly because of her mother who's so good at it. I've seen her watching her mother doing something on television and heard the Queen grind, "Oh Mummy". And I've known times when she's heard of some slightly theatrical thing that Queen Elizabeth has done and her comment has been, "Mummy *would*".'

Sir Alastair Burnet, in his tribute to the Queen Mother on her nine-tieth birthday, wrote that 'her poise, her gestures, her facial expressions are part and parcel of a theatre at the height of its art'. He might have added that the Queen Mother's extravagant dress sense is affectionately accepted by the public, whereas the Queen[*] has somehow never managed to bring forth a bundle of compliments for her own choice of out-

---

[*] Hardy Amies, for nearly forty years the Queen's favourite couturier has admitted that 'because she's only 5' 4" and not a clothes person, people wanted to make her into someone, like Givenchy did to Audrey Hepburn. That's totally against the Queen's wishes and we never attempted it.' At the same time 'I sometimes wish she had been a bit more of a clothes person. She listens to our advice and then goes off and wears shabby clothes because they're comfortable.'[9]

fits. The tilt of the head and the smile, like a break in the clouds, has become the Queen Mother's signature. Elizabeth II has a square face, and when it is in repose it is what she calls her 'po-face'. Travelling to Canada for the first time as Princess Elizabeth, she met public criticism for not smiling like her mother did. 'Look Martin,' she told her Private Secretary, 'I'm smiling till my jaws ache.' He had wanted his young mistress to ham it up more. But today sovereign and servant are that much older and opinions have changed. 'She's too honest to grin all the time,' says Lord Charteris,[8] who loves the Queen Mother dearly but admits to loving the Queen even more.

In terms of mutual strength and dependence the three women who really count within the royal family are the Queen, Queen Elizabeth and Princess Margaret. Within Palace circles they are sometimes referred to as The Triangle, or even The Eternal Triangle. The influence of the Princess of Wales and the Princess Royal is marked, but apparently is as nothing compared to that of the three older women. The turn of the younger generation will come, and is increasingly showing signs of arriving any day now, but for almost forty years the two sisters and their mother have been like a family within a family. Cross one, and you will have the others to deal with as well.

When the late Norman Parkinson was photographing his famous trio picture of the Queen Mother and both her daughters in identical blue satin capes, he was told by Princess Margaret: 'It's absolutely no use you ma'aming us like this with "chin up a little, ma'am", because we haven't the slightest idea who you are referring to. We are all ma'am.'*

Even the Duke of Edinburgh, it is said, is wary of the trio. Certainly, his plans to make alterations on the Sandringham estate were quickly dropped when he heard that the Queen Mother disapproved. But this was largely because the Queen, even though she owns the house, would never go against her mother where family sentiment is concerned. King George VI not only died at Sandringham, but of all the royal residences it was his favourite.

What surprises some people is that the three women, so disparate in personality, should get along with one another so well. They have rows, but as Princess Margaret once said in another context, within the family 'We have the occasional row, but never a rift'. The trio stood shoulder to shoulder during the Peter Townsend crisis, and again when Princess Margaret and Lord Snowdon's marriage broke down. When, in March

---

* A story is told of how, when taking a formal portrait of Prince Charles, Norman Parkinson walked over to his subject and calmly 'drew in' his subject's protruding ears by placing double-sided sticky-tape behind them.

1976, the couple mutually agreed to live apart, the Queen issued a statement through her Press Secretary saying how 'naturally very sad' she was, but added that there had been no pressure on either of the partners to take any particular course.

Perhaps the nearest the Queen ever came to falling out badly with her sister was over her friendship with Roddy Llewellyn, a baronet's younger son who was sixteen years her junior and who revived in her a *joie de vivre*.

The second son of Sir Harry Llewellyn, who won an Olympic gold medal riding the legendary showjumper Foxhunter, and the brother of Dai, then a rascal about town, Roderic's inclination was towards delicate pursuits such as planning gardens, although he had travelled abroad a good deal and worked for a time in an African asbestos mine.

His first meeting with the Queen's sister, in September 1973, came about almost entirely by chance. Princess Margaret had been invited to join a summer house party on a Scottish estate and an extra man was needed to balance the numbers. Roddy was recommended by a well-known London hostess whose nickname was 'Aunt Nose', because of her propensity to bring people together.

The mutual attraction in this case proved to be almost instantaneous. For several months the couple conducted what they hoped was a discreet friendship.

In February 1974, Roddy was invited to accompany Princess Margaret to her private villa on the island of Mustique, in the West Indies. At the time, to the outside world at least, her marriage to the Earl of Snowdon – consecrated in May 1960 – was still intact, if a little loose round the edges. But then, in June 1974, not long after the Princess and Roddy returned from the West Indies, Princess Margaret decided that her marriage could not continue as before.

Apparently, neither she nor her husband wanted a divorce at that time, but Princess Margaret did want a formal separation. She informed Lord Snowdon as they were driving down to Windsor for the funeral of her uncle, the Duke of Gloucester, on 14 June, and felt instantly 'filled with a renewal of spirit, maybe the Holy Spirit'.[10] Lord Snowdon acquiesced to a parting – he agreed not to spend his summer holiday with the family – although he was not physically to move out of the marital home in Kensington Palace until two years later.

For once, where Princess Margaret and Roddy were concerned, the other two sides of the Royal Triangle – Elizabeth II and Queen Elizabeth – were not immediately made cognizant with what was going on within their private palisade. As in the case of Margaret and Peter Townsend, things had advanced 'to a fair old state' before sister and mother were drawn in. Roddy Llewellyn, they had liked to think, was no more than a harmless distraction for Margaret and, even when whispers reached them of possibly a closer relationship, they were disinclined to interfere in any way because, as with Peter Townsend, what mainly concerned both mother and sister was Margaret's happiness.

However, once it was realized just how strained relations were between Lord Snowdon and Princess Margaret, matters took on a different complexion.

The Queen Mother, especially, has always had a soft spot for Tony Snowdon, and she was of the old school who believe that strained marriages can still be made to work if couples would only stick it out and come through on the other side of their troubles, rather like a goods train chugging out from a dark tunnel. The continued presence of Roddy Llewellyn in her daughter's life was no longer thought to be good news. He was a disruptive influence.

Elizabeth II, with her all enduring pragmatism, patiently waited on events, but with a growing sense of disapproval. Not of Lord Snowdon, nor so much of Mr Llewellyn, but of her young sister.

By the end of a year the Roddy-Margaret relationship was in something of a ferment. According to Christopher Warwick, Princess Margaret's biographer, 'Princess Margaret and Roddy Llewellyn shared nothing more torrid or passionate than what may be called a loving friendship.'[11]

Even so, it entwined its two participants in enough emotional turmoils for Roddy impulsively to fly off on his own, first to Guernsey and then to Turkey, in an effort to sort out the priorities in his life. In his absence, Princess Margaret suffered a nervous breakdown, although apparently did not, as one report suggested, attempt to take her own life. The breakdown had little or nothing to do with Roddy, but did have much to do with her husband and was, she told Christopher Warwick, 'brought about by Tony's silences and insensitivity'.[12]

At the beginning of 1975, Lord Snowdon, a successful documentary film producer as well as a photographer, was working in Australia with a crew which included Lucy Lindsay-Hogg the former wife of another film director. In June of the same year, Roddy Llewellyn joined some friends on an abandoned farm in Wiltshire with the objective of forming an 'artistic and aristocratic commune'.

The tabloid newspapers resurrected words like 'hippie' and 'flower-power' to describe their efforts, and to give some light relief to the grim reality of the nation's inflation rate, which hit 25 per cent that month. Tony Benn, the Secretary of State for Energy, watching the first North Sea oil flow into a refinery, held up a bottle of crude and declared: 'I hold the future of Britain in my hand.' And John Profumo, a disgraced former government minister who had turned to charitable work, was awarded a

CBE in the Queen's Birthday Honours.

The aim of Roddy and his friends was self-sufficiency off the land, which in its turn would cater for the restaurant, the Parsenn Sally, which the commune had opened in Bath. For a time it all worked out fairly well. Princess Margaret even visited the community, and a specially posed picture of its members sold to the *Daily Express* for £6,000. But was it the sort of thing a princess of the royal blood, the sister of the monarch, should be doing? Most people rightly suspected that the Queen thought it was not.

The first crisis came early in the following year when a Sunday newspaper published an obviously 'snatched' picture of Princess Margaret and Roddy Llewellyn, wearing swimming costumes, sitting side by side in the sun on holiday in Mustique. The suggestion, quickly accepted by readers, was that there was a romance going on between the Princess, aged forty-three, and the youth – as he always seemed in pictures – aged twenty-seven. The readers were not allowed to know that two others in the original picture, Lord and Lady Coke, friends of the Princess, had been cut out of the newspaper version, so that Margaret and Roddy were in fact not having a cosy *tête-à-tête*.

Even so, the photograph apparently provided enough evidence, if extra evidence were needed, for some people. After seeing the picture, Lord Snowdon promptly moved out of Kensington Palace - having originally agreed to do so two years previously, according to Princess Margaret – and, on 17 March 1976, the *Daily Mirror* proclaimed: 'Margaret and Tony Divorce'.

As it happened, the announcement was somewhat premature.

Although the Princess and Lord Snowdon mutually agreed to go their separate ways, there was no official word at this stage of a divorce. That particular matter would require a great deal of further careful thought, by the Queen especially.

Admittedly, a precedent had been established for a divorce within the royal family during the reign of Elizabeth II. In January 1967, the Queen's cousin, the Earl of Harewood, a grandson of George V and Queen Mary, was sued for adultery by his wife. But he was eighteenth in line of succession to the throne, whereas Princess Margaret was much closer, not only to the throne but also to her sister.

Under the Royal Marriages Act, Harewood's divorce did not formally concern the Queen. However, his remarriage did. And this was what placed her in something of a dilemma. Quite apart from her position as Governor of the Church of England, the Queen did not personally much approve of divorce. Her cousin had behaved scandalously – or, at least, that is how it would have certainly appeared to the Queen's father.

Lord Harewood had been living with his former secretary, Patricia

Tuckwell, a divorced Australian, and had had a son by her. However, when all this eventually came out, the British public did not appear to be in the least outraged. Times had changed. Sexual permissiveness was the vogue. The Queen, never one to condemn easily anyway, would have seemed out of touch with her people, and out of date, if she had taken a strong stand against a remarriage. The critics of monarchy would have had a field day, and the upholders of family virtue – of whom there were still a few – would have felt on the defensive, as they did throughout the 1960s. Yet, in her position, the Queen could not be seen to condone divorce.

In the end the solution came via the Prime Minister of the day, Harold Wilson. He took the problem to the Cabinet, and was then able formally to advise Her Majesty to grant consent to Harewood remarrying under the parliamentary Act. In other words, the decision did not technically affect the Church. The Queen was giving Royal Assent, as she might with a normal piece of legislation. This paved the way for Princess Margaret and Lord Snowdon in their dilemma some ten years later. In addition, relaxation of the divorce laws after 1967 meant that marriages could legally end without specific allegations of misconduct, provided both parties agreed to separate.

In the case of the Snowdons, the procedure should have been fairly straightforward. That was certainly the expectation of the Queen. The formal separation was in March 1976, with custody of the two children of the marriage, Viscount Linley, then aged fourteen, and Lady Sarah Armstrong-Jones, then eleven, going to their mother, with free access to the children granted to their father. There was to be a breathing space of two years – during which there was always the possibility that the couple might come together again – after which the marriage could be dissolved at any time. As with an increasing number of marriages, it seemed a sensible solution to a sad situation.

However, this was to overlook the question that every newspaper editor asks when any famous married couple, not just royal couples, separate: who are the third and fourth parties? Not always, but very often, there is at least a third party involved. In the case of Princess Margaret, of course, the editors did not have far to look.

On the day following the official separation announcement, Lord Snowdon, who was in Australia at the time organizing an exhibition of his photographs, made the sort of statement to television cameras and the press that touches some people and puts off others. It was charged with emotion. After expressing his sadness that the separation had to come, he went on: 'I would just like to say three things: firstly to pray for the understanding of our two children; secondly to wish Princess Margaret every happiness for her future; thirdly to express with the utmost humility my love, admiration and respect I will always have for her sister, her mother and her entire family.'

A week later, partly in an effort to shake off the relentless pursuit of newspapers, Roddy Llewellyn wrote his own press statement: 'I am not prepared to comment on any of the events of last week. I must regret any embarrassment caused to Her Majesty the Queen and the royal family for whom I wish to express the greatest respect, admiration and loyalty.'

Unfortunately, he also told a journalist at a different time: 'I cannot talk about my feelings for Princess Margaret or her feelings for me. That is a taboo subject.' Particularly as they were so thin on the ground, every quote held its own inference. Princess Margaret, protected by her position, wisely gave no interviews.

To the great private annoyance of the whole of the royal family, but of the Queen in particular, the whole sorry business carried on for several more months, and reached a stage where Princess Margaret's popularity with a great many people ebbed away to almost nothing.

Roddy Llewellyn launched himself on to the world, not very successfully or for very long, as a pop singer. He went on holiday to Mustique, fell seriously ill with an 'upper gastro-intestinal haemorrhage' and was visited in hospital in Barbados by Princess Margaret. This time the pictures were of Roddy sitting by his hospital bed, smiling, and of Princess Margaret swimming, walking along the beach, and 'really enjoying life on the sunny isle of Barbados', said the captions. This time, back home in Britain, the knives did come out. Willie Hamilton, the Member of Parliament who loved to hate the monarchy, questioned whether Princess Margaret earned her £55,000 Civil List allowance. 'If she thumbs her nose at taxpayers by flying off to Mustique . . . she shouldn't expect the workers of the country to pay for it.' (In fact, the Sunday *People* pointed out, in the preceding year the Princess had carried out as many public engagements as any other senior member of the royal family.) The Bishop of Truro, the Rt Revd Graham Leonard, thought that 'the thing that had to be resolved now was how far she can go on being a public person'. A withdrawal from public life might be a solution. 'This I would have thought was a possible way of enabling her to sort out her own affairs,' said the Bishop.[13]

One of the more fascinating aspects of the crucifixion of Margaret, which was how many people regarded it at the time, is the echo it had some twelve years later in the press and public reaction to the Duchess of York. Although in the summer of 1990 there was to be no suggestion of a breakdown in the Duchess's marriage, her style of life and in particular her trips abroad, brought much angry criticism – as we shall see. It is almost as if, with each new generation of royals, there has to be a 'baddie' – either one who volunteers for the part, or is created for it by the media.

It is all part of what has been called the royal soap opera, of which Prince Philip has had some pithy things to say – again, as we shall see.

The Queen's sister, although she came in for harsh criticism from several quarters during this time, was not entirely bereft of supporters. On 26 March 1978, the Sunday *People* declared that Princess Margaret 'has always provided ammunition for those who say she doesn't help to keep up the royal standard. . . . But the picture that emerges is that while Princess Margaret plays hard, she works hard too.'

The Editor of the *Daily Telegraph* warned his predominantly Conservative readers that 'it would be tempting to dismiss the present campaign against Princess Margaret as a nasty combination of envy and prurience plus that residual republican sentiment which is still part of the stock in trade of a section of the British Left.'

The charges against the Princess were lamentably unspecific, but 'there is a feeling that what, in the current jargon, is called her "lifestyle" does not befit a member of the royal family. This complaint is compounded of egalitarian resentment against expensive holidays, high-minded disapproval of "pop-culture", as exemplified by the pursuits of her friends, and a conventional prejudice against close friendships between women and younger men.'

It was all very well to point to the Queen as 'the most glittering vindication' of why Britain should maintain a monarchy in preference to a presidency, 'but to expect not only the occupant of the throne but the entire royal family to provide a perpetual exemplar of moral and aesthetic perfection is to ask too much, and would be to ask too much even in a society which was far clearer than ours is about what constitutes these ideals.'[14]

Apart from the slightly embarrassing description of herself as 'the most glittering vindication', Elizabeth II would probably have agreed with the conclusions of the *Daily Telegraph's* editor – someone, incidentally, she had met personally in his former position of government minister.* At the same time she could only regret the way that her sister had been conducting her private life over the previous few months. Their father, despite his tolerant attitude towards his younger daughter, would have been furious.

Plucked from obscurity and never quite put back into it (he now writes a gardening column and plans people's landscapes), Roddy Llewellyn, when reminded that he provided a footnote for royal histories, replies: 'I would much rather have been remembered for having

---

* William Deedes, editor of the *Daily Telegraph* between 1974 and 1986, had previously been an MP and Minister Without Portfolio in the Macmillan and Home governments.

painted a marvellous picture.'

Lord Snowdon, unlike Peter Townsend who wrote an autobiography, has so far declined to put anything except his photographs on paper, and has remained friends with all of the royal family, and on good terms with the two children of his marriage to Princess Margaret. At the same time he has somehow managed to avoid becoming a part of the strangely complicated royal jigsaw. He has strenuously defended his right to be a private citizen. As he once pointed out to the author (before his separation from Princess Margaret), 'I am not a member of the royal family. I simply married a member of the royal family.'[15] To some people Lord Snowdon has remained something of an enigma.

As for the Queen and the Queen Mother, and their attitude towards Princess Margaret during the period of her association with Roddy Llewellyn, Christopher Warwick, 'drawing on numerous conversations' with Princess Margaret writes in his biography that the Queen Mother's 'affection for Lord Snowdon meant that her eyes were not fully open to the sad truth of Princess Margaret's marriage and that she was unlikely to adopt anything but a stance in favour of keeping the marriage together'. Warwick goes on to say that 'few will know with any certainty, but what may be taken as read is that no member of the immediate royal family was enamoured of Princess Margaret's new friendship.'[16]

Someone who was in almost daily contact with the Queen at that time can recall how little she liked what was going on. 'In all honesty, she felt that her sister was behaving badly. Privately, she spoke about it in language that was quite sharp. But although she did not like the way that her sister was behaving with Roddy one bit, she never repudiated her. The family's solidarity was stronger than the revulsion, you see.'

In other words, the triangle stood firm.

Those who know her well invariably mention a compassion for others as being one of Elizabeth II's strongest virtues. But one or two may also be prepared to speak of another human attribute which is near to being the opposite. The Queen, it appears, can form deep prejudices about individuals or groups of people and, once formed, these prejudices are almost impossible to budge. It is sometimes unclear either to victims or onlookers what the origin of the prejudice is, and even more difficult to extract oneself from this unenviable form of royal displeasure when it descends. Sometimes it is better in the end simply to creep away and stay out of sight.

Historians can point to examples of some of the Queen's ancestors having a similar trait in their character. Queen Victoria, for instance, hardly spoke to one of her equerries, 'Fritz' Ponsonby,[*] for the whole of his first year in her employ because he said something that the Queen did not wish to hear. King George V took against women in smart society after witnessing the behaviour of his father Edward VII. 'We have seen enough of the intrigue and meddling of certain ladies,' he told Count Albert Mensdorff, one of the late King's cronies, 'I'm not interested in any wife except my own.' His most famous prejudice was against going abroad, which he didn't think worthwhile. 'I know, I've been there', he once told a friend.

The personal dislikes of Elizabeth II are more subtle and sometimes more difficult to detect. A courtier recalls the Queen once saying to him: 'I shall always remember my father telling me that whatever you show or say will be remembered by that person for the rest of his or her life. So you must never show displeasure unless you actually want it to be remembered.'

At least one member of the Queen's staff may have cause to muse on those words. At a Windsor Horse Show not so many years ago, on seeing two seats vacant at one end of the front row of the VIP stand, this man from Windsor beckoned to his wife to join him, and together they sat there enjoying the show-jumping – along with the Queen, Prince and Princess George of Hanover, and other guests. '*That* won't be forgotten,' said an aide.

More seriously, when Bishop Mann first arrived at Windsor Castle he found that relations between Elizabeth II and the Canons Residentiary of St George's Chapel were, to say the least, strained. The Queen's displeasure was plain. So, as a new boy, the new Dean asked the Queen's Private Secretary if something could not be done to restore good relations. 'Better not try,' was Sir Martin Charteris's response. 'We know what the Queen hates. If you remove that, she will have to find something else. And we don't know what that will be.'[17]

Others affirm that for all her undoubted kindness and tolerance, the Queen can take a strong dislike to a person, sometimes for what might be considered a trifle by others, and 'once she gets her knife into someone, then it doesn't matter what that person does, her opinion won't alter'.

When he made it known that he was retiring, Bishop Mann was asked by the Queen and Prince Philip to help find a replacement. In turn, he asked what the job description should be. 'The first thing both the Queen and the Duke said was, "Someone who can control the Canons".'

Although relations between the Queen and her Canons are apparently now back on to an even keel, the former Dean believes that the old

---

[*] Ponsonby had informed the Queen that the father of her Indian Secretary, Abdul Karim, was not surgeon-general of the Indian Army but apothecary at Agra gaol.

feelings will never be entirely eradicated.

Curiously, someone to whom Elizabeth II never showed any enmity, although she might have been expected to dislike her intensely, was her aunt by marriage, the Duchess of Windsor. Here was someone who, the Queen's mother believed, had been indirectly responsible for the untimely death of the Queen's father.

In character, interests and appearance, Elizabeth II and the Duchess of Windsor could hardly have been further apart. And yet the Queen, more than anyone else in the royal family, showed the Duchess grace, compassion and something very near to forgiveness. Allowed more freedom to follow her personal wishes, she might have managed to heal the breach between the Duke and Duchess of Windsor and the royal family in England sooner rather than later, might even have granted the Duke's greatest wish – to confer on his wife the title of Her Royal Highness. These things were discussed. But whenever it was suggested that perhaps the Windsors had been treated slightly harshly by the royal family, the Queen listened, without saying whether she agreed or not, and invariably pointed out that 'It's Mummy that matters. We mustn't do anything that hurts *Mummy's* feelings.'[18]

In 1962, ten years after her accession, Elizabeth II took the first slow step towards healing the wounds caused by the abdication of 1936. She set aside a private office for the Duke of Windsor in Buckingham Palace, and invited both the Duke and the Duchess to the public unveiling of a memorial plaque to Queen Mary in London. But after that magnanimous act nothing more really happened for another ten years, and even then mainly through coincidence.

In November 1971 it was announced that the Queen and Prince Philip would pay a State visit to France in May 1972. Preparations were well ahead when the Queen received news through a friend that the Duke of Windsor had very little longer to live. He was being treated for cancer of the throat at his home in Paris. It seemed likely that either the date of the State visit would have to be put back, or that the Queen should be prepared to run the risk of a pall being cast over the visit – which was in connection with Britain's entry into the Common Market – by the death of her uncle. After some discussion, Buckingham Palace and the Foreign Office jointly decided to go ahead with the visit despite the risk, while at the same time taking the precaution of drawing up a number of contingency plans.

Throughout the pomp and ceremony of the State visit itself, bulletins were sent to the Queen twice a day, conveying the latest news of the Duke's condition. A meeting between uncle and niece had been set for 4pm on the third day, and when the Queen, the Duke of Edinburgh and Prince Charles arrived at the Windsors' mansion in the Bois de

Boulogne the Duchess reported a 'slow, steady weakening' in her husband.

By all accounts it was an awkward meeting, eased only slightly by the Duchess of Windsor's invitation to everyone to sit down to tea. As one of those who was present recalls: 'It was all faintly sinister. There was the spotless white tablecloth, the silver teapot and water jug, and everyone made polite conversation. But the only thing that was never mentioned was the one thing we were all thinking about – the poor little man dying upstairs.'

Above the mantelpiece was the portrait of the Duchess of Windsor painted by Birley some forty years before, and sitting underneath it at the table was the Duchess herself. The jet-black colour and the shape of her hair was identical to that in the portrait, but the face in the portrait was of a young woman, whereas the woman hosting the strange tea party was now seventy-five years old.

After half an hour or so, the Queen asked if she may go upstairs to see her uncle. A servant led the way to a drawing-room on the first floor where she found the Duke of Windsor sitting in his favourite armchair wearing a smart blue blazer. He had refused to receive his sovereign in his bed in his pyjamas, all linked up to drips and tubes – 'the damn rigging will have to come out'. The task had taken almost four hours to complete, but here he was now, smart and managing a smile, though he was so ill that he could hardly manage to speak.

The Queen chatted as brightly as she could under the difficult circumstances for almost half an hour. Then she gently bade goodbye to her uncle and joined the others downstairs. In farewell the Duke had only the strength to bow his head over his sovereign's hand. In ten more days it was all over. The former King of England died peacefully in the middle of the night four weeks short of his seventy-eighth birthday.

The Queen arranged for the body, in a coffin of English oak, to be flown to London and from there to Windsor. The Duchess, who had been too distraught to travel at the same time, followed two days later and was invited by the Queen to stay at Buckingham Palace.

In their authoritative study of the Duke and Duchess of Windsor (*The Windsor Story*), the Americans J. Bryan III and Charles J.V. Murphy quote the Duchess as saying that the Queen, Prince Charles and Princess Anne 'were polite to me, polite and kind, especially the Queen'. But she adds, 'Royalty is always polite and kind. But they were cold. David always said they were cold.'[19]

The Queen is not a cold person. Neither are any of her children. But the Queen finds it harder than they do sometimes to show her feelings. Uncertainty about how precisely one should react can all too easily be interpreted as coldness or even distaste.

Although, quite conveniently, it has to be admitted, the Duke of Windsor did not die until ten days after the State visit to France, his funeral arrangements coincided with the annual Trooping the Colour ceremony in London, and this caused a problem. The parade, which celebrates the monarch's official birthday, was to take place on the Saturday, the funeral on the Monday. Should the parade be cancelled? The Queen was not sure. If possible, she would like it to go ahead. But she did not wish to seem to be showing disrespect to her late uncle, and at the same time she did not want to risk hurting her mother's feelings by putting aside an important event in the royal calendar.

After a good deal of discussion a solution was worked out that was almost inspired. When the Queen rode out on to Horse Guards Parade, before the main event the massed pipe bands of the Scots Guards and Irish Guards formed up opposite her and played a farewell lament as an act of remembrance for the Queen's uncle and their late Commander-in-Chief. In a famous picture, a photographer stationed outside Buckingham Palace caught a glimpse of a painfully distraught Duchess of Windsor pulling aside a net curtain to watch the Queen ride down The Mall at the head of her Household Cavalry.

Once the actual funeral was over, many people expected that the link between the royal family and that part of it which had broken away would also come to an end quite naturally. After all, it was not as if the dead Duke's widow was a blood relation of the Queen. But, characteristically, she showed great concern for the bereaved Duchess of Windsor. Unfortunately, this concern was not universally appreciated, particularly among some of those in the Duchess's employ. During the long years that the Duchess spent as an invalid and near-recluse in her Paris mansion, emissaries made a number of unpublicized calls on her, at the Queen's specific request. At least one of these emissaries felt each time he visited that he was regarded as a Queen's spy.

This suspicion may possibly have dated back to soon after the Duke of Windsor's funeral when Earl Mountbatten, Prince Philip's uncle and a close intimate of the royal family, was invited to Paris by the Duchess in order to help her sort out her late husband's financial affairs. Mountbatten, who was a jealous guardian of royal memorabilia, returned to London after a couple of days with an assurance from the Duchess that all her husband's uniforms, robes, Orders and decorations would be presented to the Queen. They later went on display at Windsor Castle, before being sent on to a museum. And all his private papers would also be returned to Windsor and placed in the Royal Archives. But as to the considerable fortune that the Duke left – all to go to his widow – and the pieces of inherited jewellery that the Duke had presented to the Duchess over the years, these items were to be the subject of conjecture and bitter argument for a long time to come.

The Duchess of Windsor and her shrewd advisers may have been under the impression that Elizabeth II was as interested in recovering family heirlooms as she appeared to be in the well-being of the Duchess, and this was why she sent her emissaries to Paris. However this was not the case. Certain other members of the royal family, along with sections of State management, were anxious to pursue the matter of recovery. But the Queen overruled them. In her opinion, enough distress had already been caused over the years, and an undignified scrabble after what might indeed legitimately belong to the Crown was almost bound to lead to a continuation of the kind of publicity she had never liked. So she put a dampener on it from the outset.

When Her Grace The Duchess of Windsor died on 24 April 1986, at the age of ninety (an achievement in longevity matched in 1990 by her arch enemy Queen Elizabeth, incidentally), her remains were flown to London in an aircraft of the Queen's Flight and laid to rest beside those of her husband in the grounds of Windsor. Again, this solicitude was entirely due to Elizabeth II.

Almost thirty years earlier the Duchess had persuaded her husband to buy a burial plot of ostentatious size in Green Mount Cemetery, Baltimore, because she was convinced that the British would attempt to achieve in death what they had singularly failed to see happen in life, that is, their separation.

However, the Duchess's deep suspicions were rendered baseless by the Queen's compassion. Some time after she learned of the Duchess's plans Elizabeth II let it be known, publicly, that it was her wish that when the time came the Duke and the Duchess would be laid side by side in the royal burial place at Frogmore in Windsor Great Park.

In this case, Elizabeth II's innate love of family unity and tradition had overcome any enduring family feelings of prejudice.

IO

A Question of Education

❦

A s with practically all parents, the thorny question of how best to educate their children was frequently discussed at great length by the Queen and the Duke of Edinburgh. As usual, Prince Philip was not short of questions. In the case of other children, and probably his own as well, he wanted to know, 'Is education simply a question of passing exams? Or is it a question of learning civilized behaviour, or providing young people with a capacity to earn their own living? Or is it a combination of all three?' In the end, after all four of his own children were grown up, he had inclined to the somewhat sombre conclusion that 'children grow up in spite of their parents rather than because of them'.[1] Where Prince Charles was concerned, he was aware from the outset that additional questions needed to be considered – such as, 'How early on should the heir to the throne be introduced to classes in constitutional history?' But even with their first-born the basic points that concerned Charles's parents were practically the same as those confronting millions of other parents about whether to launch their offspring on either a private or a state-sponsored education. About the only question that was unique to the Queen's son was, 'Should he go to school at all?' After all, no one in his position had done so before.

If the Queen ever had any doubts about the answer, she was soon won over by her husband. In the climate of opinion of the late 1950s and early 1960s it was almost inconceivable that a child of the sovereign should be educated by private tutors, his eyes blinkered to the outside world by the Palace walls. It may have worked with Princess Elizabeth and her young sister, but that was in wartime, and anyway – one could be chauvinist in the 1950s – it was different for girls.

The Queen was just as anxious as Prince Philip that their children – and she wanted a large family, not just one or two – should be brought up in as similar a manner to other children as possible. Furthermore, she wanted to be allowed to be a real mother to them, doing the sort of things that other mothers did. To this end she insisted on bathing all her children when they were small, making sure her official engagements ended in time to allow this to happen, and even putting back the time she gave regular audience to her Prime Minister (from 5.30 to 6.30). A time was set aside for play, and a time for reading. It was the Queen, not his governess, who taught Charles his alphabet. But the fact that special times so often had to be partitioned off emphasized just how difficult it was for the Queen ever to behave like most other mothers. Even before she came to the throne she was separated for long periods from Charles and Anne, either by protracted overseas tours or by her natural desire to be with her husband when he was doing naval service in Malta.

'The Queen and I want Charles to go to school with other boys of his generation and learn to live with other children,' declared Prince Philip, 'and to absorb from childhood the discipline imposed by education with others.' It was even suggested that Charles might endorse the spirit of post-war egalitarianism by attending a state primary school. But *that*, Prince Philip and others knew, was a forlorn hope. 'There's always this idea about treating them [Charles and the Queen's other three children] exactly like other children', he told Basil Boothroyd. 'In fact it means they're treated much worse, because they're known by name and association . . . It's all very well to say they're treated the same as everybody else, but it's impossible.'

In fact, until he reached the age of eight, Prince Charles was taught by a governess, Miss Catherine Peebles – 'Mispy' – in Buckingham Palace, with sorties outside to dancing classes with the celebrated Miss Betty Vacani (where Lady Diana Spencer was later to be a teacher for a short period), and visits to museums, and a gymnasium to develop his muscles. His mother taught him the rudiments of riding, first on a Shetland pony called Fum and then on a larger Welsh pony kept at Windsor and named William. His father instructed his son in swimming, in the pool at Buckingham Palace. His little sister Anne, always in his wake, showed early signs of being a bossy individual. 'Charles and I used to fight like cat and dog', she has confessed. Miss Peeble's brief was 'no forcing' of her young charge, whom she found to be sweet and gentle, 'But if you raised your voice to him, he would draw back into his shell and for a time you would be able to do nothing with him.'[2]

It must have been hard for the Queen to know what to do for the best, bringing up children normally in almost impossible circumstances.

'Mummy has an important job to do', her son replied when someone asked him where she was. 'She's down here', he said, pointing out Australia on the tin globe that he kept in his nursery. When he was a little older, he was found by his father pelting a policeman at Sandringham with snowballs. 'Don't just stand there, throw some back at him,' the Duke of Edinburgh commanded the nonplussed constable.

If it was difficult for the Queen and Prince Philip to strike the right balance for their son between due respect and a more normal upbringing, it was just as confusing for Charles to work out who exactly he was. He knew *how* he was supposed to behave, but he wasn't sure *why* he was expected to do certain things. 'I didn't suddenly wake up in my pram one day and say "Yippee"', he has often been quoted as recalling. 'I think it just dawns on you, slowly, that people are interested . . . and slowly you get the idea that you have a certain duty and responsibility.'[3] This suggests that neither the Queen nor Prince Philip ever sat down with their small son and told him specifically that he would probably one day be king. It was an approach that Prince Charles would have approved of. 'It's better that way, rather than someone suddenly telling you, "You must do this" and "You must do that", because of who you are.'

The Queen had it in mind that Charles should start attending a 'proper' school around about the age of eight, but felt it would be best if he were to be introduced to the daunting process gradually – say, an afternoon at a time, to start with. After all, no heir to the throne had ever been educated outside a palace before now, and there was no guarantee that it would be a success.

The school should be conveniently near to the Palace, and of course should be discreetly vetted. A number of establishments were considered before Colonel Henry Townend, founder and headmaster of Hill House, a smart day-school for boys, was invited to Buckingham Palace to have tea with the Queen, and subsequently given charge of a rather special new pupil. The Queen had been recommended to the school by friends who had sent their own children there, and was no doubt impressed by the fact that each morning the pavement outside was washed clean by the headmaster himself, and the London grime dusted from the railings. Prince Philip was encouraged by a line in the school's philosophy, displayed on a board at the entrance: 'A sense of rivalry has to be encouraged and a boy must be led to discover something in which he can excel.'

About 150 boys attended Hill House, which was run on pleasantly domesticated lines – Mr Townend's wife played an indispensable part. Discipline was of a family nature rather than of an institution. The worst crime was to disgrace the school uniform in public, punishable by confiscation of the school tie.

Prince Charles, the first heir to the throne ever to go to school, arrived by chauffeur-driven Ford Zephyr on 28 January 1957 and, half-crouching at the sight of newspaper photographers, scurried inside the building to become pupil No. 102 on the school roll. Through no fault of his own, and despite the efforts of his parents to give him as normal an upbringing as possible, he knew nothing about money and had never been inside a shop or a bus. One of the first tasks of his teachers was to explain the value of the various silver and copper coins that bore his mother's likeness.

It was to be another six months before he was given his first ride on a London Transport bus, albeit one that had been specially chartered to take him and his fellow pupils to the school sports ground. He was almost nine years old.

To the generation who have seen Prince William confidently march up the steps to his first school, and watched his mother arrive in jeans and sweater to pick him up at the end of term, it must seem almost inconceivable that William's father was quite so unprepared for the world outside Buckingham Palace. But, poor lad, apparently he was. Elizabeth II was a conscientious mother, and a loving one too, but she had none of the experience that Princess Diana enjoyed before her marriage. She had had no opportunity of working with children who were not her own, no elder sister to confer with, no knowledge whatsoever of what it was like simply to go to school and sit in a classroom with a dozen other children. Where the early education of her son and heir was concerned, the Queen was prepared to admit, 'I'm afraid I can't be of much help'.

Prince Charles would not agree. In later life, but before he married, he once told the author how lucky he counted himself to be 'because I have very wise and incredibly sensible parents who have created a marvellous secure, happy home'.[4]

Home meant everything to Charles as a boy, much more than it did to his sister who has admitted that, 'Up to my teens I don't think I went along with the family bit, not until later than everybody else'.[5] At a school dance she told a partner 'not to treat her like a piece of china'. The royal children's nanny, Helen Lightbody, who stood for no nonsense, even so found Princess Anne more than a handful sometimes. And their grandmother, Queen Elizabeth, was not naturally drawn to Anne as she was to the more gentle Charles. Anne should have been the boy, it was murmured in those early days. But Charles coped manfully. He coped with the fact that his father was not around to support his son during his first term at school (he was on his four-month tour of the Antarctic regions). He coped with the fact that his nanny retired shortly before he entered Hill House – he had spent more time with her in his short life than he had with his parents and he missed her terribly. And he coped with the ubiquitous press picking out the detail that he was the only pupil at Colonel Townend's school whose overcoat had a velvet collar.

As it turned out, Prince Charles's happiest schooldays were probably those spent at Hill House, despite their being interrupted at the beginning of each of his two terms by attacks of tonsillitis, the second attack resulting in his tonsils being removed in an operation carried out in the Buhl Room at the Palace. (The offending impedimenta remained in a jar, at Charles's insistence, on the mantelpiece in his bedroom for some considerable time afterwards.) His end-of-term reports declared him to be determined but slow. His writing was 'good, firm, clear, well formed', but his arithmetic was 'below average; careful but slow, not very keen'. The report from his art teacher most accurately presaged where one of his talents lay: 'Art: good, and simply loves drawing and painting'.

The Queen and Prince Philip cannot have been too unhappy with the report. The main thing was that Charles had successfully made the initial transition from private Palace life to a form of public life, without disgrace or too much heartache. He seemed to be happy, and in less than a year in the company of other boys had become more self-assured. As a reward his father took him off to Cowes at the end of the summer term for his first go at yacht racing, which Charles found exhilarating, once he had got over his seasickness.

The next question for his parents to answer was: where should they send their son after Hill House? The Duke of Edinburgh had already spelled out the general plan, and the first stage had been implemented at Hill House. But now that he had mingled in the company of other boys – mostly aristocrats' and foreign diplomats' sons – the next question was should the heir to the throne now be introduced to the children of less exalted people who would one day form the bulk of his kingdom and, who knows, might be asked to decide whether or not they even wished the monarchy to continue into the twenty-first century?

Would it not be prudent to sense the first faint breeze of change and absorb the advice of Labour MPs who advocated attendance at a state school? Or pay heed to the monarchist Lord Altrincham who asked if Elizabeth II would 'have the wisdom to give her children an education very different from her own? Will she, above all, see to it that Prince Charles is equipped with all the knowledge he can absorb without injury to his health, and that he mixes during his formative years with children who will one day be bus-drivers, dockers, engineers etc., not merely with future landowners or stockbrokers?'[6]

With the concept of comprehensive schools still fashionable at that time, even, or rather *especially* with many intellectuals, it was at least conceivable that the gigantic leap in one generation from private Palace tuition to playground-mixing with the populace might have taken place.

But there were too many obstacles in the way, then as now, for it ever to be carried through.

To start with, there were the problems of security within a large conurbation, and of constant press attention. Then there was the difficulty of finding a state school that took boarders – not such an important consideration to the great majority of parents perhaps, but vital to those of the Queen's acquaintance, who had always relieved themselves of their brood at the tender age of eight or nine and only received them back during the holidays. There was also the question of standard of education. Like a substantial proportion of the population, the Queen and Prince Philip were convinced that, in general, the private sector offered a better level of both education and behaviour than did state schools.

All the options were discussed, but there was very little doubt from the outset that Prince Charles would go to a private preparatory boarding school and then on to a public school – just as it is planned for his own eldest son some thirty-five years later.

The Queen and Prince Philip cast their eyes over a number of preparatory schools before deciding on Cheam, said to be England's oldest prep school, which had moved out of London to escape the Great Plague of 1665, and then in 1934 further out into the country to escape the great London urbanization. It was now situated near Headley, on the Hampshire-Berkshire border. It was Prince Philip's old school, but this was not entirely the reason that he sent his son there. The school's location was ideal. Set in sixty-five acres of grounds, it was near enough to Windsor for exeats, and far enough away from London – it was thought – to dissuade constant camping-out by the press.

Charles, like any other eight-year-old, was nervous of leaving home, and his mother was as concerned as any other parent about sending her little boy away. Neither of them really wanted it to happen, but in the end it was Princess Anne who most missed having Charles around the place. She was envious. She couldn't *wait* to go away to school.

Before term started, Charles visited Cheam with his parents and sister. 'You won't be able to jump up and down on *these* beds', the Queen told him as she inspected the wooden frame and horsehair mattress. The joint headmasters, Peter Beck and Mark Wheeler, had written to all the parents, at the request of the Queen and Prince Philip, expressing their wish 'that there shall be no alteration in the way the school is run and that Prince Charles shall be treated the same as other boys . . . It will be a great help if you will explain this.'

Of course it was impossible for any of the other pupils to think of Prince Charles exactly as one of them. At Hill House the children had been young enough not to know very much about Prince Charles's position, but at Cheam the older boys knew perfectly well. Charles himself was frightened stiff. The Queen was to recall him shuddering on the long overnight train journey from Balmoral to London, to be followed by the sixty-mile drive to Headley. Wearing his new grey school uniform, he doffed his blue cap to the headmaster and heard rather than saw his parents drive away and leave him.

The Queen anxiously waited for Charles's first letter home – by school rules he had to write to his parents at least once a week – but it almost certainly masked over his abject misery. Just a matter of hours after his arrival he had been observed by one of the school masters standing conspicuously apart in the school grounds, a slightly podgy boy 'notably in need of a haircut', who looked utterly wretched and alone.

There was not a very great deal that his masters or his parents could do about Charles's undisputed unhappiness in the first weeks. Not, that is, if he were to be treated the same as the other boys. Although aware that she could have visited her son at any time, the Queen deliberately restricted herself to the three visits a term that were the average for other parents. She and Anne would drive down from Windsor, the Queen at the wheel, and on arrival – once she had changed shoes 'to something more sensible' – would take Charles off for a walk and perhaps a picnic in the woods. She wanted to know *everything* that had happened. His favourite sport, Charles told her, was swimming. He wasn't terribly good at cricket. He preferred soccer to rugby, where, he complained, 'they always put me in the second row – the worst place in the scrum'. And what about his lessons? Well, he still wasn't very good at maths, but he was better than most of the other boys at history. And, thanks largely to Mademoiselle de Roujoux, who had been tutoring him during the holidays at Balmoral, his French was well above average. At the end of Charles's first term at Cheam his parents were relieved to receive the headmaster's report that their son was 'still a little shy, but very popular . . . passionately keen on and promising at games . . . academically, a good average'.

Gradually Charles became accustomed to school life, though he was never to be completely happy at Cheam. He was embarrassed by being who he was; lonely because he did not much like those who 'sucked-up' to him, and wary of approaching those who held back.[*] He took some solace in eating – 'all this rich food', he called the school fare compared with what he had at home – and tore into his weekly allowance of half a pound of sweets. Both his parents wrote to him several times a week. His mother sent him presents – small, inexpensive items such as a pencil-box

___

[*] While reporting a provincial tour by the Prince of Wales in 1981, the author was told by the Prince how, when touring a factory, he liked to dive into the back of a group of workers because the person who didn't push forward was often the most interesting to talk to.

– and, from his father, came a 'doodle-master' which could draw complicated patterns on paper. The disadvantage of these gifts was that every other child wanted to follow Charles's fashion and have the same items in his locker.

The gymnasium was one of Charles's favourite bolt-holes - Peter Beck, the joint headmaster, came across the Queen on one of her visits very happily trying out the parallel bars with her son. Outdoor team sports did not appeal to Charles very much as a small boy, though he was never afraid of a rough and tumble and gave as good as he got. He was somewhat deflated, however, when a boy beneath him in a collapsed rugby scrum cried out: 'Oh, do get *off*, Fatty.'

At the end of his first year at Cheam, the Queen, quite unintentionally, caused what was probably the greatest embarrassment her son had experienced thus far. On 26 July 1958, Her Majesty was due to perform the closing ceremony of the Commonwealth Games in Cardiff. However, a minor sinusitis operation prevented her attendance, and so Prince Philip took her place and introduced a tape-recorded message from the Queen, which was played over the loudspeakers of the packed stadium and relayed into practically every home in the land through television. Charles and a few of his fellow pupils were allowed into Mr Beck's study to watch. Prince Charles and Mr Beck knew what the Queen was about to say. The others did not.

'I want to take this opportunity of speaking to all Welsh people,' the Queen began, 'not only in this arena, but wherever they may be. The British Empire and Commonwealth Games in the capital, together with all the activities of the Festival of Wales, have made this a memorable year for the principality. I have therefore decided to mark it further by an act which will, I hope, give as much pleasure to all Welshmen as it does to me.' A buzz of anticipation hovered over the stadium and in Mr Beck's study. 'I intend to create my son Charles Prince of Wales today.' There was a tremendous cheer from the crowd, and in the study all eyes turned to Charles. 'When he is grown up, I will present him to you at Caernarvon.' The boys clapped and cheered and, the headmaster noted, a look of dire unease descended on the round face of the young Prince.

Prince Charles holds a clear memory of the historic occasion. 'I remember being acutely embarrassed when it was announced. I heard this marvellous great cheer coming from the stadium in Cardiff, and I think for a little boy of nine it was rather bewildering . . . later on, as I grew older, it became apparent what it meant.'[7]

Another important event of which the Prince and the Queen had prior knowledge took place in February 1960. Charles was on stage in a Cheam school play when his performance as the Duke of Gloucester was interrupted by the headmaster stepping up on to the boards to make an announcement. He was delighted to report that Her Majesty the Queen had given birth to a second son.

Prince Andrew's birth on 19 February 1960, followed four years later, on 10 March 1964, by the arrival of Prince Edward,* fulfilled the desire of Elizabeth II to have a large family, by current standards, which would ensure the succession. The reason for the twelve-year gap between the birth of her first child and that of her third was due entirely to her unexpectedly early accession to the throne. Now that she had settled to the role of sovereign, at the age of thirty-four she and the Duke of Edinburgh were to enjoy the pleasure of bringing up a 'second' family, although, history records, only hours after Prince Andrew was born the Queen was sitting up in bed and calling for 'the boxes'.

Prince Charles reached the rank of Monitor at Cheam before the time came, in 1962, for him to move on to the next stage of his education. There was to be some more serious discussion about what form this was to take. First, however, both the Queen and the Duke of Edinburgh thought it would be a good idea if their son got to know his German cousins of whom there were no fewer than seventeen. In a little over a week Prince Philip whisked Charles round his aunts and uncles, even though at the time he could not speak German, and met up with his cousin Guelf, the son of Prince George of Hanover, who had been a guest at Balmoral and who was shortly to be sent to a school in Scotland called Gordonstoun.

Right up until the present day there are question marks over whether Gordonstoun was the most sensible choice for Charles. When the alternatives were discussed among the various members of the family, Lord Mountbatten, predictably, proposed the Royal Naval College, Dartmouth, where the boy's grandfather had gone. The Queen Mother favoured Eton. There, he would be going to school with boys he knew, a few of whom might end up being his ministers in a Tory government. What if the government were Labour? Then send him to Winchester,† at that time the Alma Mater of a number of Socialist luminaries. Lord Charteris was not part of the discussion group advising on Charles's future but, even so, with hindsight he suggests that Eton might have been the right choice. 'I think it would have done him a world of good. It is a very maturing place – and the finest training ground for politicians, statesmen, and pirates!'[8] As a former provost of the college, he is in a

---

* At the 1964 New Year party at Sandringham, the Queen, Princess Margaret, Princess Alexandra, and the Duchess of Kent – all were expecting babies at various times during the following four months.
† The record to date is Eton: nineteen Prime Ministers; Winchester: two. Despite persistent press reports to the contrary, it is very unlikely that there are plans for Prince William to go to Eton.

good position to know!

Prince Philip was set against sending Charles to Eton, partly in support of the argument that it was élitist and partly because, being so near to London, and on the doorstep of Windsor itself, it would attract the worst elements of Fleet Street. At least some editors would think twice about the cost of regularly sending reporters to the frozen corner of northern Scotland where Gordonstoun was situated. Eton at that time was also thought by some to be 'not at its peak'. The headmaster and the provost, it was said, were so bored with one another that they were hardly on speaking terms.

The Queen had no firm views either way because, as she explained, she had so little knowledge of any of the great public schools. She was prepared to listen to advice before making up her mind, although she leaned heavily towards her husband's recommendation in the matter.

Charles himself, if he had any personal preference, would have quite liked to have gone to Charterhouse, in Surrey, because some of his friends from Cheam were gong there. He thought Gordonstoun sounded 'pretty gruesome'. However, some fifteen years later, in a talk with students at Chicago University that went unreported, he was to explain why he believed that certain aspects of Gordonstoun were particularly worthwhile. Included was the opportunity to challenge oneself. 'You can face the realities of modern life so much better if you've had a chance to discover what it's like actually to throw yourself against some particular new challenge. Whether it's the sea or a mountain – you're a much better person for it. You're an individual. You understand what your capacities are, your own weaknesses, your own failures, your own good points ... You could say that just sitting in a classroom, learning some form of science, just education *per se*, is the best way of preparing someone for modern industrial life. But I don't think it is. I happen to think that there's more to education than just filling someone's head with facts.'[9]

Somebody who shared this view of education was Christopher Trevor-Roberts, who today runs his own very successful preparatory school in north London. The Queen called him in to tutor each of her four children in turn. The long association began when he was asked to help Princess Anne with her Latin, in preparation for entry to Benenden school. He found Anne and, later, Andrew were very similar in that even at a young age they shared a strong sense of purpose – provided they were interested in what they were aiming at. Anne was quick to learn, had excellent concentration, and a good memory. Andrew found it hard to study and concentrate, but once he discovered which exams he had to pass in order to achieve his ambitions, he could work as hard as the best pupil.

Charles and Edward were quite different. Their tutor found them more imaginative than either their sister or Prince Andrew. 'Both of them loved poetry and literature, but where the disciplines, maths and the sciences, were concerned – where you are either right or wrong in your answers – they were less successful.'[10]

Prince Charles was utterly miserable during his first term at Gordonstoun and, although Prince Philip pointed out that it was likely to take a little time for their son to settle down, the Queen wondered whether a terrible mistake had not been made. She had visited the school prior to Charles's enrolment and had seen the asbestos-roofed stone building that he was to share with fifty-nine of the 400 other boys. But unlike other parents, she was unable to take advantage of the invitation to all parents to visit their children at weekends and half-terms and give Charles the encouragement he needed. Apart from being tied down by official engagements which she could not break, the Queen soon realized that the distance between Gordonstoun and London – some 550 miles – was a deterrent to her as well as to Fleet Street editors. On more than one occasion she asked the Dean of Windsor to fly up to Inverness and on to Gordonstoun to spend consoling time with Charles, and to bring her news on his return.

A fellow pupil was to explain part of Charles's predicament, in an article he sold to a Sunday newspaper: 'How can you treat a boy as just an ordinary chap when his mother's portrait is on the coins you spend in the school shop, on the stamps you put on your letters home, and when a detective follows him wherever he goes? . . . Most boys tend to fight shy of friendship with Charles. The result is that he is very lonely. It is this loneliness, rather than the school's toughness, which must be hardest on him.'[11]

In fact, although he was badly homesick, Charles enjoyed the solitude of his walks across the bare, wide landscape that edged on to the grey sea, and gave platform to the magnificently changing moods of sky. He was happy in the snug warmth of Bob Waddell's flat in the Round Square. Waddell was the art master, an inveterate collector of books and knick-knacks. The flat was crammed with paintings which gave Charles joy. He was less happy in the classroom where he could keep his end up when opinions or interpretations were required, but was shown up when the answer to a question required a fact or a figure, especially a figure. At such times his fellow pupils, who could be as malicious as any other fourteen-year-old boys at times, saw not the precious eldest son of the sovereign but a blushing ignoramus much like themselves.

When he came home on holiday at Easter 1963, the Queen engaged Christopher Trevor-Roberts to tutor her son in mathematics and science – 'though we also spent quite a lot of time talking about literature and reading Dylan Thomas'. The lessons took place at Windsor at a time when guests were arriving from various parts of the world for the wedding of Princess Alexandra and the Hon. Angus Ogilvy. A picture remains in Mr Trevor-Roberts's memory of a footman pausing at the door where Prince Charles was being taught and looking at how the furniture had been slightly rearranged. 'It's all right,' said Charles, 'I'll put it all back.'

'He was a sensitive, considerate boy,' his tutor recalls, 'and Gordonstoun was like a hell-hole to him at the beginning. If someone wanted to take the mickey out of him because he was snoring,* it didn't matter how nice a personality he was, it made that boy that much more clever because he was able to challenge someone who was supposed to be that much more special.'[12]

At one point early on, the Queen seriously considered withdrawing her son from Gordonstoun, but was convinced by her advisers that this would not be a solution to her son's unhappiness, and that matters would improve. Within the family, the Queen Mother was probably Charles's greatest support, giving him a warm comforting granny to call on when she was staying at Birkhall, her home on the Balmoral estate. There he could have tea and scones round an open fire, go on 'deep-breathing' walks along the banks of the river Dee, and pour out his woes to a sympathetic listener. She, in turn, could gently persuade her young grandson of the wisdom of Gordonstoun's motto: *Plus est en vous* (There is more in you).

Within the school, Robert Chew, the headmaster, and Bob Whitby, Charles's housemaster, gave all the support they could. But they had been given instructions by the Queen and Prince Philip, especially by Prince Philip, to treat their son exactly as other children, which meant subjecting him to the tough disciplines of Gordonstoun. When he could stand the noise of Charles learning to play the bagpipes no more, Whitby told him to take up some other instrument, 'and for God's sake practise it somewhere well away from here'. Charles learnt to play the cello and, despite his frustration at the slow progress, grew to love the instrument so much that once or twice he was moved to tears by the beauty of the music.

The Art School, where the art master Bob Waddell was always ready to talk, joke or philosophize, provided Charles with sympathetic adult friendship as well as an enduring interest in the arts. In 1964, a new young English master, Eric Anderson – today headmaster of Eton – and

---

* Over twenty-five years later, in a jocular aside, Prince Charles was to suggest that toothpaste up the nostrils was a good cure for snoring. Though he didn't say so, it was something that had been inflicted on him by sufferers at Gordonstoun.

155

his charming wife, Poppy, arrived just at a time when Charles was at last emerging from the misery of his first years at Gordonstoun. While the Prince of Wales has since confessed more than once that he was never totally happy at the school, the Andersons joined Bob Waddell in providing some of the encouragement he needed. Bob Waddell cultivated Charles's taste for the visual arts; Eric Anderson was able to encourage his liking for acting. First, though, there were the rudiments of public speaking to be acquired.

'The headmaster summoned me,' recalls Dr Anderson today, 'and pointed out that so far we had done nothing about teaching the heir to the throne the means by which, metaphorically speaking, he would have to earn his bread. "You are going to teach him", said the headmaster, "by setting up an option offering a course in public speaking, and I will ensure that he volunteers for it."'[13]

At the first lesson the group of six students were asked to choose any subject they liked, and to stand up and speak about it for two minutes. Charles chose polo. He was not very good. 'He had prepared carefully, but he spoke in a very halting, embarrassed way, and he looked down at his notes too much. He was also at the stage where he blushed easily.'

A forcible lady from Aberdeen came for the day and informed the class that the most important thing in public speaking was eye contact. They should pick out three people in the audience, in different parts of the room, and address their remarks in turn to each of them. It is advice which Prince Charles still follows assiduously.

His first stage performance was in *Henry V*, in which he played the Duke of Exeter. It took place in the open air. Not all among the audience – mostly local gentry, wrapped in rugs and fortified by whisky – recognized the boy behind the beard: 'Who played Exeter? He was really rather good.'

Eric Anderson agreed, and gave Charles the lead in his next production, Shakespeare's *Macbeth*. 'To me, the part is only interesting if Macbeth is not the dead butcher of the final speech, but is a sensitive and interesting person who is brutalized by the actions the man goes through. Charles is an interesting and sensitive person, and that quality came through in his performance. He has told me since then that he would have preferred to have played a comic lead. He's a good mimic, but I don't think he would have been as good as in a serious part.'[14]

His mother would have been pleased that Charles was the first to learn his lines and almost invariably the first to arrive for rehearsals. On the one occasion when he was a little late, on Remembrance Sunday in November, he explained that he had been on the telephone. 'Poor Mother. She said she was frozen cold at the Cenotaph.'

As with all school plays, rehearsals relied on a few good laughs to leaven the nerves. When Charles tried on Macbeth's crown, it slid down behind his ears: 'Good heavens, we've got better than this at home!' When, in the dress rehearsal, dried ice, a novelty in northern Scotland in 1965, was wafted across the stage where Charles lay on deer skins – borrowed from Balmoral – the physics master whispered into Poppy Anderson's ear, 'People don't normally lie down in that stuff. I hope you know it's poisonous if you inhale it.' There were a few anxious moments before she realized that he was joking.

Perhaps not so suprisingly, there were a few local girls who would have volunteered to play Lady Macbeth, but they were not allowed to. In the end the part went to a racing driver's son named Campbell.

The Queen and Prince Philip travelled up from London for the final night's performance. Eric Anderson was afraid that their presence would make the actors so tense that they would forget their lines. But in the case of Prince Charles, at least, he need not have worried. 'Oh dear, I do feel for my mother', he confided to Poppy Anderson. 'She'll be so nervous.'[15]

In fact, once she had seen her son act ('one of the best performances of Macbeth I have ever seen', says Dr Anderson), Elizabeth II was as proud and pleased as any mother could be. At supper afterwards she sparkled, telling her host how she had talked about the play with her two youngest children and gone round and round the nursery with them reciting the witches' speech: 'Double, double toil and trouble;/Fire burn and cauldron bubble.'

Unfortunately for Prince Charles, Eric Anderson and his wife had left Gordonstoun (for Fettes College in Edinburgh) by the time that Charles returned from a six-months term in Australia. During her post-coronation tour of Australia, the Queen had promised to 'send my eldest son to visit you, too, when he is older'. In the autumn of 1965, the Australian Prime Minister, Sir Robert Menzies, had been invited to Balmoral and quizzed minutely about schools in his country. The Dean of Windsor, Dr Woods, had a brother who was Archbishop of Melbourne, so he too was able to offer advice. Another who was consulted was the Australian High Commissioner in London, Sir Alexander Downer, who was an old boy of the school that Charles was eventually sent to.

Timbertop, an annexe to Geelong Church of England Grammar School in Melbourne, was 200 miles inland, on the slopes of the Timbertop mountains. Life was hard, and not unlike that at Gordonstoun, which Charles had hoped he might be escaping for a while. He wrote copious letters home about how the pupils had to shear the sheep, feed the pigs, empty the dustbins, and chop wood to heat the water. 'I was made to go out and chop up logs on a hillside in boiling hot weather. I could hardly see my hands for blisters.' But the longer he stayed the more he enjoyed the life and his contact with Australian people. His six months in Australia contributed significantly to carving out the person Prince Charles is today.

Sir David Checketts, who accompanied the Prince, and in whose family home Charles spent many happy recuperative hours, was to conclude that 'I took out a boy, and I came back with a man'.[16]

Before going to Australia, Charles had passed his O level examinations in English language and literature, history, Latin and French. He went on to take A levels in French and history. But the question still remained, what was to be Prince Charles's next step after he left Gordonstoun? The Queen would need to take advice.

In the course of finding the best way to go about this search, Sir Michael Adeane, the Queen's Private Secretary, had come across an interesting precedent.

It appeared that when Queen Victoria was considering what to do with her eldest son, the future King Edward VII, at about the same age, she called together a special committee to consider the matter. It comprised the Prime Minister, the Archbishop of Canterbury, the equivalent of today's Chairman of the Committee of University Vice-Chancellors, the Queen's Private Secretary as adviser, and the Dean of Windsor as Clerk. Good, said Elizabeth II when she heard about it, we shall do the same.

The meeting was arranged to take place at 10pm (the royal family are notoriously late bed-goers) at Buckingham Palace on 22 December 1965, following a private dinner given by the Queen for committee members. Prince Philip, naturally, was to take part in the discussions. Prince Charles was to be kept informed but was not invited to attend. The others present were the Prime Minister, Harold Wilson; the Archbishop of Canterbury, Michael Ramsey; the Chairman of the Committee of University Vice-Chancellors, Sir Charles Wilson; the Queen's Private Secretary, Sir Michael Adeane; and the Dean of Windsor, the Reverend Robin Woods. The Royal Archives recorded that Queen Victoria had also invited the Chief of the General Staff to attend as an ex-officio member of the committee. His modern equivalent was the Chief of the Defence Staff, who just happened to be Lord Louis Mountbatten. The family valued his advice, and probably would not have been able to keep him out of the discussion anyway, so he came along too.

Over dinner the main topic of conversation was the war in Vietnam and its possible consequences, with the Labour Prime Minister holding forth at length. But after dinner, while he sipped brandy and the others beer or soft drinks, he seemed more prepared to listen. He invited Lord Mountbatten to offer his suggestions about Prince Charles's further education. In typical clear-cut manner, Mountbatten proposed that his great-nephew should go to Trinity College, Cambridge, 'like his grand-father'; to Dartmouth, 'like his father and grandfather'; and then to sea in the Royal Navy, 'ending up with a command of his own'. This route, everybody agreed, was certainly a possibility.

'I know what you're thinking', said Harold Wilson at one point, turn-ing to look directly at Lord Mountbatten. 'You're thinking that I am going to propose that he goes to a redbrick university.' Lord Mountbat-ten spread out his hands and indicated that he wasn't very knowledge-able when it came to the subject of universities. 'Because', continued the Prime Minister, 'if you think that, you forget, Chief of the Defence Staff, that I am a Fellow of University College, Oxford, in my own standing. And you forget that I was educated at Oxford.'[17]

Completely unconnected with this fact (as we shall see later, she liked Harold Wilson), the Queen was disinclined to send her son to Oxford. It was too far from Sandringham, for one thing, and although she did not say so at the time, it was the university attended by Edward VIII when he was Prince of Wales. He had been something of a 'gay blade' while there, and she would not have wished Charles to follow in the wake of that reputation.

As always, Her Majesty was prepared to listen closely to her advisers. She made a point of telling her guests: 'I reckon to know the tradition of all the major units in the Army. I reckon to know the Divisions of the Royal Navy. I know nothing about universities.'[18]

Both Prince Philip and Lord Mountbatten admitted to being equally uninformed on the merits and demerits of the senior seats of learning, though at one stage in the discussion Prince Philip did question whether his eldest son, at the end of his course, 'should be constrained by the absolute need to take a degree'. For almost the entire evening the Arch-bishop of Canterbury, Michael Ramsey, a round and benign-looking man, remained silent, even though at one time he had been a professor at Oxford. In the end he plumped for Cambridge.

Harold Wilson was quite open. According to the Dean of Windsor, Robin Woods, he said that what they had to do was find a community and a college to which Prince Charles would be able to relate, and one which was big enough for him to get lost in. It had to be near enough to home (he had heard all about the early problems at Gordonstoun), and there was not to be any imposition placed on him. 'We have got to give him a very happy centre of higher education where he'll enjoy himself.' It was a sentiment that met with general approval.

When the meeting broke up, shortly after midnight, Cambridge Uni-versity was the unanimous choice, although no decision had been reached about which college the young man should go to.

Prince Charles was informed on the same day and was delighted with the outcome. Cambridge was his own option, partly because of the family connection, but also because he was told that he could have his own car for driving to and from Sandringham.*

This still left the business of choosing a college, and the subjects he should take. Charles was insistent on living-in – like Edward VIII at Oxford, but unlike Edward VII and George VI, both of whom had re-sided in large town houses in Cambridge, their tutors coming to them.

As with many other families faced with similar decisions to make, dis-cussions over college and course continued intermittently over a period of several weeks without any firm commitment being made. In the end, with so many other matters pressing, the subject somehow faded into the background and was not revived until the following November when the Dean of Windsor received a telephone call from Prince Philip. He was afraid, he said, that he and the Queen had committed something of a 'blot'. It had been agreed almost a year ago that Prince Charles should go to university, but nothing practical had been done about arranging it!

So would the Dean make arrangements immediately to travel to Cam-bridge and interview the Masters of the six colleges deemed most likely to be suitable to everyone concerned. The Queen's Private Secretary in-formed the Reverend Woods that he should report back – one foolscap page on each college, please – on the Master, the person who would be the Prince's tutor, and how the college would handle having charge of the heir to the throne. The Dean was to put up at the nicest hotel in Cambridge, at Buckingham Palace's expense, and was *not* to accept any invitation from a Master to stay in college.

Robin Woods knew Cambridge well. He had been a student at Trin-ity. His eldest son, Robert, was presently in his last year at the universi-ty, and his youngest son, Edward, was about to go up in the autumn, at the same time as Prince Charles. So altogether Robin Woods spent a pleasant week in Cambridge, going round from college to college, in-specting the premises and paying heed to the words of the Masters before returning to his hotel room to write up his confidential reports.

Sir John Cockcroft intimated that Churchill College would love to have Prince Charles, but they had not really got the resources. Sir Frank Lee feared that Corpus Christi was not large enough for the Prince to lose himself in. Jesus College wanted to have him, and Magdalen wanted to have him very much. As the Master pointed out, they enjoyed a royal tradition. Professor Owen Chadwick of Selwyn, later to be knighted by the Queen, was hesitant about accepting Charles, partly because, like the Masters of other smaller colleges, he did not feel he could offer adequate

---

* At the time, undergraduates were not allowed cars in their first year, but a blind eye was turned on Charles's first choice: an MGB with bull horn.

facilities for security, while King's had a Master who was thought to be perhaps too radical. This left Trinity College, by coincidence the Dean's old college, presided over by 'Rab' Butler.

Lord Butler of Saffron Walden was a personal friend of the royal family.* Widely regarded as 'the best Prime Minister we never had', he had been in turn Chancellor of the Exchequer, Home Secretary, Lord Privy Seal, Foreign Secetary, and Deputy Prime Minister under Harold Macmillan. He was a scholar who was not remote from the feelings of ordinary people.

'I knew in my head, while I was interviewing each man,' Bishop Woods recalls today, 'that Rab was the only one who had all the qualities to handle the job. He had five academic tutors to choose from, and 600 undergraduates. He was the only one who said to me, "It's not only a question of lodgings; we've got to know who's next door to the Prince, and who above, and who to one side, in other words whom we can trust." Within a couple of hours Rab had worked out how everything would be done. It was very impressive.'[19]

Robin Woods duly submitted his reports, on six separate sheets of foolscap, and was surprised to receive a call from the Queen's Private Secretary intimating that the Dean had omitted one vital point. He had laid out the various pros and cons, but he had failed to make a recommendation. 'The Queen never makes a decision', said Sir Michael Adeane. 'She acts on advice. And you have been commissioned to give advice.' Thus, lightly admonished, the Dean added a paragraph to his report and the Queen duly entered her son for Trinity College, Cambridge.

However, that was still not quite the end of the matter. Somewhat to the embarrassment of everyone, it transpired that Prince Charles's application to become an undergraduate had arrived after the required closing date. Trinity would not, of course, turn him away, but the authorities felt themselves obliged to set him an entry exam of some sort, and would be grateful therefore if the Prince would present himself at the college on such-and-such a date when he would be tested in a two-hour paper on his general knowledge, his literacy, and on one or two other unspecified topices. (The results of Prince Charles's A-level exams at Gordonstoun – passes in History and French – did not come through until July 1967.)

It was arranged that Dean Woods should deliver Prince Charles to Cambridge at the appointed time. Prince Philip asked if he might come too. Although, of course, this could present no problem, the Dean was

---

* In 1976 Lord Butler sold his country house at Gatcombe Park in Gloucestershire to the Queen in order that she might give it as a present to Princess Anne after her marriage.

somewhat concerned as to how he could offer interest and entertainment to the Duke of Edinburgh during the two hours that his son was sitting his exam. Then he had the brilliant idea of asking the Regius Professor of Astrophysics to meet Prince Philip at the Cavendish Laboratory and show him round the research centre for space travel.

After they had dropped off Prince Charles at the college, Prince Philip suggested that he and the Dean should walk to the Cavendish Laboratory rather than take the car. Pulling a cap from his raincoat pocket, and putting on a pair of spectacles, the Queen's husband and Dean Woods happily strolled through the streets, looking into the shop windows and gazing admiringly at the architecture of the various colleges without anyone ever recognizing Prince Philip. Then he went on to spend a fascinating hour at the Laboratory, learning about the world's largest telescope.

The Queen was not to be left out. It was her turn next. About a month later, when the college informed Buckingham Palace that Prince Charles's rooms were ready, she said that she would like to see them for herself. For one thing, she was intrigued to learn more about the 'bedder' – a term she had not come across before. Once again, the Dean was to be her companion. She wished the visit to be completely private. Off they went, with a police car in front, a police car behind, and all the traffic lights set at green. So much for anonymity! As the Queen's car drove in by the back entrance to the college square – a privilege shared only by the Master – Elizabeth II tied a silk scarf over her hair; a sure sign that she felt herself to be, if not incognito, at least off duty.

Her first impression was that her son's rooms – Number Six on Staircase E of New Court – were a bit dingy, and she expressed slight surprise that he was not to have his own bathroom. In fact, a new bathroom suite, long scheduled, had been installed on the staircase that year, but it would be for other students to use as well. Her Majesty wanted to know if it would be all right for extra furniture to be installed in her son's rooms, and when informed that all students added their own to the basics, she nodded. 'We'll make a job of it,' she said. (Soon afterwards, workmen arrived from Sandringham with carpets and curtains and a few extra items of furniture.)

The Queen had a long talk with Mrs Florence Moore, 'Mrs M' to the students, who was in her late forties and would be Princes Charles's 'bedder' – the Cambridge term for the person who dusts, cleans, and makes the beds of students. She also met Dr Denis Marrian, who was to be her son's senior tutor, and the Reverend Harry Williams, a Fellow of the college and an inspiring chaplain who had written a number of provocative books including one called *Objections to Christian Belief*. He, it is said, is the person who brought Charles to becoming a Christian believer, as opposed to being simply a member of the Christian Church. In turn, Charles was able to help his father on the way to finding answers to some of the questions that troubled him.

After lunching with Lord Butler and his wife, Lady Molly, who was to become very much a mother-figure in Charles's university life, the Queen returned to London reassured in her own mind about her eldest son's immediate future.

Previously, Lord Butler had been to tea at Buckingham Palace and, learning of Prince Charles's interest in archaeology and anthropology, suggested that these were the subjects he should pursue at Cambridge – there would be plenty of time later to learn all about British constitutional history. (Prince Charles subsequently added History to his syllabus.)

As it turned out, Lord Mountbatten's advice was followed almost to the letter. Following three very happy years at Cambridge, the Prince of Wales graduated in June 1970 with a BA Honours degree, Class II Division II. After a short spell with the RAF (he had already gained his pilot's licence), he underwent a six-week course at the Royal Naval College, Dartmouth, before joining HMS *Norfolk* in November 1971 as a sub-lieutenant, and ending up in February 1976 in command of his own ship, the minehunter HMS *Bronington*.

Throughout all that time, under the watchful eye of Elizabeth II, he was gradually introduced to the role that would one day occupy his whole life. When that day would come, no one knew. But as the representative of the sovereign he witnessed the independence ceremonies of Fiji and of the Bahamas, attended the funeral of President de Gaulle and the coronation of King Birenda of Nepal. He was invested as a Knight of the Garter at Windsor, and appeared for the first time at a Buckingham Palace garden party. All these duties and honours he carried out with dignity and aplomb, though at times he still looked painfully immature. When he left the Royal Navy in December 1976, his father was heard to say: 'What a great relief it is when you find that you've actually brought up a reasonable and civilized human being.'[20] Which was true.

Of course, at twenty-seven years of age the heir to the throne was not yet married, and marriage, where an heir to a dynasty is concerned, is always a subject for conjecture and concern. But, contrary to press reports at the time, the Queen did not worry herself at all at her son's resistance to choosing himself a bride. Judging by one or two of the girls he had been seen out with, it was probably better that he took his time, she may have thought. The Queen realized that her son, up until now, had been a late developer, and she would prefer that he waited rather than rushed into things.

As for the Prince of Wales himself, in an interview with the author in his study at Buckingham Palace in October 1975 – an interview that went round the world, ('a good age for a man to get married is around thirty'), and hung, so the Prince later claimed, like a millstone round his neck – he explained, 'It is necessary to think a bit more carefully about the whole business of getting married. It's not as simple as just falling in love with somebody and saying, "let's get married tomorrow. It will all be splendid and a bed of roses till we die, so to speak."

'Whoever it is that I marry, I hope I shall be married to for the rest of my life. It's very important to find the right partner, with whom you can be as happy as possible. In my position, obviously, the last thing I could possibly entertain is getting divorced.'[21]

This was a month before his twenty-seventh birthday, and Prince Charles was prepared to admit: 'I've fallen in love with all sorts of girls, and I fully intend to go on doing so. But I've made sure I have not married the first person I've fallen in love with. Marriage is a much more important business than just falling in love – as I think a lot of couples probably find out.'[22]

II

The Queen and her Prime Ministers

ccording to one of her former senior advisers, the Queen is
'down to earth' with all her Prime Ministers – but 'she thinks
they are all rather stupid'. He spoke only half in jest, it
seemed, and quickly added, 'Well, perhaps not stupid but
fallible'. Another source, when quoted the remark, agreed that 'this is
certainly the impression she sometimes gives – in private, that is. But the
Queen would never use those actual words, even in fun. She is far too
wise, and far too punctilious about her own role and that of her Prime
Ministers.' A third person close to the Queen commented: 'I think that
she has been in her position for so long, and seen so many people grap-
pling with intractable problems that I don't think she believes there are
very simple solutions to many problems.' Thus far into the reign, eight
men and one woman have held the post of First Lord of the Treasury
under the sovereign.* The list, following the pattern of the framed photographs that takes the visitor up the stairway of 10 Downing Street, starts
with Winston Churchill and continues through Anthony Eden, Harold
Macmillan, Alec Douglas-Home, Harold Wilson, Edward Heath, James
Callaghan, Margaret Thatcher – whose relationships with the Queen
merit their own chapter – and John Major.

Not surprisingly, the Queen has formed an opinion of each of her
Prime Ministers. And while we shall never be allowed officially to know

---

* The title 'Prime Minister' was first used in an official document in 1878 when Disraeli signed the final instrument of the Congress of Berlin as 'First Lord of the Treasury and Prime Minister of Her Britannic Majesty'.

these opinions during her lifetime, a consensus of informed guesswork at least gives a good inkling.

Churchill, it appears, she found awe-inspiring to begin with, and slightly tiresome at the end when he had become almost senile; with a period in between when she was like a young Queen Victoria to an old Lord Melbourne. Anthony Eden, who was broken by the Suez crisis of 1956, was handsome but tense and twitchy. Harold Macmillan put most things in a historical setting, which she liked. Alec Douglas-Home, the Scottish aristocrat who renounced his title in order to enter the House of Commons, was more or less one of the family and certainly 'one of us', so that was all right. Harold Wilson adored the Queen, and she quite enjoyed his kindly company, although he may have chatted on too much. She found Edward Heath much less easy to get along with – 'it was a remote relationship', according to a fellow politician who has known him for over thirty years. The avuncular James Callaghan appealed to the Queen – he used to tell her saucy stories, some of which he had picked up from Lord Mountbatten. In fact, it is sometimes suggested that it is a toss-up as to whether Harold Wilson or James Callaghan was the Prime Minister whose company she enjoyed the most. According to a Palace source: 'Labour Prime Ministers, for some reason, are better at listening than the Tory ones are.'

Richard Crossman, who was in Harold Wilson's Cabinet, but a republican himself, observed in one of his diaries: 'The nearer the Queen they get the more the working-class members of the Cabinet love her and she loves them.' But when he asked Sir Godfrey Agnew, Clerk to the Privy Council between 1953 and 1974, whether the Queen preferred the Tories to Labour 'because they were our social superiors', Sir Godfrey was quoted as saying he didn't think so. 'The Queen doesn't make fine distinctions between politicians of different parties', he replied. 'They all roughly belong to the same social category in her view.'[1] So there!

Although, obviously, their paths cross more often than this, there are three occasions in the life of every Prime Minister when he or she must have audience of the sovereign. The first is on taking up office, the second on laying down office, and the third is on Tuesday evenings when, unless prevented, the monarch and her first minister converse with one another, alone and without minutes being taken, for half an hour or longer. Usually, but not always, these regular weekly meetings take place in Buckingham Palace. The procedure, apart from the change of time, referred to in an earlier chapter, that allowed the Queen to see her small children to bed first, has not changed at all over the years.

At six o'clock the Prime Minister arrives at the side door in the courtyard of Buckingham Palace, to be met by the Queen's Private Secretary.

Together they climb a spiral staircase,* and turn left into a small room where they sit waiting to be summoned. This is never an easy time because the Prime Minister is marshalling thoughts and small talk would be intrusive. After a few moments an equerry arrives. 'The Queen will see you now Prime Minister.' He leads the way into the drawing room, then withdraws. The Prime Minister bows, or in the case of Mrs Thatcher curtsies, shakes hands, and then head of state and head of government sit either side of an unlit fireplace and talk.

That same morning the Private Secretaries of the Queen and the Prime Minister have prepared an agenda, which the Queen has on a card at her side. And the reading of foreign telegrams and papers from the Cabinet Office, which the Queen normally does in the evening, has been brought forward to the afternoon. So the Queen is well prepared – more prepared than her Prime Ministers on one or two occasions. 'Very interesting, this idea of a new town in the Bletchley area', said the Queen to Harold Wilson. The Prime Minister smiled and blinked. He had not yet read the Cabinet paper about the proposal to build the new town of Milton Keynes in Buckinghamshire. 'I shall certainly advise my successor to do his homework before his audience', he said after he retired twelve years later.[2]

'What one gets is friendliness but not friendship', James Callaghan told the biographer Elizabeth Longford. 'One gets a great deal of friendliness. And Prime Ministers also get a great deal of understanding of their problems – without the Queen sharing them, since she is outside politics. . . . Of course she may have hinted at things, but only on the rarest occasions do I remember her ever saying, "Why don't you do this, that or the other?" She is pretty detached on all that. But she's very interested in the political side – who's going up and who's going down.'[3]

While the Queen and the Prime Minister are having their *tête-à-tête* (no refreshment is offered), the Queen's Private Secretary has repaired back to his office on the ground floor of the Palace, where he has left the Prime Minister's Private Secretary twiddling his thumbs. For the next half hour or so, the two men have a convivial drink and a chat, catching up on world news, cricket scores and the like, until the Prime Minister arrives from upstairs – when they all have a drink.

It is tempting to suppose that the first question the Private Secretaries want to ask is, 'What did the Queen *say*?' But, although this may form the substance of their conversation, it could never be put as crudely as that. However, any matters arising from the audience are noted, and the following morning the Queen briefs her Private Secretary on what occurred. So the audiences are not, as generally supposed, totally con-

---

* The Queen allowed Winston Churchill the privilege of riding up in her private lift.

fidential between monarch and Prime Minister.

The universal response of all nine Prime Ministers to their Tuesday meetings with the Queen seems to be one of admiration, respect, and a warm regard. 'They all come out of the audience on the balls of their feet, having gone in on their heels', says Lord Charteris, who, as the Queen's Private Secretary, altogether saw six Prime Ministers bounce in or out of office. 'She obviously has the same tonic effect on them as she does on others.'[4]

But what power exactly does the monarch hold today? And what are her rights as sovereign?

As to power, she retains very little – although, as Prince Philip once pointed out to the author in an interview about women's rights, influence can sometimes be more important than power.

As to the role of the monarch and her rights contained therein, Elizabeth II, like her more recent predecessors, has certain undenied responsibilities which, if practised, might give her crucial power. The trouble is, until called upon by circumstance to exercise them, nobody can be certain that they are permissible or even reasonable in a country that has no written constitution.

> The Crown does still remain, despite its greatly diminished constitutional status since even Queen Victoria's, let alone George III's reign, a sort of reserve power which in certain circumstances might affect the way in which the Prime Minister operates.
>
> We live in an era when many of our time-honoured constitutional usages are being scrutinized and questioned.[5]

The words are those of Lord Blake, the distinguished modern Conservative historian, in a series of lectures that he gave as provost of Queen's College, Oxford, in 1974. But they apply equally today.

It is easier in some ways to list what the Queen constitutionally cannot do, rather than what she can. Firstly, she cannot insist that her government or her Prime Minister do as she commands, or even as she suggests. As Lord North neatly pointed out to George III some 250 years ago: 'Your Majesty is well apprized that in this country the Prince on the throne cannot with prudence oppose the deliberate resolution of the House of Commons.'[6] The key words then were 'with prudence'. Long before that, Charles I, in assertion of his belief in the Divine Right of Kings, attempted to defy Parliament and to establish a personal autocracy – and ended up on the scaffold. Forty years later, when James II was suspected of wishing to impose the Roman Catholic religion on his people, he was forced to flee the country and was thereafter decisively defeated by William III at the Battle of the Boyne. The Whig magnates who had contrived the 'Glorious Revolution of 1688' (the tercentenary celebrations of which Elizabeth II attended), subsequently imposed the Declaration of Rights which pledges the Queen not to levy taxes without the consent of Parliament, not to maintain a standing army, not to create her own private courts, and not to suspend obedience of Acts of Parliament by royal decree.

In 1700, when the last of Queen Anne's seventeen children died, Parliament passed the Act of Settlement under which the Hanoverian dynasty, in accepting the throne, was required to undertake that in future government ministers would be responsible for the acts of the sovereign.

While accepting the terms, for a while George I attempted to follow the precedent of Charles II and insisted on presiding at Cabinet meetings. However, as his native tongue was German, he found this difficult. He endeavoured, then, to converse in Latin, only to discover that Latin as pronounced at Gottingen was not at all the same as that taught at Eton, Westminster or Harrow. Bored and grumpy, he soon withdrew.

Thus came about the principle of 'responsible government' whereby the Queen, according to the famous words of Walter Bagehot, is permitted only 'to advise, to encourage and to warn' her ministers.

Of course, when it comes down to the small print, it is not always quite as straightforward as that. . .

The words 'royal prerogative' are often bandied about in discussion, and occasionally called into question. The definition of the words – 'the exclusive right of the sovereign' – causes no problem. It is the interpretation and exercise of that right that does. Or at least it has done so, before and during the reign of Elizabeth II. And there is no real reason to suppose that it may not be called into action again one day, perhaps even in the foreseeable future.

Elizabeth II has been steeped in politics ever since she took lessons in constitutional history from Sir Henry Marten as a child. At the same time, paradoxically, she has consistently preferred not to become involved in them. She tends to be interested in politicians as individuals, rather than as party members, and her regard, as one administration followed after another, has been principally for what was being done for the country as a whole, irrespective of which political party was doing it. R.A. ('Rab') Butler noticed how she always asked about prices and showed consistent anxiety in the early 1960s as inflation began to increase. In the year-long miners' strike of 1984/5, her concern was for the miners' families – she received hundreds of letters from miners' wives. But she would probably think it inappropriate to suggest, as one former Cabinet minister did, in an interview with the author, that 'In this century, whenever there has been a battle between the people and privilege, the royal family has always supported the people.'

In forty years there have been just two major political upheavals where Elizabeth II has later been accused of handling matters with an uncharacteristic lack of adroitness. Both involved Tory Prime Ministers, and both, as it happened, were concerned with privilege. In each case the sad-faced 'Rab' Butler was the unwilling centrepiece of the drama.

In January 1957, the Queen – still a young woman not yet thirty years of age, it should be remembered – was suddenly faced with the resignation, through ill-health, of Anthony Eden. His premiership had lasted less than two years and, quite apart from his sickness, his career had been ruined by the débâcle of the Suez Canal crisis.*

The process is sensibly different today (or was thought to be up until the cruel dismissal of Margaret Thatcher in November 1990), but, before Sir Alec Douglas-Home devised the new rules in 1965, when a Tory Prime Minister resigned his successor was not elected but somehow 'emerged'. Thus, acting on Eden's advice, the Queen suggested that the Marquess of Salisbury should take soundings informally among members of the Cabinet to decide upon the next Prime Minister after Eden. Lord Salisbury, of course, was the same 'Bobbety' who had advised the Queen in the matter of Princess Margaret and Peter Townsend, and was an exceedingly venerable pillar of the establishment. The other person who joined him in interviewing possible candidates was Lord Kilmuir, which caused the Foreign Secretary, Selwyn Lloyd, to object to the procedure being carried out by two members of the House of Lords. This was not very fair because the two men did, after all, hold senior posts in the Cabinet – Lord President and Lord Chancellor respectively – and, along with Winston Churchill, were elder statesmen of the Conservative Party.

The interviews went ahead anyway, in the Lord President's room in the Privy Council offices. One by one the Cabinet ministers entered – 'this is like coming to the headmaster's study' was an almost universal comment – and were asked by 'Bobbety' to choose: 'Which is it to be, Wab or Hawold?' Fortunately, all were sufficiently aware of Lord Salisbury's problem with 'R's to know that he meant that they had to decide between Richard Austen ('Rab') Butler and Harold Macmillan, the Chancellor of the Exchequer.

---

* The Suez Canal had been seized by the Egyptian Colonel Nasser on 27 July 1956, in retaliation for America's refusal to underwrite the construction of the Aswan High Dam. Half of Britain's oil passed through the canal, and the seizure was seen as being intolerable. A plot was hatched for Israel to invade, and for Britain and France to intervene, ostensibly to separate the warring nations. The collapse came within a fortnight of Britain's invasion, after America's refusal to shore up Sterling against speculation.

The world at large, including the newspapers, expected 'Rab' to win. After all, he had acted as Eden's deputy during the Prime Minister's ill-nesses, and was generally regarded as a man of ideas. But he could also be indecisive at times, and was blamed for being lukewarm towards the Suez operation – although, as he pointed out later: 'I withdrew the troops, got money out of my old friend George Humphrey, the American Secretary of the Treasury, with which to pay our loans and debts, and restored the pound.'[7]

However, in the end, Butler lost out to Macmillan, the deceptively Edwardian-looking gentleman with the charm of a steely grandpapa. (In the eyes of many, even so, or perhaps because of this, the most recent international statesman, as opposed to stateswoman, that Britain has had.) Macmillan awaited the verdict of his Cabinet colleagues, he later informed us, at the Chancellor's official residence at 11 Downing Street. 'I passed the morning in the downstairs sitting room, to which I had re-stored the picture of Mr Gladstone, and I read *Pride and Prejudice* – very soothing. At noon Sir Michael Adeane rang up and asked me to be at the Palace at two o'clock. So it was settled.'*[8]

Not quite. There were rumblings afterwards that the Queen had allowed herself to be manipulated by 'Bobbety' and his old school of thought. After all, the Cecil family, of which he was a leading member, had been of influence with the monarch as far back as Elizabeth I. But although some in Parliament felt that Butler had been unfairly treated – 'I suffered much at this time', he later admitted – most people came round to the view that Macmillan probably had a better chance of hold-ing together a solid majority in the House of Commons than Butler had.

If the Queen made a mistake, it was in not appearing to consult parlia-mentarians other than Lord Salisbury. In fact, she did speak with others, including Winston Churchill ('I told her to choose the older man' – Mac-millan was eight years older than Butler), but knowledge of this wider consultation did not emerge at the time, and it was Lord Salisbury who was seen to bring the decision of the Cabinet to the Palace. Also, if the theory of some sort of establishment conspiracy is to be followed up, it could always be pointed out that Macmillan himself, even though he was descended from a Highland crofter, was also married into the aristocratic Cavendish family. Author Robert Lacey was almost certainly correct when he wrote in *Majesty* that 'Consulting the very different Tory strain of suburban villadom represented by Edward Heath, the Chief Whip, would also have emphasized the detachment of the royal allegiance from

---

* This was somewhat different from the style of Harold Wilson almost eight years later who, on becoming Prime Minister, arrived at Buckingham Palace to 'kiss hands' with the Queen – a tradition he discovered that was 'taken as read' – with his wife, his two sons, his father, and his secretary.

any one particular faction, and would, furthermore, have provided visual evidence of the wide soundings on which her [the Queen's] decision was in fact based. As it was, Elizabeth II laid herself open to the charge of favouritism.'[9]

The question of the royal prerogative was to come up again, in 1963, this time with the resignation of Harold Macmillan and the appointment of his successor.

No Prime Minister can appoint a successor. He or she can but advise the monarch, and the monarch then asks the chosen candidate if he or she is in a position to form a government. Only after an assurance is provided can a Prime Ministerial appointment be confirmed with the traditional 'kissing of hands'.

Harold Wilson (Lord Wilson of Rievaulx) summed it up neatly: 'The traditional formula is, 'Can you form a government?', to which the traditional answer is a hurried affirmation. The alternative, in a hung election, is "Your Majesty, I will go along and try" – meaning that he will.

'In the first case the sovereign informally tells her visitor that he or she is Prime Minister, in the second he begins work on urgent problems while entering into treaty discussions with possible allies. Should all the parties, and groupings of them, fail to create a working majority, it would be her responsibility to call another election on, of course, the advice of the last potential Prime Minister she has been able to unearth. It is not her duty to assess whether a potential Prime Minister can form a government – that is his duty.'[10]

The story of the 'emergence' of Alec Douglas-Home, (Lord Home of The Hirsel), as Prime Minister has been told many times before, but, with each year almost, new fragments have emerged, to be added to the mosaic. As the episode resulted directly in a historical change in the manner in which leaders of the Conservative Party are chosen, it constitutes an important component in the Queen's reign.

Harold Macmillan was one of the Queen's greatest admirers. 'I was astonished', he wrote in his diary after a visit to America in the spring of 1960, 'at Her Majesty's grasp of all the details set out in various messages and telegrams.' Butler also shrewdly spotted how she responds to certain people. 'Like all clever women she was very interested in personalities', he wrote.

Macmillan himself, 'Wondermac' as the cartoonists drew him, was certainly a personality. He had told the British people that they had 'never had it so good', and gone to Moscow wearing a very fetching Astrakhan hat. But by the autumn of 1963 his reign was drawing rapidly to its close. The charisma was cracking. He had had to face up to de Gaulle dashing Britain's hopes of entering the Common Market, the exposure of George Blake as the 'third man' in the spy triangle of Burgess and Maclean (in 1955 he had cleared him), and, most damaging of all, in September 1963, Lord Denning's inquiry report had come out in condemnation of the way Macmillan and his ministers had handled the scandal of John Profumo, the war minister who lied to the House of Commons about his affair with a call-girl.

The Prime Minister had once before told the Queen that he might have to resign – 'apparently she did not react with the consternation he had expected', wrote his adviser on public relations. But on the opening day of the annual Conservative Party conference, taking place in Blackpool at the beginning of October 1963, after much agonizing over whether to resign or not, Macmillan told his political cronies that he *would* lead the Party into the next election. By extraordinary coincidence, on the very same night he writhed in his bed with excruciating spasms, and the next day somehow managed to preside over the Cabinet meeting, but in absolute agony. That evening his doctors diagnosed inflammation of the prostate gland 'by either a benign or malignant turmour' and unanimously proposed an immediate operation.

The Prime Minister went into hospital on the evening of 8 October, and during lulls in the pain and the fuzziness brought on by the anaesthetic the next day, he let it be known to certain Cabinet members that he would resign, but would remain Prime Minister during the process of selecting his successor.

The Queen, who was coming to the end of her summer break at Balmoral, was informed of her Prime Minister's decision and indicated that she would be guided by his advice. On a more personal level, she rang up the hospital on three occasions to have a cheering word with her friend.

Fortunately, the tumour was not malignant, and within a fortnight the patient was well on the way to recovery. However, perhaps precipitately, he had said that he would exit from Number 10, and long before he had even left his hospital bed, the wolves were snarling round the edges of the battle for the leadership. The furtive and complicated intrigues that followed were exactly of the kind that the Queen, with her penchant for working things out bloodlessly, would not have welcomed. But there was nothing she could do but await their outcome, and then set her seal of approval upon them.

There were four main contenders – five if you count the one who came in late, and reluctantly, and was finally victorious.

'Rab' Butler was once again regarded as a front runner and 'heir apparent' – although he had his problems. According to Iain Macleod, Leader of the House of Commons and also a contender, 'from the first day of his premiership to the last, Macmillan was determined that Butler, although incomparably the best qualified of the contenders, should not succeed him.'[11]

Macleod quite fancied his own chances, but was left behind in the race fairly early on. As was Reginald Maudling, the Chancellor of the Exchequer who managed only 10.5 per cent from party supporters in a newspaper poll, against a leading 38 per cent for Butler and a 27 per cent vote for Lord Hailsham.

In his memoirs, *A Sparrow's Flight*, Lord Hailsham reveals that two days before the Tory Party conference began in Blackpool, Macmillan called him to 10 Downing Street and formally intimated that he wished him to become the next Prime Minister. He remembers being 'almost struck dumb with surprise' at the news. Macmillan said he thought he would probably step down around about Christmas – but, of course, fate in the form of the prostate intervened.

The following Thursday, walking back to their hotel along the windy promenade from the Blackpool party conference, the Lords Hailsham and Home discussed the one subject on the minds of everyone – the succession – and in his customary lean-spoken way the Foreign Secretary informed Hailsham that he was under pressure to disclaim his peerage, a prerequisite to becoming Prime Minister, and throw his hat into the ring. Apparently, Hailsham was not surprised by his friend's news, partly perhaps because *The Times* that same morning had predicted that a 'fourth hypothetical candidate, the Foreign Secretary Lord Home, would probably be the choice of perfection of the party's organization men.'

However, Hailsham advised Home against standing, saying that the Foreign Secretary's knowledge and understanding of home affairs was inadequate. The opposition 'would skittle you out in six months'.

Home has a slightly different memory of that stroll along the Blackpool promenade.* 'I walked back from the meeting with Quintin who knew by then that he was Macmillan's selection, and I told him that the idea had my full support. Had I known that he intended to throw his cap into the ring within a matter of hours, I would have tried to dissuade him from it then and there, for people never like being bounced, and least of all at a time of emotional stress.'[12]

Home had an advantage. When his Cabinet colleagues had travelled up to Blackpool for the start of the party conference, he had stayed behind in London to clear his desk, and had paid a visit to Macmillan in hospital. The Prime Minister asked him why he, Home, had not thought of taking on the leadership. Home replied that he was happy at the Foreign Office and had never contemplated leaving the House of Lords. There, apparently, the matter had been left, with Hailsham still firmly in Macmill-

---

* Although in his review of Lord Hailsham's autobiography, in the *Daily Mail* of 5 July 1990, Lord Home simply wrote that he did 'not dissent from the dramatic events which followed the retirement of Mr Macmillan'.

an's mind as his successor, and Home charged with the job, as President of the National Union, of travelling up to Blackpool and informing the party faithful of Macmillan's decision in the Prime Minister's own words: 'I will not be able to carry the physical burden of leading the Party at the next general election. I hope that it will soon be possible for the customary consultations to be carried out within the Party about the leadership.'[13]

Despite the misgivings of some of his colleagues, Hailsham went ahead and very publicly threw his hat into the ring, announcing at the end of his speech to the conference that he would disclaim his titles – in other words become plain Mr Quintin Hogg so that he could stand for parliament. 'The effect was one of the most dramatic in my lifetime', Hailsham writes in his memoirs. 'The whole audience, and the platform, went mad, standing, cheering, and waving in the full light of television.'

However, by the following morning some of the euphoria had evaporated. Hailsham had not so much 'emerged' as shot himself out of a rocket, and some senior Tories thought this smacked of American presidential election methods. Others thought he had not so much shot himself out of a rocket as shot himself in the foot by making his speech. Whichever, within a few days he was out of the race. He was interviewed in the following week by Macmillan, but there was no more talk of his being a potential successor. Hailsham concluded that Macmillan 'had done another of his famous somersaults'.

That left Home, according to Macmillan, 'the preponderant first choice'. He reported to the Queen that, out of the nineteen Cabinet ministers, there were, 'ten for Home; three for Butler; four for Maudling; two for Hailsham'. And among the three hundred Conservative MPs, 'the largest group (not by much, but significant) were pro-Home'. The reluctant peer – his brother Robin Douglas-Home later wrote a play with that title – had seemingly come from almost nowhere to top the poll.

On 15 October, a week after all the to-ings and fro-ings had begun, Macmillan sent the Queen an account of events between the 7th and the 15th to prevent 'mistakes or arguments in the future'. It appeared that the choice of leader was not, after all, as clear-cut as he imagined, or desired. 'I fear that all kinds of intrigues and battles are going on.'

Late in the evening of 17 October, supporters of 'Rab' Butler made their various ways through London to the house of Enoch Powell, then the Minister of Health, in South Eaton Place. Their private conclave was to become known as 'the midnight assembly'. Iain Macleod, joint-chairman of the Conservative Party and Leader of the House of Commons, was one of those there. He and Powell both spoke to Home on the telephone. Macleod told him that if he had been a member of the House of

Commons, he could perhaps have been the first choice for Prime Minister. But those giving advice had grossly underestimated the difficulties of presenting the situation in a convincing way to the modern Tory Party. Was the Party now proposing to admit that after twelve years of Tory government there was no one among the 363 MPs in the Lower House who was acceptable as Prime Minister? That it was necessary to turn to a member of the House of Lords, no matter how greatly Home was admired and respected, as he was?

Macleod did not hear what Powell said to Lord Home, 'but I believe he spoke to him on similar lines'.

Almost thirty years after the event, speaking in the same house and in the same room in South Eaton Place, Enoch Powell was smiling as he observed: 'There are a lot of stories about that evening.' His own written account is kept under lock and key for whatever use his literary trust might wish to permit after his death. Will the document contain any surprises? Again, the smile. 'How am I to know by what people will be surprised?' More seriously, 'I think that what is publicly known is all that is significant', he added.[14]

Some hours after the meeting at Powell's house, 'Rab' Butler was approached by Reginald Maudling and Lord Hailsham at a hotel where he was staying and advised that if he would refuse to serve under Home, so would they. In that way, Home would find it practically impossible to form a government, they explained. But, Butler informed his two visitors, he had already given Alec Home his word to support him. 'Ferdinand the bull had preferred to sniff the flowers rather than take what would have been his if he had wished it', wrote Hailsham. Or as Powell said later in a television programme: 'We handed Rab a loaded revolver and told him all he had to do was pull the trigger. He asked if it would make a noise and we said, "That is in the nature of guns, Rab." He asked if it would hurt him and we said, "That too is in the nature of guns, Rab", and he said, "I don't think I will. D'you mind?"'[15]

Exactly how much or how little Elizabeth II was aware of the shenanigans that were taking place we may never know, though it seems likely that her Private Secretary, Sir Michael Adeane, like all Private Secretaries to the sovereign, had his ear close to the ground. It is part of the job. The newspapers certainly were on to something. The *Daily Express* of 18 October carried the headline in its later editions: '1 A.M. CABINET REVOLT', and *The Times* suggested 'THE QUEEN MAY SEND FOR MR BUTLER TODAY'.

In fact, it transpired that Macmillan, holding court in his hospital bed, had no intention of putting Butler 'in the frame'. He had spoken with Lord Dilhorne, the Lord Chancellor, who had taken soundings, and Macmillan was convinced that Lord Home was the person to follow him. But he had to move quickly now, if his plan was to work and the rivalry was not to overtake events.

On the morning of 18 October, Macmillan's Private Secretary delivered the Prime Minister's formal letter of resignation to Buckingham Palace. In the afternoon, to the great surprise of many, Elizabeth II went to call on Mr Macmillan, who, with advance warning, had been moved to a more accessible downstairs room in the hospital. He was sitting up, but he was still wearing his pyjamas.

'She came in alone,' he wrote, 'with a firm step and those brightly shining eyes which are her chief beauty. She seemed moved; so was I. I asked leave to read her a memorandum which I had written yesterday and brought up to date this morning. I said I was not strong enough to trust myself to speak without a text.'[16]

He thus made out his case for Alec Home, and having done so returned the papers to a large envelope and asked that Her Majesty should keep the account in the Royal Archives at Windsor as being a true account of the advice he had given her. The Queen 'expressed her gratitude and said she did not need and did not intend to seek other advice but mine.' He also advised her to act 'with speed'. And this she did. As soon as she had returned to Buckingham Palace she called for Alec Douglas-Home and offered him the premiership.* The matter was still not completely settled, however, for Home thought it necessary to ask leave first to go away and see if it were possible for him to form an administration. 'I had to enlist Butler, Maudling and Hailsham at the very least, to have the foundation on which to build a Cabinet and government which would command support in the country and respect overseas.'[17]

Butler and Hailsham both fell into line, but Macleod and Powell, 'who were not natural bedfellows, but who for the moment had got into a huddle', did not.

Almost thirty years on, Enoch Powell recalls: 'On the Friday Alec Home enquired hypothetically whether I would join a government of which he was the head, and I said I wouldn't. On the Saturday he put the same question to me as the Prime Minister holding the Queen's commission to form a government and I gave the same reply. I said "Alec, you don't expect me to give a different answer. I should have to go home and turn all the mirrors to the wall."'[18] (*The Times* once ascribed to Enoch Powell the phrase used to describe Robespierre – 'sea-green incorruptible'.)

---

* To continue the dress sense of earlier footnotes, Lord Home went to the Palace for his audience with the Queen in his everyday clothes. 'Heavens – in that suit!' exclaimed his wife Elizabeth on hearing.

With hindsight, it is questionable as to whether the Queen was wise to make her visit to the hospital and to accept Harold Macmillan's advice so readily, without calling others, such as Lord Dilhorne, to the Palace for consultation. After all, she must have known that the undisputed emergence of one certain successor to her Prime Minister had just not happened.

Enoch Powell questions whether Macmillan was even in a position to offer advice to the Queen, not because of his state of health but because he continued to play such a crucial role in the selection process after he had let it be widely known that he intended to resign as Prime Minister.

'Not for the first time,' in Mr Powell's view, 'Harold Macmillan played fast and loose with the royal prerogative in that, having announced that he intended to resign, he proceeded to go through the motions of ascertaining who might thereafter be acceptable. Now you can't say to the sovereign, "I resign my office, but I'm giving you some advice." You must do one or the other. During all that week between the opening of the Blackpool conference and the midnight meeting there had been no secrecy as to the intention of the Prime Minister to cease to be Prime Minister and proceedings were going on to see who ought to succeed him. Well, that was in fact to take away the Crown's prerogative and was incompatible with the nature of binding advice.'*[19]

It seemed at the time that perhaps the best thing to come out of what has been called 'this dubious episode' was that, during his short year as Prime Minister, Sir Alec Douglas-Home, as he became known, introduced a system for choosing the Conservative Party leader by election instead of by mysterious means of emergence. Not everyone was in favour of the change. Sir Alec himself was one of those who regretted it. 'The Magic Circle of selectors had almost everything to be said for it . . . but I then came to the conclusion that, with all its disadvantages, it was necessary to adopt a system of election of a leader, where from start to finish everything was seen to be open and above board.'[20]

One outcome of the change was that three Conservative politicians from middle-middle-class backgrounds – Edward Heath, Margaret Thatcher and John Major – were subsequently voted into highest office. And by the same means, in November 1990, Margaret Thatcher was placed in a position which led directly to her resigning the premiership.

By strange coincidence, on the very morning that Mrs Thatcher went to Buckingham Palace to inform the Queen of her intention to resign the

---

* Lord Home tells of how, while he was still Foreign Secretary, he entered the Cabinet room one day and found the Cabinet Secretary changing the seating arrangements. Had there been a government reshuffle? 'No', replied Sir Norman Brook. 'It's just that the Prime Minister cannot stand Enoch Powell's steely and accusing eye looking at him across the table any more, and I've had to move him down the table.'[21]

premiership – 22 November 1990 – Mr Denis Thatcher (as he still was), along with Lord Home, and many of her friends and colleagues were attending the memorial service of Lady Home of The Hirsel in Westminster Abbey. Four days later, Lord Home suffered a stroke and was admitted to a nursing home in Winchester.

Ironically, Harold Macmillan was to make a remarkable recovery from his illness and was to live on for a further nineteen years, during which time he made some memorable contributions to House of Lords debates. Lord Butler, if he had resolved not to serve under Home, might well have ended up as Prime Minister and gone on to win the 1964 election, defeating Harold Wilson. Thereby, as the historian Lord Blake once suggested, 'the political history of Britain might have been different'.

The royal prerogative was to play a vital role once more in the case of Heath versus Wilson in February 1974. The general election fixed for 28 February was the culmination of massive industrial confrontation, when Britain found itself virtually paralysed by strikes and a government-imposed three-day working week. Prime Minister Edward Heath's policy of wage and profit restraint had failed, but the question constantly being asked was, who ruled the country: the government or the trade unions? Perhaps leaving it a little too late, Heath decided to dissolve Parliament and go to the country to find out the answer.

At the time the Queen was visiting New Zealand and Australia, but contingency plans had been made well in advance to bring her back to England in the event of an election. 'Which was just as well,' comments her Private Secretary at the time, Lord Charteris, 'because the result did not turn out to be a clear-cut case.'[22]

At 3pm on Thursday 28 February 1974, Elizabeth II opened Australia's parliament in Canberra. She then got straight into a plane and flew to Sydney, where another plane was waiting to fly her the 12,000 miles back to London. She arrived on a freezing cold day, 1 March, to hear the results of the general election.

Labour 301 seats
Conservatives 296 seats
Liberals 14 seats
Others (Nationalists, etc.) 24 seats

In other words, there was no single party with an overall majority in the House of Commons but the choice of two *working* majorities, provided one or other of the major parties could form an alliance with the minor parties.

Despite winning fewer seats than Labour, Edward Heath was still

Prime Minister and, by long tradition, was entitled to remain so until he met parliament and secured its approval. But to gain that approval he needed the support of other parties. On the evening of the Queen's return he drove to the Palace to inform Her Majesty that he intended to try to persuade the Liberals, under the leadership of Jeremy Thorpe, and perhaps some of the Scottish Nationalist and Ulster MPs, to support him.

There were murmurings at the time, and whispers to the author since, that some senior Tories believed that the Queen would be inclined to support Edward Heath and somehow oblige him in the formation of a government. Denis Healey, who was to become Chancellor of the Exchequer in the Labour government, writes in his memoirs of how 'Ted Heath tried hard to persuade the Queen to invite him to form a government, infuriating the Palace with his assumption that the monarchy was the property of the Conservative Party.'*[23]

But Lord Charteris, who would have advised the Queen throughout, is adamant: 'There is absolutely no justice for believing the suggestion. Whether from any emotional point of view the Queen would rather have kept Ted, I don't know. But certainly from a constitutional point of view she would never ever for a second have thought of it.'[24]

Lord Whitelaw, who as William Whitelaw was Chairman of the Conservative Party at the time, agrees. 'I imagine that the Queen would always do everything she could to avoid getting into a position where she could be criticized.'[25] As it turned out, Heath was unable to recruit the support of the Liberals that he required in order to retain power. And so, on the evening of 4 March 1974, he formally resigned, and forty-five minutes later Harold Wilson arrived at the Palace to begin his second administration as Prime Minister – with a minority government.

One of the dubious advantages about a country not having a written constitution is that it, and its Head of State tend to roll along in mystery, making up the rules when circumstance demands. To a large extent precedent is what governs the royal prerogative, and even constitutional experts prefer not to be tied down to what is likely to happen in the future. But if proportional representation is introduced in Britain – and there are signs that it might well be before the end of the century – then the sovereign may find that she is called upon more often to sort out some new and very tricky situations.

---

* Precisely how Edward Heath would have gone about his ambition, if ambition it was, is by no means clear, although possibly he could have chosen to resign and then hope to be appointed as head of a national coalition government, as Winston Churchill had done in reverse in 1945 when a 'caretaker' Cabinet was approved by George VI as a stop-gap between the wartime coalition and the general election in which the wartime leader went down to defeat.

Margaret Thatcher is a well-known opponent of proportional representation, and in a typically robust interview with the biographer Elizabeth Longford in 1983 she expressed one of her reasons why. 'It means the Queen has an extremely difficult job. Look at Queen Beatrix of Holland. She can't form a government. She calls on someone to do so and they can't. So then she calls for someone else and then she gets two people trying to form a government. There is uncertainty which spreads through a whole community and the government which becomes a government doesn't stand for anything.'[26]

Proportional representation aside, there are other questions waiting to be posed. What happens if a Prime Minister refuses to resign? 'British democracy stood still while Heath was negotiating with Thorpe', Harold Wilson wrote afterwards. What if a Prime Minister asks for a dissolution of parliament and a fresh election shortly after a government has been formed, in the hope of gaining a larger majority? (Wilson might have done that after so narrowly toppling Heath.) And what about a Prime Minister who informs the sovereign of his impending resignation – impending, that is, in six months time? And only when the six months is up does he spring the news on a totally unsuspecting public, leaving them to mull over the unsubstantiated rumours that he has a terminal illness or is the subject of some Secret Service plot.

According to Lord Charteris, the following was the scenario of Harold Wilson's resignation. In the autumn of 1975 Wilson was a guest of the Queen at Balmoral, as was his Private Secretary Kenneth Stowe. Stowe took Charteris into his confidence and imparted the astonishing news that Wilson intended to resign the premiership in the following March. Charteris said that Wilson must inform the Queen, which he believes he did. As the Queen's eyes and ears, Charteris at the same time also passed on the information himself to his monarch. And there the secret remained – shared between Wilson, presumably Mrs Wilson, the Queen, and the two Private Secretaries only – for a whole two months or more. No one else had even a glimmer of Wilson's intentions until late in December, when Harold Lever, Chancellor of the Duchy of Lancaster and always exceptionally well informed, tipped off James Callaghan, the Foreign Secretary. It took some little time for Callaghan to be convinced that the rumour was true – he does not appear to have gone to Wilson himself for verification – but in the meantime he listened to his friends' advice that he must make ready for the coming leadership battle.

Prime Minister Wilson's explanation at Balmoral for his dramatic announcement was that he had not been feeling very well - he had suffered a slight heart attack the previous summer, although this again was not public knowledge - and as he was confident that there were several others in his Cabinet of prime ministerial calibre he told Charteris that he thought that it was time he made room for one of them. There was no suggestion that there was anything in the least sinister about his decision to step down. The only sensation was to be in the manner of his going.

Stowe and Charteris discussed the question of how, from a constitutional point of view, a Prime Minister resigns while still in office. 'I said that what he should do', recalls Lord Charteris, 'is resign as Leader of the Labour Party but remain Prime Minister. That would allow the Labour Party at leisure to choose the person to take his place. The Prime Minister resigns, and then the Queen immediately sends for the person who has been chosen to lead the Labour Party. That's what I proposed, and that is what happened.'[27]

First, Harold Wilson more formally informed the Queen of his intention to resign, at his weekly audience at Buckingham Palace on 9 December. (For a short while the secret date in March was moved to a date in December, but then moved back again.) On 11 March – his sixtieth birthday – Harold attended a dinner party given in his honour by the publisher George Weidenfeld, which was interrupted by a call to return to the House of Commons for a vote at the end of a debate on public expenditure. The Prime Minister invited Callaghan to ride with him to the House in his official car, and on the way finally confirmed to the Foreign Secretary his intention to step down. 'He would call a special Cabinet meeting on the morning of 16 March to inform ministers of his intention to resign, and meantime I should begin to make preparations for the inevitable contest. . . . I walked through the Division Lobby in a bemused state, hardly grasping that the Government was actually in the throes of a crisis.'[28]

On the day itself Wilson told his Press Secretary to inform the parliamentary lobby correspondents that 'you've got a little story that might interest them'. It certainly did, coming completely out of the blue.

The election of a successor to Harold Wilson as Labour Party Leader – there were six candidates altogether – went to three ballots and took almost three weeks to complete, during which time Harold Wilson remained the Prime Minister. Then on 5 April the result of the final ballot was announced – 176 for James Callaghan, 133 for Michael Foot – and within an hour the victor received a telephone call at Transport House from Buckingham Palace. 'When would it be convenient for you to come to the Palace?' enquired Sir Martin Charteris.

Over a period of forty years Elizabeth II has known, and kept, more secrets than any other person in the land. She has known what one Prime Minister tells her in confidence, and has not let on to the Prime Minister who follows. She has had this unique relationship with the eight most powerful men in Great Britain, and the one woman Prime Minister who will go down in history as possibly the greatest peacetime Prime Minister of them all. But in their time, in their various ways, they have gone, and she has stayed. She has built up a storehouse of impressions and knowledge and, by general consent, she has attained a remarkable wisdom. She has warned, she has advised, and she has undoubtedly encouraged. But she has always known her place.

According to what they have written and said, there appears to be not a single one of her Prime Ministers who has not genuinely admired and respected Elizabeth II. Indeed, they appear not to have a speck of criticism to utter, either in public or in private. Neil Kinnock has known the Queen as the Leader of the Opposition in the House of Commons, but they have still to come to know one another as sovereign and first minister. It will be interesting to see if a relationship is to develop there. According to Roy Hattersley, Kinnock's Deputy and Shadow Home Secretary, 'his views on monarchy are very like mine. He thinks it works. He will fit in very well as Prime Minister.'[29]

As for John Major, since the day he succeeded Margaret Thatcher and moved his office into 10 Downing Street in November 1990, he will no doubt have discovered, as did all his predecessors, that the three-minute drive up Birdcage Walk to Buckingham Palace concentrates the mind most wonderfully.

In typical style, the historian A.J.P. Taylor put it succinctly: 'In normal times the Queen has no important political duty except to give audience to the Prime Minister once a week. To make the Prime Minister explain himself is a useful task, often beyond the wit of parliament to accomplish.'[30]

12

A Special Relationship

❦

I t was one of those rare occasions when Elizabeth II was gracing a performance of the opera at Covent Garden. Although she has her own
box, and by tradition takes her own servants, food and refreshment
for the intermission, opera appeals to the Queen about as much as it
does to the great majority of her subjects. However, on this occasion, she
had come in a semi-official capacity. Signora Leona, the wife of the
Italian President, was on a visit to London, and an opportunity to see
and hear Rossini's *La Cenerentola*, conducted by the principal con-
ductor of La Scala, Milan – the great Claudio Abbado – could not be
passed up.

Following the performance, the Italian Ambassador invited special
guests back to his embassy in Grosvenor Square for a light supper
(Italian style). James Callaghan, at the time Foreign and Commonwealth
Secretary, was among the guests. A keen concert-goer, he was particularly pleased to be introduced, with his wife Audrey, to Toscanini's
daughter.

At the supper, the Foreign Secretary was placed next to the Queen,
and took the opportunity to describe the recent visit by Lord Greenhill,
a former Head of the Diplomatic Service, to Rhodesia. Greenhill's report, Callaghan told the Queen, suggested to him that a follow-up visit
might be worthwhile to help towards a possible settlement between the
white rebel Prime Minister Ian Smith and the black African leaders. On
the other hand, it might be better to let things simmer for the time being.
He was still considering the matter, he said.

The next afternoon, by the hand of Sir Martin Charteris, Mr Callaghan received a letter from the Queen. She had reflected on the conversation of the previous evening and 'she recognizes that any initiative you take may prove ineffective, but nonetheless believes it would be worthwhile to make the effort. Her Majesty sends you her best wishes for your efforts in dealing with this intractable problem.'[1]

In the mind of the Foreign Secretary, the Queen's opinion was enough to tip the scales. A message and a clear proposal were sent to Smith almost immediately.*

Lord Callaghan, as he became, points to the incident in his memoirs as giving substance 'to the text-book principle that the function of a constitutional monarch is to warn, advise and encourage her ministers.

'The Queen's very perceptive understanding comes not only from many years spent reading Foreign Office documents, but also from her numerous meetings with successive Commonwealth leaders and her regular overseas tours. These have given her a knowledge of Commonwealth politicians and politics unequalled by any member of the Diplomatic Service or any British politician.'

Sir William Heseltine, the Queen's former Private Secretary, speaks of an occasion – the Heads of Government conference at Lusaka in 1979 – when the Queen's calm approach, it is generally agreed, not only played an important part in cooling African anger over the Rhodesian question but also helped to 'play-in' Britain's first woman Prime Minister, who had been in office for less than three months.

'Even before the Queen arrived in Zambia,' Sir William recalls, 'there was a slight argument about whether she should be there. Mrs Thatcher wondered whether the dangers were not such as to make it unwise for her to go. But that was an occasion when the Queen's view of her role prevailed. The Prime Minister acknowledged that the Queen had a special position of her own to preserve, and it would have been unfortunate, to put it no higher, if the Queen had had to say "Sorry, but I'm not coming to your Heads of Government meeting because I'm told by my British Prime Minister that it is not safe." '[2]

The Queen had her own villa in Lusaka, in an area where all the Commonwealth leaders were staying. But she also had two houses at the conference site. One was her office, and the other was where she could rest. Throughout the conference a steady stream of national leaders called on her to discuss their worries and woes. (One of them even felt he had to go back because he had forgotten to say goodbye to Mr Bennett, the Queen's Page.) President Kaunda of Zambia probably expressed the

* An illegal declaration of independence by Southern Rhodesia on 11 November 1965, was finally terminated on 12 December 1979. Following elections in February 1980 the country obtained independence as the Republic of Zimbabwe, and became a member of the Commonwealth.

views of everyone: 'Queen Elizabeth, as always at these conferences, was a tower of strength for us. . . . First and foremost, leaders in the Commonwealth, of all sorts of different political thought, are agreed on one thing. They can *trust* her.'[3]

The effect that the Queen's presence had on the conference was an eye-opener for Margaret Thatcher, who had hinted earlier that the Rhodesian problem might be helped by trying to get recognition for the internal settlement and the lifting of sanctions. The historian Lord Blake, interviewed by Michael Charlton in a series of programmes for BBC Radio 3 in 1988, was clear about the Queen's influence: 'Her presence, undoubtedly, did make it a great deal more difficult for Margaret Thatcher to adhere to what was, in fact, the official policy of the Conservative Party, and the party manifesto. . . . One can only surmise – and one understands, and one gets to be told by various people who do seem to *know* – that the Queen herself is very "multiracial" minded, and is by no means a believer in "white ascendancy". Very far from it.'

Sir Shridath 'Sony' Ramphal, the Guyanian who was the Secretary-General of the Commonwealth from 1975 to 1990, and who has guided the Queen around many multiracial receptions, believes that she has a modern approach to multiracial society. 'She is not hung-up about race, and there is no disguise to penetrate. She will react to individuals as individuals. Whether she's talking to a white person or a black person, she's talking to a person. Everyone will tell you that. The Queen is above all happy in Commonwealth company. She is relaxed. She knows she is loved.'*[4]

The Lusaka conference ended with a decision to set up a constitutional conference in London with the purpose of bringing Rhodesia to independence. Margaret Thatcher had arrived in Zambia sceptical but, in no small part due to the Queen, left Lusaka in high spirits. After conducting her round the dance floor, President Kaunda assured the world that 'the Iron Lady has brought a ray of hope on the dark horizon'.[5]

Elizabeth II is Head of State in Great Britain. She is also Head of the Commonwealth, a conglomerate comprising fifty nations spread around the world. She is Queen of sixteen of these countries – the remainder being republics. The alliance is a huge, disparate, and complicated structure, which can give rise to many questions. For instance, if the Queen is in Australia, say, and the Australian Prime Minister gives advice which is contrary to that of the British Prime Minister, which advice should she take? According to some experts there would be a pre-eminence given to

* Even though it operates an equal opportunity policy, Buckingham Palace employs few black or Asian people, and none in a senior position. 'I think the Queen would be uneasy about doing something for the sake of making a gesture', says Sir Shridath. 'When it happens, as it will, there will be a naturalism about it.'[6]

the views of the Australian Prime Minister. And if a Commonwealth country wished to invite its Head to a meeting within its own country, and the British Prime Minister objected, whose will would prevail? It has never been made clear who can advise the Queen to attend a Commonwealth summit meeting held somewhere other than in Britain. Constitutionally, the British Prime Minister has a perfect right to advise the Queen not to leave Britain, but thus far none has actually insisted.

For millions of the Queen's subjects, the Commonwealth is something of a cosy mystery – like granny's youth. For millions of others it is an anachronism at a time when Britain's ties with Europe are being drawn ever tighter. For Elizabeth II herself the Commonwealth remains something very personal. She sees it almost in sentimental terms as a family of nations, of mixed race and creed, which she has known intimately ever since she was a child, and which, by sticking together through thick and thin, offers the rest of the world an example of informal unity. She has often expressed the ideal that 'we have been entrusted with something very special ... a potent force for good and one of the true unifying bonds in this torn world.'

At the same time Elizabeth II the pragmatist is fully aware of the political and economic alliances that are shifting the world around like the plates in some grinding geological evolution. 'I think the Queen still attaches great importance to the Commonwealth,' said a Palace aide, 'but sometimes one has the feeling that there are not all that many other people in London who feel as strongly about it as we do, apart that is from those in Marlborough House.'* Does the Queen still get excited about visiting somewhere such as Australia? 'I think she contains her excitement at the thought of visiting anywhere these days,' replied the same courtier drolly.

The modern Commonwealth, (the grandiose title 'British Commonwealth of Nations' died long ago), evolved out of the old empire, when once upon a time 13 million square miles of the world map were coloured in the familiar pink of the British Empire and 360 million people owed allegiance to a British monarch. In the beginning there were the original countries of white settlement: Canada, Australia, New Zealand and South Africa - dominions with a large degree of self-government. Then there was also the vast sub-continent of India, an empire in its own right since 1876. Scattered across the globe were the Crown colonies – acquired by fair means or foul for the improvement of trade or protection of trade routes. Finally there were the Middle East protectorates,

---

* Queen Mary's old home in The Mall was made available by the Queen in 1964 as the headquarters of the Commonwealth Secretariat, an organizational body with a staff of 232. In July 1991 the Nigerian Emeka Anyaoku completed his first year in the post of Secretary-General.

such as Egypt and Sudan, Palestine, Jordan and Iraq. 'We were, all of us, once citizens of Rome,' the former Prime Minister of Singapore, Lee Kuan Yew, was fond of saying.[7] But Elizabeth II, very early on in her reign, was anxious to persuade people that 'the Commonwealth bears no resemblance to the Empires of the past. It is an entirely new conception ... built on the highest qualilties of the spirit of man: friendship, loyalty and the desire for freedom and peace.'

To bolster this lofty ambition she was prepared to spend months away from home, visiting far-away places that her father and grandfather had only known as pinpoints on a map. Well before she reached the age of sixty-five Elizabeth II had become the most widely travelled monarch in history. In all she had visited eighty-eight different countries. The most favoured were Canada – thirteen visits – and Australia – eleven – where, in both cases, she is still Head of State. In 1985 she reached a particular milestone when she set foot in Belize, the last remaining member of the fifty Commonwealth nations that she had not visited.

A question sometimes asked, *sotto voce*, by foreign diplomats at Commonwealth social functions such as cocktail parties, is how is it that Her Majesty can be Head of the Commonwealth and not the sovereign head of every Commonwealth country?

The answer lies, first, in the Balfour Declaration of 1926 which defined the Commonwealth countries as being 'autonomous communities ... equal in status, in no way subordinate one to another in any aspect of their domestic or external affairs, though united by a common allegiance to the Crown and freely associated as members of the British Commonwealth of Nations.'

That particular piece of legal rigmarole was all very fine in the days when ideas of empire and the Raj were still hanging on like tinsel in the house after Christmas. But then there came the Second World War, and after that the demands for independence by millions of people who, even so, seemingly thought enough of their former rulers to wish to continue some kind of informal association and friendship. When India, the jewel in Britain's crown, gained independence in 1949 and became a republic, it was carefully arranged, mainly through Lord Mountbatten and Pandit Nehru, that the newly born state should retain a powerful tie by remaining a member of the Commonwealth on the basis of its 'acceptance of the King as the symbol of the free association of its independent member nations *and as such the Head of the Commonwealth.*'

Few people realize that any country can apply to become a member of the Commonwealth and, provided that the other club members agree, there is no bar to its joining. Even Japan once considered applying. Two countries, Nauru and Tavalu, are special members with the right to participate, but not to attend Commonwealth summit meetings.

However, the title of Head of the Commonwealth is not automatically vested in the Crown. So when Elizabeth II came to the throne, member nations had to vote her in, so to speak. And presumably the same will happen with Prince Charles when he becomes King, assuming, that is, that the Commonwealth is still a going concern at that time.

It may turn out to be a harder job to gain unanimity over the title than was the case in 1953, although even then there were a few voices raised in the House of Commons against certain proposals in the Royal Titles Bill. One of those voices belonged to Enoch Powell, a noble-faced gadfly on the back of British political history these past forty years, able to irritate public consciousness but not always to direct political action, who had entered politics after the war specifically with a desire to save the Empire.

Among Powell's several objections to the Royal Titles Bill was the abandonment of the word 'British' before 'Commonwealth'. 'Why is it that this "teeming womb of Royal Kings", as the dying Gaunt calls it, wishes now to be anonymous?'[8] he asked the House of Commons.

Today, almost forty years later, Powell still holds fervent allegiance to his country and his monarch – quite apart from being a member of the privy council – but still asserts that the reason that 'the humbug of the Commonwealth' was entertained at all 'was because the Brits wanted to persuade themselves that nothing had really altered. They had not really lost their great and glorious empire. It had simply been transformed into something more great and glorious still.

'I think that one might also suspect – though this would be unworthy – that the illusion of a worldwide empire perhaps dies as hard with the descendants of George V as it does with some of their subjects.'[9]

Lord Charteris, as he takes a pinch of snuff, describes the Commonwealth as 'the most civilized and sophisticated manner hitherto discovered of dismembering an empire. But it is also a great association of nations which is multiracial, multilingual, and with absolutely no political creed. My contention is that what's good – and there's a lot that's good, and a lot that's not much good – has been "midwifed" by the Queen.'

Critics point to the number of countries in the Commonwealth that are governed by dictatorships, often the result of military coups. Simon Jenkins who, before he became the editor of *The Times*, (once a veritable broadsheet of Empire), wrote in his weekly column in the *Sunday Times* that 'The Commonwealth embraces countries with some of the worst human rights in the world.' He singled out Nigeria, Zambia, Guyana, Malaysia and Tanzania – 'not one democracy among them!' This particular column appeared while both the Queen and Mrs Thatcher were attending the 1989 Commonwealth Leaders conference in Malaysia, and Mr Jenkins urged that, in future, British Prime Ministers should simply decline to attend these biennial meetings. 'We should offer to return either when it [the Commonwealth] renounces all political posturing or when it expels all members who refuse to hold multiparty elections, release political prisoners and end press censorship. The Commonwealth would then be tiny, but it might restore some credit to a body to which the Queen so closely lends her dignity.'

Sir Shridath S. Ramphal responds to the suggestion in this way: 'One doesn't have to be an apologist for things that are bad in Commonwealth countries to realize that there is value in just using the Commonwealth facility to promote international understanding, while at the same time working to get these things right. After all, there is no Prime Minister without flaw, and Britain has a long record of not choosing its friends by moral or ethical standards. One of my complaints, when I had been urging the Commonwealth to take a stand against General Amin was that Downing Street was the first doorstep that he crossed after his *coup d'état* in Uganda.'[10]

Somehow, in Commonwealth politics just as in domestic politics, the Queen has managed never to show that she is taking one side or the other – but in Commonwealth affairs she is at an advantage. Because the Foreign Office does not come into it in the way that it does with countries that are outside the Commonwealth, the Queen in a sense can think of the Commonwealth in terms of being her own domain, or if not her domain, then her extended family in which she is regarded with varying degrees of love, tolerance, awe, or boredom. But not yet as totally irrelevant.

Anyone who has witnessed the reception given to the Queen on practically any of her visits to Commonwealth countries (Quebec province in Canada might be an exception), can vouch for her popularity among the vast majority of local people. It is not the flag-waving that one sees – most of the flags that the school children wave so enthusiastically have been handed out anyway. And it is not the novelty of the occasion that draws the crowds – that applies more to visits by the younger members of the Queen's family. The Queen's attraction lies especially in the *sense* of occasion that she and the Duke of Edinburgh engender, coupled with a feeling of meeting old friends that you have known, but probably not seen, for ages. The unlikely temptation is to ask if they have time to stop for tea. Some of the people may be being fooled by some of the governments, but this joyousness at seeing the Queen is genuine. After all, the very old among them can remember her father, and still ask after her mother. Those of her own age have watched her grow up from a teenager, and seen her marry and have children and grandchildren of her own. Her Christmas broadcasts are Christmas cards, and when she comes to visit she finds herself festooned with flowers and gifts.

The rules about giving presents to royal visitors have changed very little since the 1950s when Sir Michael Adeane would send out a 6,000-word list of 'do's and don'ts' in advance to hosts. The document advised, for instance, that the presentation of a live animal is not really welcome (although the Queen has been known to accept a horse or two over the years), and when refusal of a present might offend, as it might have done in the Gambia in 1961 when the Queen was offered a baby crocodile in a pierced silver biscuit tin. Then staff may be called in to assist - in this instance her Private Secretary had to keep the reptile in his bath overnight.

Like any sensible traveller, Elizabeth II goes forth on her foreign tours armed with personal comforts; in her own case a monogrammed electric kettle, a pillow (although both she and Prince Philip, through long practice, say they can sleep anywhere) and bottles of Malvern water, which are protection against upset stomachs as much as anything.

Reporting on a visit to Brazil in 1968, the writer Andrew Duncan noted on the Queen's luggage list the inclusion of three tins of Dundee cake, six packets of shortbread, and three jars each of Tiptree raspberry and Chivers strawberry jam. At the Commonwealth Heads of Government meeting in Kuala Lumpur in 1989, Mr Edwin Le Prince, assigned by the Malaysian government to attend on the royal guests, noted that the Queen had brought her own supply of Earl Grey tea, coffee and marmalade. And she was evidently very attentive to Prince Philip. When it came to afternoon tea, 'we would have to lay the table and boil the water, but she would cut the bread and mix his tea for him'. It was also observed that, in contrast to her customary behaviour at an official banquet, the Queen scraped her plate clean when she dined in private.[11]

Those close to them say that both the Queen and Prince Philip probably enjoy most their visits to the smaller Commonwealth countries, where they can expect to be surprised by the sometimes unrehearsed behaviour and the genuine unsophisticated warmth of the people – and where, possibly, there is less chance of their eating habits being spied on!

Over a period of many years the tropical islands of Fiji were among the Queen's favourite places to visit. She always looked forward to returning there, ever since her first visit in December 1953 when she was given a ritual welcome by native chiefs, who presented her with a necklace of whales teeth (long before the Save the Whale campaign was even dreamed of), and offered her a coconut shell of the local brew, *kava*, which, as always on such occasions, she sipped tentatively and with great curiousity. She returned to the islands in 1963, 1970 and 1982. She sent Prince Charles, aged twenty-two, to witness Fiji's independence celebrations in October 1970 and the formal lowering of the Union Jack.* Princess Anne also visited the enchanting group of islands and heard her

* Fiji was a British colony from 1874 until 1970.

mother respectfully referred to by the Fijian chiefs as the Great Chief.*
All the royal family loved the place and its people, in much the same way
as the British tend to fall in love with a holiday home. They even kept a
shark carved in driftwood on board the royal yacht *Britannia* as a
memento of happy days in Fiji.

Fiji opted to remain a member of the Commonwealth after negotiating
its own independence, and for seventeen years, from a distance of some
12,000 miles, those in London who took an interest imagined that everyone was fairly happy. Then, on 14 May 1987, following a general election
the previous month, the roof fell in.

At 10am, local time, an army colonel accompanied by ten soldiers with
machine guns walked into the parliament building in Suva and
announced: 'This is a military take-over. Stay down and remain calm.'
The troops then proceeded to bundle the Prime Minister and twenty-
seven members of his coalition government into army trucks and drove
them away.

The coup took place at 11pm, London time, and the Queen learned of
it at 1.30pm the following day, on returning from a visit to the Royal
Engineers in Chatham. She was most surprised. *The Times* reported a
Fijian of long standing as saying: 'It is just so out of character with what
we have come to expect.' And an Englishman on a study exchange visit
noted: 'I only saw one soldier, and he was shopping.'[12]

It was a very gentle revolution, but nonetheless real for all that, and
very worrying. The Queen did not like to see stirrings of this sort among
her peoples.

The background to the coup was race. Of Fiji's population of 714,000,
46 per cent were comprised of Melanesian Fijians and 48 per cent of eth-
nic Indians. The Indian population had been introduced in the last
century, with the arrival of a boatload of five hundred, imported by the
British to invigorate the sugar and copra industries. When the now
deposed Prime Minister, Timoci Bavadra, had been elected just a month
previously, it marked the end of sixteen years of rule by the party domi-
nated by Melanesian Fijians.

The person responsible for the coup was Lt.-Col. Sitiveni ('Steve')
Rabuka, an extremely good-looking man of thirty-eight who had been
trained at the Royal Military Academy, Sandhurst, and been made an
officer of the Order of the British Empire by the Queen in 1981, in part
for 'his imagination and innovation' in confronting and restraining the
operations of the PLO.† He showed prowess also on the rugby field,
playing for his country. Indeed, one of the first communications he re-

---

* In Papua New Guinea the Queen is known as 'Mama belong big family'.
† Palestine Liberation Organization.

ceived from the outside world after his coup was from officials expressing the hope that he and his national team would still be able to take part
in the World Cup matches due to begin in New Zealand and Australia
the following Friday.

Elizabeth II followed events closely from London through her
Governor-General in Fiji, the highly respected Ratu Sir Penaia Ganilau,
GCMG, KVCO, KBE, DSO, whom she had known as a friend for many
years. She sent a personal message to Ganilau which he saw fit to use
when he broadcast to his people: 'The Queen wishes you to know how
much she admires your stand as her personal representative in Fiji and
the guardian of the constitution. Her Majesty is following developments
with the closest attention and hopes that you will keep in touch. We are
here to help if we can.'[13] It could have been a letter from a mother to a
troubled son. The fact that it was broadcast by the radio station taken
over by the military – Colonel Rabuka had by now been dubbed
'Rambo' Rabuka in the West – suggested that at this stage he was anxious
to observe loyalty to the Crown and retain Fiji's place within the Commonwealth.

Ganilau announced that he was assuming authority in the name of the
Queen. But Rabuka's first act was to appoint his own council of mini-
sters, which included Ratu Sir Kamisese Mara, an elder statesman of the
Pacific and a tribal chief of enormous stature – who had been educated at
Oxford. Back in London, *The Times*'s pocket cartoonist Cal greeted the
news of the coup with one person saying to another, 'Saves all the bore
of having a general election'.[14] This was at the time when Margaret
Thatcher was gearing up for her third election victory.

Eventually, and most reluctantly, the Governor-General accepted
Rabuka as chairman of a new governing council, while at the same time
maintaining that his ousting of the elected Prime Minister and his
government was an unlawful act – which it clearly was. What everyone,
including the Queen, wished to avoid was violence on the streets. Bob
Hawke, the Australian Prime Minister, watching from much nearer the
sidelines, ruled out military intervention, but still held five warships on
stand-by to evacuate Australians from Fiji if it were found to be necessary.

Then, almost as quickly as it happened, the coup seemed to fizzle out,
just four days after Rabuka had taken his soldiers into the parliament
building. The deposed Prime Minister, Timoci Bavadra, was released and
Rambo Rabuka informed his small army that as the penalty for treason
in Commonwealth countries was death, 'then if this is to be my destiny,
I accept it'. It was all very noble stuff – the kind of which the best children's outdoor games are made – but the Queen was advised that the
crisis might not be over yet.

Sure enough, within twenty-four hours word was received that the Great Council of Tribal Chiefs were considering taking steps to force the Governor-General to accept constitutional change after all. What form these threats might take was not immediately clear, but in London they were viewed seriously enough for the Queen herself to take the very unusual step of personally speaking to her Governor-General in Fiji over a secure radio link.

The uneasy peace was maintained throughout the English summer, Fijian winter. In June, as the result of a general election, Margaret Thatcher swept back into power for a third, and, as it proved, final time with a massive parliamentary majority. In September the Queen was taking her annual break at Balmoral, and preparing for a visit to Canada.

Mr Bavadra told his people in Fiji that he was going to London to see the Queen, without properly realizing that in London very few people, including Commonwealth Prime Ministers, secure an audience with the Queen without prior invitation. When he arrived in England, only to be informed that he would not be granted an audience of Her Majesty, he felt most put out. To his people back at home, talking to her Private Secretary would not seem the same at all.

Sir Shridath Ramphal, as Commonwealth Secretary-General, was fortunately placed. 'I was able to sit Bavadra down and explain to him that he had put the Queen in an impossible situation. For her to see him now would make it appear that she was interfering in the politics of Fiji. But I advised him that he should not write off the opportunity of meeting with her Private Secretary, because whatever views he expressed to him would be passed on to the Queen within a day.'[15]

By the middle of September it seemed to those in Buckingham Palace that perhaps, after all, a peaceful solution had been found, one that would satisfy both the native Fijian and Indian populations. Its basis was a bipartisan administration, with the Governor-General becoming President of a republic which remained inside the Commonwealth. It had been worked out after weeks of consultations with the two other countries most concerned after Britain and Fiji itself, that is, namely Australia and New Zealand.

However, just as the Governor-General was about to announce that the Queen welcomed the proposed arrangements, and just as the Queen's Private Secretaries were about to break open the champagne in London, Rabuka staged another coup. For a time the Palace lost contact completely with Ratu Ganilau, but on 29 September it was able to announce that 'The Governor-General has spoken on the telephone this morning to The Queen's Private Secretary and has assured The Queen that he remains at his post.'

There is a strong suggestion that the Queen spoke to Ganilau herself, from her study in Balmoral, and it is nice to speculate that she may even have rushed in from the garden to take the call. At any rate, according to the official statement issued on 29 September, 'The Queen had been pleased to give her support to the political settlement reached last week by the Governor-General and the two parties, and much regrets that this process of peaceful change in restoring Fiji to constitutional normality has been overtaken by illegal action and the use of force.' Then came the warning. 'Anyone who seeks to remove the Governor-General from office would, in effect, be repudiating his allegiance and loyalty to the Queen.'

After going on to say how much she hoped, even now, that the process of restoring Fiji to constitutional normality might be resumed, the Queen spoke of how 'deeply saddened' she would be if the bonds of mutual affection and loyalty between the British monarchy and the Fijian people were to be severed.

Senior Members of the Queen's Household at the time cannot recall a single other occasion when Elizabeth II has made known so publicly her feelings on a matter of constitutional and political concern. To the casual reader, her choice of words may not seem to be particularly passionate. But for the sovereign to take sides at all is extremely unusual, if not actually bordering on the unconstitutional. That she chose to issue such a statement, to be followed by another a few days later, is an indication of the strength of her feeling. A sentence from a leader in *The Times* may have echoed her fears: 'Yesterday's events are more than a test for Fiji. They are a test for senior members of the Commonwealth.'[16]

From this point on, events moved swiftly.

After being told by the Governor-General that he would not be given sanction to run the country on his own, Colonel Rabuka declared: 'If a republic is the only solution, so be it.'

On 29 September it was reported that the Governor-General had refused to step down, or accept the presidency of a republic under a new constitution. 'I will only leave dead, or in irons', he declared.

On 6 October, while Britain was becoming embroiled in controversy over the introduction of the Community Charge Bill, Rabuka declared Fiji a republic – a state which was not recognized by the British government.

On 15 October, however, while on a visit to Canada – another Commonwealth country with a French problem – the Queen received a message from her faithful Governor-General in Fiji finally prefacing the end of a link between the Crown and the beautiful islands that had endured for 113 years.

Your Majesty,

With humble duty I wish to submit to you the following advice, acting in my capacity as your Representative in Fiji. Owing to the uncertainty of the political and constitutional situation in Fiji, I have now made up my mind to request Your Majesty to relieve me of my appointment as Governor-General with immediate effect. This I do with the utmost regret; but my endeavours to preserve constitutional government in Fiji have proved in vain, and I can see no alternative way forward.

With deepest respect,
Penaia Ganilau.

Govenor-General[17]

It was all over. In a statement issued from the Four Seasons Hotel in Vancouver, Elizabeth II accepted that it must be for the people of Fiji to decide their own future, and prayed that peace might obtain among the people of all races in that country. Then she saw fit to add that 'Her Majesty is sad to think that the ending of Fijian allegiance to the Crown should have been brought about without the people of Fiji being given an opportunity to express their opinion on the proposal.'*

Apart from the Queen's personal sadness at losing one of the family, so to speak, the crisis in Fiji raises the interesting question, which may increasingly concern overseas realms of Elizabeth II – such as Canada and Australia – of how far they can maintain a monarchial government with a monarch who is thousands of miles away, and in other ways, too, is becoming more and more remote.

In an interview with the author in 1981, Prince Philip said that he thought that the British would always have a personal interest in the Commonwealth because many of them had relatives living in Commonwealth countries. 'They probably read more about Australia, Canada, and New Zealand than they do about what's going on in Europe.' That is unlikely to be still the situation today.

Of course there are some, Enoch Powell being notable among them, who are convinced that in any case there is an ultimate conflict between being the sovereign of the United Kingdom and being the Head of other countries which are not represented in the British parliament. 'A

---

* On 5 December 1987, Ratu Sir Penaia Ganilau was appointed President of Fiji by an Executive Council of Ministers headed by Colonel Rabuka. Ganilau called upon Ratu Sir Kamisese Mara to form another interim administration to work towards a more permanent resolution and, as at June 1989, Rabuka, now promoted to Major-General, was in charge of Home Affairs, the National Youth Service and the Auxiliary Army Services. Fiji's membership of the Commonwealth lapsed.

sovereign who believes that he or she has powers independent of the advice of ministers, or of an elected assembly,' says Mr Powell, 'is a constitutional monstrosity.'[18] He asserts that in the case of Fiji the Queen came perilously close to behaving in a manner which, constitutionally, she would have been barred from doing in Britain.

It comes as no surprise to be informed by one of the Queen's former advisers that this is not the view taken at the Palace.

However, the role of the Governor-General – the sovereign's representative in realms overseas – does from time to time cause ructions, even within the Palace. The most famous example concerned the sacking of Mr Gough Whitlam, the Labour Prime Minister of Australia, in 1975. When he came to power the Queen and he were not well acquainted, and Elizabeth II was more than slightly taken aback when she heard rumours that he intended to abolish the singing of the national anthem and inform those concerned that they would no longer be required to take oaths of loyalty to their sovereign.

Elizabeth II promptly instructed her Private Secretary to make an appointment with the Australian High Commissioner in London in order to point out to him that, while Mr Whitlam was acting quite within his entitlement as Prime Minister, if he were to do anything which affected the Queen's position as the Queen of Australia, Her Majesty 'would be extremely grateful if he would have the courtesy to tell me before he does it'.

Within three days Buckingham Palace heard that Mr Whitlam was soon coming to England and would be pleased if the Queen could see her way to giving him audience on Good Friday. There were some fears that he might be coming in order to inform the Queen of his government's intention to declare Australia a republic. But apparently this was never the case. He was more interested in mending fences. The Queen and he sat down to dinner on Good Friday, and it seems that the big man was yet another who was willingly captivated by her charm and good sense.

However, three years later things got a little rough out in Australia and the Queen was woken one morning with some quite extraordinary news. Her Governor-General had sacked the Prime Minister!

Although the titular Head of State of sixteen other countries apart from Britain, the sovereign delegates her active prerogative powers in these countries to the Governor-General, who is nominated on the advice of the Prime Minister of the land. Sir John Kerr, the son of a boiler-maker, was Gough Whitlam's choice. But this made no difference when Kerr decided to oust Whitlam from office.

Whitlam had a majority in the Lower House in Canberra, but the Upper House, the Senate, in November 1975, decided to thwart him by deferring money bills. This its members could do – unlike the British

House of Lords which had been reformed in 1911. Whitlam refused to call an election to settle the matter and so, in anticipation of ending the deadlock, Sir John Kerr invoked the 'reserve powers' of the royal prerogative and proclaimed the Prime Minister dismissed. He ended his official proclamation with the words 'God Save the Queen', to which Gough Whitlam, standing on the steps of Parliament House, added: 'Well may he say "God Save the Queen", because nothing will save the Governor-General.'[19]

Back in London Elizabeth II was aware of what had been going on over the weeks, partly because governor-generals report directly to the monarch and not to the Foreign Office. But, in the final drama, events moved so swiftly that there was hardly time for Kerr to keep the Palace abreast of what was going on. Besides, when the crisis came it was night-time in London and the Queen was a-bed.

Sir Martin Charteris was woken from his sleep, having not long returned from the Lord Mayor's Banquet at Mansion House, to be assailed by Whitlam's booming voice from 12,000 miles away. 'This is the Member for Werriwa speaking.' He was thus making the point, though perhaps it would not have been immediately clear to Sir Martin, or any other Englishman in the middle of the night, that he could no longer speak as Prime Minister of Australia but only for his constituency. 'If I didn't already know, he thought I should be informed', Lord Charteris recalls. 'Of course I didn't know, and he didn't ask me to do anything, which I was very glad about. I said I did not intend informing Her Majesty until the morning.'[20] When he did, the Queen was most surprised at the news. 'Have they all lost their heads!' was her comment.

According to Robert Lacey, in his book *Majesty*, Whitlam might have won the day and remained Prime Minister if he had telephoned Buckingham Palace before he was sacked and advised the Queen formally to dismiss the Governor-General. He was perfectly entitled to do so, and the Queen might have been hard pressed not to act on his advice. But she would not have acted instantly, without taking further opinion, and presumably Whitlam was not aware that his head was to be removed until the very last moment, when Kerr poised the axe.

What the episode does underline again are the problems that occasionally arise when you have a Head of State on one side of the world, where it is night, and a country making decisions in broad daylight while its sovereign sleeps. Many Australians were infuriated by Kerr's action, which did nothing to enhance the monarchial system in Australia. But, as he told the Queen on a subsequent visit to London, he had acted out of loyalty and he had not given intimation of his intention, because he wished to keep the Queen out of the controversy. 'Governor-Generals are expendable,' he explained, 'the Queen is not.' Even so, he did not resign.

More recently, the invasion of Grenada, eighty miles north of Trinidad, by the United States in 1983, demonstrated the problems of communication, even with the sophisticated modern communication methods available. That it should be America, the special relation, that landed on one of the Queen's possessions, without so much as a 'by your leave', was for many people temporarily unforgivable.*

President Ronald Reagan in his memoirs, *An American Life*, reveals how he was called out of a briefing to take a call from Margaret Thatcher. 'As soon as I heard her voice, I knew she was very angry ... She asked me in the strongest language to call off the operation. Grenada, she reminded me, was part of the British Commonwealth, and the United States had no business interfering in its affairs ... She was very adamant and continued to insist that we cancel our landings in Grenada. I couldn't tell her that it had already begun.'

Casper Weinberg, the American Defence Secretary, was in the next-door room. 'At the conclusion of that conversation, the President returned with a rather rueful look on his face, which made clear that even his persuasive powers had limits, and that he had not convinced the Prime Minister.'[21]

According to Palace sources, the Queen was not as obviously upset about the crisis in Grenada as she had been about the coups in Fiji. But she let it be known to her Prime Minister that she was just as angry, nonetheless. It is said that she first heard of the coup on the television news, and that when her Private Secretary telephoned Number 10 to summon Mrs Thatcher he was told that she was a little tied up at the moment. A second stiffer summons only a few minutes later had the Prime Minister hurrying out to her car, and when the two women met the Queen is supposed to have made her displeasure known by conducting the audience with her first minister while both of them remained standing.

It says a great deal about the Queen's loyalty to friends of old that where others in positions of power may have more or less written off the Commonwealth as an outworn idea, she has not. When she came to the throne as a young woman of twenty-six, she expressed her feelings on the subject in her first ever Christmas broadcast. 'My father and grandfather before him worked all their lives to unite our people ever more closely, and to maintain the ideals of the Commonwealth which were so

---

* In October 1983, disagreements within Grenada's 'people's revolutionary government' led to the Prime Minister's assassination, the arrest of the Governor-General, and the formation of a revolutionary military council. This in turn led to a request to the United States to intervene, from the Organization of Eastern Caribbean States. A phased withdrawal of American troops from Grenada was completed in June 1985.

near to their hearts. I shall strive to carry on their work.'[22]

When she was thirty-six years old, following a visit to India in 1961, she spoke of a special relationship between the ordinary people of the older Commonwealth countries which would never be weakened. 'This feeling is rapidly spreading throughout the newer members, and in its turn will help us realize the ideal of human brotherhood.'[23]

When she was forty-six years old, and Britain was about to join the European Community, she prophesied that the new links with Europe would not replace those with the Commonwealth. 'Old friends will *not* be lost. Britain will take her Commonwealth links into Europe with her.'[24]

Some twenty years on, there is not much sign that that has happened, although, according to Sir Shridath Ramphal, any blame attached should be laid at Mrs Thatcher's door. 'What she passed up was the strength in Europe that the Commonwealth would have brought her. She went alone, whereas France did not. President Mitterrand took France's over-seas connections with him, so that he stood for more than European France.'[25]

But whatever the role of the Commonwealth in the twenty-first century turns out to be, the Queen's contribution to its existence thus far cannot be overstated. She personally *cares* about the billion people who live – and in the case of millions only eke out their lives – under its umbrella. One or two of her former advisers have sometimes sensed that at the bottom of her heart she may instinctively feel even more for Com-monwealth peoples, on occasion, than she does for Europeans, including the British. Their need may appear to be greater.

In the end the one truth that does emerge, crystal clear, is the Queen's undying devotion to the *idea* of a Commonwealth, with all its faults and hypocrisies. 'We talk of ourselves as a "family of nations",' she has said, 'and perhaps our relations with one another are not so very different from those which exist between members of any family. We know that these are not always easy, for there is no law within a family which binds its members to think, or act, or be alike.'

David Lange, the former Prime Minister of New Zealand, perhaps best summed up the relationship between head and members when he said simply, although perhaps a little inelegantly: 'The Queen is the bit of glue that somehow manages to hold the whole thing together. . . . We, the Commonwealth leaders, do the fighting over the political issues. She does the unifying.'[26]

13

Monarch, Mother, Grandmother

❧

B y the time Elizabeth II reached the age of sixty – the official retirement age for women in Britain – her royal family had increased to almost forty. The clan was so numerous that, within
its circle, it was defined into those who were of chalk and those
who were of cheese. The chalk comprised the Duke of Edinburgh, the
Queen Mother, the Queen's own four children, Princess Margaret and
her two children, Lord Linley and Lady Armstrong-Jones, and, of
course, the Queen's grandchildren, then numbering four.

The cheese comprised the Gloucesters – Princess Alice, the Duke and
Duchess of Gloucester and their children; the Kents – the Duke and
Duchess and their children; Princess Alexandra and the Hon. Sir Angus
Ogilvy, and their children; and Prince and Princess Michael of Kent and
their children. The remainder of the large family was made up of the
Harewoods, the Lichfields, and various other cousins and second
cousins. Prince Philip's German relatives, who liked to come to Windsor
on high days and holidays, made up another group.

Although, like anyone else, the Queen prefers some members of her
family to others (Princess Alexandra is a favourite; Princess Michael is
thought of differently), the division into chalk and cheese has nothing to
do with preference and much to do with accommodation. Windsor, Sandringham and Balmoral may seem vast to the outsider – and they are –
but with guests bringing their nannies for their children, their detectives
for their protection, and their ladies' maids and valets for their con-
venience, the spare rooms are quickly filled.

Because in London the principal royal residences are within less than a mile of one another there is a widespread assumption that the royals are popping into one another's palaces on a fairly regular basis. It is not so. Princess Michael may be able to see into Prince Charles's bedroom from her small roof garden at Kensington Palace, and he may be able to call on his aunt Margaret just by taking a few steps along a covered way, but they are by no means constantly in and out of each other's homes. The Queen sees much less of her children than she used to, now that three of the four are married and have families of their own, and even on an administration level the various Households have surprisingly little contact. A former senior Member of the Queen's Household mentioned that months might go by without his 'bumping into' Prince Charles.

Even so, it may strike the outsider as somewhat odd that the Queen should apparently call on Prince Charles and his wife so seldom, hardly at all, at their London home, and visit Highgrove, in Gloucester, fewer than half a dozen times in ten years. But put this point to a senior courtier and he is quite arch in his relpy: 'Oh but that is because the family is where the Queen is. Whether it be Sandringham, Balmoral, or Windsor, the family congregates around the Queen. She doesn't congregate around them.' Another former Member of the Household thought that 'all the younger members of the family have always been a little in awe of her, as well as being enormously fond of her. I mean to say, if you have to drop a curtsey, it's a reminder of whom you're talking to, isn't it?*

Naturally, some are less in awe than others. The biographer Brian Hoey once asked the Princess Royal if it was difficult for her to maintain a close relationship with her mother, bearing in mind that she was also the sovereign. Princess Anne replied that he had got it wrong. It was much more difficult to remember that she was Queen. 'After all,' she pointed out, 'I've known her longer as a mother than as a queen.'[1]

Mother and daughter by all accounts have grown closer to one another as they have grown older. This was especially evident around the time of Anne's separation from her husband, Mark Phillips, in August 1989, after seventeen years of marriage. The Queen regretted being unable to help in that situation as much as she would have liked, but she showed support and understanding – and no stern criticism – which was a balm. On the whole, friends say she tends to be better at dealing with grown-up problems than with very young people's turmoils.

The Queen is not what used to be called 'a natural mother'. She tends not to coo over babies. You would be unlikely ever to find her sitting in-

---

* Princess Alexandra was touring the 1990 Chelsea Flower Show when she felt a tap on the shoulder and turned round to find herself looking at the Queen. Taken by surprise, after a kiss on each cheek, she remembered to give her cousin the customary curtsey, which should have come first. 'One does get caught out like that sometimes,' said the Queen with a beaming smile.

cognito on a park bench happily watching kiddies on the swings. She was always a much more down-to-earth kind of mother who would play, for a while, but then suggest it was time that everyone 'got out and got on' – usually a horse. She encouraged self-reliance, saying to each of her children when they were old enough to understand, 'The facts are a, b, c, and d. If you want my opinion it is this . . . but you must make up your own mind.'[2]

Prince Philip, despite his reputation for being something of a taskmaster, shared this approach towards young people. 'It's no use saying do this, do that; don't do this, don't do that. You can warn them about certain things – that's about the most you can do – or you can say this is the situation you are in, these are the choices. On balance it looks as if this is the sensible choice, go away and think it over, and come back and let me know what you think.'[3]

When he was still a young man, Prince Charles appreciated his relationship with his parents. 'My parents were marvellous in this way,' he once said, a few years ago now. 'They would outline all the possibilities, and in the end it was up to you. My father had a particularly strong influence, and it was very good for me. I had perfect confidence in his judgement.'[4]

It is always interesting to see how children turn out, and in this respect the Queen's children are no different. Charles as a boy was the arch-conformist, who in middle age is turning out to be an unusual, special kind of rebel. Most people tend to forget that Anne as a teenager, in her leather boots and acid-yellow mini-skirt with the chain belt, was something of a swinger. She was the one who went to the parties, much more than her shy elder brother who tended to stay at home. She once said that if she had been a boy she would like to have gone to sea, assuming she could overcome her seasickness. If she were challenged to do something in particular, 'perhaps the thing I might do best is be a long-distance lorry driver.' She developed an antipathy towards photographers at an early age. Cecil Beaton recalled how he dealt with a recalcitrant ten-year-old Anne who was averse to having her photograph taken in Buckingham Palace. 'You hate it, I know. But hate it by the window, there. Hate it looking this way, hate it looking that way, hate it in profile. Now *detest* it looking straight at the camera.'[5]

The Queen's 'second family', so called because Andrew and Edward arrived ten and fourteen years respectively after Anne, grew up to a certain extent in the warm shadow of their elder brother and sister. Andrew was named after his paternal grandfather, and was to remain the pride of his father, whom in some ways he resembled. Even as a child Andrew showed signs of being much more straightforward in personality than his elder brother. He was not introspective, and he was troubled by few things except boredom and rivalry. He thrived on action and was determined to emulate his elder brother, whom he worshipped as a child. When Andrew was still a schoolboy, an aide came across the Queen's second son sitting by himself in a room in the Palace, hugging a rugby ball and staring at the blank screen of a television set. Before the aide could utter a word he felt the pain of a rugby football hurled at his solar plexus and from his doubled-up positon could see Andrew's exuberant grin. The Palace staff warmed easily to Andrew. He could be arrogant, but he could also be fun. Footmen particularly appreciated the time when he hit a golf ball richochetting round the picture gallery without damaging a single vase or painting. (One of the footmen had substituted a plastic practice ball with the real thing.)

Andrew followed Charles to Gordonstoun and was much happier than his elder brother with the regime there – it had become a little less spartan by then. Less studious than Charles, he still managed to collect two more A levels than his brother. But he was not interested in following him to university. A career in the Navy held much more appeal. He followed his father and grandfather to the Royal Naval College, Dartmouth, and in 1980 entered the Navy on a twelve-year commission as a trainee helicopter pilot. He took a parachute course at the same time as Charles, and to his great delight progressed more swiftly. After one jump he handed over to his elder brother, making some facetious remark and adding, 'I *am* a card'. It riled Charles. 'One day somebody will teach that young man the meaning of modesty,' he commented to the instructor.[6]

Perhaps Elizabeth II could be accused of spoiling Andrew as a small child. But it was more a case of being won over on the occasions that he was naughty by his cheerful devil-may-care attitude. 'He'll settle down at any school once he finds out that a smile and a bit of charm won't always get him what he wants', said Prince Philip. As it has turned out, of all the Queen's children, Andrew is the one who has probably changed the least as he has grown older. The terrible suffering that he saw as a helicopter pilot during the Falklands conflict in 1982 made a profound lasting impression, and perhaps the cocksuredness is not as evident as it once was. Essentially, he is what he is, a highly regarded and conscientious Naval officer who up until now has been in his element in the close-knit, practical-joking community of the wardroom. Fortunately for both of them, he is married to someone who may be said to share the same zest for life.

The third son of Elizabeth II and Prince Philip, Prince Edward, is not as open and straightforward as Andrew, and has always been more difficult to fathom. The last of the Queen's children, as it transpired, he tended to be almost ignored by the media as a child (which gratified his mother) and even when he reached the age of going out with girls there was never the press clamour around him that there had been with Charles and Andrew. In 1990 he countered long-standing rumours by saying to a *Daily Mirror* reporter at a party in New York, 'It's just outrageous to suggest this sort of thing. It's so unfair to me and my family. How would you feel if someone said you were gay?'[7]

At school age he was generally thought to be the most brainy of the Queen's children, though the four A levels he managed to gain at Gordonstoun were only just sufficient to secure him a place at Jesus College, Cambridge. Like all the Queen's children, he enjoyed the outdoor life and was prompted to accept challenges that others might shy away from. He had qualified for his private pilot's licence even before he left school. But his withdrawal from the Royal Marines midway through a training course, which was to so anger his father in later years, and his organization of a royal family charity romp on television, which was to so irritate his mother, were examples of the streak of stubbornness and individual enterprise which runs through him. Alone among the Queen's children, he was to strike out on a career – in show-business management and production – which departed entirely from the traditional choice for the sons of British monarchs: one or other of the Armed Services.

Christopher Trevor-Roberts, who tutored all the royal children, thinks of Princess Anne and Prince Andrew as being very similar to one another because each showed a strong sense of purpose from an early age. 'They were always a bit more restless than the other two. Anne was more interested in horses than in books, and Andrew found it difficult to concentrate unless he was interested in the subject. When he was, he worked very hard. Charles and Edward, on the other hand, were alike in that they were intent on doing exactly what you told them. At the same time they were very imaginative and loved poetry and literature.'[8]

Mr Trevor-Roberts remembers Edward's courage: 'Practising cricket in the nets at Lords, with Denis Compton, Andrew would bowl very hard at his little brother and sometimes hit him. But Edward was unflinching and would never cry.' And after taking the two boys to the Tutankhamun exhibition in London: 'We went back to the Palace and over tea the Queen asked her children how the outing had gone. Edward could relate everything the guide had said, whereas Andrew just kept up a string of jokes about mummies.'

At that time Mr Trevor-Roberts personally taught many children and some, he recalls, were brought up by parents who gave them every material luxury but with very little emotional warmth. The Queen and Prince Philip's children, in comparison, were 'so beautifully and warmly brought up'. He gives much credit to Mabel Anderson who was 'firm but nice', and sounds like the ideal nanny. She, for her part, has paid tribute to the Duke of Edinburgh who 'was a marvellous father. When the children were younger, he always used to set aside time to read to them, or help them put together those little model toys.'

Bishop Michael Mann admired how the Queen and Prince Philip acted jointly as parents. 'Whenever one of the children went to the Queen with a problem she would always try to bring in their father. "What does your father say about this?" As the Queen, she could so easily have said, "This is what you will do." But she never ignored the father's role.'[9]

The problem for royal children has always been that theirs is a case where both parents go out to work. Long before Princess Diana, the Queen was the most celebrated working mother in the land. Given every assistance admittedly, but at the same time practically barred from ever ringing up a secretary to say that she would not be in today, so cancel all appointments. Royal hours are long and often erratic, and for weeks at a time may demand being out of the country on business. As Princess Alexandra and her husband the Hon. Sir Angus Ogilvy were to discover in 1990 in relation to their daughter Marina, parents – no matter how wealthy or well positioned they are – can sometimes go through purgatory worrying about where and how they might have brought up their children differently, so that they did not so completely rebel later.

One of the principle reasons why Elizabeth II hoped from very early on that it would not be necessary for her son to come to the throne while he was still comparatively young was because she wished that he and his wife could spend more time watching and helping their children through all the stages of growing up.

She once told a friend: 'I came to the throne when I was very young, and I never had the opportunity to bring up my children. The Crown separated them from me. It is something that I have regretted all my life, and I am determined that Charles shall not be put in that position. I want him to be a father to his children, because I was never allowed to be a mother to mine.'

Ideally the Queen would have preferred to have had her own family complete before she came to the throne. As it was not to be, she had Charles and Anne first, and then, seven years after her coronation, Andrew arrived. Even then, it was not a perfect solution to her unique situation. To this day it is not unknown for one or other of the royal children to complain about how difficult it is to get to see Mummy on her own, *and without the dogs*. 'Very often the only time she is free is late at night, and then she is too tired to talk.'

The Queen's corgis and 'dawgies' (an unplanned cross between corgis and dachshunds) are the only almost constant companions of the Queen who are unaware that their mistress is also the sovereign. They form as integral a part of her life as her children and 'when they occasionally fall upon one another,' a courtier relates in a resigned tone of voice, 'whoever is present is expected to haul them apart at whatever risk to hand and foot.'

In common with most mothers, Elizabeth II likes to think that she is always available if any of her children need her – even now, when they are all grown up – although she has always tended not to give advice unless asked. There have been occasions when she must have wished that affairs of State, or merely feeding the dogs, had not come in the way of having a quiet talk with one or other of her family. She is a good listener and a calmer of storms. But, partly because she does not make it her business to be, she is sometimes not fully *au fait* with the undercurrents swirling beneath the outward signs of family solidarity. Sometimes home truths only surface outside of the hothouse of London.

Sandringham and Balmoral, the Queen's private homes, have always been, since childhood, where Elizabeth II can combine relief from the grinding public role with relaxation in the company of her family and friends. Despite being only a few hours from the capital, as opposed to Balmoral which is an overnight train ride away, 'At Sandringham,' the Queen once remarked, 'I feel a great deal more remote than I do at Balmoral.'[10]

Sandringham is for Christmas and winter and the Norfolk fens grass crusted with ice. Balmoral is for summer and autumn, and sometimes the spring too. Both are for rain and Barbours, and Range Rovers and barbecues, and shooting and fishing, and horse riding, and charades after dinner ... and waving away Aunt Margaret's cigarette smoke. The sun does not need always to shine. In fact the Queen is happy in the rain. She is completely in her element in either splendid house. It is a country-house style of life that, despite reports to the contrary, has not completely disappeared from the hidden life of Britain. The Queen just carries it on a little more grandly than some and, paradoxically, in a more simple, homely manner than many who are not as overwhelmingly rich as she is.

The nervous guest who turns up at Sandringham late because of the awful fog on the A10 is likely to be greeted first by the man who takes his car away and parks it, and then by the liveried footman with brass buttons and red waistcoat who takes his coat and mysteriously vanishes, and then by the Queen herself in pastel yellow woolly jumper and tweed skirt who knows how difficult it is to find anywhere in the fog. Although everyone else has already had tea, she sits by the fire with her guest while he enjoys his, and in the sprinkling of a few minutes he is made to feel as relaxed and sparkling as his hostess looks.

Although only a few hours earlier the others in the Queen's house party had appeared a motley crew, rain-stained, red-cheeked, lining up to scrape the mud from their boots after an afternoon's shooting or just walking the labradors, by 8.30pm they are assembled for dinner, bathed and shining in their dinner jackets and party dresses. The late guest, held up by the fog, on being shown to his bedroom in a seemingly far corner of the house, has found his case unpacked, his clothes laid out. There is notepaper embossed with the royal coat of arms in the rack on the desk, with red and black sealing wax and a box of matches to hand. His over-coat is now hanging in the huge mahogany wardrobe, on a wooden hanger with 'E II R' picked out in pokerwork. Each of the books on his bedside table – a selection of crime stories and biographies – has pasted inside the cover the promise that this is 'The Queen's Book'.

Dinner is usually a jolly affair after an exhilarating day in the open air. There is much talk of 'bags' – the number of birds shot – but distraction can come, for instance in the case of the lady guest who insisted on peel-ing her grapes with a knife (Prince Philip tried to demonstrate that this was not entirely necessary by chucking one or two of his own into the air and catching them in his mouth), or in the guest who managed, when being served coffee, to flick the sugar bowl spoon into cartwheels, send-ing crystals dancing over the tablecloth. 'See if you can do that again,' said the Queen, smiling.

The royal family have a penchant for parlour games and charades. Act-ing out 'Give Us a Clue' in the saloon at Sandringham after dinner is a favourite – Princess Anne is generally the quickest at getting the answer. Passing round an orange from under one chin to under another also brings forth howls of laughter, and occasionally acute embarrassment to the person who is not a relative of the sovereign but happens to find him-self sitting next to her.

Prince Andrew has always been the most aggravatingly inventive prac-tical joker in the family. As a child he enjoyed placing whoopee cushions under bums, but after he joined the Royal Navy he returned on leave with slightly more sophisticated ideas of catching people out. While serving on the guided missile destroyer HMS *Edinburgh*, for instance, he experienced first-hand the wheeze of filling folded napkins with dusting powder, and criss-crossing thin fishing lines between wine glasses. When her children were quite small it is said, but has yet to be confirmed, a favourite practical joke of the Queen was a piece of audio equipment placed on or near a lavatory, so that a few moments after a person had sat down a voice was clearly heard to say: 'Do you mind, I'm working down here.'

The Queen's fairy-tale castle in the Scottish Highlands, close to Brae-mar, with its 11,750 acres of grouse moor and five glens spread across 50,000 acres, is for breathing deep the sharp air and feeling a million miles from cares and woes. Both she and the Duke of Edinburgh treasure the ten weeks that they have been spending there each year for the past forty years, and enjoy the house parties who come to stay for perhaps a week at a time. The Queen knows a great many people but has comparatively few friends. A countess described them as 'a fortress of friends – dull but good.' (Needless to say, she is not a very close friend of the Queen herself.) These friends, most of whom she has known for donkeys' years, number no more than twenty to thirty and are unassailably discreet and loyal – discretion and loyalty are the prerequisites of friendship with any of the royals. In the case of the Queen, it is also essential to share an interest in the horse business – racing and raising, as it is called – and preferably have a love of what a courtier termed 'shooting, dogging and stalking'. The Queen has not shot a stag herself for some twelve years or more, but she still invites friends to Balmoral to stalk – a necessary culling procedure, she would argue. According to Lord Home of The Hirsel 'Balmoral is the big rest. The Queen and Prince Philip have no wish to be away from the whole thing [of monarchy] just to have balance. The children of course keep them on the spot and up to date.'

Balmoral is where each of the children learnt to drive, on the miles of private road; where the Queen Mother taught Charles the best spots to fish on the river Dee; where the whole family can come together each year and live together as a family and not as separate entities.

A myth that has gained credence over the years is that Prince Philip uses the annual holiday at Balmoral to preside over a sort of board meeting of the family. Having got them all together in one place, it is said that he reviews the past year, hands out bouquets and brickbats for public behaviour, and proceeds to discuss calendar events for the coming year. It is a nice thought, although in fact nothing as formal takes place.* But is Prince Philip very definitely head of the family, while the Queen is the Head of State? 'I don't think anybody in the family would see it that way', Prince Philip replied when the author put the question to him in an interview in 1986. 'It's run on a sort of committee basis, really.' With Prince Philip as chairman? He smiled. 'Co-chairman. Effectively, everybody talks to everybody else, and decisions are made jointly.'[11]

In November 1977, the Queen and the Duke of Edinburgh became grandparents, when Princess Anne gave birth to a boy who was named Peter after his paternal grandfather. Because both parents wished to lead as independent lives as possible, without neglecting their royal duties in any way, Princess Anne's husband, Captain Mark Phillips, did not take a title as it was expected he might after his marriage. So both he and his two children – Zara Anne Elizabeth Phillips was born in May 1981 – re-

---

* The myth may have grown out of the biannual meetings at Balmoral and Sandringham when Prince Philip originally, and now Prince Charles, chairs meetings of the Factor from Balmoral, the Agent from Sandringham, and the Deputy Ranger of Windsor, to discuss and decide on estate matters.

main commoners. As might be expected, this has made no difference whatsoever to the Queen's outlook as a grandmother. All her grandchildren have given her enormous pleasure and regularly take their holidays at Balmoral. 'The advantage of being a grandmother', Princess Anne once said, 'is that when you feel like it you can be either as nice as you like – or as firm sometimes – without having to take the consequences that day. You can send the children home, or go home yourself.'

Prince Charles has never lost his passion for Balmoral, and is never likely to. Long before Lady Diana Spencer arrived on the scene, one of the Queen's closest aides gave it as his opinion that 'any girl who thinks she can tear Charles away from his autumns at Balmoral and plonk him down instead on some sun-baked beach, has another think coming'. The Princess of Wales has, in fact, managed to persuade her husband to spend two or three bucket-and-spade holidays with their two children at the holiday home of King Juan Carlos of Spain in Majorca. But these escapes to the sun have never lasted for more than a week, and Charles has always managed to get back to bleaker Balmoral for most of his holiday. Try as she might, Diana has never completely settled into the life at the castle, and now that both her children are at school she finally has the perfect excuse for returning to London early, so that she 'can see the boys start their new term'.

When the Queen invited Lady Diana Spencer to stay, first at Sandringham and then at Balmoral in 1980, Members of the Household imagined the nineteen-year-old addition to the house party to be a girlfriend of Prince Andrew. It was a natural assumption for them to make as Lady Diana and the Prince were of about the same age, and the press – although, in the royals' estimation, very rarely reliable in these matters – had come up with a tale of how the young lady had kept a photograph of Andrew on her bedside locker when at finishing school in Switzerland.

Prince Charles was recovering at the time from a love affair with Miss Anna Wallace, a very striking and exciting lady. She was the last of a succession of girlfriends, none of whom seemed to qualify, for one reason or another, as a suitable potential bride of the future king. On the other hand, the young Lady Diana who appeared shy, and was rather podgy and somewhat lacking in serious conversation, 'but a charming gal all the same', did not seem to be quite the sort of person who would appeal to the Prince at that stage in his development. Both the Queen and Prince Philip recognized Charles to be a late maturer, and in their opinion there was still plenty of time for him to decide about marriage. Also deep in the back of their minds may have lain the unbidden thought that if Charles were to come to serious harm because of the dangerous sports and activities that he insisted on taking up, then it would be preferable that he had got these out of his system, so to speak, before marrying and having children. If the very worst occurred, Prince Andrew would become heir to the throne; a prospect which, though they could never have wished it, sources say was not daunting to the Queen nor to Prince Philip.

It seems possible, although it should be put no higher than that, that Queen Elizabeth the Queen Mother and her friend Lady Ruth Fermoy, Diana's grandmother, played a role in bringing Charles and Diana together. Certainly the Queen Mother's comments, which behind the smile can be devastatingly frank at times, would have been listened to intently. Very little that is of importance to the future of the family is ever carried out without consultation with Queen Elizabeth, and her approval is often patiently waited upon. From the time when he was a small boy Charles in particular has always wanted to please his granny. His love of the wonderful old lady practically amounts to adoration. 'Ever since I can remember my grandmother has been the most wonderful example of fun, laughter, warmth, infinite security . . . For me she has always been one of those extraordinarily rare people whose touch can turn everything to gold.'[12]

Lady Ruth Fermoy, Diana's grandmother on her mother's side, had been a close friend of the Queen Mother for many years. The late Lord Fermoy, an Irish peer and Norfolk landowner, was a member of George VI's shooting party on the day before the King died. Subsequently, Lady Fermoy was appointed one of the Queen Mother's permanent ladies-in-waiting, and although confirmation is hard to come by, it seems inconceivable that the two women, wise and romantic, did not discuss the possibility of matching Charles with Diana – much in the same way as Queen Mary and the Countess of Airlie had talked about Philip and Elizabeth a generation before.

However, whereas with Philip and Elizabeth there had been a five-year gap, in the case of Charles and Diana the difference in ages would be nearer thirteen years, and this was a cause of concern to some members of the royal 'inner circle'.

'The Queen is such a level-headed person,' says a courtier who was close to her at this time, 'and she knows that if she tries to force something or oppose something, children are only going to rebel. So I think, in fact, that both she and Prince Philip were jolly glad that Charles had settled on Diana, because he had cast his eye at a good many girls, and when there are dynastic principles at stake there is a sigh of relief when the eventual choice comes from the right stable.'

But is that the same as saying that the Queen and Prince Philip were over the moon about Diana from the very beginning? 'No parent can be completely happy or unhappy', opined the same courtier. 'A child makes his or her choice. You might just as well ask, is a child happy with its parents? It is one of those things over which you have no control really. And therefore common sense dictates that you make the best of the situation, whatever it is, and I think the Queen and Prince Philip have made very much the best of that situation.'

Others, equally qualified to assess, express only a slightly more sanguine opinion. They say that, quite naturally, the family was as thrilled as the nation plainly was to learn of the royal romance. But concern was expressed over Diana's youth and inexperience. Did she really realize what she was letting herself in for by marrying the heir to the throne? Did she have any conception of the relentless, inescapable years of public duty that lay ahead of her? And how would she cope? Prince Charles knew precisely what she would be taking on by marrying him, and this is why he wanted Diana to think carefully about his proposal while she was on holiday in Australia with her mother and stepfather, before the official announcement of the engagement was made on 24 February 1981.

Were they in love, asked Grania Forbes, the Press Association court correspondent, at the obligatory engagement day interview with the couple? 'Of course', said Diana instantly, in that bright, youthful way she has.

'Whatever "in love" means', added Prince Charles curiously.* It seemed almost as if he were bemused, uncertain, wondering; while his fiancée was exuberant, confident, looking forward. Interestingly, within twelve months, experience had affected them both to such a degree that Diana was to come perilously close to breaking down under the onslaught of media attention and public adulation, and Charles, for a time, was to revel in having the most beautiful girl in the world on his arm. Thus, attitudes were very nearly reversed.

What very few people in Palace circles recognized immediately was the strength of Diana's resolve. Outwardly, she appeared to be the Shy Di that the newspapers loved to portray. She bit her lower lip and looked coy, and old men and young went soppy in her presence. Only one or two – those who had watched her as a child, when her family home bordered on Sandringham – suspected that she might actually be made of sterner stuff. 'Blond, blue eyes', ruminated a septuagenarian lord-in-waiting. 'Such a pin-up girl. And you know, sometimes all of us get led down the garden path a bit by all that, and don't realize what lies underneath. In reality, she is a very strong woman. Very determined that what she wants will happen.' (A very similar view was once echoed in public

---

* Speaking about choosing a partner in marriage, in his interview with the author in 1975, Prince Charles had had this to say: 'Essentially one must be good friends, and love I am sure will grow out of that friendship and become deeper and deeper.'

by Diana's father, Earl Spencer.)

Whether Elizabeth II spotted straightaway the 'core of steel' that others have since found to be in the Princess of Wales's personality is open to question. It seems unlikely that she did, or that Diana herself was aware of it. The Princess, even now, is likely to admit only that, like any other modern woman, she does not intend to be pushed around. And she might also argue, with some justification, that if she had not stood up for herself in the early days of her marriage she would have been reduced very quickly to a mere puppet by the grandees within the Palace.

On the morning of the marriage of Charles Prince of Wales with Lady Diana Spencer, on 29 July 1981, the author was fortunate enough to be in the front row of the press stand erected in the north transept of St Paul's Cathedral, and wrote in his notes at the time: 'Philip forever twisting his signet ring and joking with Queen Mother who brings out her specs to read Order of Service ... Queen looks straight ahead all the time ... shows most interest when Archbishop of Canterbury's address speaks of economic recovery meaning nothing without family unity ... Very solemn looking Queen.'

For Elizabeth II, the actual marriage service *is* a solemn occasion – all the smiles and celebration come before and after. And in this case, with television directors cutting away for reaction shots every few seconds, she would have known perfectly that it is safest to keep a straight face. In that area of her life concerned with appearances in public the Queen has long since become something of an expert. If, as a mother, she was sorry to lose a son, it is unlikely that she would have betrayed her emotion to the world at large.

14

A Very Mixed Blessing

༄

Too much publicity will stain the mystery, even the dignity of the Crown. Too little publicity will be regarded as undemocratic and will render the gulf that yawns between the sovereign and the ordinary subject an unfortunate barrier rather than a necessity of segregation.' Thus wrote Sir Harold Nicolson in 1962.[1]

'I hope to be a wall between you and the press, ma'am,' said a Buckingham Palace press secretary on taking up his appointment. 'Not a wall,' corrected Elizabeth II. 'More a sieve.'

Relations between the royal family and the media have always been a subject for discussion, and frequently of controversy. How far should the demystification go in order to make the monarchy appeal to a younger generation? Where exactly is the point beyond which demystification endangers the esteem of centuries? And, when you are a public figure as prominent as the Queen or Prince Philip, where do you draw the line where personal privacy is concerned?

According to the Duke of Edinburgh, private life only ceases to be ordinary life when it is made public on a wide scale without the person's permission. Hence, 'If I walk through Windsor, that's not private life, it's just life. But if it's projected on to the screen or put in a newspaper, it's no longer private. Similarly, when the children go shopping, or to restaurants and pubs, they do it in exactly the same way as everyone else does. But if photographers constantly turn up, it becomes impossible.'[2]

Perhaps, as a former senior aide to the Queen points out: 'The key to understanding the royal family is to appreciate that to them their way of

214

life, both private and formal, is totally natural. They do not know any other, and while most of us at some time transplant ourselves and say "how would I react if I were in their position?", and tell ourselves that we would never be able to cope with it, to them it is as natural and normal as our lives are to us.'

What is certainly true is that members of the royal family, including the Queen, go about in public, without fanfare and often without being recognized, much more than people often realize. Although to a much lesser extent than she used to – mainly for security reasons – the Queen may still occasionally stop off at some village shop on the way to visit a friend in the country, especially when she knows of a special item that would give pleasure to one of her grandchildren. Princess Diana loves shopping, and doing the 'normal' thing. Speeding up the M1 to visit a friend, it has been known for her to scream 'I'm starving', and with her police escort in tow swing off into a Happy Eater car park. The family of four sitting at a nearby table, signs of certainty growing, are politely asked by the royal security officer not to mention what they have seen – the future Queen of England wolfing down ham-salad and pinching a chip from a neighbour's plate – and they happily agree. They merely stare out of the window wide-eyed as the Princess leaves (someone else picking up the tab), and watch as she strides across the car park, patting her stomach as she goes, well satisfied.

As professional royal watchers know, not every royal story gets into the newspapers. There is even truth in the tale that one very senior member of the royal family was once the subject of a serious blackmail threat – but, for a number of good reasons, that particular story is one that is very unlikely ever to be told.

Contrary to the experience of the most exalted politician or the most world-famous film star, Elizabeth II has known from birth what it is like to be the centre of attraction. Fame did not come to her at sixteen or at sixty, but at nought. Stature was hers from the outset. And just as it began when she was born, so it will continue until she dies. She does not complain. She bows to the inevitable. And part of the inevitability is the attention of the media, sometimes sought, sometimes resented, always there, or just around the corner, or hiding behind a hedge.

Each member of the royal family has his or her own personal attitude towards the media. Prince Philip wants whatever it is that has to be done with or for the media done quickly, efficiently, and got out of the way. Prince Charles, once a willing accomplice and almost a friend of the press, has come leerily to terms with reporters and photographers, having been badly let down on too many occasions. Princess Anne mostly ignores even their presence, and Princess Diana, in her own words, 'treats them like I treat children'. For her part, Elizabeth II sails majestically among the recorders of her presence, like the flagship that she is. And woe betide any who cross her bows.

An erstwhile royal photographer, John Dixon, explains: 'The Queen doesn't treat you as a person in your own right. She regards you in the same way as the film star regards a camera. She is there doing a job, and you are there to record her doing it. She will walk straight towards you fully confident that you will get the hell out of it. And you do – that is if you're not helped by one of her security blokes in the meantime.'[3]

Apparently one of the pictures of Elizabeth II that requires the greatest patience and hard work is one which shows 'the Queen look' – that is to say, eyes sparkling, teeth showing well, tiara twinkling. A picture such as that, in an anniversary year especially, could possibly earn several thousand pounds over a period of months for the photographer. On the other hand, a fuzzy picture of Lady Diana Spencer slipping into Buckingham Palace on the eve, as it turned out, of her engagement to Prince Charles reputedly rewarded its off-duty snapper with £7,000 in one night. And a picture of Princess Diana swimming back stroke in a rooftop pool in Hong Kong in 1989 was sold by sealed bids for £12,000 to a British tabloid newspaper. (Another tabloid's offer of £25,000 arrived too late.) Offered worldwide and shrewdly handled, the very ordinary picture of an almost unidentifiable young woman could probably have earned its owners altogether something in the region of £100,000. The Queen would probably accept, with some relief, that pictures of her in late middle age are not in quite the same financial league, although a picture of her swimming in the Buckingham Palace pool would undoubtedly command a small fortune!

Among many other things, Elizabeth II will go down in history as the first sovereign of the television age. She is not very good at appearing on it – her eldest son is much better – but she enjoys watching it (the comedy *Fools and Horses* was a favourite), and, more importantly, she is conscious of the contribution that the medium makes towards the conservation of the monarchy. Its value as a public relations dispenser is one of the main reasons that she agreed to allow the BBC to spend a year making a film about her working life, as part of the programme to mark the fortieth anniversary of her accession in February 1992. In the sensitive hands of the producer Edward Mirzoeff, who had masterminded the brilliant *Forty Minutes* series of programmes on BBC 2 in the 1980s, the documentary promised well, though in the early stages there was the customary nervousness of Palace officials about letting in light on even a very ordinary day.

King George VI knew of the existence of television, but there was no mass TV audience in Britain in his day. Princess Elizabeth never lay sprawled on her stomach in front of a television set as children do now.* But her coronation was televised. Yes, but after 1953 the value of television as a communicator was virtually ignored by Buckingham Palace for several years, except by Prince Philip who made a number of enterprising programmes about his travels, and gave what today seem like illustrated lectures in black and white.

For the first thirteen years of the Queen's reign, Palace public relations – a term *never* used then, and slightly frowned upon even now within the Queen's Household – were in the keeping of a retired naval officer, Commander Richard Colville, DSC, who was a first cousin of Sir John Colville, for a time Princess Elizabeth's Private Secretary. Presumably, as with so many royal appointments in those days, family relationships played a part in securing him his job.

Colville's manner was stiff and correct. He gave the impression that he did not much like or trust the press – an attitude that, unfortunately, with the passing of years has become increasingly widespread among middle-ranking officials and the general public alike. His charter from the Queen was quite straightforward. He was to protect the royal family in their private lives, and make tidy arrangements for press coverage of their public lives. He decided for himself, with royal approval, that he was *not* expected to entertain or answer what he deemed to be questions of a trivial nature.† He was certainly not prepared to talk about the Queen's children, or what Her Majesty's preferences were in the area of food and drink. The late Douglas Dumbrell, the Press Association's highly respected court correspondent for a number of years, concluded that Buckingham Palace Press Office 'did not mind you asking anything, provided that you understood that they would probably not tell you anything.'[4] This was during the time when the first task of a reporter who was elevated – although this was not always how the appointment was regarded – to the position of court correspondent was to go out and purchase a bowler hat (Dumbrell brought his in an Oxfam shop), and, when, a little earlier, the BBC's Godfrey Talbot was ticked off by a wireless listener for referring to the Queen as 'she', instead of 'Her Majesty'.

It could be argued that Colville was only doing his job by refusing sometimes to give Fleet Street the information that it wanted, and to which it believed it was entitled. As a young woman, Elizabeth II was

---

* A guest at Sandringham recalls Prince Andrew and Prince Edward as children being severely rebuked by their father for rushing to turn on the television almost before a distinguished guest – an archbishop, it so happened – had taken his leave.
† When a reporter on *The Independent*, a radical newspaper founded in the 1980s, was informed by his editor that he was to be court correspondent, his look of displeasure, it is said, turned to relief when the editor added that the posting was purely technical. Indeed a condition of the job was that he should never write anything about the royal family.

possibly even more protective of her privacy than she is today. She was aware of chequebook journalism, and was prepared to respond to it. In 1959 an injunction was issued over a report by a former superintendent at Windsor Castle that, for reasons of economy, old bedsheets were turned sides to middle. It was the first time that the royal family had gone to court for forty-eight years.* In 1963, a relative of the Queen placed with a New York saleroom letters written by Princess Elizabeth and Princess Margaret to their childhood music teacher. They were discreetly bought, for several hundred pounds, by the British Ambassador and returned to their original recipients.

When Prince Charles was experiencing press harassment at his preparatory school (he featured in newspapers on no fewer than sixty-eight of the first eighty-eight days of his first term at Cheam) Commander Colville called Fleet Street editors to the Palace, on the Queen's instructions, and informed them in no uncertain manner that the Queen would remove her son from Cheam and have him educated privately if they did not desist. They did call off their hounds, as they always do when the Queen commands - or when she near as dammit does - and thereafter Charles was left more or less in peace.

The cynical might say that proprietors and editors, with much more chance of being honoured with a knighthood or a peerage than their royal reporters, are extremely wary of offending the monarch. But among the infantry on the ground there is also a marked reluctance to do or write anything that might reflect poorly on the sovereign. Ask a seasoned royal watcher why he might be willing to 'elaborate' on a story about the Duchess of York, say, but refuses to indulge in tittle-tattle about the Queen and he is quite clear: 'It is different isn't it? The Queen is the Queen. You don't want to knock her, now do you? She's us. She's the country.' This might partly explain why, anniversaries and national celebrations apart, Elizabeth II figures less in the newspapers than does her daughter-in-law. The fact that 'Fergie' is younger and therefore newer could also have something to do with it, as the Queen would be the first to admit.

In the late 1950s and into the 1960s the Queen and Prince Philip were also young and glamorous. However, by 1959 the excitement and optimism engendered in the years immediately following the coronation was begining to pall. And with very little 'royal' to write about, the newspapers were almost glad to latch on to the criticisms of the monarchy by Altrincham and Muggeridge and the aftermath of doubt that began to

---

* In 1910, a journalist named Edward Mylius published a story that George V, as a young naval officer, had married an admiral's daughter in Malta and had fathered a child by her before he married Princess May, later Queen Mary, Mylius was prosecuted for libel, shown to be lying, and sentenced to twelve months imprisonment.

creep in. Perhaps the whole monarchial system *was* out of date. By the time the 1960s had spun into full swing, and youth, it seemed, had taken over the Western world, thoughts of approaching middle age were bound to assail anyone born in the early or mid 1920s. The Beatles arrived, Winston Churchill died; President John F. Kennedy was assassinated in Dallas in 1963; England beat Germany to win the World Cup in football in 1966; the Berlin Wall went up at the beginning of the decade, and Concorde first flew at the end of the decade; the Queen launched the liner *QE 2*; and the hippies and the flower people congregated in the King's Road, Chelsea. It became apparent to the occupants of Buckingham Palace, along with many others, that a great deal was changing and the world would never be quite the same again.

In an editorial in 1967, the *Sunday Telegraph*, a true supporter of the monarchy, noted 'a marked change in the public's attitude to the Crown. Most people care much less than they did – particularly the young, many of whom regard the Queen as the arch square. They are not *against* in the sense of being *for* a republic. They are quite simply indifferent . . . The British monarchy will not be swept away in anger, but it could well be swallowed in a great and growing yawn.'[5]

Prince Philip was among the first to recognize that the popularity of the monarchy was in decline and might soon seem completely irrelevant to an especially vibrant up-and-coming generation. Typically, he was not prepared simply to sit back and wait for extinction. 'No one wants to end up like a brontosaurus, who couldn't adapt himself, and ended up stuffed in a museum', he told a news conference in Canberra in 1967. 'It isn't exactly where I want to end up myself!'

The question was, what was to be done about survival?

Andrew Duncan, whose book *The Reality of Monarchy* in 1970 opened up a good many eyes, realized that 'the British royal family is an adman's dream. A unique selling proposition with a pliable market strongly predisposed towards the product.' This could never be the view of Commander Colville who had warned some six years earlier that 'if there comes a time when the British monarchy ever needs a real public-relations officer, the institution of monarchy in this country will be in serious decline.'

But in February 1968, when the decline was showing, and the pliable market might no longer be so strongly predisposed, Colville retired, with a knighthood from a grateful sovereign. In his place as Press Secretary the Queen appointed William Heseltine, a dapper, approachable Australian who was to spend a total of twenty-seven years in royal service, culminating in the highest post of Principal Private Secretary to the sovereign.

Heseltine would have agreed with Colville that the job of the Palace press office was not the same as that of a public relations company. And he had great affection and sympathy for Colville personally, for whom he worked first on secondment from the Australian government as an Assistant Information Officer, and then for two years as Assistant Press Secretary to the Queen. Heseltine believes that Colville was misjudged by sections of the media. 'He had a quick naval manner on the telephone which affronted a lot of people. But he was one of the nicest and best organized men I have ever known, a marvellously tidy administrator, who did what he was charged to do. His dealings with the press were always within the guidelines given by the Queen and Prince Phililp'.[6]

Colville had arranged things so that royal events, such as parades and tours of shipyards and factories, were covered by a controlled number of accredited reporters and photographers, working from pre-fixed positions. This was to prevent the *paparazzi*, as they were to become known, swarming everywhere like locusts. He made it a firm rule not to hand out anything but the barest facts about the private lives of members of the royal family, and to forbid pictures ever to be taken of the monarch eating or drinking.

All this had worked fairly well – certainly as far as his employer was concerned – but Heseltine, coming from a less hidebound part of the Commonwealth, and with four years experience of working as Private Secretary to the Australian Prime Minister Robert Menzies, wondered if perhaps a little more could not be done to 'open up' the picture that the public had of the monarchy. 'What had slightly happened – to my mind anyway – was that the royal family had ceased to be "rounded" figures in the public imagination. One had ceased to know anything about them, except what one read in the gossip columns or what one read of their official existence. Neither of these seemed a very satisfactory way of depicting the life of the royal family. I began to think of how one could perhaps present things differently, to try and secure a better idea of the people themselves, and the work that they did. And that's when my thoughts, I confess, began to turn rather towards television and what it might be able to do.'[7]

Heseltine was fortunate in having the support of Prince Philip who to a certain extent had already pioneered the way through his own television programmes, and through what he had said on one of them. 'I think the thing, the monarchy, is part of the fabric of the country,' he told viewers of Tyne-Tees Television in March 1968, 'and as the fabric alters, so the monarchy and its people's relations to it alters. In 1953 the situation in this country was totally different. And I think young people, a young Queen and a young family, was infinitely more newsworthy and amusing. . . . We're getting on for middle age, and I dare say when we're really ancient there might be a bit more reverence again. But I would

220

have thought we were entering probably the least interesting period of the kind of glamorous existence. ... There used to be much more interest. Now people take it all as a matter of course. Either they can't stand us, or they think we're all right.'

It was one of Prince Philip's typically bluff, off-the-cuff commentaries, remarked on hardly at all at the time, which should have given a clue to the change in Palace thinking. But the film *Royal Family*, which followed the next year, and really was to become a milestone in depiction of the monarchy, also came about through coincidence rather than by shrewd design.

Back in 1958, when creating her eldest son Prince of Wales, Elizabeth II had promised that one day she would 'present him to you at Caernarvon Castle', where the only previous investiture had taken place, that of the future Edward VIII. The ceremony was planned to happen on 1 July 1969, when Prince Charles would be a few months away from his twenty-first birthday. Once the date was announced, Buckingham Palace was assailed with requests from the media for interviews with the Prince, facilities to write biographies, and from the BBC and the independent television network proposals to make a film about the life of the Prince of Wales.

Both the Queen and Prince Philip thought that their son was somewhat young to have a biography written about him – although several had been already – and they feared that a film about his life might only serve to illustrate his immaturity. After all, he had not even finished university. According to one royal aide, 'Even at twenty-one he looked as if his nanny had just combed his hair.'

So what was the answer to be? Slowly an idea evolved. 'Why not make a film for television about the kind of role that Prince Charles would one day inherit?' A film, in other words, about the Queen, her life and her work.

Elizabeth II needed to be persuaded. Such a venture had not taken place before, and where there was no precedent, she was instinctively cautious. Was it wise to let in a chink of light? What was it that Walter Bagehot had said?: 'Above all this our royalty is to be reverenced, and if you begin to poke about it you cannot reverence it . . . In its mystery is its life.'

Another consideration was the fact that the Queen did not enjoy making television appearances. She felt ill at ease doing so. 'It is no good, I am not a film star,' she had told Peter Dimmock, the producer of her first televised Christmas broadcast in 1957. On that occasion she had gone round the room in Buckingham Palace before the live broadcast began, chatting with the technicians and putting everyone at ease. But when the moment came for her actually to deliver her message to her peoples in Britain and around the world, her face froze and her eyes took on the look of faint panic. And then, the moment it was all over, her delightful smile returned – in the same moment as viewers in their living rooms were presented with a still picture of their solemn monarch and the sound of 'God Save The Queen'.

Prince Philip was in favour of making the film, provided proper safeguards were established. Initially his idea was to set up a Trust with profits from the film going to charity. Lord Brabourne, who had produced some stirring war films and was a son-in-law of Lord Mountbatten, was called in to advise. Together, along with Bill Heseltine, they managed to persuade the Queen of the wisdom of going ahead.

Brabourne approached Richard Cawston, a renowned documentary film-maker who at the time was the head of the documentary department at the BBC, but who had also been a council member with Brabourne of the British Academy of Film and Television Arts. A self-contained person, professional to the fingertips, he was ideally suited to do the job. He had made a documentary called *This is the BBC*, and another about barristers where he had been asked to treat his subjects kindly, because 'outside their courtrooms they are children'. Naturally, he felt honoured to be offered the chance of making a film about the Queen but, very sensibly, he wanted editorial freedom in doing so, and was not at all sure that he would receive it. When he raised the question at his first meeting with Prince Philip, Lord Brabourne and Bill Heseltine, he was told that he could make the film any way he liked – 'but we shall have to have some sort of editorial committee', he was warned. Cawston was wary. Why not have an *advisory* committee? 'Right, we will have an advisory committee', agreed Prince Philip. 'I shall be chairman and the four of us will be the committee.'

Cawston wanted to use his own crew of BBC cameramen and technicians. That would not be possible, he was told, because it would mean that the film was a BBC project and he could not have that exclusivity. In that case, why not bring in the commercial channel, ITV, to sell the film abroad, while the BBC looked after the organizational side and he remained the independent producer? Agreed. It was a brilliant solution from Cawston's point of view, although it did not much please ITV when they were brought in on a deal that was already a *fait accompli.**

At the outset, the film ran into problems.

As an inescapable part of her life Elizabeth II had long ago become

---

* Some sort of revenge was obtained by Independent Television News in 1986 when the company obtained exclusive rights to make a film about the Prince and Princess of Wales, at a cost of £450,000 made payable as a donation to the Operation Raleigh charity, of which Prince Charles is patron, and which at the time was in grave financial difficulties.

accustomed to film cameras mounted on tripods recording, from a distance, the more important of her official engagements. But she was not prepared for the recently introduced *cinema verité* techniques, which were all the rage of documentary film-makers in the 1960s, and which meant that Cawston's cameraman moved in and out of rooms and, in one famous scene, even sat on the floor of a Range Rover looking up at the Queen as she sat in the driving seat. ('Looking up your skirt! How perfectly dreadful', we are told the Queen Mother commented.)

The greatest concern of both the Queen and Prince Philip was Cawston's use of directional microphones. These could eavesdrop on conversations at a distance of several feet, and were used to do just that.* Again, the Queen was used to no microphones at all, or ones placed in fixed positions to pick up background sound only. Amazing though it may seem today, when video cameras with sound roam at will like sniffing dogs, Cawston was banned from using microphones at all in the first few weeks of filming. He even had a sound technician bodily removed by a policeman when he attempted to record a very public event – an inspection of a guard of honour.

Prince Philip's chief worry was that the Queen and he would be made to look silly. 'When we talk to a lot of people,' he told Cawston, 'we are bound to ask the same sort of question many times, and make the same sort of remark to more than one person. You could make us look very stupid.' Cawston said he was not making that sort of film. Prince Philip was not convinced, even so. 'Most journalists just want the shot where you're seen picking your nose', he said. Cawston replied that he was not a journalist.

Antlers were locked for almost three months.

Finally, following a particularly tricky interview with the Prince at the Palace of Holyrood in Edinburgh, Cawston was given permission to film with sound, provided that all the audio tapes were locked away at the end of each day, and that the Queen had the last word on what could and could not be used in the final film.

Cawston agreed to the conditions, and from then on things gradually became easier. The Queen instructed that Cawston should be placed next to her when the family were dining informally, so that the two of them could discuss forthcoming 'scenes'. She agreed to be filmed at her desk in Buckingham Palace, in her normal daily conference with her Private Secretary. She invited Cawston and his cameras to Balmoral, where they

---

* When, in the early 1980s, a documentary was made about Princess Anne's working life, the producer/director managed to persuade the Princess to carry a microphone concealed in her handbag on public 'walkabouts'. However, the Princess insisted on having an on/off button – which she usually remembered to turn 'off' when anything interesting was being said!

recorded the famous scene of the family preparing a barbecue. Before formally receiving a foreign ambassador she had a quiet word with him, explaining what was needed by the camera. She went out of her way to arrange one particular sequence, the meeting between President Nixon and Prince Charles and Princess Anne in the George III Room at the Palace. 'We must have something special for our film', she told Cawston.

It was characteristic of Elizabeth II that, once she had agreed to undertake a project, she wished to make sure that everything possible was done to make it a success. Her one disappointment may have been that Cawston declined to show her the rushes (the uncut film from the previous day's shooting). He explained that on previous films he had always said, 'Even if the Queen of England asked me, I would not show you my rushes.' Fortunately, the Queen understood.

Fortunately also, both the Queen and the Duke of Edinburgh approved of Cawston's final edited version. Philip was shown it first. There was only one sequence that he was slightly worried about, he said. It was where Charles was demonstrating to his little brother Edward how a cello was tuned. In tightening, a string had snapped and whiplashed against Edward's cheek, stinging him to a tear or two. Prince Philip thought that perhaps the boy's mother might not want the scene to be used. But after she had viewed the film on her own, the Queen raised no objection. 'It's the sort of thing that can happen to anyone.' (Cawston later received complaints from a few viewers that he had deliberately arranged for the string to snap!)

Royal Family went out on BBC television in July 1969 and attracted an initial audience of 23 million – 7½ million fewer than had watched the World Cup football final in July 1966, and 3 milllion less than the audience for the comedy show *Steptoe and Son*, which was about a rag-and-bone man. But a second showing produced an audience of 15 million, and over the next eighteen months there were four further showings, resulting in an overall audience of some 40 million – or four-fifths of the United Kingdom's population. The film had cost £150,000 to make, and was to produce profits of £120,000 from sales to 140 countries outside Britain.* Largely because of the film, the investiture of the Prince of Wales took on a fascination of its own and went some way to silencing those who had criticized the ceremony as being a very expensive piece of antiquated pageantry.

---

* The BBC and ITV shared the cost of making the film, and the Queen retained half of the profits. She spent some of the money on cleaning her Van Dyck paintings and putting new lighting into the Queen's Gallery, which is open to the public. Long after his film was shown, Cawston approached the Queen to see if she would donate the rest of the profits to help towards the building costs of a new home for the Society of Film and Television Arts, renamed BAFTA, in Piccadilly. She readily agreed to do so.

There were few adverse comments about *Royal Family* as an intriguing piece of entertainment, but one or two about the wisdom of allowing it to be made in the first place. Cawston could remember David Attenborough, the anthropologist and maker of highly successful wildlife films, telling him, 'You're killing the monarchy, you know, with this film you're making. The whole institution depends on mystique and the tribal chief in his hut. If any member of the tribe ever sees inside the hut, then the whole system of the tribal chiefdom is damaged and the tribe eventually disintegrates.'

The distinguished critic Milton Shulman, after acknowledging the undoubted popularity of the film with the public, posed the question in the London *Evening Standard* that had been concerning several people, and not just the one or two lord lieutenants from the shires who had written huffily to Buckingham Palace. 'Is it,' asked Shulman, 'in the long run wise for the Queen's advisers to set as a precedent this right of the TV camera to act as an image-making apparatus for the monarchy? Every institution that has so far attempted to use TV to popularize or aggrandize itself has been diminished and trivialized by it.'

In an article in the *Listener*, the well-known broadcaster and former newspaper editor William Hardcastle commented on the fact that *Royal Family* was being quickly followed by Prince Charles subjecting himself to an unscripted interview on television. Would the next step be an interview with the Queen herself? 'I doubt it', wrote Hardcastle. 'The refurbishing of the royal image that has been going on for some time now has been managed with some skill, and skill in this field involves judgement of when enough is enough. My guess is that *Royal Family* is at the completion of a process rather than a herald of further revelations to come.'

His guess turned out to be accurate. It was to be twenty-one years before facilities were once again granted, in the summer of 1990, for work on a second film about the Queen to begin, with Edward Mirzoeff as producer. This time the accent was to be more on the working side of the monarch's life rather than on her private family life. Interestingly, once again sanction to go ahead came at a time when the royal family, notably some of the younger members, were facing press criticism. On this occasion the headlines were about the spending behaviour of the Duchess of York, and the fact that the Prince and Princess of Wales were living what seemed, to some newspapers at any rate, an inordinate length of time apart from one another. It is possible that the Queen took all of this into consideration when she agreed to the film being made. But the focus was always to be the monarchy itself, and the fortieth anniversary of her accession in February 1992. The film took almost two years to complete and shows the Queen in some delightfully off-guard moments, as well as performing her multifarious official duties with a straight face and unmatched professionalism. But it was always unlikely that it would have the same impact as the first royal family film, because now we *expect* to be let into more secrets than we were permitted in 1969.

In the early hours of 21 February 1983, Elizabeth II was asleep on board the royal yacht *Britannia* as it passed through calm Mexican waters, sailing towards the fishing port of La Paz. Back in London – where it was 11am – members of her press office were examining the centre pages of Britain's biggest-selling newspaper, *The Sun*. Their eyes were drawn to a headline which read 'World Exclusive. The Astonishing Inside Secrets of the fun-loving Royals'. Underneath was an even larger headline: 'QUEEN KOO'S ROMPS AT THE PALACE'.

The source of the revelations that followed – alleging goings-on at the Palace between Prince Andrew and his girlfriend at the time, the actress Koo Stark – was, the paper told its readers, Kiernan Kenny, a twenty-year-old stores officer who had worked at Buckingham Palace for two and a half years and had left there just three weeks previously. He would be telling readers, said *The Sun* 'what really happens on the other side of the Palace walls', and what happened when 'barefoot Di buttered my toast'.

The Queen was informed of these extraordinary titbits while she ate her own breakfast aboard *Britannia*. No one was the least surprised that she showed deep displeasure. She was angry not so much with *The Sun* itself, which she had learned almost to tolerate as a purveyor of sensation, but with the betrayal of trust by a member of her staff. Within an hour, after listening to the advice of her Private Secretary and others, she had taken the extremely unusual step of instructing her Deputy Treasurer, Mr Russell Wood, in London – who technically had been Kenny's employer – to apply for an injunction to stop publication of any further material by the ex-Palace storeman. The injunction was granted by a judge sitting in chambers and, predictably, the following morning *The Sun* ran the headline: 'QUEEN GAGS THE SUN.'

The matter was not allowed to rest there. On the same day, Russell Wood took out a writ seeking to order the paper's owners to divulge the profits resulting from the publication of Kenny's disclosures. Although it was never officially confirmed, it appeared that Kenny had been paid £2,000 and given a holiday in Spain, while the paper had increased its circulation by some 54,000 copies as a result of one article and the attendant publicity. In the end, mostly to avoid further publicity, the Queen and her advisers settled out of court for a payment of £4,000 which, with a delightful touch of irony, was donated to the Fleet Street charity which looks after hard-up journalists.*

The episode serves to illustrate the extent to which some popular papers in Britain, not just *The Sun*, will venture in order to titillate their readers. But it also demonstrates how firm the Queen can be where the press is concerned, especially if she feels that trust has been betrayed. The popular conception that the royal family has no redress from unfavourable publicity is no longer true, if it ever was. Members of the royal family merely hold their fire and allow most of the potentially wounding material to pass over their heads, until something really serious happens. The Queen receives a résumé each morning of what newspapers are saying about individual members of the royal family, but rarely reacts to what she reads. The great majority of the gossip is news to her too!

The apparently insatiable appetite of the tabloid newspapers for royal stories, which became voracious during the 1980s, can at times involve very large sums of money indeed, which is another source of irritation to the royals. Prince Charles, especially, has been heard to make carping comments. Although everyone in the employ of the royal family is required to sign an agreement of confidentiality, over the years one or two have managed to circumvent their promise. The most famous of these miscreants was Stephen Barry, Prince Charles's valet for many years, whose book about his life at the Palace was never published in Britain, because of the threat of injunctions, but made its author well over £100,000 through sales in the United States and Australia alone. A sad figure, a self-acknowledged homosexual who was angry at being dismissed from service shortly after Prince Charles's marriage, he was working on another book when he died, before reaching middle age. Like 'Crawfie', his memorial may lie in the fact that many of the insights that he gave into the personality and habits of his former master live on in the 'exclusive' accounts of life at Buckingham and Kensington Palaces penned by writers less well placed than he.

Over a period of forty years Elizabeth II has become largely inured to the press and the very often hurtful stories it occasionally prints about members of her family. She is aware that press intrusion has become a penalty of the job, and that in any case there is nothing very new about the media attacking royalty. Queen Victoria was mocked as 'Mrs Brown'. *Reynolds's Newspaper* wondered whether the future Edward VII 'would have the tact and talent to keep royalty upon its legs and out of the gutter'. Her own grandfather was accused of a morganatic

---

* In 1989, *The Sun* was obliged publicly to apologize and pay £100,000 to charity after publishing a privately taken photograph of the royal family and the new-born daughter of the Duke and Duchess of York.

marriage, and her husband of a close relationship with a French woman early on in their marriage. What does infuriate the Queen is harassment of those who do not have the protection that she enjoys. The media chase of Princess Diana before her engagement was an example, although those involved would swear that for quite a lot of the time Diana really quite enjoyed the excitement. The Queen also abhors the invasion of privacy of those who become caught up in the entrails of a sensation that was none of their making. In May 1981, she was so incensed by reports that a national newspaper was planning to tell the story of Peter Sutcliffe, the murderer known as 'the Yorkshire Ripper', by paying a large sum to his relatives, that she wrote to the mother of one of Sutcliffe's victims, through her Assistant Private Secretary at the time. If the reports were true the Queen 'certainly shares in the sense of distaste which right-minded people will undoubtedly feel'.

It was an extremely rare case of Elizabeth II expressing her private opinions publicly. 'In a real sense she never demeans herself by evincing exasperation or impatience', said one of her former aides. 'But she has been known to write personal notes, always through her Private Secretary, to people she has never met who have evinced her sympathy.' During the Falklands War she communicated privately with widows of soldiers who had been sought out and written about in the newspapers. She felt that some of the interviews amounted to unwarranted intrusion into private grief.

As for press intrusion into her own privacy, this has amounted over the years to considerably less than the general public has believed it to be. And it is certainly less than her children and her sister have had to endure. Indeed, about the only time that the Queen runs the gauntlet of uninvited attention is when one of her children is about to get married, unmarried, or have a baby. And only then, when the family is staying at Sandringham or Balmoral.

At Sandringham, the stables are reached by crossing a road some distance from the house. The road is a public right of way, so the photographers – waiting often for hours in pouring rain or freezing cold for a snatched shot of a prospective bride or a pregnant princess – gather with a certain degree of immunity. However, if the Queen happens to be out riding, they are not let off without the quite withering stare of a monarch who thinks that they have no proper business to be there. Sometimes the Queen is accompanied by one of her younger grandchildren, and it is their safety that she is mostly concerned about. A camera flash could easily make a horse bolt.

At Balmoral, sections of the river Dee are visible from the public road. In the summer, at the height of royal rumour, one side is often patrolled by the royal watchers and on the opposite bank you might very occasionally see Prince Charles sprawled in the heather reading a book. It is where Lady Diana Spencer was first spotted as a potential bride for Prince Charles, in September 1980, by James Whitaker, the most unflagging of the royal watchers. Invariably, when covering a royal event, or even a non-event, he has a pair of binoculars slung round his neck. 'It is very rude to go round peering at people through binoculars,' Prince Charles once told him, not to any noticeable effect.

Why, with thousands of acres of private land into which they can virtually disappear completely, do members of the royal family insist on going to places where they can practically guarantee that they will be visible to prowling media men and women?

'The answer to that is quite simple', answered a Palace source. 'The Prince of Wales, along with other members of the family, have their own favourite spots for fishing or whatever and, like anyone else, they do not see why they should not use them. They do spend a lot of time – the majority – in other parts of their estates where the press cannot reach them. But they resent being prevented from going where they want to go just because they might run into photographers. So they go anyway.'

The next question is why do some members of the royal family, including the Queen's children, sometimes act in ways which any public relations consultant would advise them was almost certain to attract the wrong kind of publicity and do serious damage to their reputation?

'One of the nice things about the royal family', explains a one-time member of the Buckingham Palace press office, 'is that they do not make any kind of concession to public relations, saying "If this is bad PR I won't do it'. They do what they think is right and proper themselves, and sometimes you can only lament what they do if you are the chap who has to explain what has happened to the world at large. But there it is. That is how they are.'

There may indeed be an element of naivety in this behaviour, but there is also a refusal to make willingly some of the concessions the press would welcome and to organize one's life around what people, and more particularly the media, are going to say about you. The attitude runs throughout the whole family. None of them is prepared to play the political game of 'shaping one's image'.

The final question in this area is the one that is frequently asked by those who read newspapers and watch television. It is a question which, from time to time, the media addresses to itself. Why is so much gossip printed about the royal family? Why cannot the press leave Charles and Diana alone? And why for a long period did they seem to be constantly criticizing the Duchess of York in particular?

As far as the tabloid papers and women's magazines are concerned, the answers to these questions are closely tied up with reader interest, and the fierce circulation battles that break out between the major selling titles. Stories, and stories about stories, involving the royal family help considerably to boost circulation. At any time during the first five years of her marriage a picture of Princess Diana on the cover of a popular women's magazine could increase circulation by up to 100,000 copies. Tales about a rumoured rift in a royal marriage or allegations of over-spending by the Duchess of York, for instance, can easily lead to a rival newspaper trying to go one better by printing a story based more on speculation than on fact.

There *is* danger in the Dallas-Palace soap-opera syndrome, of which both Prince Philip and Prince Charles have at separate times warned, in that it might eventually trivialize the monarchy down into the status of a shooting gallery in an amusement arcade. There would perhaps be an even greater danger if the situation were ever to be reached where a size-able proportion of the press, the responsible as well as what is sometimes called the irresponsible, decided to keep up a concerted attack on in-dividual members of the family, so that the idea of the British monarchy itself was seriously threatened. Presumably, this would only happen if the papers had sufficient evidence to support their criticisms and/or felt that they were reflecting the views of a substantial section of their reader-ship.

In the autumn of 1987, in one of her typically candid off-the-cuff re-marks, the Princess of Wales answered the question of a woman in a shopping precinct by saying, 'What have the newspapers ever done for me?' Within a day *The Sun* had snapped back with an editorial:

> *The Sun* can answer Her Loveliness in one word – EVERY-THING!
>
> The newspapers have made her one of the most famous women in the world. They have given her an aura of glamour and romance. Without them the entire Windsor family would soon become as dull and commonplace as the rulers of Denmark and Sweden. Were that to happen, people might begin to ask what is the point in having royals at all. Including lovely Princess Di.[8]

The underlying message seemed to come straight out of a Hollywood producer's lexicon: 'We made you. We can break you.' Or as a veteran royal reporter once remarked: 'They might be the stars, but we write the script.' It is a childishly arrogant attitude, of course, but it holds a little truth. Whoever it was who first said, 'Don't underestimate the power of the press', it is unlikely to have been a member of a royal family, unless possibly it was Louis XVI.

Probably the feelings of a large section of the British people about how the royal family should be treated by the media was best expressed by Robert Lacey in an article published in *Time* magazine on the eve of a visit by Elizabeth II to the United States in 1983: 'One must not reveal too much of the mystery,' he wrote, 'because the royals have faults, dishonesties, nastinesses like everyone else. A lot of us happen to think that the illusions and idealization which surround this family is quite a healthy thing. Every society needs vehicles for its dreams.'

While perhaps stopping short of seeing herself as a vehicle for dreams, the Queen has never once lost sight of who she is, or more precisely *what* she is. It is one of the very good reasons, though not the only one, why not a speck of scandal has ever so much as brushed against her skirt. She regards the media as she might a barometer. Reading it every day, and giving it a tap every now and then to see that it is working properly, she steps out of her Palace and shows herself to her people in factory, hospital, or place of worship, confident in the knowledge that whatever scandals and sensations they may have read about over their breakfast cups that morning they still retain the most enormous respect and affection for the monarch and the monarchy. Privately, Elizabeth II may even agree with the late Richard Cawston who, after spending a year with the Queen and seeing the effect of his film on people round the world, came to the conclusion that 'Monarchy *is* PR . . . Public relations – a focus for public interest – is what it is all about.'[9]

15

The Yuppie Eighties

⁓⁓

I
n 1977, Britain and the other Commonwealth countries celebrated the Silver Jubilee of Queen Elizabeth II. As far as Britain was concerned, it was not the most propitious moment to do so. The country was suffering an economic crisis not so dissimilar from the one it was to face in 1980-1, and again in 1991. Enthusiasm for a giant nationwide street party was noticeably slow to gather. After meeting at 10 Downing Street in May 1977, world leaders declared that 'our most urgent task is to create more jobs while continuing to reduce inflation'.

But perhaps because they had heard that sort of talk so often before, and because the British are at their most united when times are hard, the idea of a nostalgic three cheers for twenty-five years of Queen Elizabeth II's reign gradually took wing. By the time 7 June came around (the summer date was chosen in preference to the actual date of accession in cold February), a mood of resignation or enthusiasm, depending on one's view, was clearly noticeable. 'It will give a face-lift to a very dull England',[1] assured a Birmingham clog-dancer who had taken her first booking for a street party months before.

The Queen herself was more circumspect. As with the investiture of the Prince of Wales, and the preparations to mark the fortieth anniversary of her accession in 1992, she did not wish in any way to be thought to be promoting the idea of celebration. It was entirely up to the people to do what they wanted. As ever, cost may have hovered somewhere near to the front of her thoughts. When a First Lord of the Admiralty had assured her once that it would be the government who paid for a colossally expensive refit of the Royal Yacht *Britannia*, the

232

Queen had calmly replied: 'I see. You pay and I get the blame.'[2] She did not wish the Crown to be accused of profligacy in celebrating the Silver Jubilee of her accession when the country might be said to be still in a state of near penury.

As it turned out, she need not have concerned herself. National celebrations – perhaps because they so rarely take place in Britain, compared with Continental neighbours – have a way of taking on their own momentum, more particularly if they have a royal connection which allows for deep-memory trawling. Commerce was not slow to see an opportunity. Shops took a gamble and ordered thousands of Silver Jubilee mugs and other souvenirs, such as the red, white and blue socks with the device 'Legs Warm to the Jubilee' woven into the design.* Union Jacks, some of them dating back to the coronation of George V, suddenly appeared poking out of bedroom windows. Bunting and banners were strung up across mean city streets. (Those, usually in the vicinity of places of further education, with the message 'Sod the Jubilee' were left mostly undisturbed by a tolerant celebrating majority.) In London alone there were said to be 6,000 street parties, and an interesting difference between these and those that had been organized for the coronation in 1953 was that they were not confined to the poorer areas. Television by now had become a great cross-fertilizer of social classes, showing the toffee-nosed how the other half lived, and enjoyed, their lives. 'Liz Rules – OK!', the challenging legend printed on millions of button-badges and paint-sprayed on walls, summed up the feelings of a new generation who had been toddlers when Elizabeth II came to the throne and had grown up alongside her eldest son.

The celebrations were supposed to last for a week, but went on for much longer. At the end of a year, Prince Charles, as chairman of the Silver Jubilee Appeal, was able to announce that over £16 million had been raised 'to help young people help others'. Before and after the week in June, the Queen and Prince Philip (who had celebrated their silver wedding five years earlier), travelled 56,000 miles around the Commonwealth and to the British forces in Germany.

Some two years before any Silver Jubilee plans had been arranged there had been secret government discussions about whether the Queen might visit trouble-torn Northern Ireland, and the matter was raised again in 1977. The Queen had tentatively agreed in 1975, but ministers were anxious to know the Queen's personal view of the additional risk to her life that she would be taking if she 'crossed the water' in Jubilee Year.

---

* Skinner's Departmental Store in Sutton, Surrey, put up a giant banner: 'Oh to be in England, Now that Spring is here. Oh to be in Skinner's (China and Glass), In Jubilee Year.'[3]

Lord Charteris recalls explaining to Her Majesty that if her instinct was against going she only had to say so, and her ministers would advise against the visit. But if she thought she ought to go, then this would make a big difference to their deliberations. They would still have to advise her, but they would advise more positively in his opinion. 'I remember the Queen sat quite silently for several moments after I'd spoken, then she looked up and said, "Martin, I think as I've said we're going it would be a pity if we didn't". I knew then that I had to get her to Ulster.'[*4]

Jubilee Day itself was set for 7 June, and the heart of the celebrations was the procession by Elizabeth II and the Duke of Edinburgh in the golden coach from Buckingham Palace to St Paul's Cathedral for a thanksgiving service, followed by a luncheon at the Guildhall.

Everyone who was in Britain at that time, either as a native or a tourist, has their own memory of that day, when the coronation seemed to be re-enacted in miniature and thousands lined the route and millions more around the world watched events unfold on television. Prince Charles had great fun riding behind the Queen's coach, 'which I wanted to do because my great-great-grandfather, Edward VII, had ridden beside Queen Victoria's carriage on her Jubilee. The crowds were terrific, and I'm afraid I can't really have been paying proper attention because when the Queen's coach stopped at Temple Bar, for the Lord Mayor to hand the Sword of the City to her, I very nearly ran into the back of it. And when we reached St Paul's Cathedral I nearly fell because the mounting block, which was necessary because of the size of the horse I was riding, was placed under instead of beside the animal. As it was, as I somehow descended, my bearskin slipped down over my eyes.'

Small mishaps apart, the Silver Jubilee was judged a huge success. 'People expressed amazement at the reaction to it,' Prince Charles told students at Chicago University in the same year, 'but it did not amaze me. . . . The British are a slow race in a way. They take time to show their feelings, and they need a specific reason to do so.'[5]

Perhaps the person most surprised by the public reaction was the Queen herself. For weeks afterwards she spoke about it almost continuously. 'It absolutely floored her', her domestic chaplain at the time recalls. 'She could not believe that people had that much affection for her as a person, and she was embarrassed and at the same time terribly touched by it all.'

The joy continued unalloyed until the end of the year, when her first grandchild, Peter Mark Andrew Phillips was christened in Buckingham

* The Queen made her first official visit to Northern Ireland in eleven years in August 1977.

Palace. However, the remainder of the decade was not destined to be a happy time for the Queen, nor particularly so for her subjects. Firstly, there was the matter of Princess Margaret's divorce from Lord Snowdon, and then the Pope's ban on Prince Michael of Kent marrying his Austrian fiancée, the Baroness Marie von Reibnitz, in a Roman Catholic church.[*] Just over a year later, in August 1979, Earl Mountbatten was assassinated by an IRA bomb that blew up the fishing boat which he and his family enjoyed sailing on holidays in County Sligo. And in the penultimate month of 1979 a shocked House of Commons heard from Mrs Thatcher that Anthony Blunt had been the 'fourth man' in the Burgess, Maclean and Philby spy ring for Soviet Russia.

It was the most extraordinary scandal. Blunt had been Surveyor of the King's Pictures from 1945 to 1952, of the Queen's Pictures from 1952 to 1972, and Adviser to Elizabeth II on her pictures and drawings from 1972 to 1978. But when Mrs Thatcher made her statement to the House of Commons she revealed that Blunt had confessed as long ago as 1964 to spying for the Russians during the Second World War, and had escaped public exposure and prosecution ever since then by agreeing to tell the authorities all that he knew. On the same day as the Prime Minister astounded the country with her announcement, Buckingham Palace let it be known that Blunt (who had already skipped the country, presumably after a tip-off), was stripped of his knighthood.[†] But the question that has so far not been answered is to what extent was Elizabeth II compromised? Was she informed in 1964 that a senior Member of her Household had confessed to being a spy? If she was, how could she tolerate continuing to employ a traitor for a further fourteen years? And if her Prime Minister[‡] chose to keep the secret of Blunt's confession from his sovereign, had he the right to do so?

The understanding among Palace officials in 1964 was that, in accordance with government and MI5 instructions, Blunt 'should not be disturbed', to use the Whitehall-ese. There were undoubtedly one or two among the Queen's advisers who were not pleased by this, indeed were very angry, but once having digested the news of Blunt's infamy they found it best simply to put the man out of sight and out of mind. This may well have been the Queen's attitude too. The person who took over Blunt's position at the Palace, Sir Oliver Millar, who had been Blunt's

* The couple were married at a civil ceremony in Vienna on 30 June 1978.
† 'The appointment of Professor Sir Anthony Frederick Blunt to be a Knight Commander of the Royal Victorian Order, dated May 31, 1956, shall be cancelled and annulled.'
‡ Depending on which day of the year precisely Blunt did confess, the Prime Minister would have been either Harold Macmillan or Harold Wilson, who came to power in October 1964.

assistant for many years, had no idea of the traitor's infamy until he was informed by Sir Philip Moore, the Queen's Assistant Private Secretary, in 1979. 'Something like that had just never crossed one's mind.' He recalls that his former boss always managed to get out of going to functions and parties at the Palace – 'he was never very much at home in that world. He couldn't have been.'[6] Anthony Blunt died in 1983, leaving an estate valued at £850,000. Almost half of this was accounted for in a picture by Poussin – *Rebecca at the Well* – bought for £100 in 1932, while Blunt, a young student along with Guy Burgess, was recruiting Communists at Cambridge.

If the 1970s ended with unhappy associations for Elizabeth II, the 1980s snapped open with all the bright promise of a pop-up greetings card. The family, along with the whole world it seemed, welcomed the engagement of the Prince of Wales to Lady Diana Spencer, to be followed some five months later by *the* wedding itself. 'The stuff of which fairy tales are made', rightly observed Dr Robert Runcie, the Archbishop of Canterbury. Or as our old friend Walter Bagehot would have it: 'A princely marriage is the brilliant edition of a universal fact, and as such it rivets mankind.'

This wedding certainly did that, glueing as it did an estimated 750 million people around the world to their television screens, and making Princess Diana for months to come one of the best-known images on Earth, alongside Pope John Paul and Coca-Cola.

The Queen looked on at all the hullabaloo with her customary deceptive appearance of detachment – aware but seemingly unaware - and tried her best to become used to a daughter-in-law who rollerskated over the floors of Buckingham Palace and in other ways, too, displayed a sense of independence linked to a naivety and ignorance of how a Princess should behave, according to her elders, that was quite staggering.

In those early stages of her marriage, Princess Diana by all accounts looked for and received a great deal of help and advice from the Queen. A strain in their relationship, the reasons for which were complex and manifold, did not come until later. The Queen could recall the fuss that had been made over her own wedding all those years before, and the stress it had caused, even for someone like herself who had been brought up since childhood to tolerate the attentions of the press. What she had not perhaps fully appreciated, along with others at the Palace, was the increased scope of the media, with its telephoto lenses, its satellite projection, and its ready response to a worldwide audience avid for pictures of the new Princess. Princess Elizabeth had been trained, and protected, from birth where publicity was concerned. Diana had not. In the 1940s Princess Elizabeth was seen by the public to be a modest, regal young woman with a pretty face and slim figure. Diana was something else. In an age when most girls would rather be a model than a princess, she rapidly became both. The result was mayhem wherever she went.

In her commonsensical way the Queen raised her eyebrows in surprise, but did little else besides. Until, that is, she perceived that the pressure on her daughter-in-law was becoming so great that she was in some danger of breaking down under the strain. When the two equal-best royal reporter/photographer teams in Britain sent back the famous pictures of Diana in bikini and pregnant with her first child, on a private holiday in the Bahamas, the Queen was not pleased. More especially so since only the previous December her Press Secretary at the time, Mr Michael Shea, a twinkly Scot who could darken to thunder, had taken the almost unprecedented step, at the Queen's behest, of calling Fleet Street's editors to the Palace for a meeting in the 1844 Room. After 'drawing attention' to the beleaguerment the Princess of Wales felt herself to be in as a result of press interest, the editors were shown into an adjacent room where the Queen, merely by her presence, reinforced the message.

The very real concern felt by Elizabeth II and her advisers at the time was that Princess Diana's antipathy towards the press in late 1981 might harden into a permanent antagonism, which she might even pass on to her children and which would not bode well for the future of the monarchy. Fortunately for all involved, Diana was soon to discover that a combination of co-operation and healthy suspicion dealt with most situations where most newspaper men and women were involved. So that today, photographers will swear, she positively enjoys having her picture taken – most of the time, anyway.

In order to see her own photograph in the newspapers in the early 1980s – never a particularly high ambition – the Queen, unlike her daughter-in-law, had to be engaged in something quite spectacular. This happened twice, without any prompting.

On the first occasion, on 13 June 1981, a young man stepped out into the road and fired six shots (luckily blank) at Elizabeth II as she rode down The Mall for the traditional Trooping the Colour Birthday Parade. The crowds ducked, and the Queen, showing a little concern, gave a reassuring pat to her horse Burmese and rode on.*

On the second occasion, during the early morning of 9 July 1982, a man under the delusion at times that he was the son of Rudolf Hess, entered the Queen's bedroom in Buckingham Palace and sat on her bed. 'What guts that chap had!' commented the author Roald Dahl in an interview shortly before his death. 'Waking up the Queen!'[7] Others,

---

* A seventeen-year-old youth was subsequently gaoled for five years under the Treason Act of 1842.

likely to be the majority, preferred to give the greater credit to Her Majesty for remaining so calm while the intruder Michael Fagan, in bare feet and jeans, first opened the bedroom curtains, then sat down on the Queen's bed dripping blood from his right thumb, which he had cut while trying to slash his wrists with a broken ashtray.

Fagan told the Queen all about his domestic troubles. He had a wife, four children, two stepchildren. He was thirty-five years old. 'Oh, then Prince Charles is a year younger than you', said the Queen. She pressed the night alarm button connected to the police. It was not working. She pressed the bedside bell that rang in the corridor outside. No answer. Eventually, when Fagan asked for a smoke, she found an excuse to leave the bedroom in order to look for cigarettes, and fortuitously came across a Palace maid outside her room. 'Bloody hell, ma'am,' exclaimed the Yorkshire lass, on hearing of the drama, 'he shouldn't be in there!' At the same moment a Palace footman returned from taking the Queen's corgis for their early morning airing. While he was plying Fagan with cigarettes, and at the same time fending off the snapping corgis, the police eventually arrived.

The Queen appeared to those present to be hardly ruffled at all by the whole affair, and later seemed quite to revel in recounting the experience. According to a person she spoke to soon afterwards, her main aim was to try to keep Fagan talking. 'She said that what really terrified her was the thought that Prince Philip might come in at any moment – "because I knew that all hell would break loose if that happened. That's all I was really thinking about."'*

As Home Secretary, Lord Whitelaw had to reply as best he could to questions in the House of Commons about the failures in security arrangements that had permitted Fagan to scale the perimeter railings and enter Buckingham Palace through an unlocked window. Whitelaw was also ultimately responsible for the official inquiry and the extreme tightening-up of Palace security that followed. With hindsight, he thinks that perhaps the authorities, including himself, over-reacted. 'I think that probably the Palace, and the Queen herself, felt that all the extra policing and extra security after Fagan was overdone and that probably I and others panicked too much. On the other hand, one man in the Queen's bedroom is enough!'[8]

Overall, the 1980s was not the happiest decade that the Queen had known. Hard on the heels of the Fagan affair, but in no way connected, came the sudden resignation of Commander Michael Trestrail, aged

---

* The law of trespass did not permit Michael Fagan to be prosecuted for his intrusion. Instead he was accused of burglary, acquitted of a charge of stealing a half bottle of wine from Buckingham Palace, and on the basis of medical opinion sent to a mental hospital. He was discharged in January 1983.

fifty-one and single, who had been the Queen's personal police officer for ten years. It was a newspaper, *The Sun*, that was alerted that Trestrail was a homosexual, just as it was a newspaper – the *Daily Express* this time – that had broken the story about Fagan, the Palace intruder. Both stories Buckingham Palace would have preferred to keep out of the papers, with little or no justification, and with no chance whatsoever of doing so.* However, if Trestrail had not offered his resignation so promptly and seen it accepted by his police superior, the whole matter might have been treated differently.

Once again, as Home Secretary in overall charge of the Metropolitan Police, William Whitelaw was involved. However, he was attending the Open golf championship at Troon on the Friday that Trestrail resigned and no one sought to inform the Home Secretary until the Monday morning. The Queen was not told either, because for the first time in her life she was in hospital, undergoing a dental operation.

'On balance, everyone now thinks that I should have been informed', says Lord Whitelaw. 'But whether that is right or not, I do not believe there is any way the secret could have been held. From a security point of view I feel that it would have been impossible for him to stay.'[†9]

Elizabeth II is a compassionate woman by nature, and a realist through experience. When Prince Andrew idly threatened to resign his commission in the Royal Navy if opposition were raised to his going with his unit to the war in the Falklands, his mother knew that, other considerations apart, she could not stand in his way. And when Prince Edward, in face of strong opposition from his father, decided to quit the Royal Marines when he was only a few weeks off finishing his tough officers' training course (in January 1987), the Queen was one of the first to realize that nothing would make him change his mind.

Increasingly, as the younger members of the royal family have reached maturity, and in some cases married, the question of what they *do* do with their lives has come into prominence. There have become just too many of them for each to have a job with 'the firm', as George VI called it, travelling around the country and the world, opening this, attending that, as representatives of the monarch. Besides, there is not enough money available at present to pay for them to do so.

---

* The private view of a senior Member of the Queen's Household, as expressed to the author not long after both events was this: 'I think that when such an incident does happen there is no immediate urge in an organization like ours to rush to the public prints with it because in many ways it can be best and most reasonably investigated and any fault in the system put right in private rather than in public.'

† Although for ten years he was hardly ever seen in public except at her side, Trestrail disappeared into obscurity immediately after his resignation – a broken man it is said. But the Queen has continued to keep in touch with her devoted servant in all the years since then, by letter and through friends.

'I don't think people appreciate that there are really not many work options open to them', Prince Philip has pointed out.[10]

I suppose, if they did not go into one or other of the Services, they could go into the Church. But otherwise experience has shown that if they go into any commercial or competitive activity people pick on them as the source of unfair competition. The Duke of Gloucester, for instance, was an architect. He was constantly being sniped at by other architects. He was supposed to be doing others out of a job. The same sort of thing happens with the Duke of Kent and Prince Michael. They are told that they are not going to get any more money from the State, or very little, so they go and try and get a job, and the next thing you know they are being criticized because the firm is not British, or is about to collapse, or might be involved in a scandal. In the end, if you want to keep out of that sort of argument, the only option is the Services. If one of the family went into industry and became a manager, all hell would break loose.

The Duchess of York, Prince Philip thought, was one of the few with a real advantage, because she had established a career before she became a member of the royal family, 'and I hope that she will be able to continue as a self-employed consultant. I can't see why anyone should complain about that.'[11]

The wedding of the Duke and Duchess of York at Westminster Abbey on 23 July 1986 undoubtedly gave the Queen the most enormous pleasure. Some observers thought she looked happier on that occasion than she had done at Prince Charles's wedding, and this may have contributed to the widely held opinion that the Queen much prefers 'Fergie' to Diana. It would not be so surprising if she did, if only because they share a love of the outdoors, and of horses, and, all in all, Sarah Ferguson, as was, gives a first impression of being more matey than her more soignée sister-in-law. ('Scaffolders wolf-whistle at Fergie, Diana leaves them nonplussed', says a veteran royal watcher.) Sarah, from the outset it seemed, was more ready to fall in with the ways of the Queen and her family, and show enthusiasm for the, some might think, silly parlour games played at Balmoral and Sandringham. Sarah, like the Queen, was not enthralled by fashion, which seemed at times to constitute Diana's chief interest in life. Philip liked Sarah, which counted for much in the Queen's mind. All in all, it looked as if Sarah could not go wrong. But as time has passed, she has.

At first, small things irritated. The Queen was not particularly amused when the newspapers printed the fact that Diana and Sarah had gone into a nightclub dressed up as policewomen on Prince Andrew's 'stag night'. Apparently, her face set firm when she was shown a picture of her two daughters-in-law poking their umbrellas at the backsides of men at Ascot. *Not* suitable behaviour for a princess. But much more serious was the public criticism in the late 1980s of the way in which the Duchess of York was thought to be taking advantage of her position, by allegedly accepting free holidays, and by taking some of the profits from a book that she had written for children instead of handing all the money over to a charity. Even if, whether by peradventure or design, these things happened, they should not be *seen* to be happening, some royalists – unreasonably – might argue.

The Duchess of York has caused her mother-in-law a certain amount of irritation in other ways, too. The cost of building and furnishing the Yorks' home near Windsor – a wedding present from the Queen – turned out to be much more than was anticipated; three times as much, it is alleged. And the Duke and Duchess of York's decision to invite the magazine *Hello* into their home to take intimate pictures of their two small children and themselves was an example of what some of the Queen's courtiers regard as the Yorks' propensity for acting first and thinking afterwards. 'The Queen found out about the picture session only as a *fait accompli*', says one of them. 'Had she been consulted beforehand I am sure that she would have said "this is not a very sensible thing to do".' A large fee is said to have been involved in acquiring the magazine's 'exclusive', a sum that apparently went partly towards paying the medical expenses of the Duchess's stepfather who was dying from cancer.

The Queen is not a harsh woman, and she does not like telling people off. If she does see the need, it is generally a Member of the Household who delicately delivers the Queen's message. One of the few times that those in her ken have seen Elizabeth II angry to the point of almost boiling over was when her second cousin, Marina Ogilvy, announced through the newspaper *Today* in October 1989 that she was expecting her boyfriend's baby and that, to all intents and purposes, she had been disowned by her parents Princess Alexandra and the Hon. Sir Angus Ogilvy. The Queen had loved and admired her cousin Princess Alexandra since childhood, and she was deeply shocked that Marina could so desperately hurt her parents in this way, as she undoubtedly did. But, apparently, the Queen was not as surprised as some by the behaviour of her twenty-three-year-old second cousin. Perhaps, like a few of Marina's friends, she had sensed the rebelliousness and the need for an identity not linked to royalty that Marina had wrestled with over a period of years. The Queen may also have seen the same signs in other junior members of the family from time to time. One of the most difficult lessons that the young royals have had to learn in recent years is that the chance of greater informality does not include less responsibility.

Miss Marina Ogilvy and Mr Paul Mowatt, a freelance photographer, were married in January 1990 at St Andrew's Church, Ham, Surrey. The bride's parents attended, but no other members of the royal family were present. (The Queen was attending the Commonwealth Games in New Zealand.) The Mowatts' baby, Zenouska, was born on 26 May and thus became twenty-seventh in line to the throne.

Soon after the marriage, someone close to the Queen commented to the author: 'As a good Christian I think the Queen forgives, but I don't think that she ever forgets.'

16

The Queen and Mrs Thatcher

❧

At the close of the annual Conservative Party Conference at Bournemouth on 12 October 1990 the whole assembly rose to its feet and in customary style stood smartly to attention as the National Anthem was played. As they did so, the BBC television director panned one of his cameras slowly along the platform of government ministers and, whether by accident or design, as the last words of the last line were sung out with surging feeling – LONG TO REIGN OVER US, GOD SAVE THE QUEEN – the camera arrived at the face of the leader, Margaret Thatcher, and stopped precisely on the words THE QUEEN.

For those in the hall, and those watching on television at home, it was a strangely disconcerting moment. On either side of the platform, giant screens showed the blown- up picture of Britain's Prime Minister. In her royal-blue suit, with not a hair out of place, it seemed, just for a moment, not so hard to imagine that noble profile on one side of a coin. Britannia personified.

Five weeks and six days later Margaret Thatcher's prime ministerial reign of eleven and a half years was to end abruptly in quite astonishing circumstances. At 3.09pm on Wednesday 21 November she left 10 Downing Street for the House of Commons declaring, 'I fight on. I fight to win.' At 5.30pm she arrived at Buckingham Palace for her regular weekly audience with the Queen, and stayed for thirty-five minutes. The next morning, between 7.30 and 8am, following lengthy consultation with her Cabinet ministers the previous night, Buckingham Palace received a telephone call from Number 10 intimating the Prime Minister's firm intention to stand down as Party Leader.

Was Mrs Thatcher's decision in any way influenced by her conversation with the Queen? Did the Queen use the historic definition of the monarch's role with regard to her Prime Minister – to counsel, to encourage, and occasionally to warn? It has always been assumed that the Prime Minister withdrew from the second ballot of the contest for the leadership because her Cabinet persuaded her that she would not win. But when she returned to Number 10 from Buckingham Palace, having only three hours earlier said she intended to fight on, might the seed of doubt have already been planted, not necessarily or directly by the Queen herself, but through the tenor of a private conversation between two women of the same age who over a period of eleven years had come to know, and sum up, one another very well?

It is possible that the Queen gave some kind of friendly warning, as she is entitled to, but in the opinion of those senior politicians to whom the supposition was put, most unlikely. The combined view was that the Queen would have been extremely careful not to make it appear that she was taking sides. She would have listened attentively, but offered no advice. At the same time, as other Prime Ministers have found, the Queen does make an excellent sounding board. Perhaps Mrs Thatcher applied the same attitude to the Queen as she once confessed she adopted where her husband Denis was concerned. 'Of course I listen to Denis. I'd be silly not to. Then I decide.'[1]

Whatever truth the probe of history eventually uncovers about Mrs Thatcher's dramatic resignation, the relationship in total between Britain's first woman Prime Minister and Elizabeth II makes for intriguing study and speculation.

The most commonly held view is that the two women did not get along with one another at all. Anthony Sampson may have fuelled the rumours when he wrote in 1982 that 'the weekly meetings between the Queen and Mrs Thatcher – both of the same age – are dreaded by at least one of them. The relationship is the more difficult because their roles seem confused; the Queen's style is more matter-of-fact and domestic, while it is Mrs Thatcher (who is taller) who bears herself like a queen.'[2]

However, even before she had reached the rank of Prime Minister, Grantham's proud daughter had struck some people as acting in a somewhat regal manner. 'Where's Mrs Thatcher?' piped up a girl in the crowd watching the Silver Jubilee procession to St Paul's Cathedral in June 1977. 'She'll arrive in the golden coach instead of the Queen, you'll see!' suggested a cockney neighbour.[3]

No one has been able to pin down the date when the former Prime Minister first took to using the royal 'we' (which the Queen never employs, except, ironically, when outlining the government's programme at the start of a new parliamentary session), but there are plenty of examples of her doing so. The most famous instance was when she proudly announced to the press that 'we are a grandmother'. But she also told a BBC reporter on the way to visiting Russia, 'We are in the fortunate position in Britain of being, as it were, the senior person in power.' And her proprietorial sense, if that is what it is, was displayed early on in her premiership when, in an interview with the author, she spoke of 'my coal mines'.

Many people, inside and outside parliament, were offended by Mrs Thatcher's use of the royal 'we', although they imagined that the Queen herself might be amused. Whether or not the plural was employed consciously is hard to ascertain, though it seems improbable that the Prime Minister could have been totally unaware of its effect. However, nobody close to her seems to have hurried to point out the peculiarity. Not, apparently, because it might have roused the wrath of Mrs Thatcher, but because, once drawn to her attention, it might have niggled at the back of her mind and worried her as to why anyone should see the need to mention it.

Those who know her well say that Mrs Thatcher, like the Queen, has a much more complex personality than appears on the surface. Like the Queen, she has had to succeed in what is predominantly a man's world, and perhaps as a result finds herself more at ease with men than with colleagues of her own sex. She had women in her Cabinet, but not for long. When a vacancy came up, a former Cabinet member recalls, and a colleague presumed that she would want a female replacement, he received his answer in one word, a firm 'No'.

As for Mrs Thatcher's relationship with the Head of State, no one gave much chance at the beginning of their association that the two women could ever become bosom friends. It was not just that Margaret did not shoot or fish (the majority of her predecessors had been able or willing to make a fairly good stab at both), or that she did not ride, or have a dog, or was in a position to talk about new films (which the Queen regularly has delivered to the Palace). Mrs Thatcher was something of an unknown factor to the Queen when she watched television pictures of Britain's first woman Prime Minister standing at the door of 10 Downing Street, on 4 May 1979, reciting an exhortation by St Francis of Assisi. True, she had held Cabinet office under Edward Heath, and had been Leader of the Opposition for four years. But the Queen had known most of her previous Prime Ministers reasonably well as individuals long before they achieved highest office. Mrs Thatcher was much more of an outsider.

For the first dozen or so weekly audiences, while there was little sign of nervousness on the part of Her Majesty – she, after all, had been in her job for over twenty-five years – there was a marked sense of deepest respect emanating from the new Prime Minister. Mrs Thatcher consistently arrived at the Palace at least fifteen minutes, and sometimes nearer half an hour, before the time of her appointment, causing Private Secretaries to scurry around and engage in non-controversial chit-chat with the Premier while they awaited the Queen's summons. When an aide, helpfully as he thought, suggested to the Prime Minister that perhaps she might not need to leave Number 10 quite so early, he was smilingly reminded that one could never be sure what the traffic was going to be like at that time of evening. (Perhaps it was wise of him not to go on to mention the police escort that invariably accompanies the Prime Minister's limousine.)

No one could doubt that the daughter of an alderman from middle England was the most devoted monarchist – no one curtsied lower than she. Witnessing Mrs Thatcher's deep curtsy was like watching a magnificent crimson sun sink beneath the horizon, remarked an ambassador from a Latin country who had greatly admired the lady from a respectful distance. 'A constitutional monarchy excels all other forms of government', she herself once said. 'It is not only a symbol of unity, but you respect and admire the monarch as well.'[4]

Gradually, the Queen and Mrs Thatcher may have come to realize that, affairs of State apart, there were, after all, a number of things that they had in common. Small things such as a dislike of beards, and more important things such as a loathing of litter.* Both were ladies who would not venture a step without their handbags. The Queen sometimes carried a miniature gold-plated camera in hers, and once a State paper, folded up, for which she was roundly ticked off for removing from its 'red box' by her Private Secretary at the time. The Prime Minister kept a small book of verses by her, to give inspiration at times of stress. One of these, which she had by her following the IRA's assassination attempt in Brighton in 1984,† is included in a 1966 calendar called 'Life's Tapestry'. the author is anonymous.

---

* Waiting in the old Home Office building one Armistice Sunday, prior to laying her wreath at the Cenotaph, the Queen looked out of a window and saw a pile of dirt swept into a corner of the courtyard below. 'Look!' she said reprovingly to an accompanying Cabinet minister. The following year the same Cabinet minister, having taken a peek beforehand, assured the Queen that the courtyard was clear this time. 'Yes, but I am afraid they will only have moved the dirt somewhere else', responded Her Majesty, and within a few minutes had discovered that this had indeed happened. 'She misses absolutely nothing', mused the chagrined minister.
† On 12 October 1984, during the Conservative Party Conference, a bomb devastated the Grand Hotel in Brighton, where several government ministers, including Mrs Thatcher, were staying. Three people were killed and more than thirty injured.

Life owes me nothing.
One clear morn is boon enough for being born.
And be it ninety years or ten,
No need for me to question when.
My life is mine.
I find it good,
And greet each hour with gratitude.[5]

Quite separate from politics, there are examples of both Mrs Thatcher and the Queen sharing a deep and genuine concern for someone who was known to them personally, if only slightly, and who might be in some sort of trouble or danger. When the Thatchers' son, Mark, went missing in the desert during the Paris to Dakar motor rally in January 1982 (he was rescued two days later after being spotted by a search plane), the Queen picked up the telephone and talked to Number 10, as one mother anxious for another. During the Falklands War, whenever the Prime Minister received information which she thought might indirectly affect Prince Andrew or was of especial interest to parents whose son was in the war zone, she made a point of having it relayed to Buckingham Palace.

Just occasionally, the concern and overwhelming sense of duty of both women was to lead to unfortunate clashes and some controversy. This was particularly the case at times of natural disaster, of which there were an unusually high number during the 1980s.

Mrs Thatcher's instinct is to rush to the scene of a disaster to offer comfort and help. 'She is impulsive and compassionate', says Lord Whitelaw, and the motives of being sometimes on the scene so quickly were not, he says, even partially inspired by any political advantage that might accrue.

The Queen's inclination has always been essentially practical. She has told her advisers: 'There is no point in my going, I will only be in the way.' While her advisers have sympathized with this view, and would never have urged an action which brought some nebulous advantage to the Queen alone, they believe that there have been occasions when the sovereign's appearance at the site of a disaster would have been of immense service and aid to the injured, the grieving, and the rescue services.

When asked by the author what he imagined the Queen might believe was the most unfortunate decision that she had made during her long reign, Lord Charteris replied: 'Aberfan. She always deeply regretted that she did not travel there immediately, instead of postponing her visit for a few days.'*

* In October 1966, 116 children and twenty-eight adults perished when a slagheap moved down over a school in the Welsh coal-mining village of Aberfan.

Evidence specially collated at Buckingham Palace following the spate of air and sea disasters in Britain during the late 1980s strongly suggested that those involved in one way or another with a major tragedy felt a sense of neglect if a senior member of the royal family did not travel to the scene – even if this did place an additional burden on security and rescue services. 'These things are essentially a matter of judgement', says Sir William Heseltine, who retired from being Private Secretary to the Queen in 1990. 'Each one merits a different response. The Queen's own response is generally, "I shall only be in the way if rescuers are trying to pull people out of a collapsed building." But this is not to say she does not care very deeply, or feel enormous sympathy.'[6]

Margaret Thatcher faced the dilemma of being accused of being unsympathetic and uncaring, if she did not go. Or if she did, of people saying, 'There goes Maggie, first on the scene, taking advantage of a tragedy in order to help her political image.'

Suggestions of this sort were made when she arrived on the scene within hours of the cross-channel car ferry, *The Herald of Free Enterprise*, sinking off Zeebrugge, Belgium, in March 1987, with the feared loss of 200 lives. A BBC reporter informed the Palace of the Prime Minister's impending arrival even before any arrangements had been made for a member of the royal family to visit the scene. Hugo Young, in his highly regarded biography of Margaret Thatcher, *One of Us*, states that the Prime Minister 'firmly instructed her staff to see to it that the Palace presence, in the persons of the Duke and Duchess of York, did not upstage her own'.[7] Be that as it may, a Palace source said that he would be very surprised if the Queen was not at least aware of Mrs Thatcher's plans to fly to Belgium. 'The Prime Minister has a formal obligation to let the sovereign know if she is about to leave the country – even if it is only to cross the Channel.'

According to the evidence available so far, the formal relationship between the Queen and Mrs Thatcher was not frigid, as has sometimes been suggested, but a few degrees warmer than that. The word 'cool' was used by one courtier, and 'professional' by another. A third said that Prime Minister Thatcher was 'punctilious in all modes of address and courtesies'. He went on to say that in constitutional terms Mrs Thatcher acknowledged the Queen's right to be kept informed and to be consulted. 'On the Queen's side, she acknowledges, as she must, a Prime Minister's right finally to take the decisions. But at the same time Her Majesty is very capable of offering her own opinions about things, when she holds them, and would certainly express them if they were contrary to those of her Prime Minister. However, once she had done that she would feel that she had exercised her constitutional rights and prerogatives, and it was the Prime Minister who had to take the decisions.'

One area where enthusiasms were not shared equally between the two women was the Commonwealth. Mrs Thatcher, who had seen very little of Commonwealth countries – indeed, had travelled abroad surprisingly seldom by the time she became Prime Minister - appeared lukewarm about Britain's close association. Where the Queen was a stalwart fighter for the idea of Commonwealth, Margaret Thatcher appeared more ready to spring to the defence of a sovereign Britain. According to Sir Shridath Ramphal, the former Commonwealth Secretary-General who was in a unique position to observe both women over a number of years, 'Mrs Thatcher came to the Commonwealth not knowing, not caring, very much about it. Then she came to like the style of the heads of government meetings, but grew more and more irritable with the critics of her South Africa policy. She had a schizophrenic attitude where the Commonwealth was concerned, and I must say I never felt that there was a wholly relaxed attitude between herself and the Queen. No warmth on either side.'[8]

In the summer of 1986 a major row blew up over an article in the *Sunday Times* entitled 'The African Queen'. This more than suggested that the Queen was disturbed by what she regarded as the lack of compassion in some of Mrs Thatcher's policies, and by her attitude to South Africa and whether or not to impose sanctions on that country. The article was based on conversations between the Queen's Press Secretary at the time, Mr Michael Shea (who subsequently moved to the Hanson Corporation in charge of their public relations), and a reporter from the *Sunday Times*. Buckingham Palace accused the newspaper of putting entirely false interpretations on the talks, and the editor, Mr Andrew Neil, later spoke of 'the Palace's ire. Though many of its senior officials were happy for the monarchy to be distanced from the policies of the Thatcher government, they did not want the Palace to be implicated.' As a result the pressure on the paper to recant was intense, according to Andrew Neil, 'the most serious editorial pressure I have experienced in my six years as editor'.[9] Some two and a half years later a complaint by the Buckingham Palace press office about a *Sunday Times* advertisement which stated that the monarchy had tried to 'muzzle' the paper was rejected by the Advertising Standards Authority.

So, *did* the Queen think that Margaret Thatcher's policies showed a lack of compassion for the underprivileged, that section of society, incidentally, which traditionally and somewhat paradoxically, has usually rallied to the monarchy, certainly since Queen Victoria's time? In a long letter to *The Times*, written a week after the original article appeared in the *Sunday Times*, the Queen's Private Secretary, Sir William Heseltine, described as 'preposterous' any suggestion that any member of the Queen's Household, 'even supposing that he or she knew what Her Majesty's opinions on government policy might be', would reveal them to the press. 'Whatever personal opinions the sovereign may hold or may have expressed to her government, she is bound to accept and act on the advice of her ministers ... she is obliged to treat her communications with the Prime Minister as entirely confidential between the two of them.'[10]

Four years after the event, in conversation with the author, Sir William Heseltine said that he was aware that Michael Shea had talked to the *Sunday Times* along lines which were not dissimilar to the topic treated in the paper the following Sunday, but not in such a way that suggested that 'this great rift existed between the Queen and the Prime Minister. I don't think that the Queen felt any more than I did that what appeared in the *Sunday Times* was a fair representation of her views.'

What the story encompassed, said *The Times* at the time, was the escape from captivity of 'some monstrous caged beast', namely the political opinions of the sovereign. If it did, then it was understandable that the Palace might have wished to put the dangerous animal swiftly back into its cage and in future check very carefully the credentials of anyone who wished to look behind the bars for some secret message. As *The Times* suggested, it was conceivable that the Queen's opinions might command a popularity as great as that of an elected government. And in a parliamentary democracy that would clearly never do. In any matters even verging on the political, the monarch – as far as the general public is concerned – must stay strictly mum.

What can be said about the Queen and Margaret Thatcher is that here were two women of very different personalities, of sharply contrasting interests, who probably did not always agree on the course of action that one of them, the elected one, decided to take. But in eleven and a half years the respect and admiration of one for the other only increased, and the friendship, if not close, could rely even so on loyalty and trust. Probably the greatest single difference between them was that one thrived on argument, and the other did not.

Notwithstanding this difference, Denis and Margaret Thatcher apparently quite looked forward to their summer weekend each year as the guests of the Queen at Balmoral. Golf clubs and a partner were always on stand-by for Denis (although he never made use of them) and Margaret, the Queen's Household discovered, was an easy guest to entertain. On arriving on Saturday, she would take lunch with the Queen's Private Secretary at Craigowan, traditionally his holiday home on the Balmoral estate, settle to her 'boxes' all afternoon, and go up to the castle shortly after tea for a private audience with the Queen, and then almost invariably a barbecue supper with the whole family. (Or, if the weather was too inclement, dinner in formal dress, with the Queen's piper circling the table.) Sunday morning was for church, Sunday afternoon perhaps tea at Birkhall with Queen Elizabeth the Queen Mother, after a drive round the moors and lochs with the Queen at the wheel. Monday, and it was back to work for everyone.

'That two highly spirited and very determined ladies should have been thrust together and have managed, despite all the rumours, to preserve a remarkable degree of co-operation over a period of eleven and a half years,' says a leading Conservative politician, 'is quite astonishing. It was achieved by both of them being highly skilled professionals.'

Within days of Margaret Thatcher moving out of 10 Downing Street, Elizabeth II awarded her former Prime Minister the Order of Merit, the highest award within the personal gift of the sovereign, and in Mrs Thatcher's departing honours list there was a baronetcy for her husband Denis.

Mrs Thatcher moved out, and the Queen moved on. On the morning of 28 November 1990, the Prime Minister tendered her resignation to the Queen. The Queen then received the Rt Hon. John Major, and requested him to form a government. In the afternoon and evening (the Court Circular reported) the Queen visited the Royal Military School for Music, Kneller Hall, and after receiving the Royal Salute toured the museum, unveiled a commemorative plaque and attended a concert.

Two months later the *Mail on Sunday* commented that Mrs Thatcher had begun to feel the aftermath of her resignation as reports of the Gulf War came in, and it was borne in on her that she no longer had any say in the future of the British troops that she had sent into the area. 'The trouble with Mrs Thatcher', says one of her friends, 'is that she never had any real interest in life save for politics. The strain of having this removed from her is beginning to show.'[11]

17

Seen But Rarely Reported

~~~

On 27 April 1990, the national administrator of the British Amateur Rugby League Association (BARLA), Mr Maurice Oldroyd, wrote to the Queen asking if she would open the Association's new headquarters building in Huddersfield, West Yorkshire. On 30 April he received a reply, saying that the Queen was considering the request. On 14 June he was told that she had agreed to come. And on 30 November 1990 she made the visit.

BARLA was lucky. With each morning's post Elizabeth II receives scores of requests to open this, unveil that, visit here, go there. Very few of the requests can be granted, mainly because there is just not enough free time available. During 1990, for instance, the Queen made 125 official visits, involving opening ceremonies and other appearances. She gave or was the honoured guest at fifty-nine receptions, lunches, and banquets. In addition she had a further 292 engagements outside of these categories, which included investitures.[*]

Each time a request is considered, priority of acceptance is given on a scale of one to three: one, to those organizations of which Elizabeth II is patron; two, to requests from towns or cities which she has not visited

---

[*] During the 1980s the royal family doubled its number of official engagements. In 1990 the Princess Royal covered the most ground, undertaking a total of 768 engagements, 319 of them abroad. Even more remarkable, Queen Elizabeth the Queen Mother's total in her ninety-first year, 118, was eight more than she managed at the age of eighty. The Duke of Edinburgh undertook 294 engagements at home and 260 abroad. Prince Charles's equivalent figures were smaller – 245 and 144 – but then he had suffered from a badly broken arm for much of the year.

before, or at least not for a long time; three, to events of national or topical importance, often connected with an anniversary.

Huddersfield and BARLA qualified under headings two and three.

At about the same time as the Amateur Rugby League submitted its request, the Department of Transport was also entering a bid for Her Majesty to name the new Blaydon Bridge over the Tyne, a section of the Newcastle Western Bypass. At first the Queen said no to the idea. She had already arranged to travel to Newcastle earlier in the same year for the traditional Maundy Day service. Two visits in one year to the same area might be thought to be unfair to other cities. However, there then came a request from Professor John Knill, chairman of the National Environment Research Council, to launch their new high-technology research ship, the RSS *James Clark Ross*, presently being built by Swan Hunter at Wallsend, an easy drive from Newcastle. The ship was due to be handed over to the British Antarctic Survey in June 1991, and the idea of wishing God-speed to such a useful and exciting venture appealed to the Queen. Why not see about trying to combine all three requests and make up a two-day programme, visiting Huddersfield one day and the north-east the next?

Members of the Queen's Household, notably Sir Kenneth Scott, the Queen's Deputy Private Secretary, set to work, and ran up against a problem almost straightaway. The tide, as Canute discovered, shows no preference to royalty. The word from the Swan Hunter shipyard was that in order to catch the tide the *James Clark Ross*, due for completion at the end of November, not only should be launched on a Saturday (not normally a working day for the Queen), but at 13.42 hours precisely. 'Saturday 1 December at 13.42 is the preferred date in terms of height of tide and daylight. The previous day's tide would be marginal, with risk of grounding on the launch. December 3 is the only alternative, but the tide is not till 15.30, by which time it is dark.' So Saturday it had to be. The rest of the programme would have to be worked round that date.

Lord Lieutenants are the Queen's representatives in the counties, and it is they who draw up a list of suggestions for the Queen as to which places she might visit and which people she might meet on her tours around the regions. In this case it was proposed that after the almost statutory civic reception on arrival at Huddersfield, and presentations and lunch at BARLA'S headquarters, the Queen might visit the town's sports centre (where she would be able to see the soft play area for handicapped children, and watch children at play in the combat room), and then go on to visit the Claremont Retirement Home, before returning at 5.15pm to the railway station to rejoin the royal train.

That was another thing that had to be organized – transport. The argument advanced by the Queen's advisers is that the royal train (running costs to the taxpayer in 1990 officially estimated at £1,426,000), and the Queen's Flight, (£6,745,000) both of which are used for official duties by other members of the royal family besides the Queen – are the most economic and secure ways of transporting royalty and their entourages. The train, especially, affords a place to stay, a place to work, and a place that is easier to guard than a hotel. It obviates the need, as do planes and helicopters, for the Queen to get up at the crack of dawn in order to be at the other end of her realm by midday. But normal services cannot be interrupted, and so the royal train's route and timing has to be slotted in carefully in between inter-city expresses. This requires planning.

Who to meet? The Queen looks very carefully at the file, by now some three inches thick, containing the draft programme and the names of those who may be presented. She enjoys meeting people, and she does not like to be rushed. She also likes to be sure that she is meeting the people whom she wishes to meet, and not just those who push themselves forward. When being shown round a factory or an art gallery, she does not relish being given a detailed commentary but prefers to look, and ask the questions that she wants to ask.

What to eat? On most regional tours there is at least one civic lunch, in order that some two hundred locals can say that they have had lunch with the Queen, even though they may be seated so far away from the top table that they cannot even see her hat. In Huddersfield the meal was to be a small affair in the Amateur Rugby League Association's headquarters, with just four tables for eight or nine, and no top table. It is the kind of arrangement that the Queen enjoys, but when she learned that all the 'high headians' would be sitting at her table, she suggested that everyone should be 'mixed up' a bit more. In Newcastle, two weeks before the great event, when 250 would take their places in the Civic Centre, three of the organizers tried out the official lunch, and came to the conclusion that a whole avocado for the first course, (*'each Quennel flavoured with watercress, fennel and fresh tomato garnished with fanned avocado and asparagus tips placed on an asparagus vinaigrette'*) might be too much, and halved the avocado.

Buckingham Palace requests that a choice of three menus is submitted, from which the Queen can make her choice: 'She is one of a very small number of people who knows in October precisely what she will have for lunch in December.'

By October all the plans were more or less in place. The invitations were prepared. Each of the 300 workers at the Swan Hunter yard was invited to bring up to four people to witness the launch. The bands began putting in extra practice and the ladies went shopping for hats. One Newcastle lady went down to London and only saw the label inside the hat that she had bought after she got back home: 'Not suitable for the

rain.' As always, the efficient Palace had its own wet-weather programme ready – 'usually it just consists of putting up umbrellas and
trudging along'. And the Queen had prepared her wardrobe for the
mini-tour, although no one, apart from her dresser, not even her lady-in-
waiting, is allowed to know what she will be wearing until the moment
she makes her first public appearance on the day itself. This surprising
fact needs to be explained to those who discover as a result that they cannot guarantee that the colours of their posies will match the Queen's
dress. Those who say that they would like to present a bouquet are asked
to make sure that it is not wired, in case it pricks, and also because it
makes it easier for the nurses to unravel the flowers when they reach the
local hospital, as they usually do. The question most frequently asked is:
should the ladies wear hats and gloves? And the reply from Buckingham
Palace is invariably the same: it is entirely up to the individual. The
Queen will wear a hat, because she always does, and she will wear gloves
because it is easier when shaking hands with people (who are sticky from
eating vol-au-vents, or sweaty from nerves – although this is never said,
of course). The Queen has found that people chat more easily if they
have a drink in their hands, so that is all right. Would Her Majesty care
to have something herself? A Dubonnet is her preference, or a soft drink,
or occasionally a gin and tonic, although she will probably take no more
than a sip.

As the day for actually setting out north – 30 November 1990 – drew
very near, a totally unexpected event threatened to change all the plans,
so meticulously worked out. Michael Heseltine had decided to stand for
the leadership of the Conservative Party against Margaret Thatcher, and
although she had won on the first ballot there would have to be a second
and possibly a third. The Queen had to remain in London.

Fortunately for Huddersfield and Newcastle, John Major won on the
second ballot and his fellow contenders withdrew, making a third ballot
superfluous. Even so, on the morning of Thursday, 30 November the
Queen was required to hold a privy council in the Audience Room of
Buckingham Palace to present her new ministers with their seals of
office. As a consequence, her departure to the north of England had to be
put back by nearly an hour. Happily, this did not mean that the programme had to be altered, or even speeded up very much, because the
train made up about twenty-five minutes on the run to Huddersfield.

The royal train, gleaming dark and crimson-lined, with white rims on
the engine wheels, can be made longer or shorter as required. This time it
consisted of six coaches. The Queen has her own coach with sitting
room, bedroom, bathroom, and a smaller compartment and bathroom
for her dresser. Next to it is the Queen's dining room, where she may invite accompanying Members of her Household to join her for meals.

255

They have their own coach for sleeping and working. Then there are two coaches for her servants and police officers, and another for British Rail staff. There is a spare engine at the back, in reserve. The Phantom Four Rolls-Royce in which the Queen will ride in Huddersfield and again in Newcastle had already been driven up the motorway in advance by the Queen's chauffeur, with identifying emblems and badges temporarily removed.

A royal arrival anywhere is always an anxious moment for Members of the Household, until they gauge the size of the crowds: 'It would be slightly awkward, I suppose, if no one turned up. Fortunately, it never happens.'* In Huddersfield several hundred people lined the route to cheer. Few could remember the last time that the sovereign had visited the town in 1971 and since then there had been a large influx of Asians who were particularly warm in their welcome. The Queen waved, and walked very slowly, as she always does on these occasions, and was particularly taken by how many different activities, for people of all ages, were organized in the sports centre.

After five hours of looking and listening and being scrutinized every inch of the way, it was time to return to the train, receive the farewells, and climb aboard for a welcome cup of tea and a slow chug through the Yorkshire Dales.

About one and a half hours later, like a weary horse, the royal train moved off the main line and slowed to a halt at a quiet, prearranged spot three miles from the cathedral city of Durham. Shielded by trees, and practically invisible from a nearby road, the location was a well-kept secret. But policemen, some with guard dogs, had already taken up position to surround the train, and within minutes land-lines had been plugged in to give telephone and television service to the royal party. It comes as no real surprise to learn that this whole procedure is officially termed as 'stabling for the night'.

The Queen dined at 8.30pm. As it was a Friday, fish was on the menu and, in advance, she had chosen grilled salmon. Members of her Household dined with her, and afterwards watched a tribute to Richard Dimbleby narrated by Ludovic Kennedy on BBC television. The Queen retired shortly after 10.30pm.

Sir Kenneth Scott was the first of the Household to be up and about the following day. As is his wont, he went for his early morning jog, on this occasion along an unfamiliar stretch of railway line. When he returned he was assailed by the delicious aroma of bacon and eggs, kippers

---

* The Prince of Wales once informed the author that, in his experience, the size of the welcoming crowd depended largely on the amount of publicity that he or his wife had attracted in the previous few days – 'except in central London, where most of the crowd is often comprised of tourists'.

and toast, prepared by British Rail. But there was work to be done, telephone calls to be made to Buckingham Palace, and arrangements for the
day ahead to be double-checked. Newspapers were brought to the train
and studied closely by Charles Anson, the Queen's Press Secretary.
There was nothing about the visit to Huddersfield in the national papers
– regional visits by the Queen rarely if ever get a mention, except in the
Court Circular – but the monarch was pleased to see that the *Huddersfield Examiner* had given the visit excellent coverage: 'Our Sovereign in
Town', and the next evening, 'Huddersfield Salutes the Queen's Return'.
At 9.40am the train moved off, and the Queen emerged from her coach
wearing a cherry-red coat and hat to match – which someone thought
she might have also worn on the State visit to Iceland earlier in the year.*
Twenty minutes later the train drew into the small Heworth station,
Gateshead. (Not to be confused with the Metro station next door,
warned the advance programme.) As it approached, the policemen who
had been standing guard on the platform in freezing cold for almost an
hour removed their black leather gloves to reveal white cotton ones
underneath.

First to emerge from the train was a footman carrying a tartan rug and
four leather briefcases which were conveyed to the waiting cars at the top
of a flight of steps leading up from the platform. Next there came the
Queen herself, who climbed the red-carpeted steps in strange silence, to
be greeted at the summit by Mr Edward Mirzoeff and his BBC television
crew making a film about the Queen's working life, together with a small
and surprised assortment of workmen in overalls, and mothers with
pushchairs on their way to the shopping parade to buy food for the
weekend. There was a thin cheer here and there, but it was a muted
arrival, as it was intended to be. The drive into Gateshead was equally
unspectacular, resembling nothing so much as a funeral cortège in a
slight hurry. But at the Civic Centre, where the Queen seemed to meet
just about everybody, things began to warm up.

Then it was on to the windswept Blaydon Bridge, where viewing
stands had been specially built for all those connected with the construction, and a pack of Brownies was lined up neatly, at the suggestion
of the Palace, so that the Queen could meet some really young people –
and, coincidentally, offer a photo opportunity. (The Queen was
delighted to receive appreciative letters from the den leader and her
Brownies a few days later.) The original plan had been for the Queen to

---

* When she was due to meet the Pope in October 1980, the Queen was worried that
the weather might be either very cold or quite warm. When her couturier suggested
that, to avoid any difficulty, he make two gowns, one in winter fabric and the other
in lighter cloth, the Queen protested at the extravagance, and was relieved when Mr
Ian Thomas said he would only charge for one.

open the bridge and bypass by her car driving through the ribbon and thereby cutting it. But in the end the planners reverted to the more traditional method of scissors and taste.

The luncheon at the Newcastle Civic Centre, with the 250 guests taking up the main body of the hall, was ajudged a success. (Viewed from the side, those at the top table looked rather like those nodding toys in the back windows of cars as they dipped low over their plates and passed food to their mouths, scared that they might otherwise spill on their smart new dresses or ties.) The organizers were slightly surprised to discover that, although she did not pay for the meal, the Queen was still, by protocol, the hostess. Accordingly, they had to adjust the seating plan so that the man on her left was now on her right – a fortunate change, as it happened, since it was known that one of the gentlemen was slightly deaf in one ear.

At 12.32 (it had to be any early lunch because of the launch), the Queen made a move, and naturally everyone followed – necessitating leaving one's pudding (*'three flavoured biscuits on a bed of rose scented praline sauce'*) behind, in order to board the buses going to the Swan Hunter Yard at Wallsend.

Like all ships' launches, the sending down to the water of the RSS *James Clark Ross* was exciting and romantic. Nothing went wrong, although there was a tiny moment of panic as the man with the key to the padlock that guarded the lever that the Queen had to pull in order to release the bottle of champagne, fished in his pocket to find it. The Queen, calm as ever, looked around, stretched her mouth – like Prince Charles does – and smiled sympathetically when the key was produced.

The ceremony completed, she walked through an avenue of cheering spectators ('don't she look loverly' and 'isn't she wonderful' was the most frequent response) to the Swan Hunter administration block where she was to cut a cake, receive presents and be asked to sign the visitors' book. When she paused to ask a question it was invariably of the standard sort: Do you work here? Haven't we been lucky with the weather? I hope you have not been waiting around too long? It was the Queen's smile and her modest demeanour that people recalled later, rather than what she actually said to them. Most people in a crowd are so excited at speaking to a member of the royal family that, even a minute later, they have only a hazy memory of what was actually said.

At this point the programme allowed five minutes for the Queen to 'retire', but she did not take advantage.* Instead, she moved straight

---

* Swan Hunter specially built on a toilet facility to its reception area when Queen Elizabeth the Queen Mother launched HMS *Ark Royal* in 1981. It was freshly painted and refurbished for the Queen's visit. When it is not at the service of royalty it is used by Swan Hunter receptionists.

into an adjoining reception room where she was much taken with a brooch made by a Newcastle jeweller, Jadwiga Billewicz, which was presented to her by the chairman and chief executive of Swan Hunter, Dr Roger Vaughan. Twice, as she listened to his short speech, the Queen lifted the lid of the presentation box to have a quick peek at the piece of artistry which clearly impressed and delighted her. And then it was suddenly all over. At 2.30pm the Mayor and Mayoress took their leave. At 2.50pm the Queen arrived at Newcastle airport and by 3.55pm her plane had touched down at London. At 4.15pm she was back home at Windsor Castle, in time for afternoon tea.

The two-day tour had been typical of those carried out by Elizabeth II at least once every two months over the past forty years. To the outside observer nothing about it appeared particularly strenuous or tiring, until one remembered that it had been duplicated, if not precisely, on all those thousands of other visits and engagements that had gone before. 'You try setting your face in a permanent smile for hours on end', the Queen once challenged an aide.

In terms of achievement, the value in public relations to the game of amateur rugby league and the business of ship-building is incalculable, but was reckoned by those concerned to be considerable. Against this should be set the total cost of the whole operation. In the case of Swan Hunter alone, who make a great celebration of all their launches, it amounted to over £20,000 for the day. The bill for hiring Her Majesty's Royal Marine Band alone was £2,000.

In contrast, setting aside the built-in costs of running the monarchial machine, including the royal train and the Queen's Flight, Buckingham Palace reckoned that it would probably be required to pick up the tab for just the meals on the train and the telephone calls made from the train during the forty-eight-hour excursion.

To the outside observer, what struck home most was the effect that a small woman in her sixties, slightly round-shouldered, with no benefit of spotlights or fanfares, should have on a crowd comprised of all ages from toddler to dodderer who stood in the biting cold for upwards of an hour and cheered and clapped as though their lives depended on it. Perhaps in a way they did. They were showing their admiration for the Queen as a person, but were they also cheering a way of life that most of those there wished should continue? Unemployment, hard times, the poll tax . . . all the harsh and niggling things were momentarily forgotten as fathers held up their children to see, and teenage girls, no smiles on their faces, stared inquisitively at a rather ordinary looking woman ('great make-up, though') whose photograph in coronation robes they remembered seeing every day on the wall at school assembly. However remote, she was central to their lives in a funny sort of way. They had come to see the most important symbol of themselves. At least that was the mood sensed by the outsider. Those who wanted to boo the monarchy had presumably stayed at home, or had not been allowed near.

In fact, those who probably benefited most from the mini-tour were the organizers who had put in the request for the visit to happen, and the people at whom it had been principally aimed, namely thousands of the Queen's subjects, in particular those under twelve, who, even if they managed only to catch a glimpse of what was going on, got some kind of kick out of it and are unlikely ever to forget the day that the Queen came to visit them in their home town.

18

Bones of Contention

∾✠∽

According to more than one source close to Queen Elizabeth II, if anyone were to enquire about the extent of the Queen's amazing wealth her answer would be: 'People say that I am incredibly rich, but it does not mean that I have got money to spend. I have got all these possessions, it's true, but most of them cost money to keep up and look after, and I cannot realize on them and spend the profits.'

Does the Queen like spending money? 'I don't think that she does particularly', says a courtier. 'In fact, I believe that she finds it positively painful. If she does have an extravagance it is over horses, not just race-horses. She will cannily spend money on horses that she would never dream of spending on something that you or I might want to buy, such as a luxury car or even a modern painting.'

Like most billionaires, the Queen probably has only a hazy idea of just how much she is actually worth when you add everything up, although she is quite likely to be aware if the price of a tube of toothpaste has been increased recently. Her bank, Coutts in the Strand, and her brokers, James Capel and Rowe Pitman, would be hard pressed to come up with an exact figure too. The problem has a lot to do with the fact that no one is absolutely sure what the Queen does own, in her own right, and what she holds in trust for the nation. There are a number of doubtful areas which have exercised the minds of everyone from Chancellors of the Exchequer to art historians from time to time, ever since the turn of the century.

Sir Oliver Millar, who was Surveyor of the Queen's Pictures from

261

1972 until 1988, and Director of the Royal Collection (1987-8), is in no doubt that the great historical collection of paintings and works of art, whose value on the open market is incalculable, is the property of the Crown, and that the monarch holds this cornucopia in trust during his or her lifetime. However, a question mark still arises over the future ownership of works of art purchased by a monarch.

'Queen Victoria regarded pictures bought by her uncle, George IV, as being private property', says Sir Oliver. 'and when I arrived, pictures bought by Queen Victoria were considered to be private property. After some discussion about twenty years ago it was established that everything up to 1901, when Queen Victoria died, had become part of the Royal Collection and was inalienable. I think the feeling now is that you could push the date to the outbreak of the Second World War, but it is still a slightly grey area.'[1]

Another shadowed corner of the royal treasure chest that arouses curiousity contains the fabulous gifts that the Queen and other members of the royal family, present and past, have received over the years from grateful governments, deposed relatives, or Heads of State richer even than the Queen.

The Cullinan diamond was given to Edward VII as a peace offering from the Transvaal government following the Boer War, and, after cleaving, two large sections were incorporated into the Sceptre and the Imperial State Crown. But parts three and four were made into the most valuable brooch and pendant in the world, which the Queen wears pinned just below her left shoulder. Six more pieces of the original diamond are said to have been worked into other pieces of jewellery, and if these ever reached the open market they could possibly fetch £100 million. Within the royal family they are known as 'Granny's chips'.

One of the Queen's favourite tiaras once belonged to the Grand Duchess Vladimir of Russia. When she fled the 1917 Revolution, it got left behind. An English nobleman subsequently recovered it, and the Grand Duchess's daughter sold the piece to Queen Mary. Today it is valued at well over £1,500,000.

When she was still Princess Elizabeth, and only twenty-one years old, the Queen received a present from a reclusive South African, Dr John T. Williamson, who owned a diamond mine. The gift turned out to be a twenty-three carat diamond, still the most perfect specimen in the world. When she was just five years older, at twenty five, the Princess of Wales was presented with a diamond and sapphire necklace, bracelet, and earrings by the Sultan of Oman – conservative estimate of their value: £750,000. (A little less costly, but just as acceptable presumably, was the £80,000 Aston Martin convertible that the Sultan presented to Prince Charles.)

Both *Forbes* and *Fortune* magazines, usually recognized as the arbiters of rich people's wealth, place Elizabeth II fourth in the list of the world's top owners. She comes after the Sultan of Brunei, whose personal wealth was assessed in late 1990 as being US$ 25 billion, and after the Saudi royal family who were worth only US$ 18 billion. Estimates of the private fortune of Elizabeth II are generally put at between £5 and £7 billions. But this figure is one that is necessarily plucked pretty much out of the sky, and is increasing by so many hundreds of thousands of pounds a day, anyway (one estimate early in 1991 placed the figure as high as £1.8 million a day!), that it is almost impossible to be completely up to date. Or accurate.* A belief commonly repeated over the years, that the Queen owned a part of New York's Manhattan, was roundly denied by Sir Kenneth Scott, the Queen's Deputy Private Secretary, in a reply to a letter from a member of the public: 'Her Majesty neither owns nor part owns property in Europe and America as alleged.'

Notwithstanding, in a survey of the world's twenty richest women in February 1991 *Harpers and Queen* magazine put Elizabeth II at the top of its list, with assets currently valued at £6,600 million. (Next came Johanna Quandt, who controls the BMW car group.) A large part of that fortune – whatever its true size, it is still a massive amount – has been accumulated over the years by skilful investment in property and blue-chip stocks, and by the fact that the Queen is not liable to pay any income tax. As Sir Kenneth Scott again points out to those who enquire, the Queen does surrender the entire income of the Crown Estates to the Treasury. But it comes as no real surprise that where the sovereign's *personal* finances are concerned, Buckingham Palace scrupulously avoids giving out any figures at all, and since royal wills are no longer published, as they were in the last century, we shall almost certainly never know the answer to that final demand which the living make of the dead: how much did she leave?

Almost as difficult to discover is the answer to the next question that nosy people ask: what does the Queen spend her money *on*? Apart from paying her staff and keeping up appearances, so to speak (which we shall come to in a moment), it appears that she spends, and needs to spend, very little. Like the Sultan of Brunei, she believes that even the wealthiest person can have enough of material things. 'I can see no point in just throwing money away', he once said. 'It is not necessary to buy the most expensive of everything, or indeed, everything expensive. You don't have to buy for the sake of it.'[2] The sentiments of the richest man in the

---

* In April 1991 the *Sunday Times* magazine, in a survey of Britain's 200 richest people reckoned that if the Queen retired tomorrow, stripped of her custodial wealth, she would probably be worth £1.2 billion.

world would find a home easily in the heart of the world's richest woman. Elizabeth II is never happier than when she is in old clothes, comfortable shoes, warm, in God's free air, and with wet, smelly labradors padding along in front of her. Excitement, which is subtly once removed from happiness, comes when she is riding one of her horses at the gallop, or – even better – watching one of her horses fighting for a winning place at Ascot or Newmarket. At the start of 1991 her greatest unfulfilled ambition in the racing world was to see one of her horses win the Derby, the only classic race still to fall to her. The Queen's knowledge and judgement of conformation in the collecting ring, backed up by her almost photographic memory, have earned her high respect and admiration in a world where anyone who does not know short canon bones from straight hocks is quickly rumbled. Her success in the world of breeding and racing horses is one area where no one could say she owes everything to her position.

Those who are more interested in less active pursuits, such as reading books by authors other than Dick Francis (one of the Queen's favourite story-tellers), or attending performances in the grey bunker of the National Theatre in London, sometimes express the wish that their monarch would show more interest in and patronage of what they would call the finer things in life. Elizabeth II would not say thank you for two free seats at Covent Garden – not that she would need to ask – and partly for this reason she is sometimes accused of being a philistine where the arts are concerned. There is some basis for the accusation, and equally sense in the Queen's likely response. She has told more than one person that there is no point in being what you are not, or feigning interest in something that does not rouse one's natural enthusiasm. Even in her official life, she cannot always summon up wild excitement about what she is being asked to do – and just occasionally it shows. On the other hand, there are many who would argue that, even if she is not particularly interested herself, the Queen could still give more encouragement to the arts than she appears to do, by making public donations or giving patronage in some other visible way to more modern artists and performers of one sort or another than she already does. One theory is that Elizabeth II is upper class and middle brow, a combination that has always appealed to the majority of British. And as such she watches the 'bawbies' most carefully.

To say that Elizabeth II is not an intellectual is not to infer that she is some kind of dullard where the arts are concerned. She has far too sharp and enquiring a mind to be that, and holds a genuine and expert regard and affection for the fabulous works of art of all kinds that have surrounded her ever since she was a child.

George VI made no pretence of serious understanding of painting, but took pleasure from the pictures that hung in the rooms that he regularly occupied. Queen Elizabeth the Queen Mother loves the quality of good painting and the company of artists: 'Civilized friends in a civilized setting.' Elizabeth II is interested in the historical sequence of the paintings in the Royal Collection. She was given a Dobson portrait of Charles II, for instance, which fitted in nicely; and a little time ago acquired a small Turner watercolour of Windsor, which she particularly wished to have as there was presently nothing by this wonderful artist in the Royal Collection. She studies the catalogues of forthcoming auctions, and if there is a painting that seriously interests her it will normally be brought to the Palace for her inspection. One of the problems about bidding for paintings that appeals to her historical sense is that they are becoming increasingly expensive (the Queen would argue, even for her). Because the Royal Collection is a private collection it does not qualify for consideration when pictures from other collections are bequeathed to the nation. The Queen would never buy a picture just because her advisers on art thought that it was an important acquisition or a particularly fine piece of work. As Sir Oliver Millar sensibly points out: 'A dismembered ox by Rembrandt is not particularly appealing if you do not happen to like dismembered oxen, even though Rembrandt is a good painter.'

A regret expressed by Sir Oliver and others is that so little work by contemporary artists has been acquired by the Queen during her reign. 'I think the sadness as far as pictures is concerned is that the momentum which began in the early part of her reign, even on a small scale, of purchasing pictures by contemporary British artists, has not gone forward. It is a criticism ever since Prince Albert's day that there has not really been a royal involvement with good modern painting, either significant foreign or British work. But if you don't want to buy modern pictures, why should you? You can't do it as a duty. It has to be something that springs from the heart.'[3]

The Duke of Edinburgh, whose pleasure in painting as a hobby has passed on to his eldest son, has probably acquired more modern paintings than the Queen has. Each year, over a period of years, he has bought privately a number of paintings by Scottish artists at the Royal Scottish Academy, whose annual exhibition usually coincides with the Queen's summer stay at the Palace of Holyrood in Edinburgh. Of course, the Queen herself has made a unique contribution to the nation's storehouse of art by patiently sitting for scores of portraits over the past forty years. However, again, the sadness is that practically all of these paintings have been commissioned by outside bodies, so that the finished work usually ends up in a place of honour in a company boardroom or a regimental headquarters. In the royal palaces there are practically no portraits of the Queen showing her at different stages of her life. 'It has not seemed important to the Queen to compile a chronological succession of portraits,' explains Sir Oliver Millar, 'whereas George V – who was not very good at being painted – saw that a number came into the Royal Collection. And Queen Victoria made absolutely certain that every so often there would be a new portrait of her and of members of her family.'

Cost comes into it, as it does increasingly with practically everything concerned with Britain's royal family in the 1990s. One senior retired courtier recalls that, when he first joined the royal household in the mid 1970s, the overriding criterion was to give the best possible service to the monarch. 'Today, it seems to me at least, a proviso has been added: if we can afford it. This has caused enormous tensions, with people leaving and others feeling very hard done by. Particularly at the sergeants' mess level there is deep resentment, not over salaries but over attitudes. More and more, things are run on an accountancy basis and the older members of staff resent the change from being a service to running a show. At the same time, there is no getting away from it, the royal Household has got to balance its budget like anyone else.'

Balancing the royal books has always proved something of a nightmare for those in charge of spending, and a source of confusion and some criticism for those responsible for supplying the funds in the first place, i.e. the country's taxpayers. By reverting in 1991 to a formula used when the Queen came to the throne in 1952 – a fixed sum over a period of ten years – Palace and government believed that they had simplified matters, and, by no means incidentally, removed the opportunity for annual criticism each time the figures were presented to parliament. But the changes have made it even more difficult for members of parliament and others to probe the accounts.

The first thing to remember is that the Queen's personal private income does not come into the calculations when considering what the sovereign is 'paid'. And the second point is that, strictly speaking, she is not 'paid' anything at all by the State. The large amounts of money that parliament votes to her in what is known as the Civil List are to cover the cost of running the monarchy. For the year 1990-1 this sum, according to official figures, was expected to amount to a total of £7.9 million in the case of the Queen's duties,* and £2.52 million in respect of the official duties carried out by other senior members of the royal family. In addition a further £46 million was to be set aside by a number of government departments to pay for such items as overseas visits made at the government's request (£580,000), the upkeep and running costs of the royal

---

* Shortly before her resignation, Prime Minister Margaret Thatcher informed the House of Commons that the total cost of all her offices in 1989-90 was £7,704,396. This included salaries and notional pension liability. The annual running and maintenance costs of the White House in Washington are calculated to be around £30 million.

yacht (£9,272,000), and the same for the palaces occupied by the Queen and other principal members of the royal family (£25,650,000).

For 1990 the royal accountants estimated that the Queen would be required to spend £37,950 on flowers, £149,026 on the upkeep of horses and carriages (for official use), and £63,700 on laundry bills. For donations, cups and prizes, she should set aside £9,500.

If these figures appear either small or large, modest or extravagant, depending on one's view, they do allow at least for the Queen and the various members of her family to appear in public in the kind of style and sparkling splendour which the Queen's subjects, both in Britain and in the Commonwealth, over the years have come to expect.* Twenty-two years ago, the golden encrustation on the Crown, with its thick underlay of hard-working administrators and general staff, was in grave danger of crumbling through lack of funds. In the autumn of 1969 the Duke of Edinburgh tossed a verbal firework into the arena of public debate by informing an interviewer on *Meet the Press* in Washington that the monarchy would be 'in the red' within a year.

The comment came in response to the question, 'How is the royal family coping with inflation?, and was bang on target. The Civil List that had been agreed upon at the outset of Elizabeth II's reign made some allowance for inflation, but not for the average rise in wages between 1953 and 1970 of 126 per cent. In 1962, for the first time, the Civil List expenditure exceeded the £475,000 budgeted for, and in each succeeding year the reserve fund was eaten into, until in 1970 there was only £30,000 left in the kitty to meet a deficit for that year of £260,000.

The public, who to a very large extent had been in ignorance of royal finances up until this point, began asking questions, not all of which were favourable to the royal cause. Did the cost of the Queen's Flight (two or three shining piston-engine aeroplanes manned by RAF crews) come out of the £475,000 Civil List? No, that expense (£700,000 in 1970) was born by the Ministry of Defence. As was the cost of running the royal yacht. Did the Queen pay for the stamps and telephone calls made by her staff? No, they were provided free by the Post Office, but would have cost £52,000 otherwise. British Rail paid for the Queen's official travels round the country, and the cost of maintaining the royal train (£36,000 in 1970, an officially estimated £850,000 in 1990). The Depart-

---

* Because of historical precedent the Prince and Princess of Wales do not receive a Civil List allotment from the State. The Prince's income derives from the Duchy of Cornwall estates, with land holdings estimated to be worth about £253 million which brought in a net income in 1989 of £2,515,925. Technically exempt from paying income tax, Prince Charles transfers a quarter of his annual income voluntarily to the Consolidated Fund, a sort of State piggy-bank. It is not true that Princess Diana spends the rest.

ment of the Environment paid for the upkeep of the occupied royal palaces. . . . And so it went on. When the sleuths had finished their work, after accounting for the Department Votes, as the various Ministry contributions were called, it looked as though the taxpayer was forking out something like £3½ million a year to maintain the monarchy rather than the £475,000 accounted for by the Civil List alone.

Did the Queen pay income tax on her vast personal income? No. Death duties? No.* What about the Duchy of Lancaster? Well, what *about* the Duchy of Lancaster? It was news to a great many people that the sovereign, whether male or female, is also the Duke of Lancaster and as such received, in the late 1960s, an income of over a £¼ million from an assortment of lands and property (mostly in Yorkshire, paradoxically) that have belonged to the Crown since the Middle Ages.† These were kept separate from the Crown Estates proper which were surrendered to parliament in 1760 by a debt-laden George III in return for a regular annual income from the State.‡ There were other queries, such as why were Balmoral and Sandringham considered to be solely the private property of the sovereign, when Balmoral had been purchased and extensively improved with money saved from Queen Victoria's Civil List, and the staff wages of both houses were paid out of State funds?

Prince Philip, by his frank answer to a Washington journalist's question, had not only raised a legitimate point but had also stirred up a hornet's nest. So that when the Queen's advisers formally entered a request in November 1969 that the Civil List be increased there was some support both in and outside of the House of Commons for the view expressed by Willie Hamilton MP that this was 'the most insensitive and brazen pay claim made in the last 200 years'.[4] Mr Hamilton, Labour MP for West Fife, was to become famous as a virulent antiroyalist (he incensed many people, and greatly amused others, with his book *My*

* Queen Victoria paid income tax from 1842. Edward VII continued the practice, which was dropped, by government decree, when George V came to the throne in 1910. 'It never can be . . . intended that His Majesty should take money out of one pocket to put it into another.' But George V offered to contribute to the cost of State visits out of his Civil List money, and made over £100,000 to the government during the First World War. George VI handed back the same amount during the Second World War.
† The Duchy consists of 52,000 acres of farm and moorland divided into four areas known as 'surveys'. But its most celebrated real estate lies on the south side of the Strand in London, and includes the site of the Savoy Hotel.
‡ The Crown Estates have proved to be a profitable investment. In 1988/9 the proceeds amounted to £81.5 million, of which £41 million was paid into the Consolidated Fund. Out of this fund the Civil List payment of £6,195,200 was made. This would seem to suggest that the royal family has been losing out for some time on the deal that their ancestor made, to the considerable benefit of the taxpayer. But not so if you add to the Civil List payment the amount laid out by government departments on monarchial requirements – an estimated £46 million in 1990/1.

Queen and I, published in 1975), but he was also a mouthpiece for those who earnestly wished to see a closer examination made of royal finances before any more money was voted to the Queen.

To Harold Wilson, the Prime Minister, it seemed that any increase could only be decided upon after a parliamentary inquiry had taken place. The country was, yet again, in some economic distress and an automatic increase would probably not have met with much approval.

The six meetings, in all, of the House of Commons Select Committee on the Civil List, which took place between 21 June and 27 July 1971, comprised the most thorough investigation of the official royal finances that there has ever been. The committee received an answer to practically every question asked. Even so, despite the reams of data processed, a precise picture of all the royal resources and expenditure remained hidden. 'The Officers of the Household, including myself,' explained Lord Cobbold, the Lord Chamberlain, 'do not handle Her Majesty's private funds and are not conversant with the details of such funds. Her Majesty handles these matters herself, as did the late King and earlier sovereigns.

'At the same time,' the Lord Chamberlain continued, 'Her Majesty has been much concerned by the astronomical figures which have been bandied about in some quarters suggesting that the value of these funds may now run into £50 to £100 million or more. She feels that these ideas can only arise from confusion about the status of the royal collections, which are in no sense at her private disposal. She wishes me to assure the committee that these suggestions are wildly exaggerated.' So the royal collection of pictures and other works of art, the Crown Jewels, and even the royal stamp collection built up by the Queen's father and grandfather were *national* heirlooms? 'In no practical sense', said Lord Cobbold (who once described his job as 'part-time chairman of a large company with a single active shareholder') 'does the Queen regard any of these items as being at her free personal disposal.'

As the committee's brief had been simply to examine whether the Civil List had been spent without extravagance in the past and was likely, if increased, to be administered with reasonable efficiency in the future, its members presumably felt that they could not with dignity burrow any deeper.* When the Select Committee reported at the end of 1971, its main recommendation was that the Civil List should be more than

---

* The House of Commons can be curiously reverential at times where the Queen is concerned. When, in December 1990, some members wished to ask questions about the hereditary baronetcy conferred on Denis Thatcher by the Queen, the Speaker refused them, saying that they should know the rules about discussing the royal family – 'We do not bring the royal family into our discussions' – even though, as he must have been aware, it is the Prime Minister who submits a list of such honours to the Queen, and it is the Prime Minister who is answerable for so doing.

doubled to what was then considered to be a very large sum indeed, £980,000 a year. Anticipating the reaction to its report in some quarters, committee members were anxious to make clear that the money would be reimbursement for legitimate operating expenses and in no way a salary for Elizabeth II, or anyone else in her family. 'There is, therefore, no question in any ordinary sense of a "pay increase" for the Queen', they emphasized. If the Duke of Edinburgh, who was to receive £65,000 in one year, had anything left over after paying the salaries of his staff, (estimated to total ten) and the running expenses of his office, then he would be required to pay personal income tax on the balance. This may explain the remark Prince Philip once made to the author that 'The less I do, [presumably meaning the fewer official duties that have to be attended to and staffed], the better off I am'.

The Queen had made it clear to the Select Committee that in future she wished to forego payments from the Civil List into her privy purse, an ancient practice which had added to the confusion and controversy over royal finances. In theory, the privy purse was the sovereign's pocket money, but in practice the Queen had used it to pay for both 'private' and 'public' expenditure and the demarcation line between the two had not always been made distinct. The fact that the Queen was able to pay for some public duties out of her private purse – and out of her goodwill, it needs to be stressed – at a time when, like Oliver Twist, she was asking for more, was a revelation which provided more ammunition to those who were ever ready to criticize the monarchy and the way it was administered.

By 1975, rocketing inflation had eaten even further into everyone's wage packets, and the provisions that the Select Committee had made to meet this contingency were suddenly woefully wide of the mark. The Civil List required another £½ million just to break even.

Harold Wilson, back in power after Edward Heath's resignation, had to return to the House of Commons with silver cap in hand once more. But, somewhat fortuitously, he was able to point out that royal expenses had, 'thanks to continuing economies in the administration of the royal Household, risen by considerably less than the increase in the retail price index since 1972.' The money was needed principally to meet the wage increases of the 473 members of staff, most of whom were trade union members – which cannot have escaped the attention of Labour MPs.

After a debate lasting one and a half hours, the increase was passed (£60,000 for 1974 and £150,000 for 1975) but with ninety MPs voting against the motion. It is almost certainly true to say that this opposition did not reflect any displeasure with the Queen personally, or with the increase, but with the muddle and unanswered questions that surrounded, and still surround to a certain extent, the finances of the Royal House of

Windsor. One other decision taken by parliament in 1973 was that, in future, the Civil List would be reviewed and voted on each year in the House of Commons, at around the same time as the Chancellor's budget statement. This, it was thought, would tie matters up more neatly and avoid the embarrassment of the sovereign having to come begging to the House every few years when things got tight.

Unfortunately for the Palace, that is not the way that it worked out. The annual review, which almost invariably involved an increase, led to newspapers year after year coming out with headlines about a 'Pay Rise for the Royals'. It made no matter how often Buckingham Palace pointed out that the increases were to meet running costs and did not constitute a *pay* rise, the papers and their readers went on regarding them as such. In particular, there were mumblings and murmurings, but no protest marches, when Prince Edward, hardly out of university, began receiving an allowance of £20,000 a year, and when, in 1987, Princess Margaret's 'funds to meet necessary expenditure in fulfilling public engagements' went up by £5,500 to £127,000 a year.

In 1989, the Duke of York, now a married man and father, with most of his time employed by the Royal Navy as a helicopter pilot, saw his beneficiary almost doubled to £155,400, while the hard-working Princess Royal – as the Queen had chosen to honour Princess Anne – received a more modest increase, bringing her allowance up to £140,400. The Queen's Civil List payment in 1989 was increased by £190,000 to £4,326,100. But few newspapers noted that, following precedent, she repaid £371,000 to the Treasury to cover the official duties of the Duke and Duchess of Gloucester, the Duke and Duchess of Kent and Princess Alexandra. What one or two did mention, notably the *Daily Mail*, was the Queen's sound sense of economy. 'One example of the Queen's thrift is electricity. She regularly tours the Palace ensuring lights are switched off.'

In the spring and summer of 1990, even while these increases, and economies, were being put into effect, secret consideration was being given inside Buckingham Palace to the idea of returning to the system of Civil List allowances that had operated in 1971, whereby a global sum was agreed upon and remained fixed for a period of ten years. When the ten years were up, or before if absolutely necessary, the royal trustees reported back on the current position.

The Lord Chamberlain, the Keeper of the Privy Purse, and the Queen's Private Secretary drew up the revised plan and put it to the Treasury. Apparently, the government was not all that dissatisfied with the existing system, 'but then they did not have to put up with the adverse press criticism every year', a Palace source pointed out. In a House of Commons statement on 25 July 1990, Mrs Thatcher announced that the Queen's Civil List would be fixed at about £7.9 million a year until 2001, but that during that period cost savings of £5 million were expected. In the opinion of the Prime Minister the revised measures were 'both appropriate for the dignity of the Crown and in tune with responsible management.'[5] Some Labour MPs attacked the proposed sums as excessive, although Neil Kinnock, the Leader of the Opposition, welcomed the move.

What was particularly interesting was the setting up of a new post within the royal Household, that of Director of Finance and Property Services, to be held by Michael Peat, a partner in the well-known London city accountancy firm of Peat Marwick McLintock. One of his key responsibilities would be to take over the running of both Buckingham and St James's Palaces, and of Windsor Castle. Up until now these had been in the care of the government's Environment Department and its Property Services Agency. One or two people idly wondered if the ten-year period for the new Civil List, ending in 2001, might in any way be linked to the idea of the Queen stepping down from the throne in favour of Prince Charles in that year? After all, the Civil List is always re-examined at the start of a new reign. This piece of pure speculation brought forth an enigmatic smile from the Palace, and a firm denial.

When the new plans were confirmed in a report issued by the royal trustees in the following October, press comment was mixed. Perhaps predictably, the *Daily Star* decided to have a go at the Queen's youngest son:

Prince Edward has been trying to convince us for years that he has some really useful function in life.

The only thing he seems to be able to do – with notable success – is spend our money.

The Government has now decided in the royal pay reforms to give him an £80,000 a year rise.

A few weeks ago he announced that he was setting up a theatrical business on his own.

Why should he collect a £100,000 subsidy from the rest of us?

Of course, the Queen has vast expenses from her duties and these must be met by the State.

No one objects, either to the caring Prince and Princess of Wales receiving income from the Duchy of Cornwall, or hard-working Princess Anne having money from the civil list.

But other members of the royal family don't seem to do an awful lot to earn their corn.

While most of us struggle to pay our rent and mortgages, and are told to curb pay claims, Prince Edward is being handed a 10-year rise in advance.

He doesn't have to worry about paying his gas bill, or even his gold car.

Nice work. If only he knew the meaning of the word.[6]

Couched in such a style, the message probably found approval among many of the *Daily Star*'s millions of readers. *Today*, catering largely for those in their early thirties, thought that 'The real charge against the royal family's spending habits is that they spend too much of our money and not enough of their own.'[7] While George Gale in the Tory-supporting *Daily Mail*, in his weekly column written under the title 'The Voice of Common Sense' expressed a personal and highly controversial view: 'In return [for the Civil List] we get fancy dress pantomimes of tin soldiers and a society stratified by absurdities like Ascot, the Honours List and the Royal Variety Performance.' Gale was known to be highly critical of the monarchy. Even so, his final paragraph was especially vitriolic. 'The Queen likes to pretend she enjoys constitutional influence, yet all she really enjoys is sitting atop the stinking heap of privilege which flows down from her like lava from a semi-dormant volcano.'[8] Who said that the cause of republicanism in Britain was dead!

It was left to the more sombre *Times* to reflect what was probably the view of most people to the changes: 'By common consent,' it had opined in its first leader on 25 July 1990, 'the royal family is a popular recipient of public expenditure, whose cost compares favourably with that of other Heads of State.'

However, some six months later, with the Gulf War and a deep recession combining to cause people to re-examine both values and value, there was renewed criticism of cost, and in some quarters of the behaviour of younger members of the royal family. In a newspaper poll, 47 per cent of those questioned thought that the Duchess of York was not doing enough to support Britain's role in the Gulf crisis, and 53 per cent held the same dismal opinion of Prince Edward's efforts.[*] 'A sense of unease is running through the country over the example set by the royal family during the Gulf conflict', said the *Daily Mail*.[9] Its sister paper, the *Mail on Sunday*, told its readers that 'Britain is still in love with the monarchy – but not the Duchess of York. And many people now think the royal family costs too much.'[10] The statement was based on a poll carried out by the newspaper which showed that 70 per cent of those interviewed thought that the Queen should pay income tax.[†]

* The poll was conducted by MORI for the *Daily Mail* on 11 and 12 February 1991.
† MAI UK Market Research interviewed a representative quota of 1,000 people in Great Britain by telephone on 14 and 15 February.

In 1866, the journalist Walter Bagehot had argued that we paid the Crown not in order to exercise specific functions but 'to retain the loyalty of the labourer in Somerset', who could not understand the process of government but who could respond to the drama of royalty and feel a primitive and sentimental loyalty for the personality of the sovereign.

Perhaps times were a-changing, after all.

19

Shaping Up Nicely?

❧

In January 1991, at the start of the last year of the third decade of her reign, Elizabeth II could allow herself a sigh of satisfaction. So far things had gone fairly well. The monarchy had not only survived but was still popular, despite the criticized behaviour of one or two of the younger members of the family and attacks on royal finances. She and her husband remained in robust health, although there were rumours that Prince Philip was showing worrying signs of digestive problems. Their family, apart from the unfortunate but perhaps predictable estrangement of their daughter and her husband Mark Phillips, had more or less stayed in one piece. Possibly the greatest achievement – and certainly the most popular within the family and outside – belonged to Queen Elizabeth, the Queen's mother, who had celebrated her ninetieth birthday the previous August, and showed every sign of continuing to be the favourite royal of all. In celebration of the birthdays of the Queen Mother (ninety), Princess Margaret (sixty), the Princess Royal (forty), and the Duke of York (thirty), the Queen threw a giant family party at Buckingham Palace. As much as anything, it was a reaffirmation of loyalty to the concept of family, with Elizabeth II a wise and mature matriarchal head who, on 21 April 1991, would reach her own sixty-fifth birthday.

If there were a small cloud blotting out a corner of the sun it signified the concern that the Queen, and to a certain degree the Duke of Edinburgh, felt about their relationship with their eldest son and his wife. A psychologist might suspect that what had been occurring was a classic example of a mother whose deep love for her son had not easily trans-

275

mitted itself to include the woman he married, and partly in consequence the son fiercely wished to demonstrate his independence of both women without losing the love of either. In the case of Prince Charles and Princess Diana, matters were complicated in the early years of their marriage by the disparity in their ages, and by the laser beam of publicity that in no way helped to heal the non-fatal marriage wounds that they suffered.

Few if any relationships are simple to unravel. And the amateur diagnosis given here is almost certainly not the whole truth. But it is the one offered or confirmed by a number of sound people who have been close to the royal family over a period of many years and, in view of the vast amount of speculation and sometimes misconceived notions constantly being printed by the more popular sections of the media (with no comment, confirmation or denial emanating from either Buckingham or Kensington Palaces), it is at least worth examining. After all, to put it no higher, most relationships hold interest. And the relationship between a monarch and the person who will suceed to the same throne is more important than many.

Judging by polls and other public reaction, the most commonly held view at the start of 1991 was that Prince Charles is a most likeable and highly principled person in middle age who is deeply frustrated by the absence of a strong role in his life, and that probably the best thing all round would be for him to come to the throne sooner rather than later (say, in the next five to ten years), even if it would mean the Queen abdicating first.

Setting aside for the moment the question of abdication, which we shall come to in the next chapter, the popular conception is quite a bit wide of the mark. Prince Charles, according to sources close to him over the past twenty-five years, is not frustrated at not being king. That is a duty and an inheritance that he is quite prepared to meet and take up, when the time arrives. But he is in no hurry whatsoever. Apart from anything else, short of abdication, his mother would have to die before he could come to the throne, and his daily prayer is that his mother will remain in good health for many more years to come.* What does annoy, irritate, and at times nearly drive him mad is the fact that as the Prince of Wales he can command attention for his ideas – which flood out of him, one after another, at a sometimes almost unmanageable rate – but, because of who he is, he has to feed these ideas out through the conduit of a confusing number of advisers and organizations, making scrupulously sure all the time that he is not inadvertently crossing over into the

---

* Once a year, usually before she leaves London for her summer holiday, the Queen has a complete medical check-up, including a cardiogram, for which she visits a specialist.

political arena and standing on toes. And then, once an idea is launched, he has to bow out more or less, and move on to something else.

What he would like to have been (and what he would have been very good at being) say one or two of his friends, is an MP – preferably owing allegiance to no particular party. Which of course is impossible. As a peer he can speak in the House of Lords, but has chosen to do this only twice (in 1974 and 1976), perhaps because he may think it too rarified an arena. He prefers to work largely behind the scenes, meeting people on the ground, popping up now and again with a controversial speech on the environment, architecture, education or whatever, which he knows will attract publicity, and then lending his good offices, quite literally sometimes, to help others to get *their* ideas off the ground. He is an innovator extraordinaire.

His solid work for, and in certain cases conception of, a string of organizations such as the Prince's Trust, the United World Colleges, the Prince's Advisory Group on the Disabled, Task Force, and the Prince's Youth Business Trust, far outweighs the reputation he has for being something of a slightly eccentric wimp. The Prince's Youth Business Trust alone has helped 12,000 young people to set up their own concerns, with a 70 per cent success rate. He cares more, and is prepared to do more, about the environment, about chances for youth, about racial equality, than probably any other member of the present royal family. Like his ancestor, Charles II (who was responsible for the Royal Society, the Hudson's Bay Company, and the Royal Military Hospital at Chelsea), he wishes to see a nation enriched in many areas, and a world properly warned of the environmental risks it is taking. His frustration is that while his position allows him a hearing in influential places, it also prevents him saying or doing as much as he would like.

The Queen appreciates the dilemma and admires her eldest son for his endeavours. But, from time to time, it would appear, she wonders about the wisdom of some of his actions and his choice of one or two of his advisers. The Queen is a mild-mannered traditionalist through and through. The Prince of Wales as a younger man was a traditionalist. Now, in middle age, he is much more a crusading modernist, with traditionalist undertones. And there apparently lies the rub. He also owns a raging quick temper (not dissimilar to King George VI's 'gnashes'), which at times can make him a difficult person to work for, or to be married to. It was hardly a secret that family relations in the early summer of 1991 were not as relaxed or easy as they had been, say, ten years earlier, when the Prince of Wales married.

'The Queen's role as heiress presumptive was very brief,' points out a senior courtier, 'but even if it had been long it would have been very far from her own inclination to strike out and find a role in extension to that.

'There are those who say that it was not necessary for Prince Charles to try and prove himself, for his role was already there. But I admire him without qualification for following his own instinct, which was to go and find something that he thought he had to do, something in which he could make his own impact. Even if it would not have been the Queen's way.'

Another reliable source speaks of a difficult relationship that has existed for some time between Prince Charles and his father. 'There is a tension between them. Now, as you know, the only way to handle Prince Philip in argument is to stand up to him and give as good as you get. But Prince Charles is incapable of doing that. He is too sensitive, he just curls up. So that is another reason, I believe, why he has made himself fiercely independent. He is the one member of the family, it seems to me, rather to delight in not taking his parents' advice. There have been occasions, when key appointments are being made for instance, when the Queen would normally expect to be consulted by Prince Charles. But the fact that she has made the suggestions would almost automatically mean that they were rejected.'*

Bishop Michael Mann, a former Dean of Windsor, recalls a visit to his retirement home by the Prince of Wales, at the suggestion of the Queen, to discuss a knotty problem and to seek a second opinion. 'I subsequently heard that Prince Charles's response to our long talk had simply been "generation gap". And that was that.'

As with almost any parent, the spectre of a different age, a different outlook, has undoubtedly and very naturally arisen in certain areas, affecting the relationship between the Queen and her eldest son. 'He no longer runs to his mother for advice, as he used to,' commented one courtier, 'though he still goes to his grandmother – and does not always receive the wisest advice there!'

The part played by Princess Diana in family relationships has also obviously been an important influence. As has already been noted, the Queen and her family did everything to welcome the *ingénue* Lady Diana into their midst after her marriage in 1981, and the Queen and her new daughter-in-law quickly developed a close and warm relationship with one another. However, as the years have passed, although that relationship remains warm, insiders have noticed that it is much less close than it was. Partly this is accounted for, as it is with most young married couples, by the Prince and Princess of Wales starting their own family

---

* The appointment of Major-General Sir Christopher Airey in 1990, aged fifty-six, to be Prince Charles's third Private Secretary within five years met with the Queen's full approval. A year later, however, in May 1991, his offer of resignation was accepted by Prince Charles during an 'emotional meeting'.

and thereby becoming a self-contained nucleus. But also some distancing has come about as a result of Diana's disinclination from the outset to become part of an extended family. She saw no good reason, for example, why she and her husband should automatically spend long summer and winter holidays with his parents at one or other of their country homes. Or why she should make a pretence of sharing a love of some outdoor interests, such as deer stalking, when her preference was for more popular and less muddy pursuits.

The Queen could be irritated by Diana. As when, for instance, she deliberately turned up to a formal dinner wearing jeans, or noticeably kicked off her shoes under the table, or simply walked in late for meals.

An elderly courtier attests to hearing the Queen refer to her daughter-in-law as 'that impossible girl'. Which is not such a surprising reaction from someone of the Queen's age to one or two of the early antics of the Princess of Wales. (Such as the umbrella-poking incident.) But since those early days, the Queen's first daughter-in-law has matured to a remarkable degree, without losing any of her zest or public appeal, and it is most unlikely that the Queen would make the same sort of comment today.

The original trouble, old wives will tell you, stemmed from the fact that Diana was too young to marry when she did, and Charles was too set in his ways for a man of thirty-two. The old wives were probably right. However, it may turn out yet to have been fortunate for her, and for us, that Diana did not sit down like a good little girl and behave, when she first entered the portals of Buckingham Palace. She stirred a few things up, and a few people too, including Prince Charles. He did not always like what she was doing, and for a time he almost resented the amount of attention she received from the public and the media. She changed him superficially – in the ties she chose, the way that he combed his hair – and, more importantly, showed him what it was like to think young, after a life that up until then had been spent largely in the company of people much older than himself. (As they have both grown older the age difference has mattered less and less.)

Of course, the transformation did not altogether work. As Diana discovered, Charles is not the kind of man who can be radically altered like some architectural frontage. He is too strong willed for that. Perhaps she got to him too late, or perhaps, as he once told the author, 'I may be square today, but I may not be in ten years time. And I may be square again in another twenty years time. All I know is that there are certain truths, and there are fashions.'[1] What Princess Diana perhaps did help to bring out in her husband was a submerged sense of self-confidence and independence, which he put to use in his work. Diana's own sense of independence, which she had shown ever since she was a small child, was expressed in the way that she insisted on treating her children in exactly the same way as she had treated other people's children in the days before her marriage when she worked as a kindergarten teacher, even to the extent of fetching a bucket and clearing up herself if one of them had been sick. She was determined also to keep in touch with the friends whom she had known before she met Charles, even if that did not always please him. And she did not mind telling Charles that she was not all that keen on some of his friends – 'old fogeys' was how she thought of one or two of them. She insisted on continuing to visit her friends of pre-marriage days, even if her husband was not always enthusiastic about their coming round to Kensington Palace for a meal. And she wished also to form her own set of new friends, not all of whom would necessarily be known or very acceptable to the Palace heirarchy. She thought she was being reasonable, and she was certainly being insistent.

There was a period in the mid 1980s when it seemed to one or two of those who were close to Princess Diana that she was attempting, consciously or not, to catch up on that part of her life between the ages of nineteen and twenty-five that she had missed out on because of marrying at twenty. Charles was not interested in going to night-clubs or partying. He had had the chance to do all that sort of thing before he married, without much enthusiasm. Now he was busy finding his own 'role'. So sometimes Diana just left him to get on with it, and drove off to be with friends. It is not an uncommon scenario, particularly where both husband and wife have careers.

It is hard to gauge which of them had the more influence, one on the other, in the early years, and even more difficult to judge at all correctly to what extent Prince Charles's relations with the Queen have been affected by his marriage to someone as independently minded as Diana. In family discussions perhaps he stuck up too much for his wife. Or perhaps he favoured siding with his mother too often. Either way is landmined. On occasion, notably when the newspapers commented on their lengthy unexplained separation, the Queen is said to have summoned the pair of them to Buckingham Palace for a dressing-down. That is unlikely to have happened. Even though Elizabeth II prefers to talk face to face rather than write things down (quite the opposite to Prince Charles who is a great letter-writer), she also believes very strongly in allowing people to lead their own lives in the way that they choose, with as little outside interference as possible. As Bishop Mann explains: 'The Queen feels that the room for manoeuvre for an heir to the throne is so circumscribed by birth that he or she should be able to exercise whatever freedom they have.'[2] The Queen very seldom lays down any unwritten law.

Like many other young married couples, Charles and Diana have had their ups and downs. In the mid 1980s their marriage did go through a difficult period which lasted several months. (What a large section of the public had difficulty in coming to terms with was that a fairy-tale marriage, such as Charles and Diana's had seemed to be, could possibly run up against rocks. They momentarily ignored what they knew to be fact, that royals are human despite not being like everyone else.)

There was never any serious suggestion of a third party being involved, and probably neither partner was to blame more than the other. In the end a cool assessment of the situation and a readjustment to suit was to prove the unromantic key to solving their problems. Plus an extra dollop of the mutual love that had always been there, and a greater concentration on their two children. (Those who have witnessed the Prince and Princess of Wales at home with Prince William and Prince Harry speak warmly of an obviously loving and close relationship, and of two very well brought up and polite young boys.)

An occupational hazard of royal life that will always be present is press speculation and comment, and what Charles and Diana read about themselves in the tabloids only magnified their marital problems in their own eyes and, in the opinion of the Queen amongst many others, made it even more difficult for them to find the right answers. To be fair to the press, the Prince and Princess of Wales did not make things any easier for themselves by staying apart for thirty days and then, after coming together for a public function, going their separate ways immediately afterwards. It was a course that they were urged by their advisers not to take, but perhaps Prince Charles either knew or suspected that the advice may have stemmed indirectly from the Queen. In either event, he did not heed it.

Some of the strongest differences of opinion between the Queen and the Prince and Princess of Wales have been over royal tradition and protocol.

Prince Charles would like to see a relaxation in the rules that require, for instance, that the Lord Lieutenant of a county should be present and make himself generally available whenever a senior member of the royal family pays an official visit to his particular part of the country. He would like to dispense with some of the formal welcoming receptions by mayor and local dignitaries, to allow more time for meeting the people whom he has really come to see and talk with.

The Queen's response to this proposal is that too much dispensing with protocol too quickly would not be a good thing. The formalities are a part of the dignity that encompasses and supports the throne. And in any case, those who give loyal service to their community, with or without pay, expect to be given the recognition due to them.

Here, it can be seen, there is a marked difference of approach between sovereign and heir. Normally when the Queen visits an area, she does so in order to perform a number of precise functions, carefully planned in advance, as was the case in Huddersfield and Wallsend. Prince Charles, on the other hand, more often goes to a town specifically to meet people involved with one of his charities or to draw attention to a national or international problem. A reason that he sometimes suggests that Princess Diana should not accompany him is because experience has taught that the height of her hemline almost invariably gathers more newspaper column inches and pictures than does, say, his own serious plea for action against pollution of the atmosphere.*

Princess Diana now has a large collection of her own charities, the work for which she takes extremely seriously and carries out with ever increasing aplomb. But again she insists on doing things her way. She thinks nothing of squatting on the floor to talk with toddlers, or comforting an old-age pensioner by drawing up a chair beside him and squeezing his hand. She drops off Prince Harry at school. She puts on an army camouflage uniform for a secret meeting with a regiment on active duty in Northern Ireland. She swings her skirt up at the world, and gives it an encouraging smile.

The Queen approves, but it is a qualified approval. It is the generation gap again. Or could it be more fundamental than that? In the efforts, attitude and behaviour of the Prince and Princess of Wales are we being given a glimpse of how things will be – will have to be? – after Charles III comes to the throne?

'I do not think', says a senior courtier calmly, 'that the Queen ever felt it necessary to make the populist concessions that the Princess of Wales now makes. They were not expected of her. And I think she still has her own ideas of how a sovereign should behave, and these probably apply to an heiress as well. But the young ones have different ideas, more consonant with the ideas of their own generation. We shall have to wait and see what happens.'

Dr Eric Anderson, who taught Prince Charles at Gordonstoun and is now headmaster of Eton College, at the foot of Windsor Castle, has watched his former pupil's progress with interest and admiration. 'All the good qualities are still there. He is still extraordinarily conscientious and sensitive to individual people. He has become enormously more self-confident than he was only a few years ago, and he now has a fair idea of those things that matter to him most, and where he can have an impact. I think he will represent us superbly to the world in the century that is coming.'[3]

---

* He was not best pleased with a clash of dates which resulted in his controversial news on education having to share front-page headlines the following morning – 23 April, 1991 – with a speech by Princess Diana on the subject of Aids.

20

Monarch and Monarchy

❧

When, after thirteen years of loyal service, the Dean of Windsor, and former Bishop of Dudley, the Rt Revd Michael Mann, decided in 1989 that it was perhaps time to hand over to someone else, he naturally first advised the Queen of his wish. 'Huh!' was her response. 'It's all right for you. You can retire. I never cease being a Queen.'

'And I never cease to be a Bishop', Michael Mann countered with a smile.

'Yes, but I have to be an active one the whole time,' the Queen replied.

Another source close to Queen Elizabeth II, in one of his conversations with the author, used the words 'life sentence' with reference to the Queen's reign. Is that how she thinks of it? 'She doesn't think of it in any other terms', he answered.

It seemed that this attitude was underlined during a visit by the Queen to the United States in May 1991 when in response to a schoolboy's question – 'How long have you been Queen?' – Elizabeth II replied 'Too long,' adding somewhat cryptically, 'wait and read about it in the history books.'

Many believe that in fact, the Queen feels she is answering a calling rather than serving a sentence. 'When I left Windsor,' recalls Bishop Mann, 'I would have said that the one lesson that the abdication of Edward VIII burnt deep into the souls of the present Queen and Queen Mother was that you never, never abdicate your duty. The Queen has always seen that with privilege goes responsibility.'[1]

Almost invariably, the first question people nowadays ask of someone who is known to be making a study of the Queen's life is: 'Do you think she will ever abdicate?' When given the opinion 'No', the reaction of the majority is surprise mixed with slight disappointment, which in most cases means that they are sorry for the Queen – that she cannot retire – and for the Prince of Wales, because it seems probable that he will not become King until he is in his sixties. No one, it is quickly apparent, *wants* the Queen to step down in favour of her son. But there are some staunch monarchists, an incalculable number but probably a minority, who think that perhaps within the next decade she should.

In a poll conducted for the *Sunday Times* in January 1990,* almost half of those interviewed (47 per cent) believed that Elizabeth II should abdicate 'at some stage' in favour of Prince Charles. But the Prince of Wales has never shown any strong inclination to want the job, except as a duty. As long ago as 1975 he expressed his views to the author in an interview, and there is no evidence to suggest that he may have changed his mind in this respect. (Though he did preface his remarks by saying 'Who can tell what is going to happen in five or ten years time?')

'I don't happen to believe', said Prince Charles, 'that it is a good idea for a monarch to abdicate before time, so to speak, because in the way that our constitutional monarchy has evolved it is of vital assistance, I believe, to the whole country, to the government, the older he or she is. You gain so much in experience, in understanding of events and problems, of Prime Ministers and personalities, that you are of infinitely more advantage with this accumulation of wisdom over the years. . . . I don't think people realize just how much influence the monarch does and can have. It is influence very often far more effective than direct power. Influence that is unseen and very often unfelt by the general public.'[2]

Some twenty years ago Princess Margaret ventured to predict that her sister's value to the country would increase with the passing years. 'I think she's got an aura, a twentieth-century aura. I get enormously impressed when she walks into a room. It's a kind of magic. At the moment, she's a pretty, young woman. I feel that the longer she is sovereign the more her experience will affect decisions by Prime Ministers, and she will have influence. She will be the great hope of the country in the future.'[3]

In the same interview, with the writer Andrew Duncan, Princess Margaret thought that 'Perhaps it is lucky that we've always been a little bit flexible because we have no written constitution. We can fit in with life

---

* Market Opinion and Research International (MORI) conducted face-to-face interviews with 1,075 adults aged over eighteen in 131 constituencies across Great Britain between 6 and 8 January 1990.

as it is lived in our country at any given moment in time.'

One of the strengths of the British royal family in recent years, certainly since the reign of George VI, is that, paradoxically, it has never patently tried to hold on grimly to its position. Indeed, it has sometimes shown a remarkable willingness to be shown the door, provided that it can be demonstrated that that is what most people want.

Prince Philip once told a Canadian audience that, in his opinion, it was a complete misconception to imagine that the monarchy existed in the interests of the monarch. It existed in the interests of the people. And 'I think the important thing about it is that if at any stage people feel it has no further part to play, then for goodness' sake let's end the thing on amicable terms, without having a row about it.'[4]

The Queen is herself credited with promising that 'We'll go quietly', but, even with her natural tendency towards compliance, it is more than probable that, if she ever made the remark, she was only joking. Only if she were absolutely *certain* that it was the wish of the great majority of her subjects (it would have to be more than a *mere* majority, or the outcome of a referendum) that she should step down from the throne, would she consider submiting. If parliament were ever to pass a Bill terminating the monarchy, she would be constitutionally required to give her royal assent. But that situation is also almost impossible to envisage, certainly while the present political parties inhabit the House of Commons. 'I know of no Labour Party members who are out and out republicans', say Roy Hattersley, Deputy Leader of the Party, and goes on to state why he thinks that Elizabeth II should never abdicate. 'If being monarch becomes a job that you can give up, then it becomes a job involving controversy. If the Queen can make up her mind when she should retire then some future Prime Minister can suggest to her that she should give up the throne and let Charles take over. I do not think that is how the monarchy should operate.'[5]

Actually, say people close to her, abdication is a subject which never crops up in discussions with the Queen and is one which, they believe, rarely if ever enters her head, except in relation to the legacy left by her uncle, Edward VIII, which still haunts the whole family. (The Queen Mother, it is said, even on first meeting with a person, very often introduces the subject of King George VI and how his brother's abdication was to blame for her husband's untimely death.)

Serious illness or incapacity through a dreadful accident might enforce a change of view but not of conviction. The vows which the young Elizabeth took some forty years ago at her coronation have remained as inviolable to her as any taken by the most dedicated nun or priest in holy orders.

Robert Lacey, in *Majesty*, relates a dialogue between the Queen and

Prince Philip at the meeting at Buckingham Palace in 1965 called to discuss the future of Prince Charles. 'It was in the course of these discussions that the unmentionable was touched on – and by the Queen herself. She wished to avoid, she said, "an Edward VII situation". (Queen Victoria lived so long that Edward VII did not come to the throne until the age of fifty-nine.)

'It might be wise', said the Queen, 'to abdicate when Charles could do better.'

'You might be right', said Prince Philip, smiling. 'The doctors will keep you alive so long.'[6]

Whether or not those were precisely the words used, they were spoken twenty-five years ago, when Prince Charles was seventeen. Today, reliable sources suggest, the Queen may feel that Prince Charles is not, even now, quite ready to take up his inheritance. 'She would never say so in so many words,' says one source, 'because she knows that she was not ready herself when the time came. Things may have changed, but when I was working at the Palace the Queen seemed to have this thing that so many parents have, of simply not believing that their children can ever really grow up.'

There seems to be small doubt that the monarchy in Britain with Charles as King will include a few changes that Elizabeth II would not approve of. He may, for instance, insist on continuing to speak out on subjects close to his heart, a course of action which older members of the court believe would be unwise, even impossible, after he becomes sovereign. Roy Hattersley is among those who think it will be up to Prince Charles himself to decide. 'In twenty years I have seen the monarchy become much more informal and approachable, and I think that will continue to be the pattern of development. In a modern society a monarch can quite often be controversial about issues of the day. What he cannot be is political, in the sense of being a Labour or a Tory King.'[7]

'I think that we shall have to become accustomed to a King who does occasionally speak his mind,' says Dr Eric Anderson, Headmaster of Eton and one of Prince Charles's teachers at Gordonstoun, 'and I hope that he will. There are a great number of issues which are above national politics and I think it would be rather a waste if he didn't.'

It is interesting to discover that during the last eighteen months of her premiership, Prince Charles had a number of unpublicised private meetings with Mrs Thatcher, which were not initiated by Buckingham Palace but which the Queen thoroughly approved of, when she got to hear of them. It is extremely unlikely, however, as has been suggested, that the Premier and the Prince explored a future role for Charles. It was certainly never the case that the Queen asked Mrs Thatcher to look into the possibility of the Prince of Wales taking on a job in addition to the one he already has.

A fear frequently expressed by many monarchists is that with greater informality will come loss of mystique, that strangely ephemeral substance which has enveloped and protected royalty for centuries on end. However, there is no evidence to suggest that Prince Charles would want to do away with, or even curtail, pageantry and ceremony, although he might well wish for there to be a little less pomp, or more accurately, pomposity. His response to an American university student who poured scorn on ceremony and ceremonial was unequivocal: '*I* enjoy it. . . . People talk about pomp and circumstance, but they don't really understand what it's in aid of. You only have to study anthropology for a short time to realize that ceremony performs important roles in society.'[8] And, he might have added, is essential to a successful tourist industry in Britain.

A far greater threat to the survival of the monarchy in Britain than greater informality is trivialization. On a number of occasions both Prince Charles and Prince Philip have warned of the danger of the media turning the royal family into some sort of television soap opera. The Queen, it is known, is extremely concerned about this development. And yet she might be the first to agree that the behaviour of younger and more junior members of the family continues to give ammunition to those newspapers who know what their readers like to read, even if those same readers sometimes disapprove of what they discover. An MP who is something of a modern-day Chips Channon, points out: 'Even in very informed circles there is very little gossip going on about the Queen, while there is gossip about Prince Charles circulating all the time.'

So what of the future? The celebrated diary columnist of the *Daily Mail*, Nigel Dempster (who has not always been popular with Buckingham Palace), was quoted in October 1990 as believing that the royal family would not last beyond the lifetime of Elizabeth II, the length of which he put at possibly twenty-five years hence. 'The lager louts of today are the parents of tomorrow, and I do not believe that their children will feel any empathy towards the royal family or think that Prince Charles is a good egg', he informed Naim Attollah in an interview for a book.[*]

Philip Ziegler, the author entrusted by the Queen to write the official biography of King Edward VIII, suggested in another book,[†] published the year after the Queen's Silver Jubilee, that evidence showed that the British people like their monarchs old, wise and paternal, or young and hopeful. 'In the end to hand on the Crown to a grandson of

---

[*] *Singular Encounters*, Quartet, 1990.
[†] *Crown and People*, Collins, 1978.

twenty odd would be the ideal formula for the perpetuation of the monarchy. The Golden Jubilee of 2002 might be a suitable occasion.' (When, it so happens, Prince William will be twenty!) 'This would, of course, require the premature disappearance of the Prince of Wales; a need for which he might reasonably consider inadequately proven.'

Poor Charles. In a light-hearted way he had already stated his own preference while still up at Cambridge. 'I want to be King of Europe', he told a group of fellow students discussing their future careers. At the end of 1992, when Britain is due to be fully integrated with the European Community, the ambition may not be seen to be such a joke. Might a new path for the British monarchy lie in parallel with the path for the new Europe? Might the Queen be invited to become a ceremonial Head of State for the Community, the office being occupied on a rotating basis by other European Heads of State? (Something similar operates in Malaysia.) It is an intriguing thought, enmeshed as it would be in constitutional argument and rivalry, if indeed it ever got off the ground. There are Queens Elizabeth, Beatrix, and Margrethe, and Kings Baudoin and Juan Carlos, but there is no King of France or of Germany – although judging by the interest shown in our royal family over the years, a significant part of the population in both of those countries appear still to quite like the idea of royalty, despite having chosen to get rid of their own.

Thus far, the place of royalty in the future of Europe has not been a subject on the agenda for one particular small group of men who go under no corporate name, who have no official standing, who meet irregularly and privately, but who are in the singular position of being in close and daily contact with *all* the Kings and Queens of Europe. However, according to someone on the inside, it is a subject that is likely to be raised in the very near future.

The group, which is like a small exclusive club, comprises the eight men who are currently the Private Secretaries or the equivalent to the royal Houses of Europe. They meet alternately and irregularly in one another's country on a Friday evening, often in one another's palace, and disperse after lunch on the following Sunday. On the Saturday evening the host country may invite ambassadors to dine with them. There is an agenda for their meetings, but minutes are not always circulated afterwards, and the press is never kept informed. In all but name, they are secret gatherings.

The meetings were started some ten years ago, at the suggestion of the Lord Chamberlain to the Dutch royal family, who subsequently became Ambassador to the Court of St James. The Private Secretary to Elizabeth II did not attend the first meeting, but has been present at every one since. The last one took place in December 1990 in Brussels and, although there is no fixed interval between the meetings, they usually take place once every eighteen months to two years. What is discussed at these extraordinary conclaves? 'Oh, everything that is of common interest', says someone in the know. 'None of those attending is sent with the object of negotiating, but they get a useful idea of how other people are reacting to problems connected with their jobs.' The role of royalty in Europe after 1992? 'I think that there would be much to discuss in that area', said the kindly informant. Could he elaborate? 'No', he replied with a smile, and shortly afterwards gathered up his bowler hat and tightly rolled umbrella and slipped away, quickly merging into the general scene of St James's in winter around about dusk . . .

Whatever route Britain's royal family take in the twenty-first century, Elizabeth II is already assured of a warm corner in the history books. She is too unassuming a person to have struck postures or caused any sensations, but she is loved by millions of her subjects the more for that. She has gone about her work as she believes a monarch should, and has brought up her children to have faith in God, people, and to watch the pennies. She has followed her father in a way that would please him.

Some twenty years ago a commentator wrote: 'The British monarchy is an attractive idea but the reality is, unfortunately, out of date.' Undoubtedly, there are some who would still subscribe to that view, but their number is likely to be fewer rather than larger than it was when Elizabeth II ascended to the throne in 1952. And that is due in no small measure to the willingness of the Queen to adapt but not radically to alter.

Six days after the start of the Gulf War in January 1991, while television and the newspapers were concentrating on the bombing attacks on Iraq, the Queen and the Duke of Edinburgh visited the Royal Navy's home town of Portsmouth to offer comfort and support to the wives and relatives of the men who were risking their lives in the name of their sovereign. It was not a grand, stately affair. The Queen did not look magnificent. In fact, it struck someone who was present that she looked rather small and old. 'But she was there, with us. That was what meant a lot.'

The following month the royal family, excluding the Queen, came in for some harsh criticism for not paying enough attention to the war. In what its sister paper *The Times* called 'a gleefully-promoted editorial'[9] the *Sunday Times* asked the Queen to summon the royals to Windsor and put a stop to the current behaviour of some of the younger members of the family who 'carry on regardless with their peacetime lifestyles, parading a mixture of upper-class decadence and insensitivity which disgusts the public and demeans the monarchy'. Nobody expected the royal family to cease to have any sort of social life until the war was over. 'But too many have made only token gestures and have continued to lead social lives which make no concessions to a country at war.'[10]

Buckingham Palace was angered, and swiftly responded with a list of engagements demonstrating that the Prince of Wales had been to Saudi Arabia, the Princess of Wales to visit army wives in Germany, the Queen to call on the RAF at Marham. The *Sunday Times* did concede in its editorial that 'The Queen, of course, has behaved impeccably', but intriguingly chose to end its comment with this sentence: 'In the longer run, the best hope of the monarchy lies with the Prince of Wales.'

For the foreseeable future all the evidence would suggest that the British will go on needing and appreciating having a Head of State who is not elected or appointed but who is in lineal descent from Henry VIII, whose great-great-great grandparent was Queen Victoria. There is something in the British psyche that hankers after continuity. To some, the Queen may appear to be an anachronistic totem-pole propping up a privileged and split society. And many believe that the royal financial arrangements require urgent reappraisal. But to the great majority of her people the Queen, and the Crown, remain the chief symbol of the nation, to be jealously guarded.

As she moves towards old age, and becomes possibly the oldest member of the royal family, Elizabeth II will arrive at a new stage in the nation's affections. She will become like Queen Victoria. Children of the 1980s who had grown up knowing only Margaret Thatcher as Prime Minister will marry and have children while the Queen still reigns. And those who are grandparents and great grandparents now will have lived out the greater part of their lives while Elizabeth II was monarch.

It is a sobering thought which, no doubt, may have struck the Queen too.

Epilogue

❦

efore he had even taken up his appointment as Dean of Windsor
and Principal Domestic Chaplain to Queen Elizabeth II, the
Venerable Robin Woods, Archdeacon of Sheffield, as he then
was, received a hand-written letter from the Queen's Private
Secretary, a part of which greatly puzzled him.

In this memorandum Sir Michael Adeane advised the Archdeacon that
following his installation as Dean, in December 1962, he should address
himself to two tasks which must be undertaken immediately – the word
'must' was underlined. The first of these was that he should prepare the
heir to the throne for confirmation as a believing Christian. 'Very important', wrote Sir Michael. And the second task, 'please', was that . . .
'he bury the King'.

The Dean was baffled by the request and, after consulting the Lord
Chamberlain, was surprised as anyone would be to learn that the coffin
of King George VI did not in fact lay in a tomb under St George's
Chapel, Windsor, where it had been lowered at his funeral, but was resting instead in a locked passageway underneath the deanery. There it had
remained these past ten years, draped over with the same sovereign's
standard that had lain across it when the funeral procession had passed
along the streets of London in February 1952. Two locks guarded entry
to the passageway. The key to one was held by the Lord Chamberlain,
and the key to the other by the incumbent Dean of Windsor. Both keys
were needed to open the door, and each key had been used but once.
Beyond, on stone shelves, lay the dusty coffins of George II, George III,
and William IV.

The passageway is one of several secret places linking the deanery with St George's Chapel. A corridor almost directly above that in which the King lay had been built by King Henry VIII in order that his first wife, Catherine of Aragon, could slip from her house, which once stood up against the chapel walls, into the tier storey of the chapel. In the study of the deanery itself stood the table on to which the corpse of Charles I had been lifted following the hurried journey to Windsor immediately after his execution in Whitehall in 1649. And through the same study Queen Victoria had regularly passed, to reach the roof walk to the Aragon Chantry from which she would watch the services in St George's Chapel, unobserved, in the years following the death of her beloved husband Prince Albert.

The first funeral of King George VI had taken place on 15 February 1952, in the nave of St George's Chapel. After the coffin had been lowered on a black stone slab to the crypt beneath the chapel floor, the Lord Chamberlain, following ancient royal tradition, held aloft the white staff of his office, broke it in two, and consigned it to the grave. A young Elizabeth II took grains of earth from a small silver-gilded bowl that stood on a dark Jacobean stool at her side, and scattered them over the coffin. Then Sir George Bellew, Garter King of Arms, recited the roll of titles of the dead sovereign, and repeated the stately formula for his successor – 'the most high, most mighty, and most excellent monarch, our sovereign Lady Elizabeth'. At the last moment the Queen stepped forward and reverently lay at the head of the coffin a square of crimson silk, the King's Colour of the King's Company, the Grenadier Guards, of which her father had been Colonel-in-Chief.

The service was simple, traditional, and most moving, as one would expect. But arrangements for the funeral had been necessarily hurried because of the King's untimely death. No provision had been made for a permanent tomb, and not long after the mourners had filed out of the church, the lead-lined coffin was moved to the passageway where, completely unknown to the general public until now, it was to remain for a period of seventeen years.

At some point during 1962 or 1963, in conversation with her Members of Household, both the Lord Chamberlain and the Dean of Windsor were reminded by the Queen that a permanent resting place must be prepared for her father, and dutifully they awaited their sovereign's instructions. But none came, at least not until some five more years had passed, when the Queen once again raised the matter, saying that a suitable place should now be found. It appears that she had been waiting for the approval of Queen Elizabeth the Queen Mother before making a final decision. And the Queen Mother, it seems, had not wished to endure once again the painful memories that a second funeral was bound to create. There would be time enough when she too had departed this life.

Queen Victoria had commissioned the ornate mausoleum in the Great Park as the last resting place of Prince Albert and herself. The vaults of the Hanoverian Kings and Queens were in St George's Chapel, as were the final earthly destinations of King Edward VII and George V and their Queens. But Elizabeth II did not wish to see more table-tombs in the chapel, with life-size effigies surmounting them. For her father, she desired there to be a simple slab of stone let into the floor.

However, when a careful examination of the chapel and the plans revealed that there was no suitable space for a new vault to be built, the Queen decided, after much careful thought, and with a strong sense of providence, to construct an addition, the first to be made to St George's Chapel since its consecration in around about 1475. The architects Paul Paget and Lord Mottistone were commissioned, and they prepared a design which involved piercing the north wall of the nave and adding a small rectangular chantry. This plan, even with amendments, did not meet with the approval of the Fine Arts Commission, and was eventually abandoned. Another fine architect, George Pace, was asked for his ideas. He proposed placing the chantry in the space between the angles of the north choir aisle and the Rutland Chapel. The Queen spent many hours studying these plans – they were so large that she had to lay them out on the floor. Finally, after every detail had been scrutinized and discussed, and the plans approved by both the Queen and the Queen Mother, as well as by the Fine Arts Commission and others, the painstaking work of building went ahead.

The vault was to be eighteen feet in height, ten feet in width, and fourteen feet in depth. The memorial stone covering the body of the King was to be in Belgian black marble and was to be inscribed in gilt bronze simply 'George VI'. The cost was £25,000, which was paid by the Queen herself.[1]

The reinterment took place on 31 March 1969. In the morning the coffin of the King was brought from the passageway under the deanery and raised by the chapel's eighteenth-century lift to rest in the choir, just to the east of the tombs of Henry VIII and Charles I. The sovereign's standard of 1952 still lay draped over the Sandringham oak.

In the pale, cold afternoon, with the castle closed to the general public and the Knights of the Garter seated in their stalls in the chapel, the whole royal family solemnly followed the service of burial conducted by the Dean of Windsor, the Rt Revd Robin Woods. The only absentees were the Earl Mountbatten of Burma who was in Washington attending the funeral of President Eisenhower, and the Duke of Windsor who had not been invited. At the close of the prayers and hymns the Dean recited the words of the poem that the King had haltingly spoken in his famous wartime broadcast of Christmas 1939, and which are worked into the wrought-iron gates that guard his tomb today:

> I said to the man who stood at the
> gate of the year: 'Give me a light
> that I may tread safely into the unknown.'
> And he replied, 'Go out into the darkness
> and put your hand into the hand of God.
> That shall be better to you than light
> and safer than a known way.

There is one final note to be added. The Queen's instructions to the architects were that they should produce a design for a vault with spaces enough for six. These were to allow for the final resting places of three sovereigns and their consorts: King George VI and Queen Elizabeth; Queen Elizabeth II and the Duke of Edinburgh; King Charles III and his consort, who at that time was unknown.

If there are to be Kings and Queens of the House of Windsor after Charles III and Queen Diana, new arrangements will have to be made.

Bibliography

Airlie, Mabell, Countess of, *Thatched with Gold*, Hutchinson, 1962
Alexandra of Yugoslavia, Queen, *Prince Philip: A Family Portrait*, Hodder and Stoughton, 1960
Alice, Duchess of Gloucester, Princess, *Memoirs*, Collins, 1983
Aronson, Theo, *Royal Family*, John Murray, 1983
Avon, The Earl of, *The Memoirs of the Rt. Hon Sir Anthony Eden*, 3 vols., Cassell, 1960-1965
Bagehot, Walter, *The English Constitution*, Kegan Paul, 1898
Barry, Stephen, *Royal Secrets*, Villard Books, 1985
Beaton, Cecil, *Photobiography*, Odhams, 1951; *Self Portrait with Friends, the Selected Diaries*, 1979
Blake, Lord, *The Office of the Prime Minister*, Oxford University Press, 1975
Boothroyd, Basil, *Philip: An Informal Biography*, Longman, 1971
Bryan III, J. and Murphy, J.V., *The Windsor Story*, Granada, 1979
Butler, R.A., *The Art of the Possible: Memoirs of Lord Butler*, Hamish Hamilton, 1971
Cathcart, Helen, *Her Majesty*, W.H. Allen, 1962
Channon, Sir Henry, *Chips*, Weidenfeld & Nicolson, 1967
Churchill, Randolph S., *They Serve the Queen*, Hutchinson, 1953
Churchill, Winston S., *The Second World War*, 5 vols., Cassell, 1948-54
Callaghan, James, *Time and Chance*, Collins, 1987
Carrington, Lord, *Reflect On Things Past*, Collins, 1988
Colville, John, *Footprints in Time*, Collins, 1976
– *The Fringes of Power, Downing Street Diaries*, Vols. 1 and 2, Hodder and Stoughton, 1985-1987
Cosgrave, Patrick, *The Lives of Enoch Powell*, The Bodley Head, 1989
Counihan, Daniel, *Royal Progress*, 1977

Crawford, Marion, *The Little Princesses*, Cassell, 1950

Crosland, Susan, *Tony Crosland*, Jonathan Cape, 1982

Crossman, R.H., *The Diaries of a Cabinet Minister*, Jonathan Cape/
Hamish Hamilton, 1975

Dempster, Nigel, *H.R.H. The Princess Margaret: A Life Unfulfilled*,
Quartet Books, 1981

Donaldson, Frances, *Edward VIII*, Weidenfeld & Nicolson, 1974

– *King George VI and Queen Elizabeth*, Weidenfeld & Nicolson, 1977

Duncan, Andrew, *The Reality of Monarchy*, Heinemann, 1970

Edinburgh, HRH The Duke of, and The Rt Rev Michael Mann, *A
Windsor Correspondence*, Michael Russell, 1984

– *A Question of Balance*, Michael Russell, 1982

Edwards, Anne, *Matriarch, Queen Mary and the House of Windsor*,
Hodder and Stoughton, 1984

Fisher, Graham and Heather, *The Queen's Life*, Robert Hale, 1976

Hailsham, Lord, *A Sparrow's Flight*, Collins, 1990

Hamilton, Alan, *Charles, The Man Behind the Myth*, Collins, 1988

– *The Royal Handbook*, Mitchell Beazley, 1985

Hamilton, Willie, *My Queen and I*, Quartet Books, 1975

Hibbert, Christopher, *The Court at Windsor*, Longman, 1964

– *The Court of St James's*, Weidenfeld & Nicolson, 1981

Holden, Anthony, *Charles, Prince of Wales*, Weidenfeld & Nicolson, 1979

Home, Lord, *The Way the Wind Blows*, Collins, 1976

Howard, Philip, *The Royal Palaces*, Hamish Hamilton, 1970

Hoey, Brian, *Anne, The Princess Royal*, Grafton Books, 1989

Junor, Penny, *Diana, Princess of Wales*, Sidgwick and Jackson, 1982

Lacey, Robert, *Majesty: Elizabeth II and the House of Windsor*,
Hutchinson, 1977

Laird, Dorothy, *How the Queen Reigns*, Hodder and Stoughton, 1959

Longford, Elizabeth, Countess of, *The Royal House of Windsor*,
Weidenfeld & Nicolson, 1974

– *Elizabeth R*, Weidenfeld & Nicolson, 1983

Macmillan, Harold, *Tides of Fortune*, 1945-1955, Macmillan, 1969

– *Riding the Storm* 1956-1959, Macmillan, 1971

– *Pointing the Way* 1959-1961, Macmillan, 1972

– *At the End of the Day* 1961-1963, Macmillan, 1973

McDonald, Trevor, with Peter Tiffin, *The Queen and the
Commonwealth*, Methuen, 1986

Manchester, William, *The Last Lion: Winston Spencer Churchill, Visions
of Glory 1874-1932*, Michael Joseph, 1983

Martin, Kingsley, *The Crown and the Establishment*, Hutchinson, 1962

Morrow, Ann, *The Queen*, Granada, 1983

Morrah, Dermot, *The Work of the Queen*, William Kimber, 1958

– *To be a King*, Hutchinson, 1968

Morton, Andrew, *Inside Kensington Palace*, Michael O'Mara, 1987

Nicolson, Harold, *King George V, His Life and Reign*, Constable, 1952

Pearson, John, *The Ultimate Family*, Grafton Books, 1987

Philip, HRH Prince, *Selected Speeches*, Oxford University Press, 1957

– *Prince Philip Speaks*, Collins, 1960

Rose, Kenneth, *King George V*, Weidenfeld & Nicolson, 1983

– *Kings Queens and Courtiers*, Weidenfeld & Nicolson, 1985

Sampson, Anthony, *The Changing Anatomy of Britain*, Hodder and Stoughton, 1982

Seward, Ingrid, *Diana*, Weidenfeld & Nicolson, 1988

Talbot, Godfrey, *Ten Seconds from Now*, Hutchinson, 1973

Townsend, Peter, *Time and Chance: An Autobiography*, Collins, 1978

Warwick, Christopher, *Princess Margaret*, Weidenfeld & Nicolson, 1983

Wheeler-Bennett, Sir John W., *King George VI, His Life and Reign*, Macmillan, 1958

Whitelaw, William, *The Whitelaw Memoirs*, Aurum, 1989

Williams, Marcia, *Inside Number 10*, Weidenfeld & Nicolson, 1972

Wilson, Harold, *The Labour Government 1964-1970: A Personal Record*, Weidenfeld & Nicolson and Michael Joseph, 1971

– *The Governance of Britain*, Weidenfeld & Nicolson and Michael Joseph, 1976

– *A Prime Minister on Prime Ministers*, Weidenfeld & Nicolson and Michael Joseph, 1977

Windsor, Duchess of, *The Heart has its Reasons*, Michael Joseph, 1956

Windsor, HRH The Duke of, *A King's Story*, Cassell, 1960

Woods, Robin, *An Autobiography*, SCM Press, 1986

Young, Hugo, *One of Us*, Macmillan, 1989

Ziegler, Philip, *Crown and People*, Collins, 1978

Guide to Sources

For an obvious reason, those who talked freely to the author but who, in certain instances, wished their quotations and contributions to be unattributable are not listed here.

ACKNOWLEDGEMENTS

1. Interview by author, Buckingham Palace, 20 Feb 1981
2. *Sunday Times* Book Section, 11 Feb 1990
3. Interview by author, 20 Feb 1981
4. Robert Lacey, *Majesty*, p 334
5. Interview by author, Windsor Castle, 24 April 1986

PROLOGUE

1. Leonard Harris, *Long to Reign Over Us?*, p 43
2. Ann Morrow, *The Queen*, p 1
3. Overheard by Anthony Powell, the author, quoted on television
4. Alan Hamilton, *The Real Charles*, (Fontana-Collins edition), p 143
5. *Chronicle of the 20th Century*, p 1124
6. Interview by author, Buckingham Palace, 2 October 1975
7. Vera Brittain, *Chronicles of Youth War Diary*, 11 Dec 1913

8. Lord Carrington, *Reflect on Things Past*, p 281
9. Sir Harold Nicolson, *King George V*, p 62

CHAPTER I
Accession

1. Royal Archives, Windsor, RAPE 105A
2. Sir John W. Wheeler-Bennett, *King George VI, His Life and Reign*, p 799
3. Ibid. p 785
4. Royal Archives, Windsor, RAPE 105A, Sir Philip Mitchell to Sir Frederick Browning, 7 Dec 1951
5. Ibid
6. Ibid
7. Ibid
8. Royal Archives, Windsor, RAPE 105A Sir Philip Mitchell to Sir Michael Adeane, 1 Nov 1951
9. Royal Archives, Windsor, RAGV CC 14/223
10. Royal Archives, Windsor, RAPE 943
11. Ibid RAPE 105A Mitchell to Browning, 7 Dec 1951
12. Ibid RAPE 105A
13. Ibid

14. Ibid Mitchell to Lloyd, 13 October 1951
15. Elizabeth Longford *Elizabeth R, A Biography*, pp 138/139
16. Eric Sherbrooke-Walker, *HM the Queen at Treetops, Treetops Hotel*, p 113
17. Eric Sherbrooke-Walker, p 142
18. Christopher Warwick, *Queen Elizabeth: Sixty Glorious Years*, p 93 and reporters there at the time
19. Basil Boothroyd, *Philip: An Informal Biography*, p 104
20. Longford, p 142
21. In conversation with author
22. Ibid
23. Royal Archives, Windsor, RAPE 946, 12 Feb 1952
24. Dorothy Laird, *How the Queen Reigns*, p 24
25. Longford, p 142
26. Ibid p 142
27. James Pope-Hennessy, *Queen Mary*, p 619
28. Harold Macmillan, *Tides of Fortune*, p 372
29. *Sunday Graphic*, 17 Feb 1952

CHAPTER 2
Preparation

1. Marion Crawford, *The Little Princesses*, published in the American edition but omitted from the British. Princess Margaret told Elizabeth Longford that the question was never asked.
2. Lady Cynthia Asquith, *The King's Daughter*, p 96
3. Longford, p 66
4. Crawford, p 39
5. Wheeler-Bennett, p 299
6. Warren Bradley Wells, *Why Edward Went*, pp 3/4
7. Kenneth Rose, *Kings, Queens, and Courtiers*, p 154
8. Dermot Morrah, *Princess Elizabeth, Duchess of Edinburgh*, p 62
9. Dermot Morrah, *The Work of the Queen*, p 19
10. HRH The Duke of Windsor, *A Family Album*, p 62
11. Crawford, pp 9 and 12
12. Crawford, pp 13
13. Ibid p 16
14. Longford, p 16
15. Christopher Warwick, *Princess Margaret*, p 17
16. Longford, p 60
17. Crawford, p 22
18. Longford, p 48
19. Warwick, p 16
20. Wheeler-Bennett, p 263
21. Royal Archives Windsor, quoted by Elizabeth Longford, p 71
22. Crawford, p 45
23. Pope-Hennessy, p 585
24. Royal Archives, Windsor. Included in an exhibition at the Queen's Gallery in 1990
25. Nicolson, p 525
26. Wheeler-Bennett, p 741
27. Anne Edwards, *Matriach, Queen Mary and the House of Windsor*, p 379
28. Ibid pp 379/80
29. Rose, p 203
30. Edwards, p 380
31. Princess Margaret on BBC's *Desert Island Discs*, 3 April 1981
32. Christopher Hibbert, *The Court at Windsor, A Domestic History*, p 288
33. Wheeler-Bennett, p 468
34. Ibid
35. BBC radio: *Children's Hour with Uncle Mac* (Derek McCulloch)
36. Longford, pp 93/94
37. Reminiscing to Godfrey Talbot for BBC radio, marking 40th anniversary of VE Day, 8 May 1985
38. Wheeler-Bennett, p 626

CHAPTER 3
Philip

1. Mabell, Countess of Airlie, *Thatched With Gold* p 228
2. Crawford, p 59
3. Ibid
4. Boothroyd, p 24
5. Ibid p 108
6. Ibid p 113
7. Wheeler-Bennett, p 748
8. Ibid
9. Sir Henry Channon, *The Diaries of* p xx

10. Wheeler-Bennett, p 749
11. Airlie, p 226
12. John Pearson, *The Ultimate Family*, (Grafton edition), p 123
13. Boothroyd, p 12
14. Ibid p 82
15. Interview by author, Windsor Castle, 24 April 1986
16. Boothroyd, p 24
17. Airlie, p 219
18. Wheeler-Bennett, p 691
19. Ibid p 751

CHAPTER 4
The Carefree Years

1. Interview by author, 1986
2. Interview by author, 1981
3. Lacey, p 162
4. Philip Ziegler, *Crown and People*, p 82
5. John Colville, *The Fringes of Power, Downing Street Diaries, Volume 2, 1941-April 1955*, (Sceptre edition), p 271
6. Pope-Hennessy, p 616
7. Wheeler-Bennett, p 753
8. Boothroyd, p 34
9. Wheeler-Bennett, p 753
10. Pope-Hennessy, p 616
11. Morrah, *To be a King*, p 8
12. Boothroyd, p 106
13. Ibid p 145
14. Wheeler-Bennett, p 740

CHAPTER 5
Moving Back

1. Boothroyd, p 142
2. In conversation with author.
3. Boothroyd, p 49
4. Ibid
5. Victoria Glendinning, *Edith Sitwell: A Unicorn Among Lions*, p 299
6. Channon, 18 June 1949
7. Edwards, p 408
8. Rose, p 204
9. James A. Frere, *The British Monarchy at Home*, p 165
10. Lacey, p 190
11. In conversation with author
12. Pearson, p 83
13. *Sunday Telegraph*, 9 January 1983

14. Pearson, p 86
15. Ibid p 87
16. *Sunday Dispatch*, 7 June 1953
17. Edwards, p 408

CHAPTER 6
The First Crisis

1. Mary Soames, *Clementine*, p 404
2. Longford, p 172
3. Kenneth Rose, *Twenty-five years on, Sunday Telegraph*, 20 Jan 1977
4. Sarah Bradford, *George VI*, p 416
5. Warwick, p 59
6. *The People*, 14 June 1953
7. Longford, p 152
8. Ibid
9. Warwick, p 64
10. Ibid p 74
11. 14 October 1955
12. In conversation with the author
13. *The Times*, 24 Oct 1955
14. Longford, p 177
15. James Pope-Hennessy, *A Lonely Business*, p 242
16. In conversation with author

CHAPTER 7
Inside the Palace

This chapter contains several quotes emanating from the author's conversations with Lord Charteris.

1. Boothroyd, p 50
2. In conversation with author
3. Ibid
4. Ibid
5. Pearson, p 137 and elsewhere
6. Boothroyd, p 50
7. In conversation with author
8. Interview by author 5 Nov 1970
9. Ibid
10. Ibid
11. Boothroyd, p 167
12. Longford, p 212

CHAPTER 8
Troubled Times

1. Joan Graham, writing in the *Baltimore Sun*
2. *National and English Review*,

August 1957
3. Ibid
4. *News Chronicle*, 5 August 1957
5. *Daily Mail*, 7 August 1957
6. *Sunday Times*, 2 Jan 1972
7. *Sunday Express*, 13 Oct 1957
8. *Sunday Express*, 26 Jan 1958
9. William Manchester, *The Caged Lion*, p 110
10. *Prince Philip Speaks*, Selected Speeches 1956-59, p 11
11. Ibid
12. In conversation with author

CHAPTER 9
Likes and Dislikes

1. Boothroyd, p 24
2. Ibid p 189
3. In conversation with the author, and subsequent quotes
4. November 1962: Cecil Beaton, *Self-Portrait with Friends, the Selected Diaries, 1979*
5. In conversation with author
6. Ibid
7. Longford, p 357
8. In conversation with author
9. Interview in *Woman's Own*, 28 May, 1990
10. Warwick, p 143
11. Ibid p 147
12. Ibid p 144
13. Ibid p 151
14. *Daily Telegraph*, 30 March 1978
15. Interview by author in 1976
16. Warwick, p 143
17. In conversation with author
18. Private information
19. J. Bryan III and Charles J V Murphy, *The Windsor Story*, p 551

CHAPTER 10
A Question of Education

1. Interview by author, 24 April 1986
2. Anthony Holden, *Charles Prince of Wales*, p 72
3. Prince Charles in radio interview by Jack de Manio, BBC 1 March 1969
4. Interview by author, 2 October 1975
5. Kenneth Harris, *Observer*, 17 August 1980

6. National and English Review, August 1957
7. Holden, p 104
8. In conversation with author
9. Addressing students at Chicago University, 19 October 1977
10. In conversation with author
11. Holden, p 116
12. In conversation with author
13. Ibid
14. Ibid
15. Ibid
16. Holden, p 126
17. Recollection of one who was present
18. Ibid
19. In conversation with author
20. Holden, p 188
21. Interview by author, 2 October 1975
22. Ibid

CHAPTER 11
The Queen and Her Prime Ministers

1. *The Crossman Diaries*, Selections from *The Diaries of a Cabinet Minister*, 1964-70, Introduced and edited by Anthony Howard, p 267
2. Speech at 10 Downing Street, 23 March 1976
3. Longford, p 278
4. In conversation with author
5. Lord Blake, *The Office of The Prime Minister*, p 63
6. John Brooke, *King George III*, p 222
7. R A Butler, *The Art of Memory: Friends in Perspective*, p 101
8. Harold Macmillan, *At the End of the Day*, p 184
9. Lacey, p 243
10. The Girl I Saw Become Queen, *The Times*, 6 February 1982
11. *The Spectator*, 17 January 1964
12. Lord Home, *The Way The Wind Blows*, p 182
13. Ibid
14. In conversation with the author
15. BBC 2 series: *Reputations*, 13 July 1983
16. Macmillan, 1973, p 515 ff
17. Home, p 343 ff

18. In conversation with author
19. Ibid
20. Ibid p 218
21. Home, p 192
22. In conversation with author
23. Denis Healey, *The Time of My Life*, p 271
24. In conversation with author
25. Ibid
26. Longford, p 321
27. In conversation with author
28. Callaghan, p 390
29. In conversation with author
30. A J P Taylor, *Punch and Monarchy*, p 18

CHAPTER 12
A Special Relationship

1. Callaghan, p 380 ff
2. In conversation with author
3. Widely reported in several newspapers, 6 August 1979
4. In conversation with author
5. Hugo Young, *One of Us*, p 180
6. In conversation with author
7. Trevor McDonald with Peter Tiffin, *The Queen and the Commonwealth*, p 1
8. Hansard, 3 March 1953
9. In conversation with author
10. Ibid
11. *The Times*, 24 October 1989
12. *The Times*, 15 May 1987
13. Emanating from Buckingham Palace, 18 May 1987
14. *The Times*, 15 May 1987
15. In conversation with author
16. *The Times*, 26 September 1988
17. Buckingham Palace, 20 February 1981
18. In conversation with author
19. Lacey, p 299
20. In conversation with author
21. *Sunday Times*, 29 April 1990
22. 25 December 1953
23. McDonald, p 49
24. Broadcasting to the Commonwealth 25 December 1972
25. In conversation with author
26. McDonald, p 16

CHAPTER 13
Monarch, Mother, Grandmother

1. Brian Hoey, *The Princess Royal*, (Grafton edition), p 179
2. Princess Anne, in an interview with Kenneth Harris, *The Observer*, 10 August 1980
3. Holden, p 95
4. Ibid
5. Beaton Diaries, March 1960
6. Private information
7. *Daily Mirror*, 10 April 1990
8. In conversation with author and ff
9. Ibid
10. Crossman Diaries, p 267
11. Interview by author, 24 April 1986
12. Foreword to *Queen Elizabeth The Queen Mother*, by Godfrey Talbot, 1978

CHAPTER 14
A Very Mixed Blessing

1. Sir Harold Nicolson, *Monarchy*, p 303
2. Interview by author, 24 April 1986
3. In conversation with author
4. Ibid
5. Pearson, p 244
6. In conversation with author
7. Ibid
8. *The Sun*, 22 October 1987
9. In conversation with author

CHAPTER 15
The Yuppie Eighties

1. Philip Ziegler, *Crown and People*, p 168
2. Rose, p 92
3. Ziegler, p 172
4. In conversation with author
5. Chicago, 18 October 1977
6. In conversation with author
7. *The Times*, 30 November 1990
8. In conversation with author
9. Ibid
10. Interview by author, 24 April 1986
11. Ibid

CHAPTER 16
The Queen and Mrs Thatcher

1. Interview by Terry Wogan, BBC 1, 8 January 1990
2. Anthony Sampson, *The Changing Anatomy of Britain*, p 6
3. Ziegler, p 181
4. Longford, p 286
5. Mrs Thatcher produced the poem and read it aloud during an interview she gave to the author – her first long interview after the Brighton IRA bomb explosion – 16 October 1984
6. In conversation with the author
7. Young, p 492
8. In conversation with the author
9. *Sunday Times*, 12 November 1989
10. *The Times*, 28 July 1986
11. *The Mail on Sunday*, 27 January 1991

CHAPTER 17
Seen but Rarely Reported

This chapter is based on the Queen's visit to Huddersfield and Tyneside between 30 November and 1 December, on which the author travelled, and on conversations with those involved in planning the visits.

CHAPTER 18
Bones of Contention

1. In conversation with author
2. *YOU* Magazine, *Mail on Sunday*, 18 November 1990
3. In conversation with author
4. Addressing the Select Committee on the Civil List, the report on which was published in November 1971. The figures and quotations from Lord Cobbold are also taken from this Report.
5. Margaret Thatcher, House of Commons, 24 July 1990
6. *Daily Star*, 25 July 1990
7. *Today*, 17 October 1990
8. *Daily Mail*, 19 October 1990
9. *Daily Mail*, 15 February 1991
10. *The Mail on Sunday*, 17 February 1991

CHAPTER 19
Shaping Up Nicely?

1. Interview by author, 2 October 1975
2. In conversation with author
3. Ibid

CHAPTER 20
Monarch and Monarchy

1. In conversation with author
2. Interview by author, 2 October 1975
3. Andrew Duncan, *The Reality of Monarchy*, (Pan edition), p 139
4. *The Times*, 20 October 1969
5. In conversation with author
6. Lacey p 324/5
7. In conversation with author
8. Chicago University, 19 October 1977
9. *The Times*, 11 February 1991
10. *The Sunday Times*, 10 February 1991

EPILOGUE

1. *The Times*, 29 March 1969

Index

83
Edward VIII *see also* Windsor, Duke of
Elizabeth II
  abdication, possible 276, 282-4, 285, 286, 288
  accession 9-15, 68
  and animals 20, 24, 61, 94, 94n, 95, 264
  Auxiliary Territorial Service 40
  bankers 261
  birth 19-20
  bouquets 255
  brokers 261
  Burmese 237
  business sense 103
  Callaghan, James 165, 166, 167, 184-5
  character 24, 30, 39, 81, 102-5, 124, 126-7, 130-1, 139, 141, 271
  childhood 23-38
  children 145, 201-13
    Anne 64, 65
    Charles 61-62, 277-278, 280
    education 144-63
    employment of 239-40
  Churchill, Winston 78-9, 165, 166
  Civil List 266-74, 266n, 271
  clothes 95, 255, 257n
  the Commonwealth 186-90, 199-200, 249
  confirmation 53
  corgis 20, 61, 94, 94n, 111, 206-7, 238
  coronation 70-6
  court cases 218, 226-7
  'dawgies' 206-7
  dignity, sense of 102-3
  Douglas-Home, Sir Alec 165, 166
  dress 25, 130, 130n
  and the Duchess of York 240-1
  and the Duke and Duchess of Windsor 139-43
  Eden, Sir Anthony 165, 166
  education 25-7, 29-30, 34, 38-9
  and Elizabeth the Queen Mother 27, 130-1
  Fijian crisis 192-7
  foreign tours 1-2, 3-14, 54-5, 113, 188, 190-1
  fortieth anniversary celebrations 232
  friends 209
  and George V 28
  and George VI 34, 60-1
  gifts to
    ownership of 262

  rules concerning 190-1
  governess 24, 25-7
  grandchildren 201, 209, 234-5
  Heath, Edward 165, 166
  horses 24, 123, 237, 261, 264
  House of Commons, relationship with 269n
  income 261-74
  influence of 284
  jewellery 262
  Keeper of the Privy Purse and Treasurer to the Queen 119
  letter headings 4
  litter, dislike of 246, 246n
  Low Church, preference for 124
  luncheon parties 110-11
  Macmillan, Harold 165, 166, 171, 172
  mail 96
  Major, John 165
  Malta 63-5
  marriage 43, 48-9, 105-8, 113-15
    Clarence House 58, 62-3
    engagement 53-6
    first meeting with Prince Philip 42-3
    honeymoon 61
    relationship with Prince Philip 37-8
    role and influence of Prince Philip 105
    wedding 59-61
    wedding presents 59
    whether arranged 49-51
  Master of the Horse 118
  medical check-ups 276n
  Mistress of the Robes 118
  modernization of monarchy 107, 110, 110n
  'The Monarchy Today' (article) 116-17
  multiracial attitude 186, 186n
  nanny 24-5
  1974 election 179-80
  Northern Ireland, visits to 233-4
  offical engagements 95, 111, 252-60, 252n
  official papers 96, 103
  personal staff 97-100
  personal wealth and Crown property 261-74
  politics and politicians 169-70
  power and influence 168-9
  practical jokes 208
  prime ministers 165-83
    weekly meetings with 166-8
  and Princess Margaret 30, 31, 32-3, 93, 132, 138

and the Princess of Wales 236-7, 279, 280, 281-2
private life 215
Private Secretary 103, 118
Privy Council 2
and Queen Mary 28-9
Queen's Household 97-100, 118-20
Royal Family film 221-5, 231
'royal prerogative' 169
'The Royal Soap Opera' (article) 117-18
royal 'we', use of 244-5
shot at 237, 237n
Silver Jubilee 232-4
snobbery, dislike of 102
speeches 116
spending 263-4
television appearances 221-6
Thatcher, Margaret 165, 243-51
The Triangle 131
twenty-first birthday 55
under-nurse 25
and Gough Whitlam 197-8
Wilson, Harold 165, 166, 167, 181-2
working week 95
World War II 34-41
Elizabeth, Queen Consort *see* Elizabeth the Queen Mother
Elizabeth the Queen Mother 6, 23, 33-4, 152, 201
Birkhall 61, 155
character 69, 130-1
Charles' marriage 211
death of George VI 68
dress 130
and Duchess of Windsor 139
and Elizabeth II 130-1
George VI's accession 17-19
grandchildren 147, 155
and Lord Snowdon 133, 138
marriage 19
paintings, love of 265
and Prince Charles 147, 155, 211, 278
reform, attitude towards 107
Eton College 152-3, 152n
European Community 288-9
British membership 172, 200

Fagan, Michael 237-8, 238n
Falklands War
press publicity 228
Prince Andrew 204, 239, 247
Fellowes, Sir Robert 97, 118
Ferguson, Sarah *see* York, Duchess of

Fermoy, Lady Ruth 211
Fernandes, C.N.L.
Fiji
Commonwealth membership 192
independence ceremony 163, 191
military coup 192-7
Queen's affection for 191-2
Fisher, Dr Geoffrey 60
Peter Townsend affair 88, 92
Fleming, Rt Revd Launcelot 124, 127
Foot, Michael 87, 182
fox hunting 28

Gale, George 273
Ganilau, Ratu Sir Penaia 193, 194-6, 196n
Gatcombe Park 161n
George I (King of Greece) 45
George II (King of Greece) 50
George V 24, 27, 139, 218n
death 30
income 268n
grandchildren, relationship with 28
Silver Jubilee 33
George VI 6
accession 17-19, 20-3, 31
burial 291-4
character 19, 20, 27, 33-4
and Churchill 78
coronation 32-3
daughters 34, 60-1
death 9-10
funeral 292
health 2, 5, 6, 9, 29, 63-4, 66
income 268n
and Peter Townsend 80
and Prince Philip 50, 55-6
World War II 36-7
Girl Guides, 1st Buckingham Palace Company of 30
Gloucester, Duchess of 201
official engagements 271
Gloucester, Duke of 6, 14, 151, 201
abdication of Edward VII 20
official engagements 271
Gordonstoun
Duke of Edinburgh 47
Prince Andrew 204
Prince Charles 152-7
Prince Edward 205
Grafton, Duchess of 118
Greek civil war 51
Greenhill, Lord 184
Grenada
United States invasion 199, 199n

INDEX